The Sex Directory

The Sex Directory

A guide to sexual problems and where to go for help

Compiled by
ANN DARNBROUGH and
DEREK KINRADE

Foreword by Dr Duncan Guthrie, Founder and Past Chairperson of SPOD – The Association to Aid the Sexual and Personal Relationships of People with a Disability

Woodhead-Faulkner · Cambridge

Member: Association of British Directory Publishers

Published by Woodhead-Faulkner Limited
Fitzwilliam House, 32 Trumpington Street,
Cambridge CB2 1QY, England
and
27 South Main Street, Wolfeboro,
New Hampshire 03894-2069, USA

First published 1988

British Library Cataloguing in Publication Data

The sex directory
1. Sex counselling—Great Britain—
Directories
I. Darnbrough, Ann II. Kinrade, Derek
362'.02541 HQ10.5.G7

ISBN 0–85941-163-X

Designed by Geoff Green
Typeset by Pentacor Ltd, High Wycombe, Bucks
Printed in Great Britain by J W Arrowsmith Ltd, Bristol

Contents

Foreword

by Dr Duncan Guthrie

Founder and past Chairperson of SPOD – The Association to Aid the Sexual and Personal Relationships of People with a Disability

Social historians will certainly look back at the 1960s and 1970s of this century as a time of sexual liberation. Whether it will also be seen as a time of progress or as a retrograde period will depend on personal views and, no doubt, on any fashion change that develops in social attitudes generally. For some it will have been an age of unrestrained pornography, sexual licence and the collapse of moral standards. For others it will be the time when the nation finally left behind it dank Victorian immorality with its hypocrisies and degradation of women. What is certain is that sexual liberation has not always been matched with knowledge. Through the 1980s, sex seems to have brought rather more problems than fun, and there is, in many places, a climate of retrenchment. If anything, however, the need for awareness and the information to create that awareness is greater than ever.

Everything does not of course come to us in black or white, let alone in scarlet or white, and those of us who are relieved no longer to be trammelled with many of the values and behavioural patterns of the nineteenth century may be, and should be, unhappy too at many of the persisting sexual situations. While I myself would be desperately concerned about any sexual exploitation I am, I believe, even more worried about sexual ignorance, which, in any case, is nearly always what has made the exploitation possible.

When well into my twenties I was astonished and horrified to find that I was still confusing some of the functions of the vulva, and of all things, the umbilicus. Although this was half a century ago I still tremble, not with embarrassment – fortunately the confusion was only in my own mind – but at the thought of where a young man, or woman, with this level of ignorance might well have ended up.

Although we have experienced this sexual liberation there is still a hard core resistance to sexual knowledge. Not long ago I heard a member of the House of Lords deprecatingly refer to 'the sex education industry', while the unacceptable number of schoolgirl pregnancies is clear evidence of too many girls – and boys – just not understanding the difference between what is fun and what is an enjoyable but serious responsibility.

We can be very thankful that there are skilled and dedicated people willing to counsel in this sensitive and often forbidding area. Regrettably there are still far too few of them and up to now it has been difficult for the so-called man in the street to find the advice or information he is seeking. Ann Darnbrough and Derek Kinrade must be congratulated on their initiative and their customary efficiency in marshalling a great deal of important information.

On the one hand, we have those who claim to be concerned with the moral and sexual welfare of society rushing to the courts and holding press conferences with cries of 'Filth!' 'Blasphemy!' 'Obscenity!' setting in motion the whole media train of publicity and ensuring the widest and brightest exposure possible. On the other hand, we find two people quietly setting about producing *The Sex Directory*, a book chock full of useful information which will help, directly or indirectly all who have problems or who just seek plain answers to simple questions in matters of sex. For my money I know which I would choose.

Introduction

While sexual expression, in which we include warmth, closeness and loving concern, can be the wellspring of some of our greatest joys – probably the nearest many of us come to reaching for the stars – its frustration can lead to the most profound and unremitting misery. In the course of a lifetime, there can be very few of us who do not experience some sex-related problems. We may be afflicted with attitudes shaped by a repressive and puritanical family or educational background, or we may have been taught that sexual activity is somehow dirty or distasteful, or we may have come to associate sex with giving or receiving pain, or we may simply be going through a difficult time.

Sex, unfortunately, can also be about power: used as a weapon in relationships which have gone sour, or worse, expressed in the sexual abuse of women and children. (The whole of society needs to question ingrained concepts of power when so many physically weaker members can be degraded and humiliated.)

Whatever the problem, most of us react badly. We may succumb to feelings of guilt or inadequacy and turn in upon ourselves, or push the blame and our hostility on to a partner. It would not be so bad if we had someone on hand to whom we could turn, but most of us are reluctant to discuss our sex lives with family or friends. Often, the family doctor is seen as being too close to be approached without embarrassment and may, in any case, be lacking the time or the expertise to help in sexual matters. Most of us simply don't know where to turn, so we go nowhere and our problems harden.

The main aim of the Directory is to unravel this confusion: not to provide pat solutions, but to point the way to where relevant help can be sought. While there are many books about all aspects of sexuality, some of them excellent, they generally stop short of leading the reader towards specific sources of help. We aim throughout to provide a simple and basic understanding of the subject, shedding some light on the matters of everyday concern, with what we hope is a common sense appraisal of alternative courses of action. We hope that both professionals and lay women and men will find value in our non-technical approach and guidance through the multiplicity of services which are available.

We set out in each chapter to cover a particular aspect of sexuality and to give details of national organisations known to provide help or support. Then, in Chapter 21, 'Guide to Local Services' we list those individuals and organisations working locally. Inevitably, the entries are incomplete: it is impossible to be 'comprehensive' in such a listing. We are conscious that at least in this first edition some deserving agencies will have been omitted. We hope that any we have left out will get in touch with us through the publisher. Essentially we want to show readers the variety of help available (even if sexual therapists/counsellors are far too thin on the ground), so that they may seek the sort of help which most exactly meets their needs. In such a very personal area it is important to proceed within a context in which each person feels comfortable and at ease.

In discussing sexuality and the problems which arise for both women and men, we have cast our net wide to include infertility, difficulties experienced by disabled people and the special sources of help available to homosexuals, transvestites and transsexuals. We have also felt it important to spell out, although not in precise detail, the restrictions and safeguards of the law.

Whatever the problem, we would urge readers to seek help. Sex therapists, by the very nature of their work, are usually outgoing and friendly people who have a broad view of life and who, while respecting an individual's sensitivities are unlikely themselves to be easily shocked. There is often no need to go on suffering sexual difficulties. We hope this book will provide the key to the help which is available.

Ann Darnbrough and Derek Kinrade
January 1988

Acknowledgements

We would like to thank all those people who gave us so freely of their time, to whom we are indebted for insight and information. The list is long and it would be impossible to mention everybody. However, special thanks are due to Fay Cooper, a marital therapist and Secretary of the Association of Sexual and Marital Therapists; Martin Cole of the Institute for Sex Education and Research; Mary Davies, former Editor and Training Officer of SPOD, the Association to Aid the Sexual and Personal Relationships of People with a Disability; Caroline Okell Jones of BASPCAN; the Marie Stopes House; Dateline; the Beaumont Society and the Friend Transvestite and Transsexual Group in Upper Street, London.

Very special thanks, also, go to the Family Planning Association, whose unstinting help and reading of our manuscript has been of tremendous encouragement.

In addition, we owe an untold debt to each other.

Whilst every effort has been made to verify the accuracy of the information in this book, readers are advised to make their own enquiries as to the availability of the services described.

CHAPTER 1

The Helping Therapies

Sex should be a joyful experience. But, complicated creatures as we are, things sometimes go wrong. There are few people who can claim to have had a continuously happy sexual relationship all their lives, and for most of us peaks of sublime joy are to be savoured for their comparative rarity. Even in otherwise happy relationships there are troughs when sexual activities are less than exciting. At these times we may need to take stock. If illness has intervened then plainly patience and understanding will pave the way for future happiness. If, however, our relationship is in the doldrums, and the winds of passion have stilled, then we may need to surround our sexual activities with rather more imagination and enterprise.

Sex has been described as a continuation of communication by other means. At its best it can be a wonderful communion of sensual pleasure between two people who respect each other and find fun in being together. Good sex can bring a marvellous closeness with another person, and it can also develop each one of us as individuals. As children, we learn about the world around us through our senses – our fingers opening up a world of tactile pleasure. Sometimes, as we grow up, inhibitions creep in and the pleasures of our senses may become dimmed. We need then to relearn a whole range of sensual pleasures, including that of touch. We may need to practise exploring the world around us with our sensitive fingers and consciously to develop all our senses before we are really able to enjoy the sensual delights of our own and another's body. Wood, silk, satin, flower petals and cats are delightful to touch and caress; so is flesh with its different textures and shapes. Seeing, touching, tasting and caressing the human body can be a marvellous fulfilment if our senses are awake to the delights at hand, and our mind is already attuned to natural sensuality.

Why do things go wrong? Often the problems lie within ourselves, because of unhappy experiences in our childhood or after we have grown up. Misplaced trust in another person may have damaged our ability to relate to anyone else. But sometimes the trouble is external. Our communities can be very prejudiced towards those who are different – people whose sexual expression does not conform to the 'norm', whatever that is, people who are disabled and present a different body image, people who are insecure, perhaps through lack of family support. In the end, it seems we can only share happiness if we are secure, happy personalities in our own right. Some of us need considerable help to achieve this. One of the options is to seek the advice of a psychosexual counsellor or therapist; such specialists are sometimes attached to family planning clinics, and can help people with a whole range of problems. Most clinics will require you to be referred by your family doctor, though there are some where this is not essential. Details of such services are given in Chapter 3, 'Family Planning'. Where the service is provided through the National Health Service (local family planning clinics are now part of the NHS), there will be no charge for consultation. Some counsellors also provide private consultations and you may be given that option. Other counsellors operate entirely on a private basis, though they are few and far between. To find out if there is such a person in your own locality, you should get in touch with one (or more) of the organisations listed at the end of this chapter, further details of which are provided in Chapter 21. We also list (in both places) a few organisations which themselves provide counselling advice.

The kinds of help and the forms of therapy available are various, but broadly they may be divided into two areas, the psychological and the practical, including behavioural therapy and occasionally surrogate therapy. Those therapists who are more flexible in their approach will use a combination of therapies to treat their clients' widely varying problems, and to accommodate individual personal responses.

In passing, we should also mention the use of drugs, including tranquillisers and sedatives used to calm those who may be thought to suffer from anxiety, and antidepressants which, as the name suggests, aim to lift depression and allow a person to function more happily. Nowadays, the use of drugs, except in certain specific cases, is not considered to be particularly helpful in dealing with sexual problems. They are unlikely to provide a cure, in that they treat the symptoms rather than the cause. Other therapies and ways of dealing with difficulties now exist which are likely to be far more effective.

Psychological help may be available through counselling or through psychotherapy where clients are helped to understand the nature of their own sexual problems. By learning to see their personal feelings and situation in a new light they may be enabled to help themselves. Self-help discussion groups and workshops have also proved useful to people who find strength in mutual exploration of sexuality.

A more practical approach is available through behavioural therapy, variations of which are widely practised in clinics throughout the country. Many psychosexual clinics and Marriage Guidance Councils use behavioural techniques. Given the very physical nature of sexual activity it seems a very logical step forward to treat problems in this way. Therapists practising behavioural techniques will have been considerably influenced by Masters and Johnson (*see* reviews of their books on pages 7–8), while at the same time developing their own variations of the methods of treatment. Broadly, behaviourists believe that 'bad' behaviour, having been learned at some time, can be unlearned and replaced with more satisfactory behaviour.

The new learning process will follow a clearly defined pattern. You and your partner will be asked to practise sexual techniques in between therapy sessions. If you are really motivated (and nothing can work unless you really want it to) to solve your problems and normally enjoy each other's company, this can be unexpectedly delightful 'homework'. For instance, you are likely to be encouraged to focus on feelings and sensations while positively avoiding ejaculation and orgasm. Indeed, you will be shown how to interrupt sexual activity and stimulation short of orgasm, so that the benefits of prolonged love-making may be enjoyed and the pressures to reach a 'goal' are removed. In this way it is possible to lose the distressing 'fear of failure' which can ruin a couple's happiness, while at the same time learning to savour delights which may not have been fully appreciated before.

In addition to the discussions you will have with your therapist, who will set the home practice, you will probably also be given helpful and encouraging notes describing the stages of 'sensate focus' to help you on your way. Masters and Johnson believed it was necessary to treat both partners in a heterosexual relationship, even if only one partner appeared to have a sexual problem. In turn, they felt it important to involve two therapists, a man and a woman, to balance the interaction between the sexes and to treat a couple effectively. Dual therapy is practised in some clinics in this country, but very often there are not enough resources to provide the numbers of therapists needed for such a programme. Perhaps it should be said that there is no reason why homosexual men or women should not also benefit from behavioural therapy if they feel this might help them in some way.

It is possible to practise a modified form of behavioural techniques yourself. Paul Brown and Carolyn Faulder, in their book, *Treat Yourself to Sex*, suggest ways in which you can do this (*see* page 9).

Surrogate Therapy

A surrogate is one who takes the place of another, and surrogate therapy, in the treatment of sexual problems, means therapy which is provided by a substitute partner within the context of a sexual therapy programme. The treatment may include sexual intercourse.

The word 'surrogate' was first used in this context by Masters and Johnson (*see* the review of *Human Sexual Inadequacy* on page 8), in their attempts to help people with sexual difficulties who, because they had no partners with whom to practise new sexual skills, would consequently only be able to learn these in theory. A partner was needed to share the client's interest in successful treatment and to develop physically the suggestions presented to him during therapy sessions, and Masters and Johnson responded to this need by providing 'replacement partners' for those single men who had come to them for treatment. Single women were not included in this arrangement, but were expected to take along their own replacement partner (men occasionally did this too). Masters and Johnson justified this seeming double standard by maintaining that psychosocial factors would prevent women from benefiting from such help.

Surrogate therapy is not widely practised and the only person to offer the service publicly in this country is Dr Martin Cole (*see* the Institute for Sex Education and Research, page 106), who has been prepared to stand up and be counted for his therapeutic beliefs. In taking this stand, he has recognised the desperate need of those among us who are lonely and have specific sexual problems and acknowledged their right to receive practical sexual help despite adverse criticism. As the pioneer in this form of therapy, Dr Cole employs both male and female surrogates. He has found that a range of specific sexual functions in men and women may be helped in this way. Dr Cole maintains that for clients who have no sexual partner or who have an unhelpful partner, the provision of a surrogate, simply by giving the opportunity for treatment, is of the utmost importance. He suggests that behavioural change is virtually impossible without the participation of an involved partner. We rather gathered on the grapevine that other therapists occasionally arrange for the services of a surrogate partner, but this is never openly admitted.

As we have suggested, a certain amount of controversy surrounds surrogate therapy: its opponents see it as akin to prostitution. Yet it would be an incredible situation in any other field of remedial training if theory were not extended by practice. Indeed, acceptance for this extension of behavioural therapy is quietly gaining ground. The fact has to be faced that in some cases even expert psychotherapy or practical lessons to be carried out at home may not be enough to overcome deep-rooted problems. Such a client often remains incapable and afraid when left with the loneliness of an empty bedroom or faced with an equally scared or unhelpful partner. Surrogate therapy, arranged in a wider therapeutic programme involving both sexual and social skills training, can provide the framework for people to learn to function more happily in their personal relationships.

Sexual expression employs all our senses and involves skills of mental and physical co-ordination and technique. Each of us is required to give a 'performance' to achieve our own and our partner's satisfaction. We rely partly on natural instincts and partly on acquired knowledge and experience. Sadly, natural instincts in sexual behaviour are often inhibited and some of us also miss out on that essential knowledge and experience if we come from families where our upbringing was repressive and where we were taught only to hide our feelings and to be ashamed of our bodies. As a result, we may have been burdened with guilt feelings about our sexuality which have led to unhappy and unsatisfactory relationships. Is it any wonder that in such circumstances our confidence in our own abilities becomes badly damaged and our instincts do not respond as nature intended. It can happen to anyone. The moves we long to make become clumsy and hopelessly unsatisfying to our partner and to ourselves. It is very easy to become trapped and locked in such a situation. We need help to lose damaging inhibitions and to learn or relearn happy ways of showing affection by gaining an understanding of our own and our partner's needs and of how to fulfil them.

Carefully programmed therapy sessions will be aimed at providing the nervous would-be lover with the necessary confidence and training. An experienced surrogate, who understands and is sympathetic to the problems we are suffering and accepts us as we are, may be able to take us forward in slow stages towards acquiring the confidence and sexual skills we need to function happily in a relationship. Success is difficult to measure as Dr Cole admits, and follow-up information on patients is often hard to obtain.

Therapy and Masturbation

Learning to explore our bodies and to produce our own pleasurable sensations will be one of the aims of a sex therapy programme. Many sex therapists will actively encourage masturbation, for indeed it can be a delightful way of learning about our bodies' responses. There is no reason why giving ourselves sexual pleasure through touching, exploring and enjoying our own bodies should not be recognised as a very acceptable part of celebrating our own sexuality. Apart from the sheer enjoyment of the activity and the exciting climaxes it can bring, masturbation when we have only ourselves to please, can be a good way to learn about our own responses, giving us valuable experience and understanding which we can take into our relationships with other people. Particularly for women, learning what techniques best turn us on can help overcome many sexual problems, providing a sure foundation for the intimacies we choose to share with our partners.

We first learn to enjoy our own bodies as babies when little fingers discover the pleasures of touching the genital area. Many a young mother is surprised to see the firm little erect penis her baby son proudly presents. From then on throughout childhood we are likely to finger ourselves in a natural exploratory way, from time to time progressing to full masturbation. In our teens it is likely to become a more intense activity, but girls may have conflicting emotions which prevent them from realising the enjoyment and release masturbation can bring. Some girls may be unaware of the existence of their clitoris for years and therefore unaware for a long time of their missed opportunities. Many women feel resentment at discovering what they have been missing. They are now recognising the need to educate and help each other to gain a greater understanding of the whole area of their sexuality. By joining together in self-help groups throughout the country (*see* Chapter 8, 'Women Only') they are learning about their femaleness, and to understand, appreciate and have control over their own bodies. Masturbation can be a part of this discovery of the self. It can be a liberation to have charge of our own sexuality. Such independence, far from threatening relationships (whether heterosexual or homosexual), can enhance them.

Given the joy and release that masturbation can give both men and women, it is strange to think what a very bad press the subject has had, largely as a result of various cultural and religious taboos. Early dictionaries, describe masturbation as 'self-defilement'. It is not surprising that many people feel guilty about the practice. Masturbation was presented as producing all sorts of horrific effects – madness, blindness, growing hair on the palms of the hands and so on. Finding out about our own bodily responses and trying out new and different techniques is not only fun, but it can also teach us a lot about our own capabilities, each of us learning the type of stimulation that works best for us. It can, of course, also provide a good deal of consolation to us during those times in our lives when we are without partners.

Where to Go For Help

Most services require referral from a family doctor, but if you would prefer to keep the matter entirely private, there are some clinics where self-referral is accepted if you live in their locality. Some clinics may have long waiting lists for the service you require, while others may impose unacceptable conditions – if, for example, you wish to attend as an individual and the clinic insists on counselling only 'couples' (although to be fully effective it is preferable to be seen together). It is obviously important to find the clinic which meets your needs and you may have to shop around for this. Many clinics are warm and welcoming and this, no doubt, is a happy reflection on the staff who work there.

We list in Chapter 21, 'Guide to Local Services', clinics which provide a psychosexual counselling service, but provision depends on a particular, suitably qualified person being available in a locality, so that services tend to be variable and patchy. When a counsellor moves on, any associated services may lapse.

Our list of facilities cannot be complete, so if you want to check further on services in your area ring your nearest Family Planning Clinic, (listed as such in the telephone book), to ask whether your particular problem can be dealt with (you don't need to give your name), or contact the Family Planning Information Service, 27–35 Mortimer Street, London W1N 7RJ (Tel: 01-636 7866).

We also list a number of specialist organisations, in the relevant chapters, which will be glad to help. Women might find it helpful to turn to Chapter 8 'Women Only', where self-help services are described.

Further information on marital or couple problems is available in Chapter 15, 'Marriage Guidance'. Chapter 13, 'Learning about Sex', also has useful information for those with sexual problems.

There is always someone, somewhere, who really will understand – problems should never be suffered alone.

List of Organisations, Addresses and Details of Their Activities

Alcoholics Anonymous
PO Box 1, Stonebow House, Stonebow, York YOl 2NJ (Tel: York (0904) 644026).
Heavy drinking can have a detrimental effect on sexual activity and sexual relationships. Seeking help from a specialist organisation such as Alcoholics Anonymous could help with the drinking problem.

The AA is a voluntary world-wide fellowship of men and women from all walks of life who have lost the ability to control their drinking and who meet together to attain and maintain sobriety. Members attempt to create a satisfactory way of life without alcohol and the only requirement for membership is a desire to stop drinking.

The AA does not define alcoholism, but suggests that a person may be an alcoholic when he/she repeatedly drinks more than he/she intends or wants to, or if he/she gets into trouble when he/she drinks. AA members believe there is no such thing as a 'cure' for alcoholism. They also believe they can never return to normal drinking.

Members join AA groups around the country to help them in their aims and endeavours to remain alcohol-free and to share experiences with others having similar problems. If you join the AA you need disclose nothing about yourself. No membership files or attendance records are kept.

For further information or contacts consult your local telephone directory, or telephone or write to the AA at the above address.

The Association of Sexual and Marital Therapists
PO Box 62, Sheffield S10 3TL.
Members of the Association are those who have a particular interest in the treatment of sexual dysfunction. Two of the aims of the ASMT are to promote the enrichment of people's sex lives and to foster positive attitudes towards sexuality.

In answer to an enquiry by letter, the Association will be glad to provide the name and address of a therapist living as near as possible to the enquirer. Therapy may be provided either privately or under the NHS. It is important to state which you prefer.

British Association for Counselling
37a Sheep Street, Rugby, Warwickshire CV21 3BX (Tel: Rugby (0788) 78328).
Publishes a directory of agencies throughout the country who are able to help with psychosexual problems. Price £3 to non-members, £2 to members. For those seeking counselling help, the BAC will, whenever possible, provide the name and address of a qualified counsellor or agency, as near as possible to the enquirer's home. The counsellor may be working in a clinic, a youth advisory service, or other agency or in a private house.

The BAC's quarterly journal *Counselling* is of interest to people working in the counselling field, as well as those generally interested in the concept of counselling. Price £7.50 including postage and packing.

A list of other publications of interest to counsellors is available on request – please enclose a SAE.

Catholic Marriage Advisory Council
15 Lansdowne Road, London W11 3AJ (Tel: 01-727 0141).
The CMAC is able to offer those with sexual and emotional difficulties the help of trained counsellors who are Roman Catholics. For further details of services in your area, contact the Council direct. Fuller details are given of the CMAC's services in Chapter 15, 'Marriage Guidance'.

Family Planning Information Service
27–35 Mortimer Street, London W1N 7RJ (Tel: 01-636 7866).
Will provide details of the nearest counselling and therapy service for those with sexual or emotional problems. For a full description of the information service *see* Chapter 3, 'Family Planning'.

Forum (A sex education and information magazine)
The Northern Shell Building, PO Box 381, Mill Harbour, London E14 9TW (Tel: 01-987 5090).
The editor is happy to answer any problems relating to sexuality by letter or by telephone. She is assisted by a board of eminent consultants. No fees are charged. If people wish to be seen in person they can attend the Forum Clinic at a cost of £20 per hour. For further details of this magazine, *see* Chapter 13, 'Learning about Sex'.

Institute of Psychosexual Medicine
11 Chandos Street, Cavendish Square, London W1M 9DE. (Tel: 01-580 0631).
Membership of the Institute is limited to medical practitioners, but people with sexual and related problems can obtain details of doctors qualified in psychosexual medicine from The Referrals Secretary, Institute of Psychosexual Medicine.
The function of the Institute is to promote psychosexual medicine through seminar training and research. It offers training to doctors to improve their skills with patients who seek help with sexual difficulties and related marital or psychosomatic problems. The training aims to increase skill rather than knowledge and the method of training is concerned with practice rather than theory. Doctors who seek to make this field a special interest, may be able to proceed to advanced training, leading, if successful, to the Institute's Certificate of Competence in Psychosexual Medicine.

National Marriage Guidance Council
Herbert Gray College, Little Church Street, Rugby, Warwickshire CV21 3AP (Tel: Rugby (0788) 73241).

For full details of the NMGC's activities see Chapter 15, 'Marriage Guidance'. Marriage Guidance Councils providing psychosexual services in the following towns are listed with their addresses in Chapter 21, 'Guide to Local Services'.

Aldershot
Aylesbury
Banbury
Basingstoke
Bath
Belfast
Birmingham
Blackburn
Boston
Bolton
Bournemouth
Brighton
Bristol
Broadstairs
Bromsgrove
Burton-upon-Trent
Bury St. Edmunds
Cambridge
Cannock
Cardiff
Carlisle
Castle Northwich
Cheltenham
Chesterfield
Colwyn Bay
Chichester
Coventry
Croydon (Greater London)
Derby
Doncaster
Dorchester
Dudley
Durham
Epsom
Exeter
Finchley (Greater London)
Grimsby
Guildford
Halifax
Harlow
Harrogate
Harrow (Greater London)
Hazel Grove
Hereford
Huddersfield
Ipswich
Leamington Spa
Leeds
Leyton (Greater London)
Lichfield
Liverpool
London (by borough)
Macclesfield
Maidenhead
Maidstone
Manchester
Middlesbrough
Milton Keynes
Newcastle upon Tyne

Northampton
Nottingham
Oxford
Palmers Green (Greater London)
Portsmouth
Queen Camel (Nr Yeovil)
Richmond (Greater London)
Rotherham
Rugby
St. Austell
Salford
Salisbury
Scunthorpe
Sheffield
Southampton
Sutton Coldfield
Swansea
Swindon
Taunton
Torquay
Tunbridge Wells
Walsall
Warrington
Watford
Wimbledon (Greater London)
Winchester
Wolverhampton
Worcester
Worthing
York

NAYPCAS (National Association of Young People's Counselling and Advisory Services)
17–23 Albion Street, Leicester LE1 6GD (Tel: Leicester (0533) 558763).
The Association is not itself an advisory service, but instead is the contact point for many individuals and agencies, providing a counselling and advisory service particularly for young people. It can provide local addresses and contact points for individuals who require counselling advice or information on a wide range of matters, including the whole area of sexuality.

Samaritans
The aim of this well-known organisation is to help suicidal or despairing people. Befrienders provide a 24-hour confidential 'listening ear' for those who feel they have reached the end of their tether. Sexual problems can, of course, produce acute despair and while more expert help may be needed to treat disorders of sexual function or of relationships, the Samaritans can be a valuable resource in times of crisis, which can, of course, occur at any time of the day or night, on any day of the week, when other services may not be available.

There are 183 local branches and individuals may telephone, visit or write. They can always be sure of finding non-demanding, non-judgemental friendship. Samaritan befrienders do not give advice as such, but try to help people to work through their own problems.

You will find details of your local Samaritans' branch in your telephone book, or by asking Directory Enquiries.

The Scottish Marriage Guidance Council
26 Frederick Street, Edinburgh EH2 2JR (Tel: 031-225 5006).
Local Councils in Aberdeen, Edinburgh, Glasgow, Jedburgh, and Stirling provide sex therapy. For full details of the SMGC see Chapter 15, 'Marriage Guidance'.

Woman's Own
Angela Willans (The Confidential Counselling Team), King's Reach Tower, Stamford Street, London SE1 9LS (Tel: 01-261 5000).

This magazine has advisory columns by Angela Willans and Dr Mike Smith. Both also run a service for personal, postal replies to readers who enclose a sae, and are well equipped to offer information, advice, referral, leaflets and book-lists on sexual matters.

Selected Further Information

See also Chapter 22, 'Selected Further Reading'.
Marital Therapy in Britain: Context and Therapeutic Approaches. Edited by Windy Dryden who also contributes to the main text. Published by Harper and Row Publishers, 28 Tavistock Street, London WC2E 7PN (Tel: 01-836 4635). Price: volumes one and two £8.50 each.
This two-volumed work is designed to present a comprehensive guide to the therapeutic approaches used in Britain today. The title is unfortunate in following a convention which may not be welcome to unmarried couples in committed relationships whose interests are intended to be included under the heading. We also wonder whether 'brevity' is a satisfactory reason, as stated, for continually referring to the therapist as 'him', even when in one passage the discussion is about feminist views.

The first volume is divided into two sections. Section one covers the contexts which frame marital work in Britain today; while section two is devoted to special areas of 'marital' therapy in Britain. Contributors to volume one include: Robert Chester, Jack Dominian, Jeanne Magagna, David Black, Nicholas Tyndall, Patricia Hunt, Diana Daniell, Dougal Mackay, Andy Treacher, and Michael Crowe.

In volume two contributors include: Ian Brennan, Steve Murgatroyd, Eddy Street, John Bancroft, Martin Cole, Richard Whitfield, Joy Ross, Hugh and Rachel Fielder, Lisa Parkinson, Douglas Hooper, and Paul Brown.

Therapists and counsellors will revel in the bringing together of such eminent practitioners to present not only the therapeutic practices in vogue today, but also the presentation of these practices in a coherent historical and social context. The lay person with a curiosity in these matters will also find the books of considerable interest as an insight into the world of 'couple' therapies and their exponents. Case histories provide a useful and illustrative way of setting the work in a human context. A number of the therapies seem to rely heavily on standard gender roles – the dangers surrounding 'marital' therapy can obviously include a less than flexible approach to conventions. However, the caring concern for individuals' and couples' needs is clearly shown in the varied ways in which problems and possible solutions are approached. To mention specifically just two of these approaches, in volume two John Bancroft outlines his own modified version of Masters and Johnson's treatment programme, and Martin Cole sensitively describes the controversial issue of using surrogates and the ways in which they can benefit clients with seemingly intractable problems.

Human Sexual Response by Dr William H. Masters and Virginia E. Johnson. Distributed in Great Britain and Europe by Churchill Livingstone. Published in the United States by Little, Brown & Company, Boston 1966. Price £21.25. Many modern treatments of sexual dysfunction rely heavily on the work of Masters and Johnson. Through careful research work with human models they were able to show, for the very first time, the physical reactions that occur when men and women respond to sexual stimulation, and to discredit, at last, many of the prejudices, taboos and pseudo-scientific theories which have caused such misery to so many people right up to the present day. As a result of incontrovertible evidence of physiological functioning they had gained, they were able to devise a form of therapy which, with evolving variations on the same theme, is practised widely today and which has achieved remarkable success. People who before would have been abandoned to their private miseries now have new hope offered to them.

Masters and Johnson, in their research findings and the treatment which followed, have effected a revolution in sexual understanding. The change that Masters and Johnson have brought about is so profound that one has to regard carefully, with notable exceptions, any writings on sexuality before their time. In a book published in 1951 a woman doctor could write about a separate vaginal spasm thus:

> 'Indeed, many who depend on clitoral orgasm for their enjoyment do not even realise their vaginal capacity is lacking in some way.'

The women she was treating must have been made to feel very inadequate indeed. One of the great breakthroughs Masters and Johnson made was to confirm that there is no such thing as a separate vaginal orgasm; it is direct or indirect stimulation of the clitoris which provides a woman's orgasm and which naturally, at the same time, also considerably affects the vaginal area.

Women's sexuality has long been misunderstood and women's rights to climax have either been ignored or at best placed second to those of men. Many women went through life not even knowing of the existence of a clitoris, having been taught that to touch themselves was somehow 'dirty'. New light thrown on such subjects will hopefully over the years reach people whose lives could be enriched by a greater understanding of their bodies and of their potential for sexual enjoyment.

This book represents 11 years' research into the anatomy and physiology of human sexual response and is primarily concerned with the sexual response cycles of men and women between the ages of 21 and 50. This is not to say that older people have been ignored. The authors also conducted a study into the response patterns of clients up to the age of 89, providing evidence that sexual adequacy need not necessarily decline in later years.

Sex education still does not take its rightful and dignified place within our education curricula. Unbelievably, there are today people who would argue against the provision of sex education in schools. They would no doubt agree that ignorance in other areas of our lives is undesirable – if it weren't, presumably we would have no schools – but in this one vital area of our lives ignorance is still somehow equated with innocence.

Sex educationists who are struggling for respectable recognition can now at least base their lessons more thoroughly on factual evidence. Masters and Johnson have provided

> 'physiologic fact rather than phallic fallacy to teach'.

Behaviour and education can be seen to go hand in hand, as the authors have themselves indicated. We let Masters and Johnson have the final say in our brief presentation of their work:

> 'How can biologists, behaviourists, theologians and educators insist in good conscience upon the continued existence of a massive state of ignorance of human sexual response, to the detriment of the well-being of millions of individuals? Why must the basics of human sexual physiology create such high levels of personal discomfort among the very men and women who are responsible for guiding our culture? There is no man or woman who does not face in his or her lifetime the concerns of sexual tensions. Can that one facet of our lives, affecting more people in more ways than any other physiologic response other than those necessary to our very existence, be allowed to continue without benefit of objective, scientific analysis?'

Human Sexual Inadequacy by Dr William H. Masters and Virginia E. Johnson. Distributed in Great Britain and Europe by Churchill Livingstone. Published in the United States by Little, Brown & Company, Boston, 1970. Price £21.25.
Following on the research work outlined in *Human Sexual Response* comes the practical application of what the authors had learned in the form of a programme devised to overcome specific sexual dysfunctions in men and women. Basic to all their treatment techniques is the premise that attitudes and ignorance, rather than any mental or physical illness, are responsible for most sexual problems.

Masters and Johnson have used both physiological and psychological methods to treat impotence, ejaculatory problems, including premature ejaculation, orgasm problems in women, vaginismus and painful intercourse. During 11 years of daily clinical work, Masters and Johnson's Reproductive Biology Research Foundation in St Louis treated more than 500 couples. They claim that their therapy techniques had proved successful in 80 per cent of all cases treated.

They evolved their educational and behavioural technique in order to treat couples who were seen together and who were given graded practical exercises to undertake at home. They always saw couples, because they said where sex was a problem there was no uninvolved partner. For men, they sometimes provided surrogate partners (*see* pages 2–3). An especially innovative part of their programme was the introduction of a dual therapy team, since they considered that it took both a male therapist and a female therapist to treat a couple effectively. This approach encouraged communication between partners where none had existed before.

The concept and format of the therapy programme are examined in detail in the first two chapters of the book. A full description follows of the instructions given by the therapists to effect psychosexual re-orientation of the marital partners. Analysis of each type of dysfunction, its progression and manifestations, accompanies a step-by-step explanation of practical treatment methods.

Essentially, these two Masters and Johnson books are written for professionals. For the lay person to read them from cover to cover would require considerable commitment. However, they are very interesting to 'dip' into, even for uncommitted readers. *Human Sexual Inadequacy,* particularly when discussing specific sexual problems, can be useful to the person suffering from similar difficulties, and the various case histories described provide extra insight into the subject.

Directory of Alcoholism Services Available from FARE (Federation of Alcoholic Rehabilitation Establishments), 3 Grosvenor Crescent, London SW1. Price £3.
A comprehensive national directory of alcoholism treatment services. The arrangement is by county and each county is then divided by type of service (residential facilities, day services, advice and counselling services etc.) Services are summarised by a series of symbols at the top of each page.

Human Sexuality and Its Problems by John Bancroft with the assistance of Philip Myerscough. Published by Churchill Livingstone, 1983. Price £18.
The book is divided into two main parts. Part one covers 'normal' sexuality, homosexuality and other sexual minorities. It deals with sexual development and the anatomy, physiology, biochemistry and endocrinology of sexual behaviour, in addition to sociological and psychological aspects. Part two is concerned with sexual problems – how they present, their cause, and ways in which they can be helped. Aspects covered include: types of therapy; use of surrogate partners; therapeutic aids; drugs and hormones; sexual aids; and surgical treatment. There is also a special appendix of medical practice, sexual aspects of fertility control and infertility.

Sex Therapy in Britain edited by Martin Cole and W. Dryden. To be published late in 1987 by Harper & Row, 28 Tavistock Street, London WC2 (Tel: 01-836 4635).
This book will have the most up-to-date information on sex therapy as well as the place of surrogates in sex therapy.

Sex Therapy: a Practical Guide by Keith Hawton. Published by Oxford University Press, Walton Street, Oxford OX2 6DP (Tel: Oxford (0865) 56767). Price £6.95.
The author, who has had clinical, research, and teaching experience in the field of sexual dysfunction, has written a practical account of the nature, causes, assessment and treatment of sexual problems. While, unfortunately, we have not had the opportunity of reading this book, we understand that the various stages of treatment are described in sufficient detail for therapists who are about to undergo training in sex therapy. The treatment approach includes behavioural, psychotherapeutic, and educational techniques. In addition to the treatment of couples, the management of sexual problems of individuals without partners and of physically disabled people is also described. Brief counselling and more intensive therapy are also covered.

Sex Therapy Today by Patricia and Richard Gillan. Published by Open Books Publishing 1978. Price £6.95.
We very briefly describe behavioural therapy for sexual problems earlier in this book. In the short space at our command we are only able to refer to the general theory. To learn more you could do no better than to read this

book. It describes in detail the method of sex therapy which is based on behavioural therapy, in particular the method of Masters and Johnson, together with additional behavioural methods more recently evolved.

This therapy and its variations are now widely used in treating a range of sexual problems. The authors write,

> 'One of the main principles of the treatment described in this book is the relief of anxiety associated with sexual behaviour.'

They go on to say,

> 'The sex therapist, then, aims to remove such [anxious] emotions and to replace them with emotions of pleasure, calm and sexual excitement, which will allow sexual behaviour to flourish.'

The Gillans describe the interaction this requires between therapist and client for a 'cure' to be likely, with the therapist in many ways taking over the role of an educator and the client having to work hard for the improvements he seeks and the change of behaviour which will be necessary to achieve them. They go on to describe the treatment plan and the manner of treating the problems by means of a graded series of tasks to be performed by a couple at home while they are learning to modify their behaviour. Initially these tasks are very simple, giving the couple an opportunity to gain confidence in their abilities.

We welcome the generous sharing of information regarding modern sexual therapies and the premise on which the book is based, that a person with a sexual problem who is seeking help needs to have an understanding of the treatments available to be able to come to a wise decision in his choice of therapist. The authors say that

> 'Anybody with a sexual problem would be advised to become as well informed about the alternatives as possible. This is not to say that they will be able to arrange their own treatment, but it will mean that they are in a position of greater strength and will not, like so many others, be passed off with ineffective advice or useless treatment.'

These are our sentiments exactly, and one of the reasons we have produced this Directory. Reading *Sex Therapy Today* will give you a very helpful insight into the methods of treatment now available and could, in itself, help you with specific problems you may have.

Treat Yourself to Sex by Paul Brown and Carolyn Faulder. Published by Penguin Books. Price £2.95.
The authors themselves say,

> 'We are writing for people who may, or may not, be highly experienced sexually and who, for reasons beyond their comprehension, find that sex is not the pleasure that they would like. They want to know why and they want to know what they can do about it. It is for people who are seeking honest answers together.'

They also say,

> 'We should like to help people make bad sex good and good sex better for themselves. . . Above all, however, we should like to offer this book as a contribution to the new understanding which sees enjoyable sex as a right not a privilege, of human beings.'

This book adopts a most positive approach to the matter of individual sexuality and the way in which partners relate to each other. Throughout the book the authors describe, very carefully, ways of experiencing and developing sexual enjoyment. Readers are given their very own do-it-yourself 'Sexpieces' as a means of learning specific sexual skills – based on the very reasonable assumption that sexual activity, like any other activity, has to be learned if it is to develop beyond a very basic level. Using our sexuality is as much a learned skill as any other. As you read you are learning to treat yourself. In this you could be said to be your own sex therapist and in fact the book is structured around typical weekly meetings with a sex therapist. Fun to try if you feel you are able to overcome by yourselves any inhibitions necessary to proceed through the Sexpieces.

Women's books – see Chapter 8, 'Women Only'.

Films

The treatment of sex disorders is the subject of a series of three films which were produced to provide information and guidance to those actively working in the field of sex therapy. However, they have proved to be of great value not only to those clinicians and others in charge of treatment, but also to the patients and their partners or surrogates (if they are used). It is also becoming apparent that these films are proving themselves to be of general use in sex education and are probably suitable for this purpose for anyone over 16. The films are as follows:
Female Sex Disorders. After a short introductory presentation of courtship, 'normal' sex-play and intercourse, this film proceeds to identify and describe the main sexual problems that women experience. These are heterophobia (a fear of the other sex), problems with lubrication, vaginismus, a general inability to become aroused sexually and, more specifically, a lack of orgasm. The film then goes on to discuss treatment methods currently available to help those single and married women who are distressed by these problems.
Impotence and Premature Ejaculation. This film deals more specifically with two main sex disorders of men. Firstly, it identifies the various types of impotence and then proceeds to outline various ways in which these can

be dealt with. To describe the treatment of premature ejaculation the same explicitly visual approach is used. Naturally, a description of the squeeze technique and the stop-start method are included.

Sex Disorders: an Introduction is divided into three sections. The first simply outlines the kinds of problems that are likely to be met with in the general population. This is followed by a brief and elementary treatment of the biology, anatomy and physiology of sex. The last half of the film presents a visual demonstration of a modified Masters and Johnson approach to the desensitisation of sex anxiety. The 'sensate focus' illustrated is accompanied by a commentary which emphasises the most important aspects of such a treatment programme. (For a brief description of Masters and Johnson's approach, *see* pages 7–8.)

These three films are all available from Dr Martin Cole at The Institute of Sex Education and Research (40 School Road, Moseley, Birmingham B13 9SN (Tel: 021-449 0892)). The films are available for hire or purchase and a price list is available on request. For further details of the Institute's work *see* page 106.

CHAPTER 2

Some Common Problems

In the following pages we outline some of the more common sexual difficulties. In all cases, the message is that help is available.

The list of services in Chapter 21 'Guide to Local Services' cannot be exhaustive, so if you can see no clinic near you, telephone one further away to ask their advice on the most locally available service. Alternatively, you could ring the Family Planning Information Service, 27-35 Mortimer Street, London W1N 7RJ (Tel: 01-636 7866). See also the organisations described on pages 28–31 who will be glad to help.

Dyspareunia

This is the term used to describe painful sexual intercourse experienced by a woman, often associated with vaginismus (*see* page 18).

Suffering pain during intercourse may arise from a variety of causes, which may be psychological or physical. Physical causes may include some slight malformation in the vagina which can be put right by a surgeon or which can be the result of contracting a sexually transmitted disease – again, this will respond to treatment. Scars resulting from birth difficulties may also sometimes cause problems, particularly if they have not healed properly. Certain women whose wombs rest in a tipped back position (known as a retroverted womb) may also feel pain or discomfort during intercourse. Some older women may experience some discomfort if they find their love juices flowing less freely. This can be helped by using a lubricant such as K-Y Jelly, or a doctor may prescribe hormone treatment. If the problem turns out to be psychological, as so many sexual difficulties do, it would be wise to seek advice from a skilled counsellor or therapist. Fear of pregnancy or fear of intercourse itself, for whatever reason, can lead to very real feelings of pain or discomfort during intercourse.

Whatever the cause, no woman should continue to suffer pain without seeking help, either from her own doctor or from a family planning or specialist clinic doctor. (*See also* Chapter 8, 'Women Only', which describes women's self-help groups.)

Frigidity

Although this term is not now used clinically, it is still commonly understood as a lack of sexual desire or an inability to reach a climax, and is nearly always associated with women. Difficulties with climaxes as they apply to both men and women are discussed on page 5.

Frigidity is a word which implies coldness. It is very often used in a derogatory way about women who may in fact be very distressed about being 'cold'. It can be the result of a number of unhappy conditions which make a woman unable to enjoy sex and experience orgasm. These conditions nearly all have a psychological cause and may include vaginismus (*see* page 18) and dyspareunia (*see* above).

The term 'primary frigidity' describes the situation where a woman has never experienced orgasmic release by any means. Sometimes a woman who has a severe form of primary frigidity may reject all forms of sexual contact. This can also occur in secondary frigidity, where a woman has experienced orgasm at some time, but then fails to do so. Sometimes orgasm may be reached through masturbation, but does not happen during love-making with a partner. It is in fact quite common for a woman not to experience orgasm during intercourse because the action of her partner's penis is not enough to stimulate her clitoris to orgasm. It has been shown by Masters and Johnson that it is the clitoris and not the vagina which needs to be stimulated if a woman is to achieve climax (we discuss this in greater detail on page 15). A woman who doesn't experience orgasm on every occasion of love-making need not feel any sense of failure. If a woman is to progress through the various stages of excitement to orgasm she is going to need special attention paid to various parts of her body and encouragement from her partner in every way possible. It is sad if a woman is described as frigid simply because she does not receive this loving preparation and is 'turned off'. An additional problem may be that her vagina remains dry, resulting in considerable discomfort. K-Y Jelly can be very helpful with this problem, until her love juices flow, while, of course, saliva provides a readily available alternative. Bad experiences of being 'used', lack of a good body image and poor understanding of the independent and positive role a woman can play in love-making can all lead to disappointing sexual encounters and a rejection of her own sexuality, as can conflicting ideas about purity and sin, religious taboos, fear of conception, stress and depression.

While it is possible to see how a man's poor handling of his partner may be a prime cause of her lack of interest and, therefore, of joy in their relationship, he may be acting out of ignorance of her needs and may be willing to go along with his partner to talk over problems with a psychosexual doctor or counsellor. Such consultants may in their discussions open up a means of communication between the couple, the lack of which may be partly responsible for the trouble. Any woman who is worried by an inability to reach orgasm or who is generally concerned about her own lack of responsiveness should never suffer in silence. Wonders have been worked simply by gaining a better understanding of the way a woman's body works, including the mysterious bits women themselves cannot see. In this way she may develop a pride in her ability to act as an independent sensual being. One woman speaking of her experience in *The Hite Report: a Nationwide Study of Female Sexuality* said, 'I never had orgasms during my entire marriage and its aftermath. I think what cured my frigidity was becoming my own person in other ways as well: which I did through psychotherapy and a love relationship. Orgasm for me is a part of selfhood.'

Sex therapy is available for any woman who feels she could benefit from special help. This may take different forms to suit individual needs, and may include counselling, information on contraception methods, and surrogate therapy (*see* pages 2–3). A doctor may prescibe a mild tranquilliser or recommend a bed-time sherry to bring on that nice relaxed feeling. The use of a vibrator, either alone or with a partner, might also coax a reluctant orgasm, as well as lots of other pleasant sensations (*see* page 135). *See also* Chapter 8 'Women Only', for details of women's self-help groups.

Heterophobia

Heterophobia is the term used to describe the fear of, or the dread of close contact with, people of the opposite sex.

Heterophobic people are not necessarily homosexual. Despite appearances to the contrary, their sexual behaviour and thinking may well be directed towards people of the opposite sex, but their anxieties are such that they are quite unable to form a close relationship. Some heterophobes may attempt intercourse, but are unlikely to be successful.

In the absence of a sexual partner, treatment can be difficult. Surrogate therapy (*see* page 8) may well help. Dr Martin Cole has found that good results have been obtained for some of his heterophobic patients when they have undertaken a programme of treatment with the help of a sympathetic surrogate partner.

Impotence

The inability in a man to have sexual intercourse due to erectile problems is referred to as impotence. A man is said to suffer from 'primary impotence' when he has never been able to have intercourse as a result of a failure to obtain an erection. Men who have previously adequately performed, but who then experience difficulties in obtaining an erection are said to suffer from 'secondary impotence.' Primary impotence is relatively uncommon. (*See also* 'Orgasm Trouble' page 15). To men the threat of impotence can loom large. It is not something to be admitted, only feared, and it is very often fear itself that prolongs a period of impotence. Perhaps the blustering bar-room stories of endless sexual conquests, that some men engage in represent an attempt to lay their fears at rest or are a way of bolstering their confidence. Listening to talk of this kind can easily persuade you that other men are having a far better time than you are. It is hardly surprising that many men should have difficulties from time to time in fulfilling a role that has been forced upon them. A man is often taught very early on that to be seen as really masculine he must be tough, aggressive and competitive; he must avoid softness, hide his emotions and bury his finer feelings. He must have no doubts about his prowess in the sexual act. He must accept full responsibility within a relationship for the initiation and pace of sexual activity. If he does not or, if his spirit flags, he is somehow less of a man.

Tradition has it that women expect toughness and dominance – that they want 'to be taken' as forcefully as possible and that a penis which is not hard and erect at every available moment is not worthy of consideration. As naturally passive creatures they expect their men to be powerful and to take charge of them and their sexuality – what an awesome responsibility!

While some women may encourage this belief, far

more would prefer to play a full and active role, to celebrate with their partners the delights of slow, sensuous love-making where, incidentally, insecurities in either partner are less keenly felt. In a relaxed and comfortable situation, where no goals are pursued or set, there is space and time for partners to express themselves.

It is the continuing and unrealistic demands which are so often placed upon a man's capabilities which are liable to create penile insecurity leading to impotence. Both sexes need to give and receive gentleness in their lives, to be touched and loved for their own sakes, but as a man you may have been brought up to believe that talking about your own feelings is somehow weak and that love-play must always lead to intercourse or, conversely, that it is not worth bothering with unless it does. Touch in such circumstances can never be enjoyed for its own sake: it is a challenge rather than a delight to be savoured for itself. You may feel you have to avoid touching if you don't think you can 'follow it through' to the ultimate 'goal' of intercourse. On these terms many women are left emotionally stranded, fearing the touch which treats them only as sex objects.

Many men, during their lives, will experience periods when they are unable to achieve or maintain an erection. This may be due to psychological or emotional causes, to ill-health or sometimes to drinking too heavily. These phases are usually fleeting and with understanding from a partner will not develop into a long lasting problem. It is important to recognise that occasional failure, even when there appears to be no reason for it, is a common experience and should be accepted without too much concern.

Certain drugs prescribed for high blood pressure or for other conditions, and some tranquillisers and anti-depressants may also cause impotence as a side effect. If you feel this may be the case it is important to discuss the matter with your doctor who may be able to restrict the dosage or substitute another form of treatment.

Other causes of impotence include genital diseases, prostate problems, hormonal disorders, surgery or accident affecting the spinal cord, and sometimes other long-term conditions like diabetes and multiple sclerosis. (*See* Chapter 12, 'Sexuality and Disability'). In other cases, the cause can be wholly psychological. Some men who fail to have an erection with a sexual partner may nevertheless be able to achieve erection and ejaculation by masturbation. This suggests that if feelings of excessive shyness, guilt, fear of women or other psychological 'blocks' can be removed, the man will be able to enjoy normal sexual relations.

Orgastic impotence, where a man is able to have intercourse to the point of ejaculation, but then finds that ejaculation is an anti-climax and not attended by particularly intense feelings, may derive from the same causes as erectile impotence. There may also be particular psychological reasons for the condition, for example if a man has an unusually undemanding attitude towards his own sexual needs to the point where because of his low self-esteem his motivation is lost.

Masters and Johnson, by gaining a greater understanding through research and observation of human sexual behaviour, were able to evolve treatments which are practised by many psychosexual therapists and which have a high measure of success. A better understanding of the fine line between potency and impotency and of the fragility of men's confidence in this respect has led to more successful therapies to help this most distressing condition. Knowing that there is understanding help at hand may be half the battle. Certainly there is no need to suffer such a problem alone. Any clinic where there is a psychosexual counselling service should be able to help.

If you can be fairly certain that your impotence has no physical cause, a course of treatment involving sexual therapy may prove helpful. You can learn, or relearn, forms of sexual expression which will, by focusing on varied ways of pleasuring, 'take the pressure off your penis'. You may come to realise that all is not lost because you don't have an erection absolutely to order. As Starr and Weiner say in their report, *Sex and Sexuality in the Mature Years*,

> 'As we have constantly emphasised sexual energy exists regardless of erection or ejaculation, it resides in the vitality of the individual. Therefore it is possible to have powerful fulfilling sexual experiences with or without an erection.'

Bernard Zilbergeld in his splendid book, *Men and Sex*, (*see* Chapter 22, 'Selected Further Reading') writes,

> 'If your penis doesn't work the way you want it to, remember that it's trying to tell you something. It's not your enemy. It was made for sex, it likes sex. If it's not working the way you like, it's telling you that there is something wrong with the way you are going about sex. If you want better sex, you need to start deciphering your penis's message'.

Those who suffer from primary impotence may at first be difficult to help, since men who have this problem are unlikely to have sexual partners. However, it is now possible for female sex partners to be found who work as surrogates (*see* page 2) and who have proved to be of considerable benefit to their clients. Dr Martin Cole (*see* page 106), who pioneered work of this type in the UK, claims a marked improvement in performance and confidence in about 75 per cent of cases treated.

Sex aids (*see* chapter 17, 'Sex Aids') sometimes prove helpful with erectile dysfunction, for example, a penile splint – a soft rubber cylinder which will keep a soft penis sufficiently rigid for intercourse, even though there is no erection, and leaves the glans of the penis uncovered to permit sensitive contact with the vagina. The use of such aids may reduce anxiety about the need to have an erection and the ability to satisfy a partner. If the impotence is not longstanding, a suitable device may provide the encouragement a man needs to be able to return to independent intercourse. A vibrator can also sometimes be useful in reducing anxiety when unable to achieve penetration.

There is no reason why impotence should necessarily be associated with mature years, but a number of factors which may cause difficulty are discussed in Chapter 16, 'Sex in Later Life'.

Loss of Libido

Libido is the term used to describe sexual drive or energy.

Libido is, without doubt, a central driving force in our personalities, but it varies in strength from time to time, from person to person and with age and one's state of health. The intensity of libido is closely related to hormone levels in our bodies. These levels vary from time to time in men, and in women they vary in tune with the menstrual cycle. However, it is encouraging to find that our production of hormones is quickly stepped up when we respond to whatever turns us on. A loving partner can work wonders in this way.

Libidinous drive as a basic life force is considered to affect not only the degree to which we seek sexual gratification, but other inter-related aspects of our nature. Conversely our libido may be adversely affected by poor health, depression or tiredness. Alternatively, we may have purposely damped down the sexual fires, fearing the strength of our own desire and being inhibited about expressing our feelings.

Many people fear loss of libido in old age, very often unnecessarily, and we discuss this in Chapter 16, 'Sex in Later Life'. That is not to say that libido is not age-related. Manifestly, problems may be overcome simply by taking more rest, having more fun, being prepared to take time to enjoy sexual activity, and being alert and receptive to different kinds of stimulation. Whatever the problem, if your libido is letting you down and your own measures don't seem to be working, a doctor or a psychosexual counsellor will be glad to discuss possible causes and treatment.

Non-consummation

When a husband's penis enters his wife's vagina for the first time, their marriage is considered to be consummated. If the wife is a virgin, the hymen, a membrane which at birth covered the vagina, may need to be stretched and sometimes torn sufficiently to allow an erect penis to pass through. The hymen rarely offers much resistance to firm but gentle stretching.

There is something old-fashioned about the word 'consummation'. It conjures up those cultural values which require brides to keep themselves pure and unsullied for their future husbands. It is part of the belief that a wife somehow belongs to her husband. Consummation takes place on the wedding night and the couple are then considered to have completed the process of becoming husband and wife. Indeed, it is possible to seek a declaration to make a marriage null and void in many situations in which consummation does not take place. Among those people who believe virginity to be important for religious or social reasons, husbands have been known to feel cheated if there are no signs of blood on the bridal sheets after their first intercourse. However, this is an unreliable test of virginity. It is true that if the penis in addition to stretching the hymen also tears it slightly there may be a little blood to show for its endeavours. However, the hymen may have been previously stretched in some other way, perhaps through energetic exercise or using tampons or by a doctor. Then there would not necessarily be any bleeding – virgin or not.

Aside from a couple making a rational decision to share their lives but not their beds, and therefore to remain celibate, there is a variety of reasons why an intended sexual relationship may not be consummated. A couple may wish to enjoy intercourse as part of their love-making, but somehow find themselves unable to go through with the act. It is rarely that one partner is entirely to blame for any difficulties and attributing blame, in any case, can only make matters worse. Dr David Delvin in *The Book of Love* (*see* page 214) describes how a man suffering from impotence was seeking treatment alone because he blamed himself for the marriage's failure, while his wife, who firmly rejected any responsibility for the problems, was found to have married twice before, but had somehow managed to remain a virgin throughout! She had long suffered from a severe case of vaginismus. In fact this condition is a major cause of non-consummation.

Obviously then, where there are difficulties over consummation and in starting a happy sexual life as a couple, it is important for the man and woman to seek help together. Any couples with this problem may approach their family doctor; alternatively, they may prefer to talk to someone who has a special understanding of psychosexual problems. Some counsellors and therapists are prepared to make appointments direct with their intending patients, while others will require referral from a family doctor.

Before treatment begins a doctor will examine you to check that there are no physical abnormalities preventing intercourse and that the rest of the body has developed and is functioning well. The most common causes of non-consummation are impotence in men (*see* page 12) and vaginismus and dyspareunia (*see* pages 18 and 11) in women. More often than not, these conditions can be satisfactorily treated. Many couples now leading happy and mutually satisfying sex lives had difficulties at the beginning in overcoming prejudice, inhibitions and fears. It is always worth making the effort to seek help. The basis of a happy life together may be at stake. Simply gaining a better understanding of our own and our partner's needs and how our bodies will work for us if we let them, can resolve the difficulties.

Orgasm Trouble

Orgasmic dysfunction is the term used to describe difficulty in achieving orgasm – in women this may be one of the problems associated with frigidity (*see* page 11) or dyspareunia (*see* page 11), and in men, with impotence (*see* page 12). Alternatively, in men there may be problems with premature ejaculation (*see* page 16), or retarded ejaculation, (*see* page 17). Failure to achieve orgasm can be primary, where it has always been difficult or impossible to climax either during intercourse or masturbation, or it can be secondary where the difficulty has occurred after a period of normal sexual functioning.

There are many possible reasons for problems with climaxes. Disease, certain drugs, spinal cord injury, accident or surgery may cause loss or reduction of sensation. It is important if you think you may have a medical problem that you check with a doctor. More often than not, however, orgasm difficulties are psychological, and can be overcome by wise counselling.

Orgasms in themselves are a marvellous way of casting aside inhibitions, in fact they rather depend on it. Most women find that orgasm can only result from all the stimulation they are receiving from themselves or from a partner if they are prepared to 'let go', if they can abandon themselves to sheer delight. Sometimes, the problem may be simply a lack of privacy, or an inexpert or insensitive partner, but the most persistent enemies of orgasm are those deeply ingrained inhibitions which hold us in their grip. We may have been brought up very strictly by parents who never even mentioned sex and showed no physical affection for each other in our presence. We may have learned that parts of our body were 'dirty' and not to be touched. We may also, in consequence, believe that a naked body is a thing of shame, to be kept hidden from our partners and even from ourselves. We may suffer from all sorts of religious taboos. If we feel guilty about 'indulging' in sex, it is not surprising that orgasms are difficult or impossible to achieve, because they require an imaginative commitment to freedom of expression. We cannot help our upbringing, but if we recognise the problems we are halfway to solving them. We may need help in this, however, and a psychosexual counsellor may be able to provide the sort of advice and supportive encouragement we need to leave behind the unnecessary guilty feelings with which we have been burdened and to help us function as we would wish.

Most men reach orgasm easily, probably thousands of times during their lives; but a much smaller proportion of women will do so and less often. Indeed some women, having little understanding of their own sexuality, may not even know they have the ability to achieve orgasm. It is not surprising that women are so confused, since it is only recently that the myth of a separate vaginal orgasm was finally laid to rest by Masters and Johnson. We now know that although during intercourse the vagina is an area affording much pleasure for a woman, it is not the source of her climax, and orgasm cannot be reached through vaginal stimulation alone. It is the clitoris which is comparable in sensitivity to the penis and which when correctly stimulated directly or indirectly, provides her pleasure. Given the position of the clitoris, above and somewhat away from the vaginal area, we cannot be surprised that only relatively few women regularly achieve orgasm during intercourse without additional stimulation. However, indirect stimulation to the clitoris, when the skin around the clitoris may be moved back and forth as the penis thrusts, can sometimes give sufficient stimulation for orgasm to be reached during intercourse. It can also be stimulated by hand, mouth or vibrator during love-making, separately from the act of intercourse. One of the commonest sources of difficulty arises because most men reach climax quite quickly, whereas a woman takes longer. If sexual intercourse alone is relied upon, this often results in a sense of inadequacy in the man and frustration in the woman. A man needs to know that a woman's response is more subtle than his, and is greatly influenced by emotional factors. She is likely to take longer to get 'turned on' and may need quite prolonged stimulation to reach orgasm.

In men and women the experience of orgasm may be similar (who knows?), but the road towards climax tends to be very different. The triggers in love-making for women depend to a much greater degree on the active consideration of their partners, whereas men can often achieve climax in a crude way without much involvement of the woman: a sad and, in the end, unsatisfying experience for both partners. Men have not always understood the equal need a woman has to achieve orgasm and therefore they have tended to deny this vital area of a woman's sexuality, causing the frustration and the boredom many women feel in their sexual relationships. One woman in *The Hite Report: a Nationwide Study of Female Sexuality* summed it up:

> 'Whoever said orgasm wasn't important for a woman was undoubtedly a man.'

Sex therapists will sometimes actively recommend masturbation to their clients to help them to achieve orgasm and thereby build up their own confidence in this respect. For a woman, masturbation may not only help to encourage orgasm and self-confidence, but also to establish a healthy and guilt-free familiarity with her own body. Women concerned with questions about masturbating and sexuality generally may be encouraged by identifying with the women's self-help movement (*see* details in Chapter 8, 'Women Only').

Vibrators may be helpful to achieve climax, especially for women who find that manual caressing does not provide sufficient stimulation. They can be particularly helpful to people whose sensations have been diminished by disability. For some disabled people, masturbation can present problems, particularly where there is a lack of privacy or where they need help to make the necessary movements. Yet such people would especially enjoy the relief and pleasure orgasm can bring. Staff in homes and institutions, as well as parents, usually prefer to deny sexuality in the people they see as being in their care, and are reluctant to respond to an obvious human need. Anyone who is so denied may benefit from the help of a counsellor who has received special training and has experience of such situations. SPOD (*see* page 91) would be able to advise on local help available.

No one would sensibly deny the importance of orgasm – this great explosion of pleasure and relief. But it is not the whole of sex, and sex can be perfectly valid and joyful without it. Women, in particular, may prefer relationships which are less goal-orientated. Love-making does not have to be fast and furious, with only one end in view. Sexually liberated people who are not locked into the traditional sex roles so often forced on men and women can more easily enjoy slow sensuous love-making with no precise demands being made on either partner, simply a sharing of pleasuring. Such activities within a loving relationship can unlock undreamed of areas of joy and allow partners time and opportunity for full expression of their individual sexual identities. In such an atmosphere, when vitality and virility allow, orgasms are much more likely to flourish.

Premature Ejaculation

Ejaculation which occurs too easily and too quickly in sexual activity with a partner, either before intercourse or immediately after penetration, is referred to as premature ejaculation. In other words it is a matter of a man reaching his climax too early for his partner's satisfaction.

Premature ejaculation, or 'hairtrigger trouble' as it is sometimes known, is one of the most common male problems. Quite the reverse of impotence, it can nevertheless cause serious distress to a man and also to his partner, who may be left feeling unsatisfied and 'unwanted', having had too little time to reach a high level of excitement. For the man, the normally pleasurable sensation of release associated with ejaculation is spoilt by feelings of anxiety and failure.

The causes of premature ejaculation are still imperfectly understood, but it is a problem which can be overcome. Given that over-anxiety about sex is sometimes the cause of the difficulty, you may find that a couple of stiff drinks relax the tension just enough – but beware the 'brewer's droop'! Or you could visit a sex shop and buy one of those anaesthetic sprays which can be applied to the glans of the penis. These are calculated to delay ejaculation by deadening feeling!

In many cases, however, premature ejaculation should be taken very seriously. Because it is so potentially destructive of sexual harmony, it is advisable to seek help from a doctor or psychosexual counsellor as soon as possible. Some doctors will prescribe drugs – certain tranquillisers or anti-depressants – which may delay ejaculation, but which, unfortunately, may have side effects. There is also the problem that when you stop taking them the problem of premature ejaculation is likely to return.

Natural methods of control are to be preferred wherever possible and there are two happy and appropriate ways of dealing with the problem, provided a man has an encouraging and co-operative partner. The first method is for her to accept an initial premature ejaculation, seeing it as a relieving of tension, and then for her to go on to stimulate the man to encourage him to try again. The second attempt at intercourse, with some of the tension resolved, may be more successful, providing just the confidence the man needs.

Another technique, developed by Masters and Johnson, and reported in *Human Sexual Inadequacy* (*see* page 8), is known as the 'squeeze' method. Again an understanding partner is essential. She must be willing to control the reactions of the man's penis in its response pattern. After initial stimulation of the penis she must apply firm pressure, squeezing it between fingers and thumb just below the corona of the glans, that is, below the head of the penis. She squeezes quite hard and holds the pressure for about four seconds. This way ejaculation will be prevented. This may need to be repeated several times before intercourse and also while intercourse is being attempted. Apparently, this method of control does not work if the man applies the pressure himself.

In either method the co-operation of a partner is essential. However, where a man has no current partner or only an unco-operative one, he may wish to consider surrogate therapy, where an experienced substitute sexual partner will help him to learn the techniques to prevent premature ejaculation. Dr Martin Cole (*see* pages 2–3) has a special treatment programme using the natural methods described above which sometimes includes surrogate therapy.

Retarded Ejaculation

This is the opposite extreme to premature ejaculation, when a man, although able to achieve and maintain an erection, takes a very long time to reach orgasm and ejaculation, perhaps never getting there at all. The problem may be primary where a man has never ejaculated or secondary where a man who has had no particular previous difficulty finds this condition arising as a reaction to a sexually stressful situation. Some men, although able to 'come' through masturbation or, perhaps, oral sex, find themselves unable to release their seminal fluid and to experience orgasm through intercourse.

The reasons for this difficulty are various. A man may be anxious lest his partner conceives, or have an irrational fear of 'contaminating' her with his seed. He may be subject to deep-rooted inhibitions implanted during a strict upbringing, or have feelings of fear or hostility towards his partner or towards women generally. Such problems can often be helped by discussion with a sexual therapist who may suggest a programme of love-making activities for the man who has a co-operative partner. He may also be encouraged to masturbate to learn how to ejaculate and achieve a climax. Using a lubricant such as K-Y Jelly may also be recommended.

Where there is a fear of conception, a thorough discussion of various contraceptive methods should allay anxiety. Sometimes surrogate therapy (*see* page 2) may be helpful. Where there are problems of this kind in our sexual lives, the sooner help is sought the better chance there is for success, leading to loving and fulfilling sexual relationships.

Sex and Alcohol

We are very much aware that many sex and marital problems are closely linked with heavy drinking habits.

The 'soft lights and sweet music' setting will nearly always have alcohol to aid and abet the romantic turn-on. Without doubt, a little alcohol does wonders for releasing our inhibitions and chasing away our anxieties and fears. That stirring in the genitals as the liquid courses down can be a glorious prelude to love-making.

The trick lies in knowing our limits, because more than that small and magic amount can land us in trouble. The difficulty is in recognising the borderline beyond which alcohol affects our nervous system seriously enough to lead to sexual failure and marital and social difficulties. Under the influence of too much drink both men and women can be adversely affected, but it is the man's performance which is likely to suffer most. He may find himself suffering from 'brewer's droop'. All that anticipation, then nothing doing.

Alcohol acts as a depressant on the nervous system, and taken in quantity it is an enemy of erection and sex, along with other activities. As Shakespeare said in *Macbeth* :

> 'It [drink] provokes the desire, but it takes away the performance.'

Chronic and heavy drinking will not only eventually dampen down sexual desires, but will also drastically affect sexual functioning. Therapists and doctors say that this can happen long before the stage of alcoholism is reached. Masters and Johnson in their book *Human Sexual Response* (*see* page 7), when discussing the ageing male say:

> While under its [alcohol's] influence, many a male of any age has failed for the first time to achieve or maintain an erection of the penis. Secondary impotence developing in the male in the late 40s or 50s has a higher incidence of direct association with excessive alcohol consumption than with any other single factor.

If you have a 'drink' problem or are prepared to admit that your drinking could cause problems in the future, it is wise to seek advice. It is a difficult problem to face alone. Some towns have special centres where you can go for advice and where you can be seen in privacy and with complete confidentiality. Your local Alcoholics Anonymous group (*see* page 4) will have information on local services. You would not need to be an 'alcoholic' to seek advice.

In Chapter 21, 'Guide to Local Services', we give details of two organisations in London who help people within their stated areas: ACCEPT and the Alcohol Counselling Service. ACCEPT has some useful publications, including *It's Your Life – a Guide to Survival in a Drinking Culture* and *I Never Thought It Could Happen to Me*.

Vaginismus

Vaginismus is a condition in which a woman involuntarily contracts the muscles surrounding her vagina in a sudden and sometimes painful muscular spasm making intercourse impossible. If intercourse is nevertheless attempted, the act can be extremely painful for the woman. Although she may not intend this, it is her way of saying 'no' to an experience she fears. Vaginismus may also be accompanied by dryness of the vagina, because only when a woman is relaxed and happily anticipating the act of love-making will her love juices flow.

Vaginismus is a troublesome condition, but is one of the easiest sexual dysfunctions to treat. The problem can be improved and very often cured if a woman is given the sympathetic help she needs from someone who understands the difficulty. This could be her doctor or a psychosexual counsellor or therapist. Any sexual partner must also learn to show extra sensitivity and tolerant understanding of the reasons lying behind a woman's fearful rejection of love-making. If she is suffering dryness of her genitals, perhaps through lack of stimulation or inability to respond in a relaxed way, then this will cause considerable discomfort. K-Y Jelly can be very helpful or saliva will provide a readily available alternative.

The cause of vaginismus, which is usually psychological, may be found in a repressive childhood where sexual matters were considered 'dirty', where a girl was taught to hide her body and to be especially ashamed of her genitals. She may also have been taught by female relatives to fear men and their 'unreasonable' demands to which she would have to be a martyr. The 'hidden' parts of her sexual organs may have remained a mystery even into womanhood, a mystery she would be afraid to feel, touch and explore.

Women's groups (*see* Chapter 8, 'Women Only') and some therapists and doctors are now encouraging women to become better acquainted with their own bodies and to learn to explore the vagina with their fingers or with dilators of graded sizes. A mirror is often used so that a woman may see how those inside parts look and also see just what she is doing to herself. Familiarity with her sexual organs will help her to dispel ignorance and to be at ease with herself. She may experience a new sense of pride in her vagina and all its workings. She may learn that this marvellously warm and cushioned passage is plenty big enough to accept and welcome any size of erect penis, offsetting any fear that she will be hurt or damaged in any way by the act of intercourse. For virgins who suffer from vaginismus this may be a very real fear. Other women may suffer vaginismus after a bad sexual experience, especially after the horrific experience of rape.

It is important that the male partner should be part of any treatment or discussion. Intercourse, when there are difficulties, may be easiest with the woman on top of her partner, lowering herself gently on to the man's erect penis. Having command over the act of intercourse may provide a woman with just the confidence this delicate occasion needs to ensure a happy coupling.

For those women who have no partner, perhaps because they fear the sexual outcome of any friendship with a man and their own inability to cope, there may be a case for suggesting surrogate therapy. An understanding male may, over a period of time and in a therapeutic programme, be able to give just the confidence needed.

There are, of course, also a number of physical causes of painful sex, which will temporarily cause a woman involuntarily to 'shut off' her vagina. These include some gynaecological and skin conditions which a doctor trained in psychosexual medicine should be able to diagnose and for which he can provide suitable treatment (*see* 'Dyspareunia', page 11). Whatever the cause, it is important to seek skilled help as soon as possible. The sooner an understanding of the problem is gained, the easier the solution will be. We list in Chapter 21, 'Guide to Local Services', those places where psychosexual counselling is available. All of these would be able to help to encourage sexual and personal confidence in any woman suffering from the problems of vaginismus.

Deviations and Perversions

These are variations from normal behaviour beyond the limits generally found acceptable to the mainstream of public opinion.

A sexual deviant could be described as someone who is aroused and takes sexual pleasure from variations of sexual expression not usually accepted as normal. But what is normal? Anything we don't personally do, we rather suspect.

Opinion as to what is sexually abnormal varies from time to time, and from person to person. Deviancy can be defined only on a sliding scale in relation to what may loosely be described as the current climate of opinion, which itself, of course, is made up of a wide range of personal preferences and prejudices. A more satisfactory approach, perhaps, is that nothing is perverted if it is engaged in by consenting adults and does not damage anyone psychologically or physically. Certainly we would not attempt to say where normality ends and deviancy begins, but it is appropriate to caution that some forms of deviancy are potentially very dangerous, sometimes even fatal. They can become compulsive and obsessive, and are increasingly dangerous as fulfilment becomes harder to achieve. For instance, very serious risks are run by masochists who are without willing helpers and who force themselves to carry out increasingly bizarre and gruesome rituals on themselves. Attempts at partial strangulation can result in death and other self-inflicted punishments can go tragically wrong.

Many people who associate sex with pain may have had a heavily disciplined childhood. A parent who doled out physical punishment in the name of love will have imprinted a growing and vulnerable child with strange and paradoxical feelings. In adulthood, he or she may find it difficult to relate to another person in a warm and loving way and may forever associate love and sexuality with pain and punishment. Repression causes grave damage to impressionable children who may find their only pleasures as adults are austere and solitary.

Rather than continuing to take ridiculous and life threatening risks, it is important for people whose deviation is out of reasonable control to ask for help in order to try to adjust more suitably to the deviation. It has to be said that treatment which seeks to modify such obsessions can be difficult, given that the motivation for change is unlikely to be strong. A clear-cut desire to modify behaviour has to be the basis for any therapy.

Aversion therapy has occasionally been practised to discourage deviations and perversions, but it is questionable if this is a desirable way to attack the problem; it may indeed be counter-productive. Associating the deviation with a painful experience, rather than allaying the problems, could serve to heighten them.

Drug treatment may sometimes be recommended to reduce sex drive. Psychotherapy may also be helpful in gaining a greater insight into personal feelings and the reasons for deviant behaviour.

A number of the many deviations are briefly described below.

Bestiality and Zoophilia

Where people are sexually attracted by animals, and sometimes seek to have illegal intercourse with them (*see* page 153).

Body Piercing

Often a part of bondage (*see* below). Rings may be attached to the foreskin, vaginal lips and nipples, to which may be linked padlocks or stainless steel shackles. Needless to say, do-it-yourself piercing can be very dangerous.

Bondage

When a person in a sexual relationship is restrained by all manner of straps, ties, ropes, chains, gags and other restraints to induce sexual excitement.

Coprophagia

The consuming of the faeces of a sexually admired person.

Coprophilia

A morbid attraction for excrement, usually but not always human. A wish to be debased and made filthy and therefore unworthy by wallowing in faeces may be part of a masochist's sexual fulfilment (*see* below).

Exhibitionism

Most of us exhibit ourselves at some time or other by dressing up in sexy clothes or undressing for our lover. We are here referring to exhibitionism in a narrow sense where a person (usually a man) deliberately exposes his genitals in public to women or children to gratify his sexual needs. Such a man is popularly called a 'flasher' and is committing an offence known as indecent exposure (*see* page 157).

Fetishism

We all have a variety of personal triggers which turn us on. A fetishist, however, is someone who cannot be aroused to sexual excitement without the stimulus of a very specific object or material such as leather, rubber, boots or shoes or some other very specially revered article. In these cases the normal object of sexual love is replaced by the fetish. There has been a redirection of the sexual instinct towards an object. Sometimes this may be carried to the point where a sexual relationship with another person is virtually impossible.

Flagellation (or whipping or flogging).

Flagellants obtain sexual pleasure by whipping themselves or others (*see* also Sadism and Masochism).

Masochism

Where pleasure is derived from the experience of pain or humiliation. This may be inflicted by another person or may be self-inflicted (*see* Sado-masochism).

Necrophilia

Sexual attraction to corpses, sometimes leading to intercourse. Most necrophiliacs are male and may well have normal sexual relations as well.

Necrosadism

Where corpses are subjected to wanton mutilation as part of sexual activity.

Paederasty

Sodomy or anal intercourse with a boy or a young man.

Sodomy is illegal except between consenting male adults over 21 years of age in private.

Paedophilia

Sexual attraction to children, whether male or female, sometimes leading to fondling, sex games, masturbation and intercourse. When the child is a member of the offender's immediate family then the question of incest arises (*see* Chapters 9, 'Sexual Abuse', and 20, 'Sex Law'). Incest is a serious criminal offence and, in any case, sexual activity with children under the age of 16 is illegal in the UK. Such activity, given the trust a child should be able to rely on in an adult, can cause lifelong emotional damage to the child.

Sadism

Where pleasure is derived in response to inflicting or thinking about inflicting pain on other people. (*See* also Bondage and Flagellation.)

Sado-masochism

Sexual activity in which one partner (the sadist) enjoys inflicting pain, while the other partner (the masochist) enjoys receiving it.

Urolangia

A fascination with the passing of urine by a sex partner, possibly by watching the person urinate, or by urinating on or being urinated upon. There may be a desire to drink urine or to smell it – say on a pair of knickers while masturbating. Some women experience intense sexual pleasure while urinating when they are already sexually aroused, and young girls may enjoy wetting their knickers.

Voyeurism

The condition of deriving sexual pleasure from watching activities which may be associated with sex, from watching a partner undressing in preparation for bed to watching explicit sex shows or couples making love in the bushes. When a voyeur creeps up to people's windows to peep inside hoping to see sexual activity or nudity, he is known as a 'Peeping Tom'. Clearly though, we all enjoy a good deal of mild voyeurism and it is only a question of degree as to when the practice becomes unacceptable.

Water Pleasure

Water and soap together are for many people powerful arousers. Shared baths and showers and copious soapings can provide just the right ingredients for exciting love play. Some men and women go a stage further and enjoy water sensations in the rectum or vagina, by means of special enema or douche equipment. The advertisements often talk about high colonic irrigation when these services are provided by prostitutes.

CHAPTER 3

Family Planning

The first birth control societies, operating in the 1920s, had as their slogan 'Children by choice not chance'. Thanks to their pioneering work, a woman can now be in command of her body rather than a slave to it.

Moreover, with improving medical care and a better understanding of hygiene, at least in industrialised countries, women need no longer fear dying in pregnancy or childbirth, and babies will usually survive birth and the vulnerable early years. Women no longer need to bear ten children, hoping that two will survive. They can plan their families and their lives and are refusing to accept an unremitting cycle of child-bearing. At the same time, sexual activity has been relieved of the fear of unwanted pregnancy, and can be indulged in with uninhibited love, and for pleasure as well as for procreation.

Women now have real choice. We can decide in the first place whether to have children at all or, if we do want a family, how many children we want and when. This means not just that as adults we can please ourselves whether we become parents, but also that we can ensure that all babies born to us are wanted and much desired additions to our families. Through the vital element of choice the quality of parenthood is greatly enhanced.

Family Planning Clinics

Family planning clinics provide a wide-ranging service covering various forms of birth control. However, there are regional variations in the provision of services, particularly in the availability of sterilisation and abortion. We would urge you to contact your local clinic. If the clinic is unable to help you with a particular problem, they can usually recommend you to another source of help. If you prefer, you can contact your nearest Family Planning Association Regional Office (*see* page 28), or telephone or write to the Family Planning Information Service at 27-35 Mortimer Street, London W1N 7RJ Tel: 01-636 7866). The Scottish Health Education Group, Woodburn House, Canaan Lane, Edinburgh EH10 4SG will provide information on family planning clinics and other appropriate services in Scotland.

There are now nearly 2000 family planning clinics throughout the UK, operating as part of the NHS. They are mainly run by district health authorities or occasionally on behalf of these by other organisations, such as the Family Planning Association or Brook Advisory Centres. They operate from health centres, hospitals and local authority premises. To find the address of your local clinic you need only look under 'Family Planning' in the telephone directory or Yellow Pages. Post offices, Community Health Councils and Citizens' Advice Bureaux will also be able to tell you the address of the nearest clinic.

In addition to the NHS services, certain charitable organisations provide birth control services on a fee-paying basis. These include the British Pregnancy Advisory Service (*see* page 29) and Marie Stopes House (*see* page 175).

Most family planning clinics prefer to serve those people who live or work in their immediate neighbourhood and, apart from a few which provide a 'walk-in' service, will usually ask you to make an appointment. But if you have a particular problem which you feel needs immediate attention a clinic should arrange for a member of staff to see you on the spot. Anyone may attend a clinic, regardless of their age, and whether or not they are married. All personal information will be treated as strictly confidential. It isn't necessary to have a referral letter from your family doctor, even for your first visit. Mostly, you need not give the name of your doctor at all, although the clinic will usually ask for his or her name, as the person responsible for your health. Your doctor need be informed only if you decide to take the pill (*see* page 22), to use a coil (*see* page 24) or to be sterilised (*see* page 24). However, the clinic will at all times ask your permission before informing your doctor. Confidentiality is always respected. The service is free to all UK residents, together with any supplies which are provided.

Specialist Services

Some agencies provide specialist services. The Brook Advisory Centres, for instance, aim to cater for young people's needs (*see* page 30) and a few NHS family planning clinics also specialise in young people's services. In some areas, domiciliary or home-visiting services are available for women who are housebound or who find clinics and surgeries intimidating, though in recent years there has been a cutting-back of such services. Where available, a woman may be referred to the service by a midwife, health visitor, doctor or social worker. The service and any supplies are provided free of charge. (For information on contraceptives as they relate to women with disabilities, see *Toward Intimacy: Family Planning and Sexuality Concerns of Physically Disabled Women*, details on page 99). Pregnancy testing for those who are more than 14 days overdue with their period is carried out by some family planning clinics, but there may be a charge (*see* page 27).

General Practitioners and Family Planning

Family doctors joined the family planning part of the NHS back in 1975. Now most general practitioners provide a contraceptive service, though this service may be limited by comparison with the services provided at family planning clinics. In practice this means that they will prescribe the pill, while only a small proportion will fit IUCDs or the diaphragm. A very small number of practices will undertake vasectomies. Some will provide pregnancy testing, though there may be a charge. No family doctors provide condoms or the contraceptive vaginal sponge.

As a patient, if you decide you would prefer a family doctor rather than a clinic to provide this service for you, you are entitled to ask your own doctor (unless he is one of the few who has opted out) or if for any reason you prefer not to discuss birth control with your own doctor, you are entitled to go to another family doctor of your choice. A list of general practitioners offering a contraceptive service in your area is provided by the local Family Practitioner Committee and is available at post offices or from your local Community Health Council or from Citizens' Advice Bureaux. Health visitors and midwives would also have a list.

The service is free to all UK residents irrespective of age or marital status, together with any supplies which are provided.

Birth Control Methods

Alas, the perfect birth control method has not yet been developed and, except for the ubiquitous male sheath, it is still the woman who usually has to take the responsibility and the precautions. It is to be hoped that before too long researchers will come up with new contraceptives which are effective and more convenient to use.

It is important to choose carefully the method of birth control you feel will best suit your needs and lifestyle – medically and psychologically. For a woman, the anxiety of inefficient contraceptives or the lack of them can ruin all hope of carefree sexual activity, while, in addition, her nervous reaction is bound to affect a sensitive partner.

Basic methods of birth control are described very briefly below. For further information it would be best to talk to your family doctor or make an appointment at your local family planning clinic. It is important to bear in mind that some methods of birth control, to achieve a high 'safety' rating, require very careful adherence to precise instructions for use.

The Pill

The pill (of which there are several types, varying in hormone content and action) prevents an egg ripening in the ovary and being released. It is considered the most reliable form of birth control and is reversible simply by ceasing to take it. Taken regularly as instructed, the chance of pregnancy occurring is very small. It also has another tremendous advantage in that it does not interfere at all with love-making and in this way can add considerably to the spontaneity of sex by relieving a woman of the need to prepare or speculate on her needs in advance.

Having said that, there are drawbacks. Some women are warned against taking the pill for health reasons. Those who are likely to be susceptible to thrombosis, strokes or raised blood pressure will be advised against taking the pill. Such women may include diabetics and cigarette smokers.

Supply of the pill can only be on a doctor's prescription (given by your family doctor or family planning clinic doctor). Before starting the pill it will be necessary to have a medical examination and regular check-ups are essential while taking it.

The Family Planning Information Service, 27–35 Mortimer Street, London W1N 7RJ, has a useful leaflet, *The Pill.*

'Morning After' Contraception

'Morning after' contraception, as it is familiarly known,

consists of either a special dose of pills or the insertion of an IUD (for those women who cannot use hormonal methods). It may be considered appropriate for women who have been involved in an act of unprotected intercourse or of rape, and are worried they could become pregnant as a result. Both methods act by preventing implantation of the fertilised egg. This method of 'emergency' contraception could never be considered a suitable means of regular birth control. Women with regular sexual partners will be advised by clinics to use a more appropriate long-term contraceptive method for their continuing sexual activity.

In the case of the hormonal method, treatment must be started within 72 hours of intercourse, and before prescribing it, a doctor will make a physical examination to exclude the possibility of an existing pregnancy or any condition which might make the treatment unsuitable. Women with high blood pressure, jaundice, blood vessel disease and other conditions would not have the 'pill' prescribed for them. The IUD can be fitted up to five days after unprotected intercourse.

With the hormonal method, some women suffer side-effects which may include sickness, headaches and dizziness, but these have greatly diminished in recent years with modern hormonal combinations. Your family doctor may provide this treatment if he or she is convinced it is suitable, or you could contact your local family planning clinic (*see* page 27), the Family Planning Information Service (*see* page 28), a Brook Advisory Centre (*see* page 30) or the British Pregnancy Advisory Service (*see* page 29).

The Sheath

The sheath (condom, french letter, Durex or rubber) is a male contraceptive device. It is a thin rubber sheath worn over an erect penis to contain the sperm after ejaculation and so prevent their entry into the vagina. It is still a popular form of contraception, being easy to obtain and to carry around and therefore readily available at a moment's notice. In addition, its use requires no medical supervision and there can be no side-effects whatever. It also provides some protection against sexually transmitted diseases and cancer of the cervix.

However, some men do not enjoy wearing a sheath, claiming that it diminishes the sensual pleasures of feeling the vagina directly in touch with their penis. Manufacturers have tried to overcome this reluctance by producing numerous imaginative varieties of sheath. Sheaths in the past have been made from all sorts of substances which really must have been uncomfortable. Until the middle of the last century they were mostly made from skin (some still are), then crepe rubber and, more recently, we have seen the development of pre-lubricated, shaped, coloured and spermicide-coated condoms. These may be bought in chemists, barbers' shops, slot machines, and from 'small ads' in a variety of magazines. Family planning clinic doctors may also provide sheaths on prescription. Family doctors cannot provide the sheath.

The sheath has been found to be a reliable form of birth control so long as it is used carefully. It must be put on the penis before there is any contact with a woman's sex organs, because sperm may be released at any stage before ejaculation. The penis must also be withdrawn very carefully before the erection wears off to make sure that no semen containing sperm escapes into the vagina.

The Diaphragm or Cap

The diaphragm or cap is another 'barrier' contraceptive. Four types are available: the Dutch cap or diaphragm, the cervical cap, the vault cap and the vimule cap. They all work on the principle that by covering the opening of the cervix they stop sperm from entering the womb during sexual intercourse.

Initially the cap must be individually fitted by a doctor or specially trained nurse to ensure that you have the cap best suited to your needs and that it fits exactly and will therefore act as a barrier to stop a man's sperm getting into the womb as a result of sexual intercourse. The cap is put in by the user before intercourse and left in position for at least six hours afterwards. It must be used together with a suitable birth control cream, jelly, pessary or foam which is applied to the cap before inserting it. A new form of cap, still in the experimental stage, is tailor-made to fit the individual cervix. It has a one-way valve to allow menstrual fluid to escape, and can be left in place over several cycles.

Contraceptive reliability depends to a large extent on the woman being conscientious in the way she uses the cap and in having regular check-ups every six to twelve months to make sure the fitting is still correct. The cap or diaphragm also needs to be checked after any weight gain or loss, after abortion or miscarriage or after birth. Caps may be fitted by family doctors or family planning clinic doctors or nurses and are available under the NHS free of charge.

The Family Planning Information Service, 27–35 Mortimer Street, London W1N RJ or your FPA Regional Office, (*see* page 28), has a useful leaflet, *Barrier Methods of Birth Control*, discussing the use of the cap with spermicide and sheath.

IUCD (Intra-Uterine Contraceptive Device)

The IUCD loop or coil has proved to be a reasonably reliable and reversible form of birth control for those women whom it suits. Once it is in place in the womb it needs little attention except a monthly check of the strings to ensure it is still there and still in place. The failure rate in such circumstances is very low. It is a small flexible device and is inserted into the womb by a doctor or a trained nurse. Nobody actually knows how it works, but it appears to stop the fertilised egg from settling in the womb. Sometimes an IUCD may be fitted within five days of unprotected intercourse or rape. It then works by preventing implantation of the fertilised egg. Unfortunately, the coil sometimes comes out, and the user may not realise this has happened and thus be left, completely unprotected against possible pregnancy. Women usually learn to feel the threads of the coil in the vagina, so that they may reassure themselves of its presence. Once a month, after a period, is a useful time to check.

The coil is not suitable for all women. Some are unable to tolerate its presence – they may suffer severe backache, irregular bleeding and sometimes heavy periods. If such symptoms continue the coil is usually removed. There can also be some risk of pelvic infections which could result in infertility.

Occasionally, a woman becomes pregnant despite having a coil in place. She is then more likely to suffer a miscarriage than in normal pregnancy. Occasionally, when a pregnancy has occurred despite the use of a coil, it can develop outside the womb, usually in the Fallopian tube. In this case immediate treatment is needed. However, where a pregnancy develops normally and a woman decides to continue with it, there is no evidence of any foetal abnormality arising out of the use of an IUCD – whether it is made of plastic or plastic wound with copper wire.

The device can be fitted at hospitals or family planning clinics. Some family doctors also provide this service. When NHS facilities are used, supply is made on prescription. Services are also available from private clinics for which, of course, a charge will be made.

The Family Planning Information Service, 27–35 Mortimer Street, London W1N 7RJ or your FPA Regional Office, (*see* page 28) has a useful leaflet, *Intra-uterine Devices*, and also lists clinics where the service is available.

Spermicides

Spermicides (contraceptive creams and jellies, pessaries and aerosol foams) are chemicals put into the vagina just before intercourse which are intended to destroy the man's sperm before they enter the neck of the womb.

While definitely better than nothing, spermicides are not considered very reliable when used on their own. However, the combination of a spermicide and a cap (*see* page 23) can be very effective. You may find some spermicides are more pleasant to use than others. Not everyone, for instance, likes the fizziness of the foams, although it is possible they are more effective than the other varieties.

Spermicides are available from chemists and you do not need any medical advice in order to use them. They may also be supplied on prescription from family planning clinic doctors or from your family doctor.

Contraceptive Sponges

Contraceptive sponges are popular in America but have been shown in British trials to be disappointingly less effective than their nearest rival, the diaphragm, with a success rate of only 75–91 per cent. Consequently, the Family Planning Association and family planning clinics do not recommend the sponge. It is also considered to be rather expensive.

The appeal of the sponge is its simplicity – it contains spermicide, is made in just one size, and is just like a tampon. Unlike a diaphragm, which is fitted individually to ensure maximum efficiency, the sponge adapts to each user and therein lies its weakness as a method of contraception.

The sponge is available on open sale through chemists' shops.

Sterilisation

Male and female sterilisation (known as vasectomy in men) is essentially a permanent method of birth control for both men and women. You need to think very carefully before taking a decision which will deprive you of the ability to have your own children. However, you may have decided that you have completed your family or that you do not want children of your own, for whatever reason. Then, indeed, by making a mature, mutual and informed decision and by removing the worry of unwanted pregnancies, you could be opening the way to a happier and more fulfilled sex life. Certainly this form of birth control is becoming increasingly popular with both men and women.

Sometimes people are dissuaded from the operation, not because they are undecided about the size of their family, but because of fears of losing their 'femininity' or 'masculinity' – of somehow being less of a woman or man. It must be stressed, therefore, that sterilisation has no effect on the workings of the sex organs or on the male or female hormonal systems. Nothing is taken away except the ability to have children. However, should you have any doubts at all in the matter, you should not go ahead. In any case, it is wise to seek counselling help before finally making up your mind on a matter of such major importance, the consequences of which are not always easy to see. We can none of us foretell when our circumstances might drastically alter.

While you do not have to seek your partner's permission before deciding to go ahead and be sterilised, on the principle that each of us alone hold the rights over our own bodies, nevertheless, for those in stable relationships it would obviously be advisable to reach agreement on such a major issue affecting both partners. Some doctors would insist on this and on seeing the couple together when making the decision.

In some cases it may be possible to reverse the operation, but this chance should never influence a decision about which you are uncertain. The chances of success in reversal operations are not high, so a decision to have the operation should always be regarded as a permanent step. Anyone who is, nevertheless, considering an attempted reversal operation should consult his or her family or clinic doctor. The British Pregnancy Advisory Service (*see* page 29) has two useful leaflets, *Sterilisation Reversal* and *Vasectomy Reversal*.

If there is a risk of passing on an hereditary disease, one or other of a couple may decide to be sterilised. It is essential in such cases to consult a genetic counsellor (*see* Chapter 5, 'Genetic Counselling and Pre-natal Diagnosis'). Such counsellors seek to be non-directional and non-judgemental. Their role is to provide you with accurate information on which to base your decision.

You can get more detailed information about sterilisation at a family planning clinic or from your family doctor. Both male and female operations are free under the NHS. However, in some areas it can be difficult to get the operation done for other than strictly medical reasons, unless you seek private treatment. NHS waiting lists also tend to be rather long, and you may prefer to visit a private clinic rather than accept a long wait. Some charitable organisations, like Marie Stopes House (*see* page 175) and the British Pregnancy Advisory Service (*see* page 29), will perform operations for a basic fee. The Family Planning Information Service, 27–35 Mortimer Street, London W1N 7RJ, or your FPA Regional Office (*see* page 28), has a useful leaflet *Male and Female Sterilisation*. They will be glad to provide you with the names of suitable clinics, including those that provide a private service and make a charge for the operation. The Scottish Health Education Group, Woodburn House, Canaan Lane, Edinburgh EH10 4SG (Tel: 031-447 8044) has a splendid booklet, *Male and Female Sterilisation – a Guide to Help You Make the Decision.*

Female sterilisation is somewhat more complicated than is vasectomy for men, but although the length of time spent in a hospital or clinic varies, it can now be as little as one day. The length of time depends on the method used and that, of course, depends on what the surgeon considers best for the individual. The operation blocks the Fallopian tubes, so that the egg cannot travel down them to meet the sperm and possibly start a pregnancy. There are several ways this can be achieved. The three most often used methods are laparotomy, when the Fallopian tubes are reached directly through a small incision in the lower abdomen, under general anaesthetic (this may necessitate three to five days in hospital); or mini-laparotomy, when a smaller incision is made, necessitating a shorter stay in hospital; or laparoscopy, when the tubes, uterus and ovaries can be seen via a delicate optical instrument (a laparoscope) which enables the doctor to carry out the simple operation through a very small incision. The procedure may be carried out under a local anaesthetic if both doctor and patient agree to this. The operation may take place in a hospital or in a specially equipped clinic.

The Family Planning Information Service, 27–35 Mortimer Street, London W1N 7RJ or the FPA Regional Office (*see* page 28) will be able to give you details of local family planning clinics where the service is free. They are also able to send you leaflets describing the operation and details of private clinics where a charge would be made for the operation. The approximate cost is £120 to £200. The British Pregnancy Advisory Service (*see* page 29) conducts sterilisation operations on a fee-paying basis. Details of charges are given on page 30. The BPAS has a helpful leaflet, *Sterilisation*, describing the services. Women's Health Concern (*see* page 62) will also provide advice.

Male sterilisation or vasectomy is a minor procedure in which the tubes (vas deferens) through which sperm travel from the testicles to the penis are cut or blocked so that sperm can no longer become part of the ejaculate (the seminal fluid a man releases when he climaxes). To do this, one (or two) small incisions are made in the skin of the scrotum. As the sperm is in fact only a tiny part of the seminal fluid, its absence is not noticeable. Climaxes will be at least as good as before, perhaps better for having any fear of causing a pregnancy removed. It will be necessary for a while to continue to use effective methods of contraception, as it will take several months for all the remaining sperm to be cleared from the vas deferens above the place where the doctor cuts. In practice two sperm samples are taken after a vasectomy to ensure negative sperm counts.

It is now possible to take, freeze and store sperm

before the operation for possible use through artificial insemination at a later date (*see* page 51). This service is not available on the NHS.

Vasectomy is likely to be carried out under local anaesthetic (although you may have a general anaesthetic if you prefer) and the operation usually takes only a few minutes. It may be carried out as an outpatient procedure in a hospital, in a specially equipped family doctor surgery or in a family planning clinic. Your local family planning clinic secretary will advise you which clinics provide this service, or you may write to or telephone the Family Planning Information Service, 27–35 Mortimer Street, London W1N 7RJ (or your FPA Regional Office (*see* page 28). The FPIS will also be able to give you details of private clinics where a charge would be made for the operation. The British Pregnancy Advisory Service (*see* page 29) conducts vasectomy operations on a fee-paying basis, and also has sperm freezing and storage facilities. For details of sperm freezing services *see* page 51. The BPAS has a helpful leaflet, *Vasectomy*, describing its services.

Other Methods of Contraception

Withdrawal

Withdrawal or *coitus interruptus* is probably the oldest form of birth control and is still practised today by many couples who do not like or do not have available at the time more reliable methods of birth control. It simply involves the man withdrawing his penis just before he climaxes, so that he ejaculates his sperm outside the vagina. This can be unreliable because sperm may be emitted long before he ejaculates, or he may not withdraw quickly enough. This method may also be inadvisable because it places considerable strain on the man and may spoil the spontaneity of the act of intercourse as a part of love-making.

Breast Feeding

Breast-feeding does not always prevent pregnancy, but it is more likely to when breast-feeding the baby every two to four hours day and night.

Douching

Douching is considered useless as a contraceptive measure.

Natural Family Planning

Some people, for religious or personal beliefs, prefer not to use forms of birth control which they think of as 'unnatural' – those methods where some kind of intervention is used to stop a pregnancy occurring, as in barrier methods (cap, sheath, spermicide), chemical contraceptives (the pill), the coil or through sterilisation.

To try to avoid pregnancy they restrict intercourse to those days in a woman's monthly cycle which are referred to as the 'safe' period. This is the time around her menstrual period when, theoretically, a woman is unlikely to conceive. Couples using this method otherwise avoid intercourse especially at the time of egg release (ovulation), which is when a woman is most likely to become pregnant. This occurs over a number of days mid-way between a woman's menstrual periods. The fact is that while this can be a reasonably effective method of birth control for women with completely regular periods who are trained to follow the chosen regimen, it can be unreliable for those with somewhat irregular periods and a preference for spontaneity of love-making throughout the monthly cycle.

There is a variety of ways in which a woman may work out her fertile and infertile times. These include the temperature method, based on the fact that a woman's temperature changes very slightly at the time of ovulation; the cervical mucus method involving observation of the mucus produced by the cervix which noticeably increases and changes in consistency at the time of ovulation; and the calendar method, which involves understanding the regularities and irregularities of the monthly cycle (the calendar method should not be used as a sole indicator). She can, of course, use a combination of these methods.

The point to be stressed about natural family planning is that it needs to be learned from a specially trained teacher, so it can be used correctly. It will involve abstaining from sex or at least abstaining from full intercourse for at least two weeks in every month.

Free family planning advice and supplies, which may include fertility thermometers and booklets for recording temperatures, are available from most family doctors and family planning clinics. The Natural Family Planning Service, Catholic Marriage Advisory Council, 15 Lansdowne Road, London W11 3AJ, has booklets on the method, and supplies free thermometers, charts and a list of teachers. The Family Planning Information Service 27–35 Mortimer Street, London W1N 7RJ, will give you information about local services. It also has a useful leaflet on *Natural Family Planning*. See also details of the books *Fertility* and *Natural Birth Control* at the end of this chapter.

Depo Provera

Depo Provera is a hormonal contraceptive, given as an injection. It works as a contraceptive for three months. There are other injectable contraceptives, available here and in other countries e.g. Net Oen, which are similar to Depo Provera and have similar effects.

Depo Provera, known also as DP and 'The Jab', has its advantages and disadvantages, like all methods of contraception. But as it is an injection, lasting three months, it is a method over which women have little control. For this reason, it is open to abuse, for example, women may be given DP without their knowledge or consent or not given full information about its side-effects.

The advantages include the following:

It is almost 100 per cent effective as a contraceptive.
You don't have to do anything else to prevent pregnancy.
No one can interfere with your using it, for example, your partner, if he objects to contraception.

The disadvantages include:

The majority of women experience a change in their periods, e.g. irregular, frequent or heavy bleeding, sometimes continuous bleeding or no periods at all.
DP should not be given in the first six weeks after childbirth, as heavy bleeding is likely.
You might find it difficult to get pregnant for at least eight months and possibly up to two years after the last injection.
Other side-effects include weight gain or loss, headaches, back pain, depression, stomach discomfort, nausea, breast tenderness, dizziness, and tiredness. These can also happen on the Pill, but you can stop taking the Pill.
DP can affect the body for an average of eight to ten months, even though the contraceptive effect lasts for only three months.
Research into the long-term effects of DP, e.g. on cervical cancer, is inadequate. The effect of DP combined with other drugs is unknown.

If you need further information about DP or if you are concerned about your treatment regarding the use of DP, you can contact the Women's Reproductive Rights Information Centre, 52–54 Featherstone Street, London EC1. (Tel: 01-251 6332). The Centre has a free leaflet (please send sae) *Depo Provera an injectable contraceptive* and a booklet *Who Needs DP* containing detailed information about this drug. The booklet costs £1.18 including postage and packing.

Pregnancy Testing

This section concerns what to do when you're overdue with your period. If you had been planning for a baby, then you can enjoy a happy period of anticipation. However, if you are facing an unwanted pregnancy, then it's a worrying time.

Either way, it is useful to have a pregnancy test and to make plans for coping with the situation. If it is definitely an unwanted pregnancy and you really have no doubts about this, then the sooner you can arrange for a termination the better. In the early stages of pregnancy (certainly before 12 weeks), the operation is a minor procedure. For details of abortion services see Chapter 4, 'Abortion'.

Family Doctors

Pregnancy tests are available through a number of family doctors – some 14 days after your missed period. If the doctor agrees to provide the test there is likely to be a few days' wait for the result. There is no charge for this service. The doctor may also be able to determine pregnancy by a physical examination on around the 28th day after a missed period. At the same time he may decide to use a chemical test to confirm his diagnosis.

NHS Family Planning Clinics

Some clinics will provide a pregnancy testing service for those who are 14 days overdue, but there may be a charge. Results will often be available on the spot.

Other Clinics

The Family Planning Association (*see* page 28), Brook Advisory Centres (*see* page 30) and the British Pregnancy Advisory Service (*see* page 29) provide pregnancy testing services in different areas around the country. Other organisations exist which provide a similar service in one place – for instance, in London, Marie Stopes House (*see* page 175) and the Pregnancy Advisory Service (*see* page 181). These organisations usually provide a walk-in service, with on-the-spot results. A small charge is made for this service.

Chemists' Shops

A number of chemists provide a pregnancy testing service. Where this applies a sign advertising the service is usually displayed on a door or window or other prominent position. The result is usually available in a very short time – perhaps half an hour. There will, of course, be a charge for this service.

Do-it-Yourself Kits

A number of kits are available from chemists. These include the following:

1. Discover-2, price £6.35 (two tests), Predictor, price £6.75, and Confirm with which you can test your own urine to determine whether or not you are pregnant. These tests can be carried out after a period is overdue. If instructions are carefully

followed the manufacturers claim an accuracy rate of 98 per cent. In the case of Predictor the test may be carried out from the sixth day after a missed period, and with Discover-2 one day after a missed period. Since Discover-2 provides two tests, you can double check the results five days later. Discover-2 and Predictor are produced by Chefaro Proprietaries Limited, Cambridge Science Park, Milton Road, Cambridge CB4 4FL. (Tel: Cambridge (0223) 312956.

2. Discover Colour, price £6.50, is a single test with a 30-minute result. Also available from chemists' shops, it is produced by Carter-Wallace Ltd, Wear Bay Road, Folkestone, Kent CT19 6PG (Tel: Folkestone (0303) 57661).
3. Clearblue home pregnancy test system, price £6.75, provides a 30-minute result. Each pack contains two tests – the first can be used from the first day after a missed period. The makers claim 99 per cent accuracy. Clearblue is available from chemists' shops and is produced by Unipath Limited, Norse Road, Bedford MK41 OQG. (Tel: Bedford (0234) 47161). There is an advice service for any queries about carrying out the test or its result – tel: (0232) 50408.

All the above pregnancy tests are available from chemists' shops.

Without calling the reliability of the kits into question, it might be unwise to place absolute faith in such tests; for one reason or another it is possible to get mistaken readings.

Perhaps the biggest snag about finding out for yourself, particularly if any pregnancy is unwanted, is simply that you may be left alone to face difficult decisions. Or you may find a partner or family unhelpful or confused as to what to do. If your test is done in a clinic, there will be staff who can advise and counsel on the options open to you and the ways in which they are able to help you.

Helpful Organisations

Family Planning Association Services

Family Planning Association
27–35 Mortimer Street, London W1N 7RJ (Tel: 01-636 7866).
In 1974, when the majority of FPA-run clinics were handed over to the NHS, the FPA began to reorganise itself. By 1976 it had set up a structure of 11 regions throughout England, Scotland, Wales and Northern Ireland, each with a regional office managed by a regional administrator who carries out information and educational activities in that region.

Each office is equipped to provide free literature and also information on the whole range of family planning services, both NHS and private, available within their specific areas. These regional offices and the areas they cover are listed below, together with details of any extra services they provide, including those clinics which continue to be run by the FPA, either privately (when fees are charged) or on behalf of the NHS. Where there are private clinics for vasectomy services, fees are liable to be between £60 and £70 to cover counselling, surgery and pathology tests. All enquiries should be made to the regional office.

Where there are book centres, the publications cover such subjects as child care and pregnancy, birth control, sex education, sexual development and relationships, women's health, psychology and medical or nursing topics.

All information services provided by the FPA are free.

Family Planning Information Service
27–35 Mortimer Street, London W1N 7RJ (Tel: 01-636 7866).
The FPIS is a service jointly run by the Family Planning Association and the Health Education Authority to provide information to ensure that people are aware of and make use of the free NHS family planning facilities. The FPIS provides information by answering individual enquiries by letter or telephone (Monday to Friday 11 a.m. – 3 p.m.) and by the provision of free leaflets, help sheets, and posters and some other publications on all aspects of family planning and reproductive health care. The FPIS enquiry service is able to help you with personal problems and will also give you details of family planning and related services in your area.

Related services may include pregnancy testing and advice, psychosexual counselling, vasectomy services, menopause and pre-menstrual tension advice, special services for young people, and subfertility advice. The FPIS also has details of private clinics providing similar services and of other help agencies.

At a local level, there are regional administrators who will be glad to help with enquiries and supplies of leaflets. *See* pages 165–212 for addresses.

For further details of the service and of the leaflets and publications available, ask for the leaflet, *How the FPIS Can Help You*. This includes an order form.

Family Planning Association Regional Offices
National Head Office (co-ordinating the regions): 27–35 Mortimer Street, London W1N 7RJ (Tel: 01-636 7866). In addition to information services there is also a book centre.

Regional offices are situated in each of the following areas. Addresses are listed in Chapter 21.

ENGLAND

GREATER LONDON
See Chapter 21 – GREATER LONDON, Hammersmith
Area covered: London.

NORTH OF THE THAMES
See Chapter 21 – BEDFORDSHIRE, Bedford
Areas covered: Bedfordshire, Berkshire, Buckinghamshire, Hertfordshire, Northamptonshire and Oxfordshire.

SOUTH-EAST ENGLAND
See Chapter 21 – EAST SUSSEX, Hove
Areas covered: Kent, Hampshire, East and West Sussex, Surrey, and the Isle of Wight.

SOUTH-WEST ENGLAND
See Chapter 21 – DEVON, Exeter
Areas covered. Avon, Cornwall, Devon, Dorset, Gloucestershire, Somerset, Wiltshire.

EASTERN ENGLAND
See Chapter 21 – NORFOLK, Norwich
Areas covered: Cambridgeshire, Essex, Lincolnshire, Norfolk, Suffolk.

MIDLANDS
See Chapter 21 – WEST MIDLANDS, Birmingham
Areas covered: Herefordshire, Worcestershire, Leicestershire, Shropshire, Staffordshire, Warwickshire, West Midlands.

NORTH-WEST ENGLAND
See Chapter 21 – MERSEYSIDE, Liverpool
Areas covered: Cheshire, Cumbria, Greater Manchester, Isle of Man, Lancashire, Merseyside.

YORKSHIRE AND NORTH-EAST
See Chapter 21 – SOUTH YORKSHIRE, Sheffield
Areas covered: Cleveland, Derbyshire, Durham, Humberside, Northumberland, Nottinghamshire, South and West Yorkshire, Tyne and Wear.

WALES
See Chapter 21 – WALES, SOUTH GLAMORGAN, Cardiff
Area covered: Wales.

SCOTLAND
See Chapter 21 – SCOTLAND, STRATHCLYDE, Glasgow
Area covered: Scotland.

NORTHERN IRELAND
See Chapter 21 – NORTHERN IRELAND, Belfast
Area covered: Northern Ireland.

Other Services

Birth Control Trust
27–35 Mortimer Street, London W1N 7RJ (Tel: 01-580 9360).
The Trust produces publications and provides information on all aspects of fertility control (abortion, contraception and sterilisation). These mostly consist of papers providing information and statistics on the provision of birth control and abortion in this country. (*See* also Chapter 4, 'Abortion'.)

British Pregnancy Advisory Service (BPAS)
Austy Manor, Wootton Wawen, Solihull, West Midlands B95 6BX (Tel: Henley-in-Arden (056 42) 3225).
The BPAS was formed in 1968 by a small group of volunteers in Birmingham to meet the specific need for abortion advice and services. It is now a national organisation (*see* details of branches and services below), and is a non-profit-making registered charity. It offers help, information and counselling for any problem connected with pregnancy, contraception, infertility or sexuality, including 'morning after' birth control (available at some clinics), and artificial insemination (*see* Chapter 6, 'Infertility'). Pregnancy testing, for those who are more than six days overdue with their period, is carried out at all branches and pregnancy counselling is available to any woman who needs it. Whether or not she decides to go ahead with her pregnancy or seeks a termination, the BPAS offers continuing support.

To seek help from the BPAS, you do not need professional referral. Referrals to other organisations, where necessary, are made available to you concerning adoption, accommodation, welfare rights and so on.

For details of the the BPAS infertility services, *see* Chapter 6, 'Infertility'.

Abortion services are available through the BPAS, which has its own nursing homes at Brighton, Doncaster, Leamington Spa, Liverpool and Bournemouth, where experienced doctors perform the operations. The length of stay in the nursing home depends on the stage of the pregnancy and varies from a short day-care stay to up to three days for later pregnancies.

Contraception services include general information and supply of contaceptives, as well as male and female sterilisation.

Charges are made for all services. The BPAS is a non-profit-making registered charity and its funds come from its patients' fees. Limited help may be given to those who would have difficulty paying the fees. Charges in 1986 were as follows:

Pregnancy testing: £3.
Termination of pregnancy assessment, and referral if appropriate – including pregnancy test (if required), counselling and any necessary examinations £24.
Note : the £24. fee is chargeable to all patients when they see the lay counsellor.
Actual cost of termination (depending on surgical method employed and length of pregnancy) £120 to £255 plus £24 as above.
Fertility control clinic. Per visit fee for contraception advice, including coil fitting, if required: £15 (plus supplies at recommended retail price).
Sterilisation assessment, including counselling, any necessary tests or examinations and post-operative check £24.
Sterilisation operation: £135, plus £24 as above.
Sterilisation reversal assessment, including counselling and any necessary tests or examinations: £75.
Sterilisation reversal operation
Pre-operative laparoscopic examination (one to two-day stay): £125
Operation (seven-day stay): £625.
Vasectomy, including lay counselling and examination: £21.
Operation and sperm tests: £48.
and any necessary tests or examinations: £75.
Vasectomy reversal operation, including operation and sperm count (two to three-day stay): £420.

The BPAS has a range of leaflets on all the above services.

BPAS branches in the following places – *see* Chapter 21 for full addresses.

ENGLAND

AVON, Bath

BEDFORDSHIRE, Bedford, Luton, Milton Keynes

CAMBRIDGESHIRE, Peterborough

CHESHIRE, Chester

DORSET, Bournemouth

EAST SUSSEX, Brighton

GREATER LONDON

GREATER MANCHESTER, Manchester

HAMPSHIRE, Southampton

LANCASHIRE. Preston

MERSEYSIDE, Liverpool

SHROPSHIRE, Dawley

SOUTH YORKSHIRE, Sheffield

WARWICKSHIRE, Leamington Spa

WEST MIDLANDS, Birmingham, Coventry, Sandwell, Wednesbury, Wolverhampton

WEST YORKSHIRE, Bradford,Leeds

WALES

MID GLAMORGAN, Pontypridd

SOUTH GLAMORGAN, Cardiff

SCOTLAND

STRATHCLYDE, Glasgow

Brook Advisory Centres
153a East Street, London SE17 2SD (Tel: 01-703 9660/ 7880).
These Centres were set up by Helen Brook in 1964 to cater for the sexual and emotional needs of young people. Workers at the Centres, who include doctors, nurses and social workers, will listen to problems and will also provide advice and practical help with all matters relating to birth control, as well as pregnancy testing and counselling (including termination of pregnancy where this is appropriate).

The Centres set out to create a friendly and informal atmosphere where young people (there is no lower age limit) will feel at ease. Brook Centres understand that it takes considerable courage for a young girl to admit that she is having sexual intercourse and a good deal of self-confidence to go for help to discuss matters which may be difficult to put into words. Brook Centres maintain that they essentially listen to young people on their terms, and respect them as individuals by providing them with good information and non-directional services. Mostly they see people up until about age 25, but Brook Centres are flexible about this.

Brook Centres offer a contraceptive service; infection testing (Birmingham, York Road clinic); counselling for emotional or sexual problems; pregnancy testing, for those who are more than 14 days overdue with their period, carried out on the spot; and counselling for unplanned pregnancies, so that no decision need be made alone as to whether to carry on with a pregnancy or to seek termination. Where appropriate, referral may be made to NHS or voluntary charitable agencies for further advice and for help with motherhood, adoption or abortion.

Brook Centres will also, in certain cases, prescribe 'morning after' contraception where there has been recent (within 72 hours) unprotected intercourse.

There are now 20 Centres, most of them in London and Birmingham, but there are also Centres in Bristol, Burnley, Coventry, Edinburgh and Liverpool. Details of these are given in Chapter 21 in the areas listed below.

It is not necessary to obtain a doctor's or parent's permission to visit a Centre, and everything you discuss will be regarded as private and confidential.

No charges are made for supplies or services, except in Birmingham (York Road) where there is a fee for infection testing. There is also a per visit fee for psychosexual counselling.

Some useful publications, including *Safe Sex* and *A Look at Safe Sex*, are available from the Education and Publications Unit in Birmingham.

Brook Centres are located in the following places – full addresses are given in Chapter 21.

ENGLAND

AVON, Bristol

GREATER LONDON – see under the following boroughs: Camden, Hackney, Islington, Lambeth, Lewisham, Newham, Southwark, Wandsworth

LANCASHIRE, Burnley

MERSEYSIDE, Liverpool

WEST MIDLANDS, Birmingham, Coventry, Handsworth, Saltley

SCOTLAND

LOTHIAN, Edinburgh

Community Health Councils (CHCs)
CHCs offer a wealth of information regarding health services in their areas, including family planning services, (clinics and general practitioners), etc. Look in the telephone book for your local CHC.

International Planned Parenthood Federation
Regent's College, Inner Circle, Regent's Park, London NW1 4NS (Tel: 01-486 0741).
For further details of this organisation, *see* Chapter 13, 'Learning about Sex'.

The Natural Family Planning Service
Catholic Marriage Advisory Council, 15 Lansdowne Road, London W11 3AJ. (Tel: 01-727 0141).
Has booklets on the 'safe' period or rhythm method and can supply free thermometers, charts and a list of teachers.

Women's Health Concern
Ground Floor, 17 Earl's Terrace, London W8 6LP. (Tel: 01-602 6669).
For further details of this organisation, *see* Chapter 8, 'Women Only'.

Women's Reproductive Rights Information Centre
52 – 54 Featherstone Street, London EC1Y 8RT. (Tel: 01-251 6332).
WRRIC is performing an invaluable service in providing the information and the support necessary to women to enable us to claim our reproductive rights. They say in their literature

> 'Until we can control our reproduction in the ways that we want, women will always be subject to experimentation, abuses, cuts and lack of information. But we want to make our own decisions, not have them made for us by people who think they know best.'

WRRIC gives support and information such as where to go, your rights, etc., on the following topics: abortion; contraception; sterilisation; infertility; artificial insemination; pregnancy testing; reproductive technology; reproductive health (including health and safety at work).

WRRIC produces a wide range of literature – details on their publications list – and a bi-monthly newsletter which contains information on reproductive rights issues, news and information about meetings, publications, events and campaigns. Subscriptions to individuals: waged £7.50, unwaged £3, to local groups and organisations: £15, to national organisations and student unions £30.

Selected Further Information

Family Planning Association Book Centre
27–35 Mortimer Street, London W1N 7RJ (Tel: 01-636 7866).

The Centre has a range of books on matters relating to birth control and sexuality, including sex and relationships; sex education; family planning; birth and child care; books especially for women; birth control; abortion; pregnancy; general health, physical and emotional; subfertility; sexually transmitted diseases; psychosexual problems.

Books may also be sent by mail order. We recommend you send for the book list.

Choices in Contraception by Zandria Pauncefort. Published by Pan Books. Available from the Family Planning Association. Price £1.75 + 32p postage and packing.

In this illustrated book the author gives the FPA's assessment of the risks, benefits and effectiveness of all available methods of contraception, for the consumer and the professional. The book also covers services, new methods, research, and effects of contraception on relationships.

Contraception by John Guillebaud. Published by Churchill Livingstone, Robert Stevenson House, 1–3 Baxter's Place, Leith Walk, Edinburgh EH1 3AF (Tel: 031-556 2424). Price £4.95.

This book has been recommended by the Family Planning Association. It is intended primarily for general practitioners and family planning doctors but will also be of interest to other health care professionals and to lay people who have basic medical knowledge in this field and who want to be well informed. The question and answer format provides clear guidance on reversilble methods of contraception. Each chapter discusses a different type of birth control in depth. The queries posed are mostly based on questions asked by doctors arising from their clinical experience, and in a concluding section to most chapters there is an assortment of practical questions asked by patients.

Fertility: a Comprehensive Guide to Natural Family Planning by Elizabeth Clubb and Jane Knight. Published by David & Charles. Price £5.95.

Written by a doctor and an experienced teacher of natural family planning methods, this book covers all aspects of the subject in detail. Couples can use the natural fertility awareness they learn from the book to achieve pregnancy where this has proved difficult, or to limit and space their family as desired.

Make it Happy: What Sex is All About by Jane Cousins. Published by Penguin Books 1980. Price £2.95.

A lovely, lively book which is direct and down-to-earth. Written especially for young people, it manages to inform without being in the least patronising. There are useful chapters on birth control, pregnancy and abortion and much more besides. For a fuller description, see Chapter 22, 'Selected Further Reading'.

National Marriage Guidance Council
Herbert Gray College, Little Church Street, Rugby, Warwickshire CV21 3AP (Tel: Rugby (0788) 73241).
Has a very good list of books and publications on subjects concerned with marriage and relationships and with sexuality. Books may be ordered by post.

Natural Birth Control by Katia and Jonathan Drake. Published by Thorsons Publishing Group Limited. Price £3.50.

The authors are qualified teachers of natural birth control who have themselves experienced problems with such methods as the pill and the coil. They have written a guide to contraception through fertility awareness, which, they say, is what natural birth control is all about.

Our Bodies Ourselves: a Health Book by and for Women. British edition by Angela Phillips and Jill Rakusen. Published by Penguin Books. Price £8.95.

Has a chapter on birth control and in its thorough style discusses the issues of birth control and then goes on to describe very fully, with all the implications, the various contraceptive methods available. For a fuller description of the book *see* Chapter 8, 'Women Only'.

The Vasectomy Book: a Complete Guide to Decision Making by Marc Goldstein and Michael Feldberg. Published by Turnstone Press Limited. Price £4.95.

Vasectomy is chosen by millions of men as the male form of contraception. It is a simple enough operation but it is a big decision to decide whether to go ahead. While the operation may be reversible, it should never be undergone with that possibility in mind. Some men also suffer psychological problems in making the decision. In this book, the authors discuss the subject in depth.

Chapter 1 presents the historical background to the operation. Chapter 2 takes a detailed look at how the male reproductive system works and how vasectomy affects its functioning. Chapter 3 provides a method for men and couples to assess whether they are ready to adopt permanent contraception and whether the male or female is the more appropriate partner for sterilisation. In Chapter 4 there is a preview of what to expect from the experience of the vasectomy procedure, including how it will probably feel, and advice is given on taking care of yourself for the first few days after the operation. The potential for subsequent emotional problems is the topic for Chapter 5, which profiles individuals who have had difficulty making psychological adjustment to sterilisation. Chapter 6 outlines all the known and suspected medical risks. Chapter 7 weighs the advantages and disadvantages of vasectomy against other methods of contraception. Final chapters discuss reversal, and the future possibilities of male birth control.

The Which? Guide to Birth Control by Penny Kane. Published by the Consumers' Association and Hodder and Stoughton, 1983. It is available from bookshops or the Consumers' Association, P.O. Box 44, Hertford SG14 1SH). Price £5.95, including postage.

This illustrated, practical guide looks at all the methods of birth control available in the UK today. It explains marvellously clearly how each of them works, and assesses their safety, effectiveness, availability and acceptability. They include traditional methods such as withdrawal and breastfeeding; barriers such as condoms, diaphragms, caps, and spermicides; the pill in all its forms, including the 'morning after' pill; injectable contraception; periodic abstinence; sterilisation and abortion. There is also a chapter on new developments in contraceptive research. Warmly recommended.

CHAPTER 4

Abortion

Abortion is the interruption or loss of a pregnancy before the foetus is viable, that is, before it can survive outside the womb.

Controversy over abortion continues to rage, but an increasing number of women are maintaining their right to terminate unwanted pregnancies. They are becoming increasingly determined to be responsible for their own fertility by choosing to bear children only when and if they feel ready to take on the responsibility of caring for them.

Abortion has been practised at all times in history and by all civilisations, and until relatively recently was about the only way for a woman to reject child-bearing. Even today, in those countries where abortion is illegal, many women die at the hands of back street abortionists. The liberalising of the abortion laws in the UK has mercifully stopped the horrors wrought by unqualified abortionists to whom women turned in their desperation. Throughout history women have shown that they were prepared to accept pain and risk, mutilation and death, rather than carry on with unwanted pregnancies.

Having said this, even legal abortion can never be seen as a desirable form of birth control. We need constantly to be seeking ways to reduce the need for women to resort to this last option. However, for one reason or another, there will always be occasions when a woman feels the need to have an abortion. If she has been raped, she is likely to wish to abort any resulting pregnancy. A variety of medical reasons, including danger to her own health or the fear of having a severely handicapped child, will also lead many women to choose abortion rather than continue with a pregnancy. Then there are the occasions when a woman has simply forgotten her contraceptive or has acted rashly by having intercourse and chancing to luck. Then again, she may have been let down by an unreliable form of birth control. Indeed, the various methods of contraception available at present are simply not living up to the promises made for them. There is still no method which is 100 per cent reliable while at the same time being wholly acceptable to a majority of women throughout their fertile years. Isobel Allen, author of *Family Planning, Sterilisation and Abortion Services* says,

> 'The pill and IUD were an enormous breakthrough, offering freedom for millions of women, but there has been surprisingly little development in the last 20 years, and, in fact, the choice of birth control methods remains remarkably small.'

Certainly the best way to reduce the abortion rate is to improve family planning and contraceptive services and the contraceptive methods used.

The following remarks of Professor Francis Lafitte, Chairperson of the British Pregnancy Advisory Service Trustees, seem to us to place abortion in a proper context within the whole area of fertility control:

> 'With our preference for contraception and sterilisation and growing stress on education in sex and inter-personal relations, we should be able to keep abortion at a modest level, as a necessary back-up for other forms of birth control, not a substitute for them. But if we are to do this we must assign abortion to its rational place in our family planning services.'

Am I Eligible for an Abortion?

Abortion is available under the NHS and in private clinics, provided that the abortion surgeon has the signed authorisation of two doctors. These two doctors must have satisfied themselves that in their opinion you are eligible for an abortion under the 1967 Abortion Act (*see* Chapter 20, 'Sex Law'). They must each give an opinion in good faith that

(a) to continue the pregnancy would involve risk to your life or a risk to the physical or mental health of you or your existing children greater than the risk involved in terminating the pregnancy (in determining this, account may be taken of your actual or foreseeable environment); or

(b) there is a substantial risk of the child being born with a serious physical or mental abnormality.

If both doctors are in agreement, an abortion can be carried out in an approved hospital or nursing home. If you are under the age of 16, one of your parents must sign the form consenting to the operation. If you are 16 or more, you can sign the consent form yourself.

What Will an Abortion Cost?

Abortion is free to residents of the UK (excluding Northern Ireland) under the terms of the 1967 Abortion Act. NHS provision, however, is patchy, and in some areas virtually unobtainable, so that many women may have to turn to private organisations where a fee will be charged (*see* below).

When Should an Abortion be Performed?

The earlier an abortion can be performed, the easier the procedure is and the less chance there is of complications occurring. Despite this wisdom, many women are still kept waiting until a later stage in their pregnancy, to the further detriment of their mental and physical health. When an abortion is performed under 12 weeks, the usual method is vacuum aspiration. This is the removal of the contents of the womb by mild suction. This operation may sometimes be carried out on a day-care basis and a local or general anaesthetic may be used. If you have any preference you can discuss this with your doctor. From the fourth month of pregnancy onwards more complex procedures become necessary. The earliest possible detection of an unwanted pregnancy is therefore desirable. For details on pregnancy testing *see* Chapter 3, 'Family Planning'.

Where to Go for Help

To find out about having your abortion carried out under the NHS, you should contact your family doctor or a doctor at your family planning clinic or a Brook Advisory Centre (*see* Chapter 3, 'Family Planning').

Abortions for which a fee is charged may be carried out by private or charitable organisations. *See* Chapter 3, 'Family Planning' for information on the British Pregnancy Advisory Service, Marie Stopes House, the Pregnancy Advisory Service and the Family Planning Information Service, who will also advise you about local clinics. Your local Community Health Council (*see* the telephone book) will have information on local services.

If you are undecided whether to seek an abortion or to continue with your pregnancy, these agencies all provide counselling services to help you and to support you in whatever decision you make. Should you decide to go ahead with the pregnancy, counsellors will refer you to helpful organisations which can offer you advice and assistance about bringing up a child in difficult circumstances or about adoption or fostering agencies.

Abortion Law Reform Association
88a Islington High Street, London N1 8EG (Tel: 01-359 5200).
The ALRA acts as a pressure group to change the law on abortion and press for improved facilities on the NHS when women need them. The ALRA believes that abortion should be a woman's choice not a doctor's decision.

A membership subscription costs £7.50. Members receive the ALRA's magazine, *Breaking Chains*, every two months. A publications list is available.

Birth Control Trust
27–35 Mortimer Street, London W1N 7RJ (Tel: 01-580 9360).
The Trust produces a number of publications on the subject of abortion. These mostly consist of papers providing information and statistics surrounding the provision of abortion services in this country. A bi-monthly newsheet, *Abortion Review*, is also published – it is intended to be a useful source of information for anyone interested in, or working in this controversial area. Topics covered in the news-sheet include: reporting and analysing current research in this country and abroad; recording and interpreting the latest abortion statistics; public and medical opinion polls; monitoring the administration of the abortion law and parliamentary activity. Subscription is £5 a year.

For further details of the work of the Birth Control Trust *see* Chapter 3, 'Family Planning'.

Doctors for a Woman's Choice on Abortion
101 Burbage Road, London SE24.
This organisation unites a group of doctors who believe that the law should be changed to allow the woman herself to decide whether or not to have an abortion. They consider that in the past, when the medical termination of pregnancy involved a dangerous operation performed only for urgent medical reasons, it was reasonable that a doctor should make the decision whether or not to operate. However, now that abortion is so safe, particularly when carried out within the first three months of the pregnancy, they believe that women should be able to make the decision for themselves – all the more so, because when a doctor decides whether or not to allow an abortion, this is not usually a medical

decision but one which depends on moral and social factors and therefore not a decision for a doctor to make. The DWCA say,

> 'It is not for doctors nor anyone else to impose their moral or religious beliefs on others. No one can know better than the woman herself what is right for her. It is the woman and not the doctor who goes through the abortion operation or continues the pregnancy and has the baby.'

They go on to say that many women are delayed and unnecessarily upset by having to convince two doctors of their case. Doctors vary in their interpretation of the law, so that the ease with which a woman can have an abortion on the NHS depends mainly on the views of the doctors in her area, rather than on her circumstances.

This organisation does not offer personal services, but its members work in close co-operation with the Co-ordinating Committee in Defence of the 1967 Abortion Act (*see* below) and are individually able to provide counselling and referral for their patients, although not for the general public.

Membership of the DWCA is open to all qualified doctors in Britain (£10 per annum) and associate membership is available to medical students (£2 per annum).

Other interested individuals and organisations are invited to keep in touch with the activities of the DWCA by subscribing to the mailing list (£4 per annum).

National Abortion Campaign
Wesley House, Wild Court, London WC2.
A feminist organisation campaigning for a positive change in law and practice to give women the right to decide whether to continue or terminate a pregnancy. They work both nationally and through local campaigning groups around the country as well as with other organisatons. The Campaign produces a quarterly magazine, an internal newsletter and has a wide range of informational material and an extensive publications list.

Northern Ireland Abortion Campaign
Belfast Women's Centre, 18 Donegal Street, Belfast (Tel: Belfast (0232) 243363).
This is mainly a campaigning organisation, seeking to change the law to make abortion available in Northern Ireland. It will also help women seeking abortion by providing advice on where to go, the cost involved, and contacts who will help once in England.

Rape Crisis Lines
If you are seeking an abortion as a result of rape, and feel the need to discuss the problems and your feelings with women who have a special understanding, we would recommend you to contact a Rape Crisis Line or similar organisation as mentioned in Chapter 9, 'Sexual Abuse'.

Women's Reproductive Rights Information Centre
52–54 Featherstone Street, London EC1 (Tel: 01-251 6332).
WRRIC publishes a range of information on relevant subjects including abortion. We recommend sending for the publications list. For further details on this organisation *see* Chapter 3 'Family Planning'.

Selected Further Information

Abortion: the Whole Story by Mary Kenny, Published by Quartet Books. Price: £9.95.
It is a bit worrying that anybody can consider they are able to tell the 'whole story' as suggested in the title, however, the author does cover a wide range of issues. She explains how the operation works and how it changes in relation to the pregnancy's advancement. She suggests ways in which women might cope with different social attitudes towards the subject, as well as their own personal reactions, and she explains what rights they have. Using medical data, interviews, and statistics, she also places abortion in a wider historical context, setting out the arguments for and against. She also discusses what other options are open to women.

Abortion Questions and Answers. A helpful leaflet available from Marie Stopes House 108 Whitfield Street, London, W1P 6BE (Tel: 01-388 0662/2585).

British Pregnancy Advisory Service
The BPAS offer a number of helpful leaflets on all their services, including those for unwanted pregnancies. Details are available from BPAS, Austy Manor, Wootton Wawen, Solihull, West Midlands B95 6BX (Tel: Henley-in-Arden (056 42) 3225).

The Dilemma of Abortion by Edwin Kenyon. Published by Faber and Faber. Price £6.50.
In this book Dr Kenyon, a consultant psychiatrist with a special interest in abortion, discusses the important background factors to the abortion debate – moral, religious, legal, medical, psychological, and political issues are all covered. In addition, there is a critical look at the Warnock Report; comment on the Gillick case and subsequent judgement by the Law Lords; a description of current methods of inducing abortions together with an indication of possible complications; and an explanation of the ways by which foetal abnormalities may be detected before birth.

Make it Happy: What Sex is All About by Jane Cousins. Published by Penguin Books, 1980. Price £2.95.
Has a useful and very practical chapter on abortion. For full details of this book *see* Chapter 22, 'Selected Further Reading'.

Our Bodies Ourselves: a Health Book by and for Women. British edition by Angela Phillips and Jill Rakusen. Published by Penguin Books. Price £8.95. (For a fuller review of the book *see* Chapter 8, 'Women Only')
The chapter on abortion and unwanted pregnancies is marvellously full and complete, dealing with practicalities as well as all the emotional issues. The different ways of doing terminations are described in detail. Information is based on a woman's right to choose and a woman's right to know all the details which enable her to make informed decisions with which she can comfortably live. Information includes: a history of abortion laws and practice, the anti-abortion movement, the pro-abortion movement, how to know when you may be pregnant, deciding what to do, adoption, bringing up a baby alone, a full description of medical techniques for abortion, the service you may expect from your family doctor and pregnancy advisory services.

Understanding Abortion by Mary Pipes. Published by The Women's Press, 34 Great Sutton Street, London EC1V ODX (Tel: 01-251 3007). Price £3.95 plus 60p postage and packaging.
In telling us as women all we need to know when faced with a decision about whether or not to terminate an unwanted pregnancy, the author draws on the experience of numbers of women who have themselves had abortions, and who are able to describe what happened and how they feel about it. There is information on pregnancy testing, counselling, NHS and private facilities as well as medical procedures.

CHAPTER 5

Genetic Counselling and Pre-Natal Diagnosis

For those of us who, rightly or wrongly, are worried about passing on a handicap to our children, the study of human genetics provides an opportunity to consider carefully our own, our family's and our partner's genetic inheritance before we decide whether or not to have children. We can seek guidance as to whether in our own particular coupling there is any risk of producing a handicapped child.

Genetic Counselling

Genetic counselling consists essentially in giving as accurate information as possible, to the extent that knowledge permits, on the risks of transmission of inherited or partly-inherited conditions.

By advising us about any potential risks, a genetic counsellor will clarify our options, and then, by giving us the information we need, will enable us to make up our minds on this complicated issue. We may decide to plan a family of our own despite any risks there may be, but being aware of the dangers, we will be ready to seek early medical help for a handicapped infant if necessary. Alternatively, should an unwanted pregnancy occur, we may wish to seek an abortion (see Chapter 4, 'Abortion').

Where a male partner has a serious disease, some women may wish to consider artificial insemination by a donor – further details in Chapter 6, 'Infertility'.

Genetic counsellors are not there to tell us what to do, but should be prepared to present us with the fullest understanding of any disease risk, its implications, and the options available. We will then need to talk and think the issues through, and the doctor should be prepared to stand back to let us make our own informed decisions. Neither an outsider's religious beliefs, which may encourage acceptance of the birth of a child (however handicapped), nor the beliefs of a doctor concerned with eugenics who might strongly discourage a couple from having a handicapped child, should be allowed to interfere.

Pre-Natal Diagnosis

A number of diseases and abnormalities can be detected by a simple test in pregnancy, although there would be little point in undergoing this procedure unless you were prepared to seek termination of the pregnancy if the foetus were found to be abnormal. It is now possible to determine the sex of a foetus. This may have practical application where the mother is a carrier for a sex-related condition and there is a one in two risk of a son being affected but no risk to a daughter. In such a case, couples might wish to consider selective abortion, only seeking to abort a foetus of the endangered sex.

The Maternity Alliance, a charity concerned with improving Britain's maternity services, wants screening for spina bifida available for all women, and screening for Down's Syndrome to all women over 35. At present, these services are patchy throughout the health authorities.

Where to Go for Help

Initially, your family doctor should be consulted for referral to a local genetic advisory centre (we list these on page 39), which may provide diagnosis, a biochemical testing service and genetic counselling. Not all centres provide the full range of services.

Voluntary Organisations

The following voluntary organisations can also offer valuable information and advice:

Association to Combat Huntington's Chorea
34a Station Road, Hinckley, Leicestershire LE10 1AP (Tel: Hinckley (0455) 615558).
For details of this organisation's publications, *see* page 42.

Down's Syndrome Association
12/13 Clapham Common South Side, London SW4 7AA (Tel: 01-720 0008).
See page 42 for further details.

Muscular Dystrophy Group of Great Britain and Northern Ireland
Nattrass House, 35 Macaulay Road, London SW4 0QP (Tel: 01-720 8055).
The Group has a list of centres for diagnosis and genetic counselling and will be glad to advise people with muscular dystrophy – or their relatives – where to go to find the most appropriate service to meet their needs.
See also the list of publications on page 43.

NHS Genetic Advisory Centres

ENGLAND

AVON

Bristol
Department of Child Health, Bristol Royal Hospital for Sick Children, St Michael's Hill, Bristol BS2 8BJ.

BEDFORDSHIRE

Bedford
Bedford General Hospital, South Wing, Kempson Road, Bedford.

Luton
Luton and Dunstable Hospital, Children's Annexe, London Road, Luton.

CAMBRIDGESHIRE

Cambridge
Regional Genetic Advisory Service, Addenbrooke's Hospital, Hills Road, Cambridge CB2 2QQ.

CHESHIRE

Chester
Genetic Advisory Clinic, Maternity Wing, West Cheshire Hospital, Liverpool Road, Chester CH1 2BA.

CLEVELAND

Stockton-on-Tees
Genetic Clinic, North Tees General Hospital, Children's Outpatients Department, Hardwick, Stockton-on-Tees.

CUMBRIA

Carlisle
Genetic Clinic, Children's Department, Cumberland Infirmary, Carlisle.

Whitehaven
Genetic Clinic, Child Assessment Unit, West Cumberland Hospital, Hensingham, Whitehaven.

DEVON

Exeter
Paediatric Research Unit, Royal Devon and Exeter Hospital, Gladstone Road, Exeter EX1 2ED.

Plymouth
Scott Hospital, Plymouth.

ESSEX

Colchester
Genetic Clinic, Pathology Department, Turner Village Hospital, Mile End, Colchester CO4 5JP.

GREATER LONDON

Galton Laboratory, Department of Human Genetics, University College Hospital, Wolfson House, 4 Stephenson Way, London NW1 2HE.
Genetic Clinic, Institute of Child Health, The Hospital for Sick Children, Great Ormond Street, London WC1N 3JH.
Genetic Clinic, Moorfields Eye Hospital, City Road, London EC1V 2PD.
Genetic Clinic, The National Hospital for Nervous Diseases, Queen Square, London WC1N 3BG.
Genetic Clinic, Paediatric Department, North Middlesex Hospital, Sterling Way, Edmonton, London N18.
Genetic clinic, Paediatric Department, University College Hospital, Huntley Street, London WC1E 9AU.
Genetic Clinic for Skin Disorders, Institute of Dermatology, St John's Hospital for Diseases of the Skin, Lisle Street, Leicester Square, London WC2H 7BJ.
The Maudsley Hospital, Denmark Hill, London SE5 8AZ.
Middlesex Hospital, Mortimer Street, London W1N 8AA.
Northwick Park Hospital, Watford Road, Harrow, Middlesex HA1 3UJ.
Paediatric Research Unit, The Prince Philip Research Laboratories, Guy's Hospital Medical School, Guy's Tower, London Bridge, London SE1 9RT.

Queen Charlotte's Maternity Hospital, Goldhawk Road, London W6 0XG.
Queen Mary's Hospital for Children, Queen's Drive, Beeches, Carshalton, Surrey SM5 4NR.
Regional Cyto-Geneticist, Wandle Valley Hospital, Mitcham Junction, Surrey CR4 4XL.
St George's Hospital, Blackshaw Road, London SW17 0QT.
St Mary's Hospital, Praed Street, London W2.

GREATER MANCHESTER

Manchester
Assessment Unit, Booth Hall Children's Hospital, Charlestown Road, Blackley, Manchester M9 2AA.
Department of Clinical Genetics, Royal Manchester Children's Hospital, Pendlebury, Manchester M27 1HA.
University Department of Medical Genetics, Manchester Royal Infirmary, Oxford Road, Manchester M13 9WL.
University Department of Medical Genetics, St Mary's Hospital, Whitworth Park, Manchester M13 0JH.
Willink Biochemical Genetics Laboratory, Royal Manchester Children's Hospital, Pendlebury, Manchester M27 1HA.

HAMPSHIRE

Southampton
Genetic Clinic, Department of Child Health, Southampton General Hospital, Tremona Road, Shirley, Southampton SO9 4XY.

HEREFORD AND WORCESTER

Hereford
The County Hospital, Hereford HR1 2ER.

Kidderminster
Kea Castle Hospital, Wolverley, Kidderminster DY11 6XN.

Worcester
Worcester Royal Infirmary, Castle Street Branch, Castle Street, Worcester WR1 3AS.

HERTFORDSHIRE

Radlett
Kennedy Calton Centre, Harperbury Hospital, Harper Lane, Radlett WD7 9HQ.

MERSEYSIDE

Liverpool
Cytogenetic Unit, Royal Liverpool Hospital, PO Box 147, Liverpool L69 3BX.
Genetic Advisory Clinic, Assessment Centre, Alder Hey Children's Hospital, Eaton Road, West Derby, Liverpool L12 2AP.

Wirral
Genetic Advisory Clinic, Cerebral Palsy Unit, Clatterbridge Hospital, Bebington, Wirral L63 4JY.

NOTTINGHAMSHIRE

Nottingham
Regional Genetics Service, City Hospital, Hucknall Road, Nottingham NG5 1PD.

OXFORDSHIRE

Oxford
Department of Medical Genetics, Old Road, Headington, Oxford OX3 7LE.

SHROPSHIRE

Shrewsbury
The Royal Shrewsbury Hospital, Mytton Oak Road, Shrewsbury SY1 1DY.

SOMERSET

Taunton
Musgrove Park Hospital, Taunton, Somerset.

SOUTH YORKSHIRE

Sheffield
Centre of Human Genetics, (Sub-department of Medical Genetics), Longhill, 117 Manchester Road, Sheffield S10 5ND.

STAFFORDSHIRE

Burton-on-Trent
The General Hospital, New Street, Burton-on-Trent, Staffordshire.

Stafford
Staffordshire General Infirmary, Foregate Street, Stafford ST16 2PA.

Stoke-on-Trent
Central Out-Patients Department, North Staffordshire Royal Infirmary, Princess Road, Hartshill, Stoke-on-Trent ST4 7LN.

SURREY

Caterham
St Lawrence's Hospital, Caterham, Surrey CR3 5YA.

SUSSEX

See West Sussex.

TYNE AND WEAR

Newcastle upon Tyne
Regional Genetics Advisory Centre, University Department of Human Genetics, 19 Claremont Place, Newcastle upon Tyne NE2 4AA.

WARWICKSHIRE

Nuneaton
George Eliot Hospital, Nuneaton CV1D 7BL.

Rugby
Hospital of St Cross, Barby Road, Rugby CV22 5PX.

Warwick
Warwick General Hospital, Lakin Road, Warwick CV34 5BW.

WEST MIDLANDS

Birmingham
Birmingham and Midland Eye Hospital, Church Street, Birmingham B3 2NS.
Infant Development Unit, Birmingham Maternity Hospital, Edgbaston, Birmingham B15 2TG.

Coventry
Exhall Grange School for the Partially Sighted, Wheelwright Lane, Coventry CV7 9HP. Sherbourne Fields School, Rowington Close, Coventry.

WEST SUSSEX

Chichester
Royal West Sussex Hospital, St Richard's, Spitafield Lane, Chichester, West Sussex PO19 4SE.

Horsham
The Forest Hospital, Crawley Road, Horsham, West Sussex.

WEST YORKSHIRE

Leeds
Genetic Clinic, The General Infirmary of Leeds, Great George Street, Leeds LS1 3EX.

WILTSHIRE

Salisbury
Department of Cytogenetics, Salisbury General Infirmary, Fisherton Street, Salisbury SP2 7SX.

YORKSHIRE

See West Yorkshire and South Yorkshire.

WALES

GWENT

Abergavenny
Nevill Hall Hospital, Abergavenny, Gwent (referral through Paediatric Department).

Newport
Royal Gwent Hospital, Newport, Gwent (referral through Paediatric Department).

GWYNEDD

Bangor
St David's Hospital, Bangor, Gwynedd LL57 4SL (referral through Peadriatric Department).

SOUTH GLAMORGAN

Cardiff
Child Health Laboratories, The Department of Child Health, Welsh National School of Medicine, Heath Park, Cardiff CF4 4XN.
Wales Medical Genetics Clinic, The Section of Medical Genetics of the Department of Medicine, Welsh National School of Medicine, Heath Park, Cardiff CF4 4XN.

WEST GLAMORGAN

Swansea
Morriston Hospital, Morriston, Swansea (referral through Paediatric Department).

SCOTLAND

GRAMPIAN

Aberdeen
Department of Medical Genetics, University Medical Buildings, Foresterhill, Aberdeen AB9 2ZD.
Genetics Clinic, Royal Aberdeen Children's Hospital, Cornhill Road, Aberdeen AB9 2ZG.

HIGHLAND

Inverness
Paediatric Unit, Raigmore Hospital, Inverness.

LOTHIAN

Edinburgh
Medical Genetics Clinic, University Department of Human Genetics, Western General Hospital, Crewe Road, Edinburgh EH4 2XU.

STRATHCLYDE

Glasgow
West of Scotland Genetic Advisory Centre, University Department of Medical Genetics, Royal Hospital for Sick Children, Yorkhill, Glasgow G3 8SJ.

TAYSIDE

Perth
Consultant Paediatrician, Perth Royal Infirmary, Taymount Terrace, Perth PH1 1NX.

NORTHERN IRELAND

Belfast
Department of Medical Genetics, Institute of Clinical Science, Grosvenor Road, Belfast BT12 6BJ.

Selected Further Information

Association to Combat Huntington's Chorea
For address *see* page 00

Helpful publications include:

Huntington's Chorea: a Booklet for Families, which describes the disease and its effects and carefully illustrates the inheritance factors. Every child born to a parent with Huntington's Chorea (the symptoms of which usually do not appear until mid-life) has a 50 per cent chance of inheriting the defective gene and therefore of developing the disease in later life. Price 35p, plus postage.

Living with Huntington's Disease by Dennis H. Phillips. This is a paperback book covering all aspects of the condition for patients and families, including reference to sexual aspects. Price £1.95 plus postage.

Tomorrow's Child? A booklet discussing the problems of and alternatives to parenthood in a Huntington's Chorea family. Free on receipt of a stamped, self-addressed envelope.

What is HC?. A comprehensive question and answer leaflet on Huntington's Chorea. Free on receipt of a stamped self-addressed envelope.
The Association also provides individual fact sheets on specific aspects of Huntington's Chorea. A list is available from the Association.

The Dilemma of Abortion by Edwin Kenyon. As well as discussing abortion this book also has an explanation of the ways by which foetal abnormalities may be detected before birth. For fuller details of the book see Chapter 4, 'Abortion'.

Down's Syndrome Association
12/13 Clapham Common South Side, London SW4 7AA (Tel: 01-720 0008).
The Association publishes a pamphlet *The Genetics of Down's Syndrome (An Account for Parents)* by M. d'A. Crawford, written to give parents a reasonably detailed explanation of the chromosomal abnormalities. Price £1.70 including postage and packing.
A range of leaflets is also available on all aspects of Down's Syndrome.

Genetic Counselling in Mental Handicap by Brian Kirman. Published by the Royal Society for Mentally Handicapped Children and Adults (MENCAP). Available from the MENCAP Bookshop, 123 Golden Lane, London EC1Y 0RT. Price 50p, plus 25p postage.
Brief, but informative, explanation of the nature of genetic counselling, why it is necessary, what it involves, and ethical considerations.

Human Genetics. Available free from the Department of Health and Social Security, Room B1305, Hannibal House, Elephant and Castle, London SE1 6TE.
A helpful booklet concerned with the medical implications of human genetics and, in particular, the role of genetic counselling. It is presented in a simple and straightforward style and gives only the bare outline of the subject. The main types of inheritance: dominant, recessive (including the implications between blood

relations), and sex-linked (X-linked), are explained and some examples given. Also discussed are conditions caused by chromosomal abnormalities and those with partial and complex inheritance.

While this booklet is primarily intended to alert doctors to the problem of genetic disease in the community and therefore presumes a knowledge of medical terms, it is, nevertheless, written in such a way that a lay person would also find a good deal of it accessible and informative.

Inheritance and the Muscular Dystrophies: a leaflet containing basic information for people concerned with muscular dystrophy, available from the Muscular Dystrophy Group of Great Britain and Northern Ireland, Nattrass House, 35 Macaulay Road, London SW4 OQP (Tel: 01-720 8055).

The Group has a range of helpful leaflets all of which are free.

The Maternity Alliance report of a survey *It all depends where you live* by Catherine Boyd is available from the Alliance at 309 Kentish Town Road, London NW5 2TJ. Price: £1.50 plus 20p postage and packing.
This survey is aimed at informing women of what screening facilities are available and persuading district authorities to adopt comprehensive and uniform policies.

See also the review of *Sex and Young People with Spina Bifida and Cerebral Palsy* in Chapter 12, 'Sexuality and Disability'.

CHAPTER 6

Infertility

Infertility affects at least one in ten people. Roughly the same proportion of marriages in the United Kingdom are still without children after ten years. In some marriages, of course, this may be a perfectly acceptable state of affairs, but for many couples inability to conceive causes deep distress, even desperation, and creates a need for help as yet inadequately met.

Although for many people conception seems all too easy, the reproductive process is not a simple one. It requires a chain of events in which each link is viable and interconnected at the right place, at the right time and in the right conditions. The process can break down at any stage and for a wide variety of reasons: sometimes the problem lies with the man, sometimes with the woman, sometimes with both. (A summary of the main causes of infertility is included in the British Pregnancy Advisory Service (BPAS) leaflet FER 1 – *see* below). In some cases, a solution may be simple, in others the problem may lie deeply concealed, requiring intensive investigation by a number of highly trained specialists. A couple may need the help of a considerable range of medical resources and expertise. In our view, the starting point should always be the general practitioner. He or she has a broadly based overview of your health and can help to ensure that any intervention to deal with your infertility does not conflict with treatment for any other condition, or *vice versa*. If your doctor has a personal interest in infertility, he or she may well be able to provide help in some cases. In any event and at the very least, he or she will be able to refer you to an infertility clinic equipped to seek out the cause of your problems and hopefully to provide a solution.

Infertility Services

The first thing to be said is that these are inadequate. According to a report prepared for Frank Dobson MP, *Infertility Services in the NHS; What's Going on?*, only 71 of the District Health Authorities in England and Wales have specialised infertility services, and only 27 of the authorities provide donor insemination. The second problem is that it is extremely difficult to discover details of such services. They certainly exist, but the authoritative listing by the Royal College of Obstetricians and Gynaecologists is available only to professionals and cannot therefore be published. With some regret we must refer readers seeking information about services available to them to, in the first instance, their general practitioner, or, if this is not fruitful, one of the organisations listed below.

Helpful Organisations

British Pregnancy Advice Service (BPAS)
Head Office: Austy Manor, Wootton Wawen, Solihull, West Midlands B95 6BX (Tel: Henley-in-Arden (056 42) 3225).
For those who can afford fees for private consultations or treatment, the British Pregnancy Advisory Service offers a wide range of services. These include the following:

Fertility counselling, screening and treatment;
Artificial insemination by husband or donor (see pages 49 and 51);
Sperm freezing and storing facilities (see page 51).

Some services are available only at certain branches, and it would always be wise to check with the BPAS Head Office.

The BPAS also makes available a series of helpful leaflets, including:

Infertility Investigation
Sperm Counts and Semen Analysis
Sperm Freezing and Storage Facilities
Artificial Insemination (by donor)
Artificial Insemination (by husband)

BPAS charges are as follows:
Infertility investigation (including counselling, examination and tests): £170

Additional (as required):

Semen analysis	£ 23
Sperm count	£ 6
Semen/mucus cross hostility (per test)	£ 30
Hormone assay (per test)	£ 9
Medical examination (per person)	£ 17
Antibody screening (per test)	£ 25
Smear only	£ 10
Chlamydia serology (per test)	£ 12
Laparoscopy and dye instillation	£150
Counselling only	£ 35

Artificial insemination: see pages 49 and 51
Sperm freezing and storage: see page 51.

CHILD

367 Wandsworth Road, London SW8 2GJ (Tel: 01-486 4289). Gen. Secretary: Dorothy Bull, 'Farthings', Gaunts Road, Pawlett, Nr Bridgwater, Somerset (Tel: Bridgwater (0278) 683595).

Founded in 1979, CHILD is a registered charity concerned with infertility research, education and counselling. It is a young and vital organisation whose members share a high level of involvement and commitment. It raises funds for and promotes research into the causes of infertility and is very active in stimulating public awareness of the problem of infertility and its emotional and psychological effects.

It provides counselling for couples based on the most up-to-date information available, and seeks to allay anxiety. Counselling work is particularly concerned with the effects on the female partner. CHILD can call on medical advisers to help those who need expert medical advice.

There is a 24-hour answering service ('Link-line') and through both this and the post, thousands of enquiries are dealt with each year in strict confidence.

CHILD has an impressive educational programme which includes regular meetings with distinguished guest speakers, and a quarterly newsletter *CHILDchat*. In this work it has the support, advice and encouragement of eminent specialists in all relevant aspects of infertility.

Over the years, a number of important articles have appeared in the newsletter, of which the following are available as fact sheets (these are free to members; non-members please send £1.50 in stamps to cover postage and packing for up to three fact sheets – send applications to Sally Tottle, The Red Cottage, Enmore, near Bridgwater, Somerset.)

1. *Methods of Infertility Investigation*
2. *Artificial Insemination by Donor*
3. *Adopting from Abroad*
4. *The Exchange Service of British Agencies for Adoption and Fostering*
5. *Adoption*
6. *Induction of Ovulation*
7. *In Vitro Fertilisation*
8. *Mucus Hostility*
9. *Artificial Insemination by Husband*
10. *Reversal of Sterilisation*
11. *Book List*
12. *Male Infertility*
13. *CHILD*
14. *The National Children's Home*
15. *British Pregnancy Advisory Service*
16. *Endometriosis*
17. *Parent to Parent Information on Adoption Services*
18. *Dr. Barnardo's*
19. *The Church of England Children's Society*
20. *The Catholic Children's Society*
21. *The Miscarriage Association*
22. *Placental Insufficiency*
23. *Artificial Insemination Centres in the UK*
24. *Birthright*
25. *Recurrent Miscarriages*
26. *In Vitro Fertilisation Centres in the UK*
27. *CHILDchain – Friends to Contact.*

Membership costs £8 per year.

Endometriosos Society

Ailsa Irving, 65 Holmdene Avenue, Herne Hill, London SE24 9LD (Tel: 01-737 4764, evenings and weekends).

The Group was formed in 1981 by women suffering from endometriosis. The link between endometriosis and infertility is not entirely certain, but roughly 40 per cent of women who have the condition are infertile. The group aims to support and share the problems encountered by members and will pool information about symptoms and treatment, learn what sufferers have found effective and helpful and discover what research is being done. There are 85 groups nationwide. Regular meetings are held and a newsletter is circulated bi-monthly.

National Association for the Childless (NAC)

318 Summer Lane, Birmingham B19 3RL (Tel: 021-359 4887).

NAC was founded in 1975, and is helped by the DHSS. Like CHILD, it is a vigorous and far-sighted organisation which recognises the importance of providing its members with relevant and open information and advice about the causes and treatment of infertility.

A quarterly newsletter is distributed to members, and the following fact sheets are available to members of the Association on request:

1. *Miscarriage*

2. *Endometriosis*
3. Discontinued
4. *Drugs Used in the Treatment of Infertility*
5. *Male Infertility*
6. *Blocked Tubes and Microsurgery*
7. *Artificial Insemination by Husband*
8. *Artificial Insemination by Donor (including a list of clinics)*
9. *Infertility Tests*
10. *Test-tube Babies (including a list of clinics)*
11. *Mucus Hostility*
12. *Ectopic Pregnancy*
13. *Ovulation Disorders*
14. *Unexplained Infertility.*
    Booklist
    Glossary

NAC has several lively branches around the country which organise their own meetings and are always ready to welcome local members.

The DHSS advisory panel for NAC has several eminent gynaecologists and infertility specialists among its number, as well as advisors on adoption, fostering and the psychological and sociological aspects of childlessness.

NAC hopes to establish its own infertility clinic in the future, and is always prepared to advise members where to go for appropriate treatment. In addition to the work of the national office, NAC acts as a self-help group with a nationwide network of members prepared to offer counselling and personal contact to those with similar problems.

Membership costs £12.50 for the first year and thereafter £8 a year. Couples pay the same charge as individual members.

Progress
27–35 Mortimer Street, London W1N 7RJ. This is an umbrella organisation formed in 1985 to protect controlled research into human reproduction. It aims to increase knowledge about research into the earliest stages of human conception through a wider exchange of discussion between the general public and scientists.

Its sponsors came together following attempts during 1985 to ban all research on pre-embryos, in the belief that exaggerated and emotive propoganda had distorted the facts and caused confusion and anxiety. They are now concerned that there should be a wider and informed debate in order to help the introduction of any necessary legislation, and represent the view (shared by the authors of this *Directory*) that further research is needed to discover why problems occur during reproduction, such as miscarriage, infertility and genetic disorders, in order to prevent and treat them.

SPOD (The Association to Aid the Sexual and Personal Relationships of People with a Disability)
286 Camden Road, London N7 0BJ (Tel: 01-607 8851). Sometimes infertility occurs as a result of disability, for example, spinal injury. A specialist voluntary organisation, SPOD is always ready to help and has a wide range of information (*see* Chapter 12, 'Sexuality and Disability', for full details).

Selected Further Reading

How to Get Pregnant by S. Silber. Published by Peter Owen (1980). Price £8.95 (hardback)
Includes a section on how not to get pregnant!.

The Gift of a Child by Robert and Elizabeth Snowden. Published by George Allen & Unwin, 1984. Price £4.95. This book is about male infertility, drawing attention to its prevalence, and supporting a more open and honest attitude towards donor insemination. The authors distinguish between voluntary and involuntary childlessness, and in the latter context consider the feelings of inadequacy commonly experienced by men when they find they are infertile, and the need to face the situation honestly and with understanding. They go on to discuss various courses of action, first examining the options of remaining childless and of adoption, before turning (at only page 23) to artificial insemination.

A detailed consideration of AI by donor (*see* page 47 in this Directory) occupies the remainder of the Snowdens' book, drawing on the collective experience of approximately seventy couples who have achieved a family by this means. Separate chapters examine the development and technique of AI by donor, its availability, what it entails, the selection and use of donors, the potential effects on marriage and parenthood, the question of secrecy, and the situation of resulting children. Any couple faced with the problem of male infertility will find this easily digested book of considerable help.

Infertility – A Common Sense Guide for the Childless by Dr Andrew Stanway. Published by Thorsons Publishing Group, 1986. Price £4.99.
This is a reprint of the revised 1984 edition of *Why Us?* The subject is one which, as the author admits, could occupy a volume at least twice the size. As it is, Andrew Stanway does not wholly avoid a doctorish style in giving us practical advice. He first suggests simple self-help methods which may be successful, but goes on to describe the many forms of treatment available if infertility persists, with chapters on male and female infertility and medical investigations.

Dr Stanway has also included valuable contributions on psychological factors which may contribute to as well as arise from infertility. There is a chapter on miscarriage, and finally, if all else has failed, a consideration of the prospects for childless couples.

Infertility – A Sympathetic Approach by Robert Winston. Published by Macdonald & Co. (originally Martin Dunitz, 1986). Price £9.95.
An outstanding book. Robert Winston's dedication sets the tone for the whole text, which is engagingly personal. Throughout the book, the author tries to expose what he believes to be mythology associated with the subject. He is not afraid to spell out the full facts, but they are presented in a way which the lay reader can readily grasp without feeling patronised.

Early chapters discuss the 'experience' of infertility and examine in detail possible causes, both male and female. The author argues cogently that diagnosis should come before treatment, that the diagnosis of 'unexplained infertility' is really no diagnosis at all, and that treatment – which can be stressful and expensive – in the absence of diagnosis is questionable. He explains, as a gynaecologist active in the field, the pros and cons of in vitro fertilisation (*see* page 52 in this *Directory*), and discusses (in rather less depth) GIFT, donor insemination, adoption and surrogacy. Finally, there are generous reviews of other literature on infertility, and, in keeping with the spirit of concern which pervades the whole book, ten basic points for infertile couples to consider.

Robert Winston's approach is more than sympathetic. He sheds light upon darkness, and dispels the commonplace confusion between infertility and sexuality. He offers a well presented blend of information and advice – both positive and negative – which, in a context of realism, will bring enlightenment and encouragement to many infertile couples.

Test-Tube Conception by Professor Carl Wood and Ann Westmore. Published by George Allen & Unwin, 1984. Price £4.95.
We found the print size in this book initially off-putting and the language of the Australian authors high-flown. We think that infertile couples will not necessarily be familiar with terms like 'psychological ambivalence', 'peer group pressures', 'the pro-natal views of latter-day theologians and the high value they place on monogamy' and 'the kaleidoscope of motivational factors' (to go no further than page 5!). The style improves, however, and the authors provide a great deal of detailed information on how pregnancy occurs (with clear diagrams), infertility, and the development and use of in-vitro fertilisation (*see* page 52 in this *Directory*). Making it clear that IVF is not the answer to all problems, they explain the demands the procedure makes on couples, the chances of success, and the associated legal and ethical problems. This is a useful contribution to the emerging literature on IVF, but we think that the ordinary couple contemplating the treatment will find Robert Winston's 1986 book on *Infertility* (see above) rather more accessible.

Artificial Insemination by Donor

So-called 'artificial' insemination (AI) has been with us since the late eighteenth century (even earlier if we include its use on animals). Technically it is a simple process in which a small quantity of semen is injected into the cervical canal at a woman's most fertile time (ovulation). The semen may be either fresh or from frozen stock, although fresh semen generally seems to improve the chances of success. In AI by donor, the sperm comes from a man other than the woman's partner, although by using semen from the same donor for a subsequent pregnancy it can be assured that the children of the same mother are fully and truly related to one another. It is a technique which may be appropriate (other possible forms of infertility treatment having been excluded) where a woman is normally fertile and healthy, but one of the following applies:

(a) her male partner has been found (after proper investigation) to be infertile or has been vasectomised; or
(b) her male partner's blood group is not compatible with her own; or
(c) there is a risk of passing on a serious familial or hereditary disease; or
(d) she is without a male partner.

AI by donor would not, of course, be appropriate if the woman was herself infertile or had other problems in conceiving or bearing children. The success rate is quite high, but in a proportion of cases pregnancy does not result, even after repeated inseminations, and infertility investigations may be needed. The incidence of abnormality in children conceived by AI by donor under medical supervision is reported to be no higher than in normal conceptions. Provided the donor has been carefully selected and screened, there should be no risk over and above that which attaches to any pregnancy.

There are, however, some significant religious, legal, emotional and social implications. Some of the more orthodox Churches remain antagonistic to AI by donor, seeing it as contrary to the natural order and akin to adultery. The law, too, has so far (change is on the way) implied disapproval by declaring any child born by AI by donor to be illegitimate and by making it a criminal offence falsely to register paternity at birth. In practice, such an offence would be difficult to prove and no one has ever tried. Effectively, there has been a presumption that any child born in wedlock is legitimate (which in many cases, where intercourse continues while AI by donor is carried out, it might well be). Often the woman's partner registers as the father. Women without male partners usually enter 'father unknown' on the birth certificate. But the present legal position is less than satisfactory. There are problems inherent in the use of AI by donor should the facts ever come to light. If the relationship of the natural mother and the 'adoptive' father breaks down or if the truth is known in the wider family, it is possible, as things stand, that the rights of the child – particularly to inherit – may be open to legal challenge. There is also the chance, if the woman has gone ahead without her husband's consent, that her treatment could provide grounds for divorce.

What matters above all else is the welfare of the child. It is to be hoped that people will approach the opportunities offered by AI by donor responsibly and seriously, giving careful thought to the level of support, love and stability which they can give to a child, in the long term as well as the short term. Skilled and experienced confidential advice from counsellors who understand the profound emotional, social and spiritual implications is surely indispensable.

Where male/female couples are concerned, the use of AI by donor should be acceptable to both partners. A woman wanting a child may well find the opportunity to become pregnant a very attractive one, fulfilling her natural aspirations. Many women regard the option as preferable to the often tortuous and uncertain procedures of legal adoption. But the attitudes of a male partner are likely to be more equivocal. He may feel threatened by AI by donor, and see his partner's recourse to another man's fertility as a sign of fading love, and regard it, however illogically, as a confirmation not only of his infertility, but of sexual inadequacy. He may, moreover, feel a deep-rooted antipathy to the introduction of another man's seed into his partner, even though sexual intercourse is not involved. If such feelings are strong, it would be unwise to proceed. There would be a real danger that the child would not be fully accepted. Any future stress in the parental relationship or perceived defect in the child or its behaviour might lead to it being rejected, with a shifting of blame to the unknown donor. It would also be thoroughly unwise to seek AI by donor in the hope that a child may save a rocky marriage. Approached from another point of view, however, the acceptance of a child by AI by donor is not so very different from taking on a partner's existing offspring by an earlier marriage. Indeed, in many important respects it is a far better situation.

Any doctor advising a couple would certainly wish to be satisfied as to the health of both partners and may also address him/herself to their motivation, the stability of their relationship and whether the man is truly reconciled to the prospect of fathering a child which will not be, biologically speaking, his own. The couple need to be personally honest and open with each other, to be frank with their advisers and to consider the marital, psychological, ethical, moral and legal implications for themselves. They must be prepared to accept that the donor will always remain unknown, as they will to him and to accord to the child normal privileges and rights.

If both partners, after careful consideration, find AI by donor acceptable, it is nobody's business but their own, and our firm advice would be to keep it that way. One does not, after all, discuss with others the manner in which a child is ordinarily conceived; neither ought we to do so when AI by donor is involved. There is no question of it being a guilty secret; it is simply a private matter between two people. The question of whether eventually to tell the child can be a worry to parents. Opinion is divided about this; in the case of adopted children current thinking tends towards the view that they should be told. But with AI by donor, the child is accepted from the moment of conception, to be born, raised and loved by the natural mother and the 'adoptive' father as their own and so recognised by everyone else. In a stable marriage, it is doubtful if there is any virtue in raising worries about identity and paternity where none exist, unless there is some compelling reason for doing so – say, for example, where the 'adoptive' father is suffering from a serious communicable disease which the child may think he/she is in danger of having inherited.

Donors used by AI by donor clinics are checked for mental and physical health (you would be wise to ask about the extent of such screening – it should certainly include testing for sexually transmitted diseases and AIDS and an examination of the donor's family history to guard against the transmission of a genetic disease). Semen specimens are taken and analysed to ensure that the donor's sperm counts are sufficiently high and blood groups are determined. Physical characteristics are also noted to permit a broad-based match with the recipient parents. Selected donors must formally disclaim all legal rights and responsibilities over any child born of the donated semen and agree not to seek to identify the recipient. It should be mentioned that there remains a small risk, as there is from adultery, that offspring of the same biological father (who are therefore related) may unwittingly marry.

Apart from its use in heterosexual partnerships, AI by donor is obviously attractive to lesbian couples who enjoy a stable relationship and want to have a child, and to single women who want to get pregnant without sexual intercourse with a partner. Clinical services, however, (all of which have long waiting lists) tend to discriminate against women who do not have a male partner. As far as we know, only the British Pregnancy Advisory Service (BPAS) and the Pregnancy Advisory Service (PAS) are prepared to help and even then this is quite expensive. In these circumstances, women may try self-insemination, using either frozen semen from a clinic (if it can be obtained) or fresh semen from a donor, who may or may not be anonymous. From the point of view of avoiding custody battles, anonymity is the preferred option, and some women use more than one donor so as to obscure the identity of the father. It may, however, be difficult, through a third party, to find suitable willing donors. Anonymity, as we have already mentioned, may also be difficult to explain to a child when it wants to know who and where daddy is. The truth may hurt and fail to satisfy a deep emotional need. Self-insemination is technically simple (The Women's Reproductive Rights Information Centre, 52–54 Featherstone Street, London EC1Y 8RT (Tel: 01-251 6332) has produced an information sheet on the subject), but there are obvious health dangers in the use of unscreened sperm, not least from AIDS.

Where to Go for Help

Ordinarily, AI by donor will present itself as an option at the end of fertility investigations, and this may point you in a particular direction. It is available both on the NHS and privately. The NHS provision is patchy and there are long waiting lists. Referral by a general practitioner or subfertility clinic is necessary. Both the NHS and private practitioners may choose to whom they will give the service. Some stipulate that the couple must be married.

British Pregnancy Advisory Service (BPAS)
Austy Manor, Wootton Wawen, Solihull, West Midlands B95 6BX (Tel: Henley-in-Arden (056 42) 3225).
The British Pregnancy Advisory Service has a completely 'open door' policy and will help anyone, even women without a partner. The BPAS is a non-profit-making charitable trust, but charges have to be made for all services, including initial counselling and medical screening. At some branches there is a waiting list which may cause some delay.

Initial counselling and medical screening are available at six BPAS branches in England, as well as in Glasgow (see Chapter 3, 'Family Planning') and can be arranged by contacting the nearest BPAS branch. When writing for a place on the waiting list, the BPAS asks that you give as full a history as possible, with details of any fertility tests (male or female) already carried out and of any menstrual records kept. Treatment is carried out at the BPAS nursing homes in Brighton, Doncaster and Leamington Spa, and at its branches in Brighton, London, Birmingham, Liverpool and Glasgow. Further facilities are planned for South Wales.

BPAS charges for AI by donor are as follows:
Initial counselling, tests and medical assessment £80
AI by donor per cycle £40

The Family Planning Information Service
27–35 Mortimer Street, London W1N 7RJ (Tel: 01-636 7866).
The FPIS is able to provide details of private AI by donor facilities in your locality.

Women's Reproductive Rights Information Centre
52–54 Featherstone Street, London EC1Y 8RT (Tel: 01-251 6332).
Offers support and information on infertility and artificial insemination. Has a self-insemination group. Further details in Chapter 3 'Family Planning'.

Selected Further Reading

The Artificial Family: a Consideration of Artificial Insemination by Donor by R. Snowden and G. D. Mitchell. Published by Unwin (paperback edition, 1983). Price £2.95.
Artificial Insemination. British Pregnancy Advisory Service leaflet. *See* page 44.
Artificial Insemination by Donor. CHILD Fact Sheet No. 2. *See* page 45.
Artificial Insemination by Donor. National Association for the Childless, Fact Sheet No. 8. *See* page 46.
Considering Parenthood: A Workbook for Lesbians by Cheri Pies. Published by Spinsters Ink, San Francisco. Available from Sisterwrite Bookshop, 190 Upper Street, London N1. Price £6.95 plus postage.
Rocking the Cradle: Lesbian Mothers – a Challenge in Family Living by Gillian E. Hanscombe and Jackie Forster. Published by Sheba Feminist Publishers (1982). Price £3.50 (paperback). For further details of this book, *see* Chapter 18, 'Homosexuality'.

Artificial Insemination by Husband or Partner

Except that the semen is provided by the recipient's partner, the procedures for AI by husband are the same as those for AI by donor. Obviously, the man must be able to produce (albeit sometimes by extraordinary means) viable sperm capable of fertilising the woman's ovum. If the sperm are of such poor quality that fertilisation does not occur in normal intercourse by ejaculation, then AI by husband will not improve matters. In a few cases, however, where the sperm are viable, but the count is low, AI by husband may help by facilitating the introduction of the sperm at exactly the right place and keeping them there (with a cervical cap) for an hour or so. This may enhance the possibility of good sperm reaching the uterus (but *see* page 52 for better prospects using IVF).

Apart from the scruples of some religious people who object to masturbation, it is difficult to envisage any objection to AI by husband. It is no more than an intervention to overcome some impediment which stands in the way of natural conception.

AI by husband may be indicated in a variety of circumstances, including:

(a) where there is a physical problem which precludes sexual intercourse or ejaculation through intercourse;
(b) where there is an aversion to sexual intercourse (although here it would seem more satisfactory to attempt to overcome the mental block before resorting to AI by husband – particularly if only one partner is so affected);
(c) where the man suffers from retrograde ejaculation (*see* below);
(d) where the volume of ejaculate is abnormal;
(e) where semen must be treated before use;
(f) where semen cannot reach the uterus because growths, infection, or mucus in the cervix prevent the passage of sperm (a specialised insemination technique can be used where the semen is introduced directly into the uterus: it is rarely successful);
(g) where for some physical reason the man's ejaculate consistently fails to reach the cervix;
(h) where the man has become sterile or has had a vasectomy, but has taken the precaution of storing sperm in deep freeze (*see* page 51).

Mostly, these problems lie with the man; for one reason or another he will have had difficulty in impregnating the woman in the usual way. He may have erectile or ejaculatory trouble and this may be psychological or physical in origin or a combination of both. Naturally, the first intervention would seek, wherever possible, to rectify these handicaps and to restore or improve natural function. But where this is impossible or unsuccessful and a couple wish to have children, AI by husband may be considered.

Many men, although unable to have intercourse or to ejaculate through intercourse, can nevertheless produce semen through masturbation and if this is viable and the partner is fertile, conception may well be possible. AI by husband is often carried out at home (*see* below) when the fresh semen can be introduced without delay. Men who suffer from retarded ejaculation (*see* Chapter 2, 'Some Common Problems') may find that they are able to produce semen through prolonged masturbation. In research with disabled people, Professor G. S. Brindley has found that ejaculatory problems can sometimes be overcome by the application of a powerful vibrator to the glans of the penis. He has successfuly used the Ling 201 (a heavy duty industrial vibrator). The Pifco body massager, though less powerful, sometimes suffices. Battery operated vibrators are unlikely to be sufficiently powerful, but *see* Chapter 17, 'Sex Aids' for a general description of aids of this kind.

Electroejaculation

In a limited number of cases and under medical guidance, another possible approach is to encourage ejaculation through drug therapy or by electrical stimulation. Electroejaculation is another technique researched and developed by Professor Brindley, who has been able to effect the emission of semen in about two-thirds of men suffering from spinal injury with complete cord lesion, even, in some cases, without erection. The semen may, of course, contain less than the normal number of sperm, but Professor Brindley suggests that with repeated electroejaculations the count and motility of sperms may improve. Wives can be taught the necessary techniques to electroejaculate their husbands, but, at £300, the equipment is expensive for domestic use.

Ejaculation, including electroejaculation, may sometimes be retrograde: the semen, instead of being emitted normally, passes backwards into the bladder. Although sperm cannot survive long in urine, it may be possible, by urinating into a washing solution immediately after a retrograde ejaculation, to retrieve sufficient live sperm by centrifuging to make AI by husband worth a try. 'Washing' of semen is also necessary where a man ejaculates normally, but is producing antibodies to his own sperm.

Self-Insemination

The actual process of AI by husband is so simple that it can easily be carried out at home, and some clinics favour this approach, given that insemination can proceed at leisure with the minimum of stress and fuss. Guidance is given, so that insemination can be timed to coincide with ovulation. One couple reported success using a piece of rubber connecting tube and a plastic medicine bottle! But it is more usual to use a syringe which has no needle (available from chemists) or an appliance which incorporates a cervical cap which allows the semen to be held in contact with the cervix. The process need not be coldly clinical. There is no reason why the use of AI by husband should not be seen and practised as an act of love. CHILD (*see* page 45) make available (but only to members) a 'do-it-yourself' kit; send a cheque or postal order for £5.25 made payable to CHILD to Pam Adler, 83 Evelyn Drive, Pinner, Middlesex, allowing 28 days for delivery. The Women's Reproductive Rights Information Centre, 52 – 54 Featherstone Street, London EC1Y 8RT (Tel: 01-251 6332) has a self-insemination group, and publishes an information sheet on self-insemination.

Where to Go For Help

There is the same range of options as for AI by donor (*see* page 47), but there is rather less opposition to AI by husband and you may find it easier to get NHS treatment. The starting point for state services is again your GP or subfertility clinic.

The British Pregnancy Advisory Service (BPAS)
Austy Manor, Wootton Wawen, Solihull, West Midlands B95 6BX (Tel: Henley-in-Arden (056 42) 3225).
The BPAS has specialist expertise and experience in this field.
BPAS charges for AI by husband are as follows:

Initial counselling, tests and medical assessment	£80
AI by husband (frozen semen) per cycle	£30
AI by husband (treated semen) per insemination	£40

Selected Further Reading

Artificial Insemination by Husband. British Pregnancy Advisory Service leaflet (*see* page 44).
Artificial Insemination by Husband. CHILD Fact Sheet No. 9 (*see* page 45) and National Association for the Childless, Fact Sheet No. 7 (*see* page 46).
Male Fertility after Spinal Injury. SPOD (The Association to Aid the Sexual and Personal Relationships of People with a Disability) Information Sheet (September 1981). Includes notes on electro-ejaculation.

Sperm Freezing and Storage

The British Pregnancy Advisory Service (*see* page 29) offers facilities for depositing semen for storage in liquid nitrogen at −196°C. In these conditions, semen will retain its potency almost indefinitely. The 'sperm bank' is appropriate for men who are contemplating vasectomy, who work under hazardous conditions or who feel that their future fertility may be in danger for any other reason, e.g. because they are about to undergo chemotherapy or radiotherapy.

A preliminary screening is carried out by testing a semen sample for the number, motility and normality of the sperm and their reaction to freezing and subsequent thawing. Any adverse results are reported to the client and he is made aware of the implications.

Samples are produced by masturbation, processed for freezing, 'packaged' in plastic straws, identified (with the utmost care), colour-coded, frozen, stored and recorded. A deposit consists of 38 to 42 straws and takes about a month to establish. As a safeguard against accidental loss, the straws can be divided and stored at three different centres.

Where to Go For Help

The British Pregnancy Advice Service
BPAS charges for sperm freezing and storage are as follows:

Initial screening	£13
Establishment of deposit	£85
Storage per year	£13
Establishment of deposit plus five years' storage	£140
Test thaw (one straw)	£6

For further information or for an appointment, please contact the BPAS at any one of the following addresses:

Birmingham
Birmingham Branch, 1st floor, Guildhall Buildings, Navigation Street, Birmingham B2 4BT.

Bournemouth
Dean Park Nursing Home, 23 & 25 Ophir Road, Bournemouth BH8 8LS.

Brighton
Wistons Nursing Home, 138 Dyke Road, Brighton, BN1 5PA (Tel: Brighton (0273) 506 263).

Doncaster
Danum Lodge Nursing Home, 123 Thorne Road, Doncaster DN2 5BQ.

Leamington Spa
Blackdown Nursing Home, Old Milverton Lane, Blackdown, Leamington Spa, Warwickshire (Tel: Leamington Spa (0926) 34664).

Liverpool
Merseyside Nursing Home, 32 Parkfield Road, Liverpool L17 8UJ (Tel: 051-727 1851).

Solihull
Austy Manor, Wooton Wawen, Solihull, West Midlands B95 6BX (Tel: Henley-in-Arden (056 42) 3225).

London
London Branch, 7 Belgrave Road, London SW1V 1QB.

In Vitro Fertilisation (IVF)

This is a technique, pioneered by Dr Robert Edwards and Mr Patrick Steptoe and first successful in 1978, in which eggs are taken from a woman's ovary, fertilised with male sperm in a laboratory glass (in vitro) and returned to the womb.

After the initial success of Edwards and Steptoe, IVF clinics have been set up in various parts of the world. There are no indications that the technique is anything but safe or that there is any risk of abnormalities greater than occurs in natural conception. There is, however, some vehement opposition to IVF. Those whose God wants things done in a traditional way regard it, even more than other techniques, as 'against nature'. There is also a view in some quarters that the minute cluster of cells triggered by fertilisation is already a child in the making. People of such persuasion react to research on fertilised eggs or the disposal of surplus pre-embyros as though a baby was being tortured and sacrificed. They are unlikely to be impressed by information that at this early stage an embryo has not yet been formed and that nature is itself profligate in shedding such eggs and wasting potential pregnancies. But that is not all. Where the sperm used are donated, IVF is susceptible not only to those objections discussed in relation to AI by donor but also the concern that IVF goes a stage further in making possible the transfer of fertilised eggs to a recipient other than the woman from whom they were taken, thus facilitating the carrying by a surrogate mother of a child which is biologically parented by two other people. Although it is illegal for third parties to make surrogacy arrangements on a commercial basis (*see* Chapter 20, 'Sex Law'), there does not appear to be any impediment to an IVF centre making such arrangements provided that no charge is made for that service. While there is no reason to think that such a practice would be anything other than exceptional, it does give genuine cause for concern. Finally, in this catalogue of disapproval, there is some anxiety that the present limited clinical use of IVF and associated research could be extended into the darker areas of genetic engineering. In our view, such speculation is not very realistic. Research of that kind is not being undertaken, and is neither proposed nor contemplated. IVF is being used, and researched, only to try to help people to have babies, and to avoid the distress of genetic handicap.

Nevertheless, the setting up of the Voluntary Licensing Authority for Human In Vitro Fertilisation, following recommendations in 1984 of a Committee of Enquiry chaired by Mary (now Baroness) Warnock, is entirely welcome. The Authority's first report issued in 1986, indicates that the development of IVF and the approval of both clinical and research programmes is being handled (in advance of appropriate legislation) in a responsible and sensitive way.

The problems for which IVF may be appropriate include the following:

(a) where there has been irreparable disease or surgical loss of the Fallopian tubes;
(b) where infertility is unexplained;
(c) where cervical hostility prevents passage of sperm;
(d) where the tissue lining the womb (normally shed each month at menstruation) overgrows or appears elsewhere (endometriosis);
(e) where the man's sperm count under natural conditions or AI by husband is too low to achieve fertilisation (oligospermia).

The ova are 'harvested' through an instrument called a laparoscope which is inserted through a small incision in the abdomen. Fertility drugs can be used to stimulate the production of more than one egg and ovulation can be monitored and then triggered by the use of a further drug to occur at a time when it is convenient to carry out the laparoscopy. The recovered eggs are allowed to mature for some hours in a culture medium before sperm are introduced. Once one gets through, all others are precluded. The fertilised eggs are incubated for two or three days, before one or more is transferred to the womb. Where the man's sperm count is low, IVF may enhance the prospects for fertilisation.

After transfer of the fertilised egg(s) to the womb, nature must take its course. Of course, if more than one egg is returned the chances of conception improve, but there is also a risk of a multiple pregnancy. In natural circumstances, a pre-embryo has roughly only a one in four chance of implantation and development, and the success rate for IVF, at present, appears to be even lower. There is also at least a similar risk of subsequent miscarriage. Some women seem to be inherently more receptive than others in the reproductive processes and IVF cannot alter these facts of life. It is not the answer to every fertility problem, and there will certainly be very many disappointments among those accepted for treatment. Bearing in mind the considerable emotional demands of going through the IVF process and, if private facilities are used, the high financial cost, it would seem prudent to explore other avenues first, and to persevere with investigations to establish the cause of infertility before trying IVF. On the other hand, IVF does succeed in some cases. If there is any realistic chance, however small, if time is running out and infertility investigations are getting nowhere slowly, some couples will wish to take that chance.

Gamete Intra-Fallopian Transfer (GIFT)

Finally, we should mention a treatment similar to IVF (though with important differences) known at GIFT – Gamete Intra-Fallopian Transfer. Whereas in IVF eggs and sperm are allowed to fertilise in a laboratory glass and are only then transferred to the uterus as a pre-embryo, in GIFT the eggs and sperm are simply mixed and immediately put into one of the Fallopian tubes for fertilisation to take place within the body, if it will.

As with IVF, there is quite a high failure rate, with the further disadvantage that it is not possible to know whether failure was attributable to a fertilisation problem or some other cause. On the other hand, in common with IVF, GIFT sometimes succeeds where natural intercourse has failed, and it may appeal to those who have moral qualms about IVF.

Where to Go for Help

The following list of approved clinical IVF centres has been provided by the Voluntary Licensing Authority for Human In Vitro Fertilisation and Embryology, and is reproduced by that body's kind permission. It must be stressed that nearly all centres have long waiting lists. For NHS services you may have to wait four or five years! At present, only one – St Mary's in Manchester – is supported by the NHS alone as part of an infertility service for its patients. Some of the NHS centres ask patients for a specified donation, but others do not stipulate a set fee and do not press patients to contribute. Centres also differ as to the number of attempts they will allow, which in some places may be only one. Private clinics, of course, tend to have fewer restrictions, but are seldom able to offer a full range of infertility investigations and treatment. Some centres will, if requested by both partners, use donated sperm.

ENGLAND

AVON

Mr D.N. Joyce, University of Bristol, Department of Obstetrics and Gynaecology, Southmead Hospital, Bristol BS10 5NB.
Mr M.G.R. Hull, University of Bristol, Department of Obstetrics and Gynaecology, Bristol Maternity Hospital, Bristol BS2 8EG.

CAMBRIDGESHIRE

Mr P. Steptoe, Bourn Hall, Bourn, Cambridge CB3 7TR.
Dr P.R. Braude, Embryo and Gamete Research Group, Department of Obstetrics and Gynaecology, The Rosie Maternity Hospital, Robinson Way, Cambridge CB2 2SW.

GREATER LONDON

Mr R.M.L. Winston, Institute of Obstetrics and Gynaecology, Hammersmith Hospital, Du Cane Road, London W12 0HS.
Professor R.W. Shaw, Academic Department of Obstetrics and Gynaecology, Royal Free Hospital School of Medicine, Pond Street, London NW3 2QG.
Dr K.K. Ahuja, IVF Unit, Cromwell Hospital, Cromwell Road, London SW5 0TU.
Mr I. Craft, Humana Hospital, Wellington Place, London NW8 9LE.
Dr B.A. Mason and Professor S. Campbell, The Hallam Medical Centre, 77 Hallam Street, London W1N 5LR.
Mr D.K. Edmonds, Department of Fertility, Chelsea Hospital for Women, Dovehouse Street, London SW3 6LT.
Mr M.E. Setchell, Department of Obstetrics and Gynaecology, The Royal Hospital of St Bartholomew, London EC1A 7BE.
Professor S. Campbell, Department of Obstetrics and Gynaecology, King's College Hospital, Denmark Hill, London SE5 8RX.
Dr J. Glatt, The Infertility Advisory Centre, 144 Harley Street, London W1N 1AH. (Not approved by the VLA at the time of writing).

GREATER MANCHESTER

Dr B.A. Lieberman, Regional IVF Unit, St Mary's Hospital, Whitworth Park, Manchester M13 0JH.

HAMPSHIRE

Mr G.M. Masson, Department of Human Reproduction and Obstetrics, Princess Anne Hospital, Coxford Road, Southampton SO9 4HA.

LEICESTERSHIRE

Professor J. MacVicar, Department of Obstetrics and Gynaecology, Clinical Sciences Building, Leicester Royal Infirmary, PO Box 65, Leicester LE2 7LX.

NOTTINGHAMSHIRE

Mr J. Webster and Dr S. Fishel, Park Hospital, Sherwood Lodge Drive, Arnold, Nottingham NG5 8RX.

OXFORDSHIRE

Dr D.J. Little, Mr P.D. Bromwich and Mr D.H. Barlow, Nuffield Department of Obstetrics and Gynaecology, John Radcliffe Hospital, Headington, Oxford OX3 9DU.

SOUTH YORKSHIRE

Professor I.D. Cooke, University Department of Obstetrics and Gynaecology, Jessop Hospital for Women, Sheffield S3 7RE.

WEST YORKSHIRE

Mr D.R. Bromham, Department of Obstetrics and Gynaecology, St James' University Hospital, Leeds LS9 7TF.

SCOTLAND

GRAMPIAN

Professor A.A. Templeton, Department of Obstetrics and Gynaecology, University of Aberdeen, Royal Infirmary, Foresterhill, Aberdeen AB9 2ZB.

LOTHIAN

Professor D.T. Baird, Department of Obstetrics and Gynaecology, University of Edinburgh, 37 Chalmers Street, Edinburgh EH3 9EW.

STRATHCLYDE

Dr W.P. Black, Dr J.R.T. Coutts and Professor M.C. Macnaughton, Department of Obstetrics and Gynaecology, Royal Infirmary, 10 Alexandra Parade, Glasgow G31 2ER.

TAY

Dr J. Mills, Department of Reproductive Medicine, Ninewells Hospital, Dundee DD2 1UD.

At the time of writing the following additional centres may be setting up in the near future (in England):

GREATER LONDON

Professor J.G. Grudzinskas, Department of Obstetrics and Gynaecology, 4th floor, Holland Wing, The London Hospital, Whitechapel, London E1.

GREATER MANCHESTER

Dr P.J. Haynes, Department of Obstetrics and Gynaecology, University Hospital of South Manchester, West Didsbury, Manchester M20 8LR.

HUMBERSIDE

Mr A.G. Gordon, Gavis Brown Clinic, Princess Royal Hospital, Saltshouse Road, Hull HU8 8HE.

WEST MIDLANDS

Professor J.R. Newton, Department of Obstetrics and Gynaecology, Queen Elizabeth Medical Centre, Birmingham B15 2TG.

CHAPTER 7

Menstruation, Pre-menstrual Syndrome and Menopause

Menstruation

Menstruation is a monthly bleeding from the vagina occurring during a woman's child-bearing years. Every month, the womb prepares to receive a fertilised egg. If, however, the egg remains unfertilised, it does not implant itself in the womb. Hormone levels drop off, and the egg is discharged from the body with fragments of the wombs lining, ready for the process to begin again.

Usually, menstruation starts at around 11 or 12 years of age, though it may begin at any time from 9 to 18 years. Certain medical conditions may mean it is delayed longer. Few women have continuously regular menstrual cycles: the length of a menstrual cycle usually ranges from 20 to 36 days, with the average being 28 days. A normal period may last for anything from two to eight days, with four to six days being the average. Many of us have a particular time during our cycle when there is a feeling of special well-being and enthusiasm, with a strong upsurge of sexual desire. This is likely to be when the period is over. But, of course, intercourse is fine at any time, even during the period, and many women do, in fact, feel aroused at this time. At other times during our cycle we may feel somewhat depressed and have a good deal less 'get up and go'. However, these feelings and their extremes vary considerably from woman to woman.

Women are said to suffer from amenorrhoea if they have no menstrual periods – considered 'primary' if a girl has not started by the age of 18, and 'secondary' if a woman's periods cease at any time. Of course, periods cease if a woman becomes pregnant, but they may also stop through stress, malnutrition, obesity, taking the pill and certain illnesses.

Most women consider their periods a very mixed blessing. They can cause pain, inconvenience and, at the very least, some discomfort. For a few days each month our hair is likely to go lank, and our eyes to be emphasised by dark shadows. Our periods force us to keep closely in touch with our bodily functions. It is not so easy to be as consistently carefree as in our childhood period-free days when, as adults, we are bound into our monthly cycles, having to fuss over our bodies to a degree healthy men never experience.

Difficulties with periods arise for a number of reasons, not all of them being easy to put right. As women, we tend to be indoctrinated into believing that we must simply suffer such 'womanly' complaints. The medical world regularly reinforces this view when we present them with problems of heavy or unreliable periods, backaches and headaches, and it is sometimes suggested either that these difficulties are 'all in the mind' or are no more than we can expect and nothing that a few tranquillisers won't put right.

Fortunately, many women are now prepared to challenge such attitudes and are learning to be a lot more open about their periods with each other and with male partners. Certainly, it is wise to learn as much as we can about these special workings of our bodies. Understanding can help us to cope with difficulties and enable us to ask the right questions and to find the most appropriate services and treatment for physical problems. Women's groups, which are now appearing around the country (*see* Chapter 8, 'Women Only'), can be marvellously supportive in this, and books written on a woman-to-woman basis can be both enlightening and practical. See especially the references to *Our Bodies Ourselves: a Health Book for and by Women* in the 'Selected Further Information' section in this chapter.

Pre-menstrual Syndrome

Throughout our fertile years, which may range from age 9 to 55, many women will suffer from pre-menstrual syndrome (PMS) to a greater or lesser degree. If this is serious it may result in a combination of depression, headaches (migraines may be at their worst at this time), backaches, lethargy, irritability and numerous other symptoms.

However, not every woman who has any or all of the symptoms is necessarily suffering from PMS and it is important to check carefully whether your symptoms occur in a regular pattern each month, that is in the week or ten days before your period, with freedom from symptoms during the rest of the month. By keeping a careful chart for two or three months you could easily check this and such a chart would be useful to convince your doctor of the seriousness of your claims.

Where to Go for Help

See your family doctor first. While male doctors have often been less than sympathetic and some downright dismissive and patronising, many doctors are now recognising the very serious problems women can experience before and during their periods and are more prepared to pay serious attention to our problems, rather than simply sending us away empty handed or with a prescription for tranquillisers. She or he may decide to prescribe a diuretic which will help with the problem of water retention by increasing the volume of urine produced. It is thought that the build-up of fluid which occurs before a period may be the cause of some of the problems associated with PMS. Or she or he may prescribe treatment based on hormone or vitamin replacement therapy, where it is considered that your problems are caused by a hormone imbalance or a vitamin deficiency. You may also find counselling and psychotherapy beneficial to help with the emotional problems which may be interwoven with the physical ones.

If necessary, your doctor may refer you to a special PMS clinic. Your Family Planning Association regional office (*see* Chapter 3, 'Family Planning') would be able to give you details of the nearest clinic. If you feel unable to approach your own doctor you could go to see a family planning clinic doctor (*see* Chapter 3, 'Family Planning').

Other helpful services are provided by:

The Premenstrual Society (Premsoc)
PO Box 102, London SE1 7ES
Premsoc invites membership from anyone interested in helping women who suffer from PMS and their families. The aims of the society are to promote research and educational courses on PMS and to support individuals and organisations aiming to start self-help groups, local part-time clinics, telephone helplines, etc.

The membership subscription is £5 per year (full time students and the unwaged £2.50). The benefits include four newsletters per year and reduced rates on some books on PMS and other aspects of women's health. Members are invited to enquire about 'starter packs' for self-help groups and about ideas for fund raising. It is hoped in the future to start a helpline.

Premsoc's professional advisors will reply by post to general queries from members (a stamped, addressed envelope is essential). It is not possible to answer queries by telephone.

Women's Health Concern
Ground Floor, 17 Earls Terrace, London W8 6LP (Tel: 01-602 6669).
Will advise you on PMS. They have a useful booklet, *Pre-menstrual Tension and Period Pains*, price 85p, including postage and packing.

The Menopause

This is the time in a woman's life when she permanently ceases to menstruate (that is, to have monthly periods), because the ovaries stop producing an egg cell every four weeks. She is then no longer able to have children. She will also experience a decrease in the body level of oestrogen (the female sex hormone).

The menopause is most likely to happen from around the mid-forties to the mid-fifties, but it can sometimes begin as early as the mid-thirties. Monthly periods may end abruptly or they may continue with long intervals in between before finally stopping. It is possible to become pregnant until about two years after the last period (one year if this occurs after age 50), so birth control measures need to be continued during this time.

Having had all those years of monthly periods we might be expected to be glad when they are over, but to many women they may represent a lost youth. The menopause is often referred to as the 'change' and indeed we do then have to come to terms with a different view of life. Many women worry that their sex lives will be harmed, but this most certainly need not be so. In fact, relieved from the problems of unwanted pregnancies, many women blossom forth and positively enjoy a new lease of life. They glory in relaxed and worry-free love-making. Certainly, many women feel no lessening in their sexual desires.

Some women sail through the menopause without too much trouble, seemingly very little affected by the change in the balance of sex hormones in their bodies, while others may experience a number of problems which may be mild to severe and which may include hot flushes, palpitations, dryness and lack of suppleness in the vagina. Sexual intercourse can obviously be very uncomfortable if there is too little lubrication. This problem on its own can be helped by using a product like K-Y Jelly, available in chemists' shops. Some women may also suffer emotional problems, suffering loss of energy, feeling irritable, and associating the menopause with getting older and less attractive.

Hormone Replacement Therapy (HRT)

When menopausal problems are clearly interfering with a woman's lifestyle and the difficulties we have described become unmanageable, doctors will sometimes prescribe hormone replacement therapy (usually consisting of oestrogen and progestogen in the smallest possible dose necessary to alleviate the symptoms). For vaginal dryness alone it may be sufficient to use a cream.

However, not all women would be considered suitable for this treatment, since they may be at risk from serious side-effects. HRT is not usually prescribed for women with kidney or liver disease, heart disease, diabetes or high blood pressure. Women who smoke heavily or who are overweight may also be recommended to steer clear of HRT.

A good deal of controversy still surrounds the use of HRT and the risk of cancer has still not been completely ruled out. But potential risks are being minimised by careful selection of patients and by careful prescribing. Certainly, HRT does remove unpleasant physical and psychological symptoms of oestrogen deficiency in middle age, and taken under careful supervision can be of considerable benefit to women whose lives are being disrupted by serious menopausal complications.

Where to Go for Help

Your family doctor may be able to help you. However, too many male doctors still tend to dismiss menopausal symptoms, telling the patient that she is being neurotic. They seem to remain oblivious to the very real distress a woman is suffering. If you feel that your doctor is being less than helpful or that you are being unnecessarily prescribed tranquillisers when you have real physical symptoms for which you are seeking relief, you can ask to be referred to a menopause clinic.

Family Planning Information Service
27–35 Mortimer Street, London W1N 7RJ (Tel: 01-636 7866).
The FPIS or the FPA regional office will be able to provide you with details of local facilities. (*See* Chapter 3, 'Family Planning' for further details of clinics.)

Women's Health Concern
Ground Floor, 17 Earls Terrace, London W8 6LP (Tel: 01-602 6669).
Has a list of menopause clinics and would be glad to provide advice.

Selected Further Information

The Menopause by John McQueen. Published by the Women's Health Concern, Second edition 1982. (*see* page 62). Price £1, plus postage and packing.
This very straightforward little booklet explains the various aspects surrounding the menopause, including symptoms and also describes the function of the sex hormones (oestrogen and progesterone) and why the oestrogen levels decrease. The author briefly describes hormone replacement therapy. There is a very useful list of NHS and private medical facilities offering help and guidance to women.

Once a Month by Katharina Dalton. Published by Fontana Paperbacks, 1982. Price £1.50.
The 'curse of Eve' is here described very fully. The author gives us the benefit of her experience in working with women patients over 30 years. She describes pre-menstrual syndrome and all the other sometimes serious discomforts which can occur at period time. She points to the insensitivity of so many doctors in dealing with the very real problems of their women patients and talks about the

> 'shamefully neglected subject of menstruation'.

The author also discusses the menopause and describes it as the

> 'Gateway to serenity, for the postmenopausal years are characterised by confidence, calmness, sophistication, stable mood and endless energy.'

As to what to do, Dr Dalton shows that in most cases women can treat themselves and that in some more severe cases progesterone treatment can be highly effective.

While agreeing with the author that women's menstrual problems merit urgent and serious attention (and she has done more than most to bring this matter to attention), we need to be cautious in accepting a too simplistic view of our condition which may provide ammunition for those elements in our society who are only too ready to look for reasons to keep a woman 'in her place'. Dr Dalton explains that one of the reasons for writing the book is to help men to understand the capricious and temperamental changes of women, so that the image of women as uncertain, fickle, changeable, moody and hard-to-please may go, to be replaced with the recognition that all these features can be understood in terms of the ever-changing ebb and flow of her menstrual hormones. The danger of this proposition is that it can easily be used to reinforce the stereotype of woman as being essentially unstable and therefore incapable of serious responsibility. Would that it were as easy to explain men's irrationalities, fickleness and moodiness!

Our Bodies Ourselves: a Health Book for and by Women British edition by Angela Phillips and Jill Rakusen. Published by Penguin Books. Price £8.95.
Includes informative and encouraging sections on menstruation and the menopause, discussing attitudes and experiences, while also providing full and useful information on medical and non-medical treatment, including hormone replacement therapy. (For full details, *see* page 57).

The Premenstrual Syndrome: the Curse That Can be Cured by Dr Caroline Shreeve. Published by Thorsons Publishers Limited, Denington Estate, Wellingborough, Northamptonshire NN8 2RQ (Tel: Wellingborough (0933) 76031). Price £3.95.
This practical self-help guide gives advice on coping with PMS – at home, at work or at school. As a former GP and herself a PMS sufferer, Dr Shreeve explains the various ways of alleviating the symptoms and discusses a natural cure which has been clinically tested and which, it is suggested, has transformed the lives of thousands of women. The natural cure has dietary implications and involves topping up the essential fatty acids in our bodies – the deficiency of which, it is considered, can be a significant cause of PMS. In addition to alterations in diet, taking of Oil of Evening Primrose is recommended and the reasons for this are clearly given.

Pre-menstrual Tension: What It Is, How to Recognise It and How to Cure It by Judy Lever with M. Brush and Brian Haynes. Published by the New English Library, 1980. Price £1.50.
A readable booklet which aims to strip away the mysteries surrounding PMS and urging women who may suffer from this problem to seek help or, if the PMS is present in only a mild form, to try a little self-help and healthy living.

The author claims that scientific evidence has now finally established that PMS has a physical cause. She says that

> 'In those women who suffer from it there is a malfunction in the production of hormones during the menstrual cycle, in particular the female hormone progesterone. This upsets the normal working of the menstrual cycle and produces the unpleasant symptoms of PMT.'

She goes on to say,

> 'As a result of this discovery, treatments have been devised which are simple, safe and remarkably successful. More than three-quarters of women who have been treated appear to be completely cured or helped to the point where their symptoms are easily bearable.'

Ms Lever points out that not every woman who has one of the symptoms or even a collection of them necessarily has PMS; she explains how to recognise your own symptoms for what they are. A useful book, covering every aspect of the problem, including what to do about it.

SisterWrite Bookshop, 190 Upper Street, London N1 1RQ (Tel: 01-226 9782).
This is a cooperative women's bookshop selling books which provide a penetrating feminist insight into women's issues. Monthly booklists of new titles are available on subscription of £1.75 for six months. For further details *see* Chapter 8, 'Women Only.'

Toward Intimacy: Family Planning and Sexuality Concerns of Physically Disabled Women by The Task Force on Concerns of Physically Disabled Women, edited by Susan Shaul, Lane Bogle and others. Published by the Human Sciences Press, 3 Henrietta Street, London WC2E 8LU (Tel: 01-240 0856). Price £5 plus postage and packing. For further details, *see* Chapter 12, 'Sexuality and Disability'.

CHAPTER 8

Women Only

Women are becoming more and more determined to express their own unique sexual identity. We are refusing to accept a role and a sexual caricature imposed by men, which contradicts our inherent femaleness, and implies that our own image is somehow not good enough.

Over the centuries women have donned ridiculous clothing – wasp waists, bustles, stiletto heels – to contort their bodies and restrict their movements, all so that they should appear attractive to men, while at the same time remaining essentially helpless, firmly under the control of, and even in the ownership of, the men in their lives.

Times are changing, and women are learning proudly to present their natural selves to the world, with only as much artifice as pleases them. Now they are choosing to wear clothes which are fun, but which also allow the wearer natural, relaxed movement and which enhance bodily grace, while permitting participation in life on equal terms with men.

The women's liberation movement, the backbone of the struggle for change in a largely male-dominated society is, without doubt, the greatest self-help movement there has ever been. Women band together to fight for equal rights and for a change in a patriarchal society's attitudes towards them; they also band together in supportive sisterhood to help each other and to help individuals under stress. It is the women's movement which has provided refuges for women who have been battered and has made available practical help, advice and comfort for women who have been raped. It is women who are emerging to help women who have suffered incestuous sexual abuse and who are planning to provide refuges to meet a very specific and desperate need. Women are also coming together to explore their own sexuality and by gaining an understanding of their own bodies are learning to have control over them.

They have learned to enjoy masturbation for its own sake and as a means of understanding their own bodily responses. Some have found the courage to take sexual pleasure from each other; the majority remain heterosexual but are clear about their sex lives – they do nothing they don't like, but having learned to appreciate their own bodies they are able to take a full and equal part in love-making.

While sex can be the source of some of our greatest joys, tragically it can also bring with it horrific violence and degrading misery. So much of this can be traced directly to the institutionalising of an inferior role for women. Women are seen as 'pure' or 'impure', as 'sex objects' or 'domestic'; always under the command and alleged 'protection' of men.

Double standards abound. Our society, through distorted advertising and in a million other subtle ways, reinforces the message. Pornography flourishes on the debasement of women. Girls are brought up to 'please' men and to wait for the knight in shining armour who will sweep them off to a marital bed of roses. As a result, women at the very least are disappointed and men at their worst become brutal. So many female/male partnerships are built on shifting sands of misunderstanding. The relationship is a disaster precisely because each goes into it with false expectations of the other, based on learned stereotypes, which at the same time encourage men and women to make too many allowances one for the other. Unquestionably, men must be made fully responsible for their own mindless violence towards women, but could women sometimes foresee that a man whom they mistakenly think in their courting days looks so attractive with his tough, 'macho' pose, is, in fact, a dominating brute and a battering husband in the making?

Only by refusing to accept these standards, by developing their own standards, by seeking to change the law and demanding that the authorities no longer tolerate domestic and other violence towards women, by repudiating the brain-washing and stereotyping carried out in families, at school and in society generally, will women gain the strength and understanding to develop their own individuality and to promote a more harmonious and peaceful society.

Lesbian women are coming forward to enjoy each other's company and to share a mutually enjoyed homosexuality. They have something to teach all women about a genuine appreciation of female sexuality as a force in its own right. Heterosexual women, hopefully now more confident in their sexuality, want to share with men the tremendous pleasure such joys can bring when the relationship is relieved from any exploitative or dominating aspects.

To take this forward as women we may well have to teach the other half of human kind that they don't own the world or us and that mutual harmony can be a whole lot nicer than taking us on as vassals.

Where to Go for Help

Women's Centres
Exist throughout the UK to provide advice, information, support, and solidarity to women in all aspects of our lives.

The Feminist Self-insemination Group
c/o Women's Reproductive Rights Information Centre, 52 – 54 Featherstone Street, London EC1Y 8RT (Tel: 01-251 6332).
This group has produced a guide, *Self-Insemination*, which offers advice on the use of AI by donor without recourse to a clinic.

Gingerbread Association for One-parent Families
35 Wellington Street, London WC2E 7BN (Tel: 01-240 0953).
An association for one parent families with 300 self-help groups in England and Wales which give advice and support on practical and emotional problems. Contact the national office for details of local groups.

King's Cross Women's Centre
71 Tonbridge Street, London WC1 (Tel: 01-837 7509).
Mailing address: PO Box 287, London NW6 5QU.
The centre provides a very useful contact centre, covering a wide range of subjects where women can help each other to help themselves. Women outside London with particular needs will be put in touch with local women's groups for supportive help or with other agencies sensitive to women's needs – solicitors, doctors, rape crisis centres, etc. The Centre has extensive files on women's issues, useful for students or others pursuing specific campaigns. The Centre is open Monday to Thursday 11 a.m. – 5 p.m. A free legal advice service is available to women. The Centre has a number of groups working on specific areas of interest. These include:

ROW (Rights of Women); 52–54 Featherstone Street, London EC1Y 8RT (Tel: 01-251-6577). ROW is a feminist organisation of women interested in the law or campaigning to make changes in law. They say that

> 'as women we have all experienced coming up against a male-dominated legal system. We got together because we think it is important for women to help each other find our way around the many man-made laws that affect our lives, and make legal services responsive to women's interests.'

There is a women's resource centre, which provides help and information on the law and legal services. Applications for membership by women are welcome – for details send a stamped addressed envelope for a subscription form.

Sex, Race, and Class Discussion Study Group – combines support with discussion and study by sharing individual experiences as black and Third World women from different communities, cultures and backgrounds. The group focuses on what they share in common as the basis for building unity among British communities of black and Third World women.

Young Women's Group – brings together black and white women under the age of 25 with and without disabilities, lesbian and non-lesbian, of different backgrounds and occupations. The group aims to make visible the contribution made to society by young women, whether or not they have waged jobs, as well as to build a national and international network of young women.

International Wages for Housework Campaign – aims to campaign for wages for all women from all governments. Currently organising to implement the 1985 UN decision to count women's waged and unwaged work in the Gross National Product of every country.

International Black Women for Wages for Housework – similar to above and aiming to make visible black women's needs and priorities and their right for economic and social power in Third World and metropolitan countries.

Wages Due Lesbians – similar to above and also providing information and advice on child custody cases, rape and assault, discrimination at work, in housing, etc.

Wages for Housework Campaign – which has branches throughout the country.

Women Against Rape (*see* Chapter 9, 'Sexual Abuse').

WinVisible – for women with visible and invisible disabilities. For further details *see* Chapter 12, 'Sexuality and Disability'.

Peace Collective – women working to make the connections

among all our struggles for peace against nuclear weapons/ power, poverty, sexism, racism, ecological devastation and overwork which military expenditures cost us.

English Collective of Prostitutes

Mailing address: PO Box 287, London NW6 5QU (Tel: 01-837 7509/01-459 1150; or Bristol (0272) 422116).

The ECP campaigns to abolish all laws against prostitutes and for the state to provide support in housing and money to any woman who wants to leave the game. The Collective also helps with cases – soliciting and loitering, brothel keeping, child custody, social security, etc.

The ECP has produced a useful leaflet, with the information clearly set out, *A Guide to the Rules of the Game: A – Z for Working Girls*. A number of other publications are available, including *Prostitutes – Our Life*, published by the Falling Wall Press, 1980. Price £3.50. Available from the King's Cross Women's Centre as above.

A Woman's Place

Hungerford House, Victoria Embankment, London WC2 (Tel: 01-836 6081).

This is a women's liberation information service completely run by women volunteers within a collective. They are available Monday to Friday 12 noon – 7 p.m. and Saturday 12 noon – 6 p.m. and will provide information on matters specifically affecting women. They can advise you about local women's groups and other sources of help. A bookshop is run as part of the service and contains books and pamphlets of special interest to women.

Women's Aid Federation

National Office – England

37 – 39 Jamaica Street, Bristol. New telephone number unknown at time of going to press.

The Federation is organised around individual, autonomous Women's Aid Groups, who carry out a very specific function in providing refuge and support for battered women and their children.

The national office co-ordinates 104 refuges in England and can put individuals in touch with a local group. Nationally, the Federation has an 'open door' policy, which means that they work on a collective basis to ensure that no woman is ever refused refuge. If a woman contacts a refuge and women there feel they are unable to accept her because the refuge is already crowded, they will tell her of or accompany her to the nearest alternative refuge.

For any woman who does not necessarily want to go to a refuge, but wants to discuss her problems, the local refuge will have someone who will be glad to listen and give information on legal, financial and housing rights.

The national office also sends and receives information about legislation, etc. affecting battered women and campaigns for legal and social change. This office will also give help and contact to women wanting to start up a new group. The aims of the Federation through its local refuges are:

(a) to provide temporary refuge on request, for women and their children who have suffered mental or physical harassment in their relationships or sexual harassment, rape or sexual abuse;
(b) to encourage the women to determine their own futures and to help them to achieve this, whether this involves returning home or starting a new life elsewhere;
(c) to recognise and care for the emotional and educational needs of the children involved;
(d) to offer support, advice and help to any woman who asks for it, whether or not she is a resident and also to offer support and aftercare to any woman and child who have left the refuge;
(e) to educate and inform the public, the media, the police, the courts, social services and other authorities, with respect to the battering of women, mindful of the fact that this is a result of the general position of women in our society.

Essentially the work of the Federation is based on self-help, and women living in refuges support each other both emotionally and practically. A publications list is available from the National Office.

Regional Offices are located at the following addresses:

ENGLAND

GREATER LONDON

Women's Aid Federation 52 – 54 Featherstone Street, London EC1Y 8RT (Tel: 01-251 6507). Hours: Monday to Friday 10 a.m. – 5 p.m. (24-hour answerphone service).

GREATER MANCHESTER

Northern and Publications Office, 116 Portland Street, Manchester M1 4RP (Tel: 061-236 6540). Hours: Monday to Friday 10 a.m. – 4 p.m. (24-hour answerphone service).

NOTTINGHAMSHIRE

Women's Centre and Women's Aid, (Tel: Nottingham (0602) 476490). Hours: Monday, Tuesday, Thursday,

Friday 10 a.m. – 3 p.m. (24-hour answerphone service.)

WEST YORKSHIRE

Leeds Women's Aid (Tel: Leeds (0532) 444060). Hours: Mondays and Thursdays.

The following national bodies of the Women's Aid Federation fulfil a similar function to that described under 'National Office – England'.

WALES

Incentive House, Adam Street, Cardiff CF1 2FJ (Tel: Cardiff (0222) 462291), or Welsh Women's Aid Rural Office, 9 Castle Street, Aberystwyth SY23 1DT (Tel: Aberystwyth (0970) 612748). Co-ordinating body for the Women's Aid Groups and refuges in Wales. A newsletter is available called *Women's View* and a range of leaflets including: *Divorce: Your Rights*; *Domestic Violence* and *Housing*.

SCOTLAND

Scottish Women's Aid, 11 St Colme Street, Edinburgh EH3 6AG (Tel: 031-225 8011 – 24 hour answerphone service). Co-ordinating body in Scotland for local Women's Aid Groups. A Scottish Women's Aid newsletter is available (£6 subscription). A publications list is available. There are Women's Aid Groups based all over Scotland.

NORTHERN IRELAND

143A University Street, Belfast BT7 1HP (Tel: Belfast (0232) 249358).

Women's Health Concern
Ground Floor, 17 Earl's Terrace, London W8 6LP (Tel: 01-602 6669).
The WHC aims to provide an information and counselling service to women with obstetric or gynaecological conditions. These may include dysfunctional illness such as post-natal depression, menopause problems, premenstrual syndrome; all kinds of common infections like cystitis, thrush, and herpes and a variety of sexually transmitted diseases; all kinds of urinary problems; infertility and psychosexual problems; loss of periods after taking the pill or following anorexia; complications after sterilisation; epilepsy; pre-operative and post-operative worries; and disharmony in marital and other relationships.

They may be contacted by letter, (include stamped, self-addressed envelope) or telephone, or you can make an appointment to visit.

The WHC has found that all too often a woman's problems have not been sorted out by a doctor and she needs somewhere else to turn to for sympathetic advice and help, before returning to the doctor or some other appropriate source of help. The WHC gives general counselling sessions to women by appointment in London. For these the clients give donations of anything up to £15. Psychotherapy is also available.

Women's Reproductive Rights Information Centre
52 – 54 Featherstone Street, London EC1Y 8RT (Tel: 01-251 6332). WRRIC give support and information on reproduction issues stressing women's rights. For fuller details see Chapter 3, 'Family Planning'.

Women's Therapy Centre
6 Manor Gardens, London N7 6LA (Tel: 01-263 6200). The Centre provides a programme of workshops for women clients only and is committed to facilitating London-based self-help therapy groups by putting women in contact with one another and by providing back-up for groups that are having problems.

In the workshops a wide range of subjects is covered (send a stamped, self-addressed envelope for details), including 'Bodywork on Boundaries', for women who would like to assert their boundaries more, say no without feeling guilty and be better able to enter and close a contract; 'Myself in Relationship with Others'; 'Co-counselling'; 'Women and Men and Anger'; 'Sexuality and Pleasure' (providing time to learn, share and get in touch with your unique sexual energy and expression); 'Pre-orgasmic Women' (for women who have never had or who have difficulty in having an orgasm); 'Menstruation and Pre-menstrual Tension' (the group shows both positive and negative feelings and attitudes towards menstruation, including myths and taboos, and also explores PMS both in its physical and emotional aspects); 'Post-abortion' (exploring issues around feminity, womanhood, sexuality and fertility emerging before or after an abortion).

Selected Further Information

Cystitis: the New Approach by Caroline Shreeve. Published by Thorsons Publishing Group, Denington Estate, Wellingborough, Northamptonshire NN8 7RQ (Tel: Wellingborough (0933) 76031). Price £3.99.
Dr Shreeve sets out to provide a clear idea of what happens inside the bladder to cause cystitis. She outlines the numerous factors that can trigger an attack and discusses the preventive measures available and the

orthodox approach to treatment, along with a comprehensive guide to supplementary or alternative treatments including diet, herbalism, homeopathy, and aromatherapy. Also included is a self-help programme aimed at helping you to avoid attacks or alleviate one which has already been started.

Down There: an Illustrated Guide to Self-exam, written and compiled by Sophie Laws, with help and advice from the Onlywomen Press Collective. Printed and published 1980 by the Onlywomen Press Ltd, 38 Mount Pleasant, London WC1 (Tel: 01-837 0596). Price £1 plus 35p postage and packing. Speculum available for an additional 85p. Also available from SisterWrite Bookshop, 190 Upper Street, London N1 1RQ (Tel: 01-226 9782). The thought of self-examination may worry some women. We are so used to leaving everything 'down there' to doctors, having been taught that this vital part of our anatomy does not really belong to us at all, or even that it is something to be ashamed of. As the author explains,

> 'Learning to do self-exam with a speculum is an important part of the process of women beginning to take control of and responsibility for our own bodies.'

It is also explained just how useful it can be to look at your cervix regularly, learning to spot changes, early signs of infections, pregnancy and cellular changes, which might indicate problems.

> 'Basic self-exam is a first step towards coping with all kinds of things for ourselves – the treatment of some infections, menstrual extractions and self-insemination for example.'

It is made clear that

> 'speculum self-examination is not a way of detecting cervical cancer – pap smears taken at regular intervals throughout every woman's adult life are the way to screen for this cancer'.

It is considered that the best way to learn about self-exam is with a women's liberation group – either a general or consciousness-raising group or one specifically focused on women's health. Certainly, an understanding and a sense of ownership of all our body including this very special area, provides us with the confidence to enjoy our sexuality and to express it and enjoy it in any way we choose.

Speculums are also on sale at SisterWrite Bookshop (*see* address above) price 90p, at A Woman's Place (*see* page 61) and at some local women's centres.

For Ourselves: Our Bodies and Sexuality from Women's Point of View, English translation from the Dutch by Ann Oosthuizen, with help from Marij van Helmond. English edition edited by Jill Nichols, with help from Tina Reid. Published by Sheba Feminist Publishers, 1981. Unfortunately now out of print, this book is available in libraries, and may be reprinted.

This book is a joyful celebration of women as we really are, our hopes, aspirations and fears – and most of all our sexuality. As the publisher says it dismisses

> 'once and for all the passive Playboy image that has for so long been called our sexuality'.

They go on to say,

> 'This book describes how we can learn to assert ourselves even when it comes to sexuality. How we can begin a romantic affair with our own bodies. Or with a woman. Or with a man. And how our sexual freedom is determined by how much freedom we have in the rest of our lives.'

The book, which is copiously illustrated, has a lyrical, imaginative quality combined with a wealth of practical information and encouragement. It was written by one woman, but much of the time she is drawing on the experiences of women whose words are quoted. A lot of collective thought has also gone into it from the health group in the Sara Collective who first published the book in Dutch.

Our Bodies Ourselves: a Health Book by and for Women. A product of the Boston Women's Health Book Collective. British edition by Angela Phillips and Jill Rakusen. Published by Penguin Books. Price £8.95.
A marvellous book which has virtually become a bible in this country, and no doubt in the United States, for all those women who are seeking to take control over their own bodies – to become the keepers of their own health and their fertility.

Although it was written in the first place for women in the United States, it has travelled well. The editors have done an incredibly good job, extensively overhauling the text and the resources to ensure its practical and cultural affinity. The style of the book is attractive. The writers are women who identify with their readers throughout; you know that somehow, no matter what, they are always on your side.

As well as discussing women's health and bodily functions, they also describe in very precise details how our bodies work and what we may expect when we seek treatment or services. A good deal of emphasis is laid on the help women can give each other, the power of shared information, how we ourselves can explore our own bodies and become not only familiar with their workings, but also proud of the parts and the whole. The material covered includes anatomy, sexuality, relationships, lesbianism, nutrition and health, venereal disease and common ailments, birth control, abortion, considering parenthood, child-bearing, menopause, the health care system and how to use it. Also included is a valuable list of reading and resources at the end of each chapter.

Scottish Women's Aid
11 St Colme Street, Edinburgh EH3 6AG (Tel: 031-225 8011).
Scottish Women's Aid have a publication list available.

SisterWrite Bookshop
190 Upper Street, London N1 1RQ (Tel: 01-226 9782). Open Monday to Saturday 10.00 a.m. – 6.00 p.m. (Thursday 10.00 – 7.00 p.m.).
SisterWrite is a co-operative women's bookshop stocking a wide range of titles by and about women and also children's books. Sections include fiction, health, therapy and psychology, sex and birth and childcare, sexuality, history, women's studies, biography, education, art, poetry, and writing by Black, Irish, Jewish, and lesbian women.

SisterWrite has a worldwide mail-order service, and monthly booklists of new titles are available on subscription: £1.75 for six months in UK, £2.25 in Europe, £2.50 elsewhere. Send a large SAE for details of the mail order service.

Spare Rib
The monthly newspaper of the women's liberation movement. In addition to news and features it carries a mass of information about women's campaigns, meetings and social events. You can also write to *Spare Rib* for contacts in local women's organisations, including those concerned with health and sexuality. Available at bookstalls and from 27 Clerkenwell Close, London EC1 OAT (Tel: 01-253 9792).

Women's Aid Federation (England) (WAFE)
116 Portland Street, Manchester M1 4RP (Tel: 061-236 6540). Women's Aid Federation (England) has a publications list available, and some very useful leaflets including: *Are Children Safe in the Home*; *Will I Be Safe: Battered Women and Injunctions*; *Women and Housing*; *Unhelpful Myths and Stereotypes about Battered Women*; *What is Women's Aid?*; and *Women Demand Control over Their Lives*.

WAFE has also produced a video *Judy Punches Back* in which women answer the question 'why are men violent to women?' This video concentrates on four women and the episode in each of their lives when they were receiving violence from a man. It starts with them leaving the violent situation, and looks at their expectations and feelings about themselves while living in that violent relationship, comparing them with their feelings and expectations about themselves now. It shows how, with the support of other women, they have got together new homes, rebuilt their lives, friendships, confidence and re-claimed their own identity. The video is available from Manchester as above.

The Women's Press
124 Shoreditch High Street, London E1 6JE (Tel: 01-729 5257).
Has a most interesting catalogue which is a joy to read in its own right. It lists a wide range of books covering feminist issues with topics ranging far and wide. We recommend you send for it and see for yourself.

CHAPTER 9

Sexual Abuse

Many people are reluctant to acknowledge the darker side of sex. They would prefer to deny its very existence. And yet unless we are prepared to bring out into the open those sexual activities which, far from being joyful, seriously damage people, those who are caught up in them will go on suffering in silence and being seriously psychologically and emotionally damaged as a result. The question of rape is thankfully being discussed more widely now, though there needs to be a significant change in attitudes by those in a position of authority if the woman's perception of this act of personal violation is to be understood. Child sexual abuse, on the other hand, is still very much a taboo subject, despite recent studies pointing to the fact that it is much more widespread than had been previously thought.

For those brought up in sexually abusing families or suffering a marriage in which sex and violence seem inextricably and inexplicably interwoven, sexual activity can only be equated with fear and with personal humiliation. The innocent pleasures of awakening sexuality in children who trust and love their parents, and the joys of sexual loving that many adult couples share, are worlds away for people whose homes are devastated by sexual abuse and violence.

We are talking about an abuse of power which allows a physically and socially stronger person sexually to abuse a physically and socially weaker person, whether this be a child or woman. Sexual abuse of another person can only result in abuse of that individual's whole identity, never allowing them to be themselves – they are forever 'owned'.

We are also talking about the betrayal of a child's normal expectations of trust and safety from the adults around her, when vulnerability is exploited rather than protected. As those who have suffered know, and as statistics clearly show, the sexual abuser is more than likely to be known to the victim – the enemy within. Child sexual abuse is overwhelmingly a family crime, predominantly carried out by fathers against daughters. It rests firmly on a base, generally sustained by society at large, of patriarchal authority and power. It is not only an abuse of power, but power to abuse, which can be sustained as though by right. Small wonder that many women come to see themselves as survivors in adulthood, rather than victims. The whole subject is surrounded by myth, mostly tending to stereotype familial roles and to shift responsibility towards those abused.

The subject of rape has been similarly treated for many years, but is at last being discussed more openly. Women are making known their feelings on this horrific offence. They are refusing to accept the simultaneous roles of 'victim' and 'guilty enticer', thrust upon them by an ambivalent society. They are questioning the male orientated values which perpetuate the idea that females of any age exist for the pleasure of the male, at his direction and command. Women are making known to male authority figures – the police, the judiciary, the legal profession and others – that they are not prepared to accept responsibility and blame for what is a male crime.

For a society to remain healthy it is essential that sexual abuses, of whatever kind, should be widely understood and that services should be provided to help both victims and perpetrators. Society has for too long preferred to brush the subject of domestic violence, especially sexual violence, under the carpet. Incest, in particular, is more often than not a well-kept secret. Victims commonly keep quiet for fear of being disbelieved or blamed or because they sense that they would be striking at the roots of the cherished ideals of family order. Society seems, on the whole, to prefer the secret to be kept, finding it a subject of profound distaste which it would rather avoid. Even social workers are largely silent, uncertain perhaps as to how they can cope with the consequences of exposure. It is this guilty conspiracy of silence, this tolerance of 'sex behind closed doors' which allows these abuses to continue unchecked, very often for years on end. The family itself sadly tends to be bound even more closely within the shackles of its guilty secret.

Opening up the whole area of sexual abuse for general discussion can only lead to greater understanding. Until this happens to a much greater extent than at present, services to help families in distress will continue to be woefully inadequate.

Child Sexual Abuse, Including Incest

We give a legal definition of incest in Chapter 20, 'Sex Law' and this may be summarised as

> 'sexual intercourse between persons who are so closely related that their marriage would be prohibited'.

We also describe, in Chapter 20, the law relating to the sexual abuse of children. A wider definition which gives sensitive expression to a child's situation has been expressed thus:

> 'the involvement of dependent, developmentally immature children and adolescents in sexual activities they do not truly comprehend, to which they are unable to give informed consent or that violate the social taboos of family roles.'

(From *Child Abuse* by R. S. Kempe and C. H. Kempe. Published by Fontana/Open Books, 1978. For further details see page 74).

A MORI poll conducted in 1985 for a Channel 4 programme on sexual abuse used the following definition:

> 'A child (anyone under 16 years) is sexually abused when another person, who is sexually mature, involves the child in any activity which the other person expects to lead to their sexual arousal. This might involve intercourse, touching, exposure of the sexual organs, showing pornographic material or talking about sexual things in an erotic way.'

We are mainly concerned here with parent/child incest. Sex between brothers and sisters is not, of course, uncommon, but the experience does not necessarily have all the damaging consequences of an adult/child relationship. Children within a family, who are of a similar age, may explore their sexuality as a result of natural curiosity and the episode may be no more than a fleeting experience. There need not be a betrayal of trust and violation of dependency as there is with adults and, of course, in such situations both partners are typically sexually naïve. However, in instances of sibling incest where age gaps are wider and force or threats are employed, the damaging effects of the experience can remain to blight adult emotional relationships.

Sexual abuse need not include intercourse and can still be horrifying and damaging to a child. Parents may sexually assault their children in a number of ways. A father may ask to be masturbated or demand that his daughter perform a variety of acts. Erin Pizzey, who has done so much to bring the cause of 'battered' women to light, has described the sexual abuse of children, in whatever form it occurs, as

> 'an act of violence against children and an act of treason against children'.

She has also spoken of the horror of the child's lack of real choice. Either the child opts in to the situation out of fear of the man or she opts out and is severely punished.

Parents who abuse their children – or who acquiesce in their abuse – exploit and betray their position as guardians and protectors. One survivor of childhood sexual abuse described in a radio programme the constantly terrifying experience when your molester lives in your own home.

> 'You feel that no place in the world is safe – if you cannot be safe in your own home and your own bed.'

Terror of sleep is a natural result in such circumstances, when a full and satisfying night's sleep is impossible for fear 'he' might appear.

The Scope of the Problem

There is a growing recognition that the problem of child sexual abuse is much greater than may have been realised. Criminal statistics give no real indication of the scale of the problem in that they represent only those cases which come to the attention of the police and result in prosecution. Similarly, registers of children at risk of abuse and neglect often fail to distinguish those cases which involve sexual abuse. None of the figures reflect in any way the undoubtedly large numbers of people who keep the secret to themselves. The findings of a survey conducted in 1981 in the United Kingdom suggested that there could be 'an absolute minimum' of 1,500 cases of sexual abuse of children every year and that this may represent just the tip of the iceberg. It reported that 85 per cent of sexually abused children in the survey were girls and 15 per cent boys – a third of the girls and half of the boys were under the age of 11 years. The youngest child reported was nine months old and was a victim of attempted sexual intercourse. The study also showed that the majority of child sexual abuse was, as we have already indicated, carried out by family members or close acquaintances. The NSPCC is now dealing with more cases of sexual abuse than previously. They say that prior to 1980, sexual abuse counted for only 1 per cent of all NSPCC maintained registrations. In 1985 that share was 14 per cent. Moreover there appears to be an increase in younger children being registered as victims. In 1984, 4 per cent were aged less than five years old, and in 1985 this rose to 14 per cent.

It was only in 1980 that the DHSS issued a circular recommending that the criteria for placing children on Registers of Suspected Non-Accidental Injury be broadened to include other forms of abuse than physical injury. The types of abuse mentioned included neglect, non-organic failure to thrive, and emotional abuse. In addition to those types of abuse, many areas also decided to include cases of sexual abuse among their criteria for registration.

Many people will stop short at reporting the offence for fear of splitting up the family. Professional intervention may result in prosecution of the father and a gaol sentence, and possibly the reception of the child into care. On top of all their other troubles, the victims may well find themselves blamed for the disintegration of the family and, in addition, may have the horrific ordeal of appearing as a witness in a criminal court case. During the proceedings the child will be cross-examined as a witness for the prosecution and is likely to suffer further humiliation and discredit at the hands of the defence counsel – 'legal child abuse', as it has been described. Clearly there is a need for child witnesses in criminal cases to be afforded greater consideration in the court setting in a variety of respects.

Treatment and Services

In the provision of help we are facing a 'chicken and egg' situation; we can be sure there are many children and families who need help, but we don't provide the services, because they don't come forward and make their needs forcibly known. But they don't come forward because our services are inadequate and special treatment facilities geared to meet these families' needs are virtually non-existent.

Victims are also often reluctant to come forward, fearing that their problems will not be understood or will be dismissed. Adults who have been abused as children have described the insensitivity, lack of understanding and disbelief with which they were met when they plucked up courage to seek help. When turning to a teacher or a doctor, for example, they found their stories of their fathers' treatment of them shrugged off as fantasies – a further indication to the child of her own powerlessness and lack of self-worth. To be disbelieved on such a matter can cause only profound mental agony and confusion and will hardly be likely to encourage the child to seek further help. To make matters worse, professionals who are concerned to help may be reluctant to do so, feeling that they have few ways of assisting the child without involving the full weight of the law and the added distress this is likely to bring to a child.

In the United States different approaches to the problem are being developed. Sexual treatment programmes in the United States combine legal and therapeutic interventions and involve all family members. They also rely on the co-operation of all those official agencies responsible for such matters, including social and mental health workers, probation officers, lawyers, judges and the police. The offending person is likely to have to spend time apart from the family, while every effort is made to keep the child who has been abused within the family home wherever this seems viable. All the family members receive treatment on an individual basis, as couples and also in self-help groups. These are considered to be a vital part of many treatment programmes. While the offender is clearly required to take responsibility for the sexual abuse that has occurred, he is not excluded from the treatment process. By contrast, in the United Kingdom our response to the offender is still essentially primitive and punitive. Notwithstanding that punishment for its own sake is unlikely to achieve any positive benefit.

The message emanating from various treatment programmes in the United States is that families in which child sexual abuse has occurred need not inevitably be destroyed in order to protect the child, although the amount of therapeutic input to reverse such families' situations is considerable. Redressing the harm done may be even more difficult. Adults who were sexually abused as children testify to the lasting damage they have suffered. Many of them have married, but have experienced serious difficulties in establishing satisfactory sexual relationships with their partners and close, warm relationships with their children. They commonly express feelings of confusion, of low self-worth, of their lives being ruined and of social isolation, and they may need considerable therapeutic support before they can fully adjust to adult roles and regain a sense of personal identity and value.

In some areas of the United Kingdom the different professions and agencies involved with the problems of child sexual abuse are beginning to come together to work out a way of providing more appropriate intervention (*see*, for example, the details on SAIF on page 74). Where the police also agree to be involved in meetings of this kind, they will often co-operate by not taking unilateral action. In these situations it is possible for an overall plan to be devised to help the whole family.

At the same time, it must never be forgotten that it is the abused child who requires the most urgent attention and whose needs must remain paramount. Preservation of a family structure which puts further responsibility on the abused child's or teenager's shoulders to preserve relationships which can only continue to damage her will result in further disabling trauma which is likely to make recovery that much harder. Sarah Nelson, in her book *Incest: Fact and Myth* (*see* page 75), discuss implications such as these.

Rape

We have been discussing child sexual abuse, which tragically includes rape. Here we are discussing rape as it affects women. A legal definition of rape is given in Chapter 20, 'Sex Law', but the Rape Crisis Centre in London has a wider definition, which includes any unwanted, forced or coerced sexual attention.

While rape is a vicious crime, nevertheless, in the eyes of the law, a woman cannot be raped by her husband. Forced intercourse is apparently regarded as no more than a man's claiming of his conjugal rights; the law upholds the view that a woman must submit to his demands, however unreasonable she finds them. Should he knock her around at the same time, the wife may then be able to bring a charge of assault, but even this can prove difficult, since the police may take the view that they cannot 'interfere between a man and wife'. Right up to the present day, even severe physical injury suffered by a woman may be seen as nothing more than a man's right to impose his will in 'domestic' matters. Even when a woman is raped by a stranger, she may be blamed for being in a certain place at a certain time, for being provocative or simply for being a woman.

One of the disturbing elements of rape is that a woman is liable to be accorded at least a part of the blame, even if this is only 'contributory negligence', as the presiding judge suggested in the infamous case of *R*. v. *Allen* in 1981. No wonder women feel that the legal process is still weighted against them. They may even have the problem of having to prove their credibility when they seek help.

It has often been felt that the police act with a profound lack of sensitivity. There may be an implication that the woman has secretly enjoyed it or, as one rape victim put it when discussing friends' reactions,

> 'As far as they were concerned, rape was simply a matter of having sex with someone you didn't particularly fancy, at a time when you didn't feel particularly like it.'

This particular victim made it clear that she believed rape was

> 'about violence – a very special sort of violence, the sort which has its roots in male inadequacy (whether emotional, sexual, social or whatever) and manifests itself in a hatred of women.'

It is no wonder that women are angry about rape and one of the things that makes them most angry is other people's attitudes to those who have been violated. Rape is not only a violation of body but also a violation of personhood. If women really are to receive justice in this area, there will have to be a considerable change in attitudes by those in authority and by society generally. It would be strange indeed if a woman really could be said 'to have asked for it', but this is frequently suggested.

When women have been raped they suffer (apart from the terror of the attack itself) devastating feelings of worthlessness, of being used, of being dirty. After such an experience it is not surprising that the raped woman should suffer a major psychological upheaval, for the feelings of gross humiliation are overpowering. And yet she seldom receives the sympathy and understanding she needs.

Rape victims have consistently suffered from callous disregard of their plight. It is not surprising then that women have taken matters into their own hands and have provided the understanding and supportive help that is needed when a woman who has been raped is suffering the desperate after-effects of an attack. We describe and list on page 70 the Rape Crisis Centres which exist around the country where any woman can go with the assurance of complete confidentiality. We also recommend you turn to Chapter 8, 'Women Only', where other women's organisations are described.

Where to Go For Help

Child Guidance Clincs

These clinics offer services to families where the children are experiencing difficulties. They may be found through the local telephone directory or through your Social Services Department or Community Health Council.

Incest Survivors' Campaign

c/o A Woman's Place, Hungerford House, Victoria Embankment, London WC2.

This is a women-only campaign with nationwide contacts, whose main aim is to set up refuges for girls. It provides a contact service for women in any part of the UK to set up self-help therapy; gives talks and workshops to women's groups and conferences; refers women to rape crisis lines; and campaigns against sexual abuse of girl children and young women. The problems dealt with include adult women's reactions to sexual abuse in their childhood.

Contact should be made by post at present. There are no fees. Stamped, self-addressed envelopes would be appreciated.

Incest Survivors' Groups
A number of these exist around the UK, your local Women's Centre will be able to advise.

National Association of Victims Support Schemes
17a Electric Lane, London SW9 8LA (Tel: 01-737 2019/ 326 1084).
The National Association co-ordinates and develops local schemes to assist victims of crimes. Some local schemes restrict themselves to helping people who have suffered from a particular category of crime, for example burglary, but a number of the schemes now offer support in a broad area, helping victims of sexual assault and other violence.

By October 1986 over 300 schemes were affiliated to the NAVSS in England and Wales. A separate association has been formed in Scotland. For details of these contact the above address.

A newsletter is available, containing new developments, members' views and experiences, and information about other agencies, new books and films.

National Children's Home – Family Network
85 Highbury Park, London N5 1UD (Tel: 01-226 2033 – administration only – during office hours).
The NCH is a voluntary childcare organisation, providing a wide range of residential and community services for children and families.

The Family Network provides a number of services, including a confidential telephone enquiry and help line, groupwork, and face-to-face counselling. In some areas there are drop-in centres. The broad range of problems dealt with includes child sexual abuse.

The Family Network is active in the following towns at present.

ENGLAND

BEDFORDSHIRE

Luton
(Tel: Luton (0582) 422751).
Hours: Monday to Friday 10 a.m. – 2 p.m. and 6 p.m. – 9 p.m.

ESSEX

Ilford
(Tel: 01-514 1177).
Hours: Monday, Wednesday, Friday 10 a.m. – 4 p.m. and 7 p.m. – 9 p.m.

GLOUCESTERSHIRE

Gloucester
(Tel: Gloucester (0452) 24019).
Hours: Monday and Friday 1.30 p.m. – 9 p.m.; Tuesday, Wednesday, Thursday 6.30 p.m. – 9 p.m.

GREATER MANCHESTER

Manchester
(Tel: 061-236 9873).
Hours: Monday to Friday 9.30 a.m. – 9.30 p.m.

KENT

Maidstone
(Tel: Maidstone (0622) 56677).
Hours: Monday to Friday 9.30 a.m. – 9 p.m.

LANCASHIRE

Bamber Bridge
(Tel: Preston (0772) 24006).
Hours: Monday to Friday 9.30 a.m. – 9.30 p.m.

NORFOLK

Norwich
(Tel: Norwich (0603) 660679).
Hours: Monday to Friday 10 a.m. – 4 p.m. and 6 p.m. – 9 p.m.

WEST MIDLANDS

Birmingham
(Tel: 021-440 5970).
Hours: Monday to Friday 10 a.m. – 4 p.m. and 7.30p.m. – 10 p.m.

WEST YORKSHIRE

Leeds
(Tel: Leeds (0532) 456456).
Hours: Monday to Friday 9.00 a.m. – 9.30 p.m.

WALES

SOUTH GLAMORGAN

Cardiff
(Tel: Cardiff (0222) 29461/2).

Hours: Monday to Thursday 10.00 a.m. – 3 p.m. and 7.00 p.m. – 9.00 p.m.

SCOTLAND

FIFE

Glenrothes
(Tel: Glenrothes (0592) 759651/2).
Hours: Monday to Friday 10 a.m. – 10 p.m.

STRATHCLYDE

Glasgow
(Tel: 041-221 6722/3/4).
Hours: Monday to Friday 10 a.m. – 10 p.m.

National Society for the Prevention of Cruelty to Children (NSPCC)
67 Saffron Hill, London EC1N 8RS (Tel: 01-242 1626). The NSPCC aims to protect children and prevent child abuse in all its forms. It provides a 24-hour service to families with children. The charity's primary focus is on the needs of children who are at risk of abuse, or who have been abused. The Society has considerable knowledge of dealing with abused children and over recent years has developed skills and expertise in dealing with sexual abuse victims and their families. As well as dealing with the children who have been the victims of sexual abuse the Society also helps families in which the parents are having difficulties in parenting their children, as a result of physical or sexual abuse they themselves experienced as children.

The NSPCC is developing a network of 60 Child Protection Teams which will be completed by the end of 1988. In close liaison with local authorities, selected Teams are developing methods of working with sexually abused children and their families and are offering consultation and training sesrvices to local professional workers.

The NSPCC is authorised by statute (along with the police and the local authority social services departments) to take action to protect children when necessary. If anyone suspects that a child is being abused, either physically or sexually, the NSPCC advises them to contact the Society itself, the police or the local authority social services. Referrals to the NSPCC are treated in the strictest confidence. While the Society deals primarily with children and families, if individual adults who have been sexually abused contact the local office of the NSPCC, they will be referred to the most appropriate agency. The address and telephone number of local NSPCC offices can be found in the telephone directory.

The NSPCC has a range of Information Briefings and Research Briefings some of which are especially concerned with child sexual abuse.

OPUS (Organisation for Parents Under Stress)
106 Godstone Road, Whyteleafe, Surrey CR3 OEB (Tel: 01-645 0469). OPUS is the umbrella name adopted by various groups throughout the country who have come together with the common aim of trying to help parents under stress, who may physically or emotionally abuse their children.

The National Co-ordinating Committee of OPUS works to bring the groups together. OPUS groups use different names, for example Parent Lifeline, Parents Anonymous, Families under Stress, Parent Helpline, etc. They are all completely autonomous and self-supporting. The majority of groups provide a confidential telephone listening service, some have a network of befrienders to visit parents, some provide a drop-in centre or place for parents to meet regularly and some offer practical help. OPUS groups provide help for mothers, fathers, grandparents, friends and sometimes for children.

Many parents feel frightened of asking for help from the traditional sources and desperately need the anonymity an OPUS group offers. Many callers have no one they can go to who they can trust, no one they know who will not criticise. Sometimes, after talking the problem through with an OPUS group volunteer, a parent will have the confidence to approach another source of help. No professional referral is required and all contact is completely confidential.

A quarterly newsletter is available entitled *Parent Newslink*. Membership fees to individuals who want to receive the newsletter are £3. Associate members pay £10 a year.

(*See* details of the Parents Anonymous Group in London in Chapter 21, 'Guide to Local Services'.)

Rape Crisis Centres
These now exist around the country and we list the telephone numbers below. Many of those listed also counsel women who have been sexually abused as children.

A woman's life can be totally disrupted by being raped and she may not know where to turn for help or comfort. She may feel that people close to her simply will not understand. Also there are some immediate problems to overcome. Has she caught an infection? Could she be pregnant? She needs specially supportive and understanding help to assist her in making the right decisions. If she decides, and it is entirely her decision, to report to the police, she may want a friend to go with her.

Alternatively, workers at the Centres are always ready to accompany a woman who has been raped to court, as this is likely to be a particularly gruelling ordeal.

Rape Crisis Centres, in helping women to cope with sexual abuse, widen the definition of rape (a legal definition of rape is given in Chapter 20, 'Sex Law') to say that any unwanted, forced or coerced sexual attention is a form of rape and therefore they prefer to assure women that they will be supportive and helpful to any woman who has been forced to take part in a sexual situation, and that they will treat her feelings with equal care and gravity, however the sexual abuse occurred. The Centres listed below offer a free and confidential service. Help offered includes: emergency and on-going support; information about pregnancy prevention after rape, pregnancy tests, abortion and infections; accompaniment to special clinics, doctor, police or court; explanation about police, court or medical procedures; information about applications to the Criminal Injuries Compensation Board for financial compensation as a result of rape or sexual assault.

Rape Crisis Centres are located at the following addresses:

ENGLAND

AVON

Bristol
(Tel: Bristol (0272) 428331).
Hours: Phone lines open Monday to Friday 10.30 a.m. – 2.30 p.m., but appointments may be made at other times. 24-hour answerphone service.

BEDFORDSHIRE

Luton
(Tel: Luton (0582) 33592.
Hours: Monday to Friday 9 a.m. – 5 p.m; Monday and Wednesday 7 p.m. – 10 p.m.

BERKSHIRE

Reading
(Tel: Reading (0734) 55577).
Hours: Sunday 7.30 p.m. – 10 p.m.

BUCKINGHAMSHIRE

Milton Keynes
(Tel: Milton Keynes (0908) 670333)
Hours: Monday 7 p.m. – 9 p.m.

CAMBRIDGESHIRE

Cambridge
(Tel: Cambridge (0223) 358314).
Hours: Wednesday 6 p.m. – 12 p.m.; Saturday 11 a.m. – 5 p.m.

Peterborough
(Tel: (0733) 40515).
Hours: Tuesday 7.30 p.m. – 10 p.m.; Saturday 10 a.m. – 12 noon.

CHESHIRE

Runcorn (Halton)
(New centre not yet open at time of writing)
(contact tel. no. 092 85 63624).

CLEVELAND

Middlesbrough
(Tel: Middlesbrough (0642) 225787) 24-hour answerphone service.
Hours: Monday to Wednesday 10 a.m. – 3 p.m; Thursday 7.30–9.30 p.m.

CUMBRIA

Kendal
(Tel: Kendal (0539) 25255).
Hours: Monday 7 p.m. – 10 p.m; Wednesday 12 noon – 3 p.m.

DERBYSHIRE

Derby
(Tel: Derby (0332) 372545).
Hours: Thursday 7.30 p.m. – 9.30 p.m.

DEVON

Exeter
(Tel: Exeter (0392) 30871) 24-hour answerphone service.
Hours: Monday to Friday 10 a.m. – 5 p.m.

Plymouth
(Tel: Plymouth (0752) 23584)
Hours: Thursday 7.30 p.m. – 10 p.m.

EAST SUSSEX

Brighton
(Tel: Brighton (0273) 699756) 24-hour answerphone.

Hours: Tuesday 6 p.m. – 9 p.m.; Friday 3 p.m. – 9 p.m.; Saturday 10 a.m. – 1 p.m.

ESSEX

Chelmsford
(Tel: Chelmsford (0245) 467075).
Hours: Friday 7.30 p.m. – 9.30 p.m.

Grays Thurrock
(Tel: Grays Thurrock (0375) 380609) 24-hour answer-phone service.
Hours: Monday 6 p.m. – 9 p.m; Tuesday 7 p.m. – 10 p.m; Wednesday 1 p.m. – 5 p.m; Thursday 12 p.m. – 4 p.m.

GLOUCESTERSHIRE

Gloucester
(Tel: Gloucester (0452) 26770).
Hours: Monday 7.30 – 9.30 p.m; Thursday 11.30 a.m. – 2 p.m.

GREATER LONDON

Central London
London Rape Crisis Centre, P.O. Box 69, London WC1X 9NJ
(Tel: 01-837 1600 24 hours; 01-278 3956 office).

Croydon
(Tel: 01-656 5362).
Hours: Saturday 3 p.m. – 6 p.m; 7 p.m. – 10 p.m.

Southwark
(Tel: 01-639 1106).
Hours: Tuesday 7 p.m. – 10 p.m; Thursday 2 p.m. – 5 p.m.

GREATER MANCHESTER

Manchester
(Tel: 061-228 3602).
Hours: Tuesday and Friday 2 p.m. – 5 p.m.; Wednesday, Thursday and Sunday 6 p.m. – 9 p.m.

Rochdale
(Tel: Rochdale (0706) 526279).
Hours: 7 p.m. – 10 p.m.

HAMPSHIRE

Portsmouth
(Tel: Portsmouth (0705) 669511).
Hours: Wednesday and Friday 7 p.m. – 10 p.m; Sunday 3 p.m. – 6 p.m.

Southampton
(Tel: Southampton (0703) 229288).
Hours: Mondays 7 p.m. – 10 p.m.

HUMBERSIDE

Hull
(Tel: Hull (0482) 29990).
Hours: Thursday 4 p.m. – midnight.

Scunthorpe
(Tel: Scunthorpe (0724) 853953).
Hours: Monday 7 p.m. – 9 p.m.

KENT

Canterbury
(Tel: Canterbury (0227) 450400).
Hours: every evening 6 p.m. – 9 p.m.

LANCASHIRE

Lancaster
(Tel: Lancaster (0524) 382595).
Hours: Tuesday 7.30 p.m. – 9.30 p.m; Friday 1 p.m. – 3 p.m.

LEICESTERSHIRE

Leicester
(Tel: Leicester (0533) 666666).
Hours: Tuesday 7 p.m. – 10 p.m; Saturday 2 p.m. – 5 p.m.

LONDON – *see* Greater London

MERSEYSIDE

Liverpool
(Tel: 051-727 7599).
Hours: Monday 7 p.m. – 9 p.m; Thursday and Saturday 2 p.m. – 5 p.m.

NORFOLK

Norwich
(Tel: Norwich (0603) 667687).
Hours: Monday 6 p.m. – 8 p.m; Thursday 8 p.m. – 10 p.m; Friday 11 a.m. – 2 p.m; Saturday 4 p.m. – 6 p.m.

NOTTINGHAMSHIRE

Nottingham
(Tel: Nottingham (0602) 410440).
Hours: Tuesday to Friday 10 a.m. – 4 p.m; Saturday 10 p.m. – 1 p.m.

OXFORDSHIRE

Oxford
(Tel: Oxford (0865) 726295).
Hours: Monday and Tuesday 7 p.m. – 9 p.m; Wednesday 2 p.m. – 10 p.m. Thursday and Friday 2 p.m. – 4 p.m.

SOUTH YORKSHIRE

Sheffield
(Tel: Sheffield (0742) 755255).
Hours: Monday to Friday 11 a.m. – 4 p.m; Tuesday 7.30 p.m. – 9 p.m.

STAFFORDSHIRE

Stoke-on-Trent
(Tel: Stoke-on-Trent (0782) 414288). 24 hours in conjunction with Birmingham.

SUSSEX – *see* East Sussex and West Sussex

TYNE AND WEAR

Newcastle upon Tyne
(Tel: Newcastle upon Tyne (0632) 329858; office (0632) 615317).
Hours: Monday to Friday 10 a.m. – 5 p.m.; Saturday and Sunday 6.30 p.m. – 10 p.m.

WARWICKSHIRE

Leamington Spa
(Tel: Leamington Spa (0926) 832529).
Hours: Tuesday 7.30 – 10 p.m.

WEST MIDLANDS

Birmingham
(Tel: 021-233 2122 24 hours, 7 days a week; 021-233 2455 office).

Coventry
(Tel: Coventry (0203) 76606).
Hours: Monday to Friday 11 a.m. – 3 p.m;

WEST SUSSEX

Littlehampton
(Tel: Littlehampton (0903) 726411).
Hours: Monday 7 p.m. – 10 p.m; Thursday 7 p.m. – 10 p.m.

WEST YORKSHIRE

Bradford
(Tel: Bradford (0274) 308270).
Hours: Monday 1 p.m. – 5 p.m; Wednesday 12 noon – 3 p.m. Thursday 6 p.m. – 10 p.m.

Leeds
(Tel: Leeds (0532) 440058; office (0532) 441323).
Hours: Monday to Sunday 12 noon – 4 p.m., Monday to Friday 7 p.m. – 10 p.m.

YORKSHIRE *see* South Yorkshire and West Yorkshire

SCOTLAND

CENTRAL

Falkirk
(Tel: Falkirk (0324) 38433).
Hours: Monday and Thursday 7 p.m. – 9 p.m.

GRAMPIAN

Aberdeen
(Tel: Aberdeen (0224) 575560) 24-hour answerphone.
Hours: Monday 6 p.m. – 8 p.m; Thursday 7 p.m. – 9 p.m.

HIGHLANDS

Inverness
(Tel: Inverness (0463) 220719).

Hours: Monday, Thursday, Saturday, Sunday 7 p.m. – 10 p.m.
(Incest Crisis Line Tel: Silloth (0965) 31432).

LOTHIAN

Edinburgh
(Tel: 031-556 9437).
Hours: Monday 1 p.m. – 2 p.m; 6 p.m. – 8 p.m; Thursday 7 p.m. – 10 p.m; Friday 6 p.m. –8 p.m.

STRATHCLYDE

Glasgow
(Tel: 041-221 8448).
Hours: Monday, Friday, Wednesday 7 p.m. – 10 p.m; Thursday 11 a.m. – 1 p.m.

NORTHERN IRELAND

Belfast
(Tel: Belfast (0232) 249696) 24-hour answerphone service.
Hours: Tuesday and Friday 7 p.m.– 10 p.m.

WALES

SOUTH GLAMORGAN

Cardiff
(Tel: Cardiff (0222) 373181).
Hours: Monday and Thursday 7 p.m. – 10 p.m; Wednesday 11 a.m. – midnight.

WEST GLAMORGAN

Swansea
(Tel: Swansea (0792) 475243).
Hours: Tuesday 7 p.m, – 9 p.m; Friday 10 p.m. – midnight

SAIFLine
The Link Centre, 7 Southbrook Terrace, Great Horton, Bradford, West Yorkshire (Tel:Bradford (0274) 309909).
SAIFLine (Sexual Abuse in the FamilyLine) is a service which offers telephone and face-to-face counselling for people who are concerned about child sexual abuse in the family. They may wish to talk about an incident in the past or a present situation. Professional workers may also contact SAIFLine for support and advice. The telephone counselling service is available each Wednesday from 10.00 a.m. to 1.00 p.m.

Women Against Rape (WAR)
PO Box 287, London NW6 5QV.
WAR actively campaigns to end rape in all its forms, including rape in marriage, racist sexual assault, and sexual abuse of power and authority. WAR is a member organisation of the International Wages for Housework Campaign.

Selected Further Information

Child Abuse by Ruth S. Kempe and C. Henry Kempe. Published by Fontana/Open Books, 1978. Price £2.50.
The authors have many years of experience of working with abusive families in the United States. They maintain that abusive parents can be predicted, with 76 per cent accuracy, from simple observations made in the first 24 hours after childbirth. They demonstrate that the abusers can be helped in four cases out of five – by a mixture of therapy, help through crises and visits by caring lay personnel. However, they also consider that there is a hard core of 'incurable' abusers and that in those situations, re-uniting families should not be the overriding goal and the children should be removed immediately and permanently.

One chapter is given over to 'Incest and Other Forms of Sexual Abuse'. It was the Kempes who coined a more sensitive definition of child sexual abuse than that embodied in legal language. They say,

> 'sexual abuse is defined as the involvement of dependent, developmentally immature children and adolescents in sexual activities that they do not fully comprehend, to which they are unable to give informed consent, or that violate the social taboos of family roles.'

They discuss the nature of sexual abuse, exploring paedophilia, violent molestation and rape, and incest. In writing about incest the authors have no hesitation in upholding the taboo against the practice on the broad social grounds of protecting the immature members of the family, as well as for genetic reasons. They say,

> We believe that all sexual exploitation is harmful. This does not imply that criminal sanctions must always follow, what is clear is that the child may need months of individual or group psychotherapy to come to terms with the event and to integrate the sometimes puzzling, sometimes frightening, and sometimes guilt-laden occurrence back into a normal and secure environment. Here the growing child increasingly assumes charge of his or her control over body and mind. Failure to treat the victims is a far more serious societal deficiency than failure to punish the perpetrator.

Incest – a Family Pattern by Jean Renvoize. Published by Routledge & Kegan Paul. Price £6.95.
In a thorough discussion of the whole topic, Jean

Renvoize examines the less well-known aspects of incest, as well as the more common ones, including in her study mother/son, brother/sister, father/daughter and other forms of incest. This discussion is viewed in the context of family relationships in general.

The author looks at various research findings and discusses work being done by professionals and amateurs in the field; in particular, she discusses the work being undertaken in the United States and quotes from Hank Giarretto, who was behind the first-ever child sexual abuse programme in San Jose, California. This treatment programme now helps whole families, also taking into account the rehabilitation needs of the offender.

Her chapter on the pro-incest lobby brings out into the open the body of opinion which suggests that incest may be permissable, and that it is just our reaction to it which is wrong. A number of people have claimed that their incestuous experiences were positive and beneficial. It was noted that nearly all of these were sibling sex. The author seriously considers the claims, but is able to put the idea into firm perspective by countering with evidence of damage suffered by abused children, which continued into adulthood and which exhibited itself in a variety of ways, including periods of delinquency, and an inability to develop relationships in later life.

A moving part of the book concerns personal stories. In one, a young woman is mourning for the father figure she never had. In adult life, having moved some distance from home, she continues to yearn for this figure. She goes back to confront her father to try to awaken him as a parent. Despite a supportive and understanding husband, she says,

> 'Even though I was so many miles away I wasn't free of what he'd done to me. It was devastating my whole life.'

The father/daughter relationship was not to be, even years after the incest episodes. He was quite incapable of relating to her in this way. She describes her feelings,

> 'I'm going to have to mourn. . . for the father who is dead. I've already mourned for the little girl who lost her father. He's my father, but I'm not his daughter, and that's hard for me, very hard. This is what it is for a victim of incest.'

Incest: Fact and Myth by Sarah Nelson. Published by Strathmullion, a Scottish-based feminist publishing collective, second edition 1986. Price £4.95 plus postage.

This book, in disentangling fact and myth, demolishes the illogical arguments of the 'experts', caring agencies and legal profession, which serve to justify their own inaction and which underpin current professional practice. We are shown the extent to which our particular society upholds a man's rights over the women in his family, while at the same time devaluing the roles women and girls are expected to play.

The author sets up the myths and knocks them down with fact and common sense. She concentrates her attention on the most common form of incest, that between daughters and their fathers or step-fathers. She contends that, far from being small-scale and unusual incest is widespread; that in the great majority of cases we cannot talk of meaningful consent by the child; that incest causes serious physical and psychological harm to victims, and is a significant cause of adult mental illness; and that the cause of incest is not complex and mysterious. Instead, it is a simple and straightforward form of sexual abuse and exploitation of female children by adult men, for the selfish purpose of sexual gratification.

Ms Nelson questions the assumption that the family must be preserved at all costs if something that corrupts and mocks the institution of the family is allowed to flourish unchecked. She also questions the validity of some of the treatment programmes whose aim is to preserve the family. She mentions that Hank Giarretto (*see* above) lists the first goal of the Child Sexual Abuse Treatment Programme in San Jose as rehabilitation of the family and marriage. Ms Nelson writes,

> 'Those who genuinely feel that every effort should be made to keep incestuous families together might ask themselves why is it only in family crimes – and only in certain family crimes – that they call for offender and victim to be kept together?'

She maintains that prison may be useless in many ways, but it is the only way we have of expressing our condemnation of certain acts:

> 'For you cannot remove or lessen responsibility from a crime without also making a statement about its gravity in the eyes of society.'

She goes on to say,

> 'The other danger in decriminalising an offence is that deterrence may be reduced. It is said that more children might report incest if they knew their fathers would not go to prison. This would not help much overall if more fathers indulged in incest because they no longer feared serious legal consequences.'

In discussing the way forward the author says that victims and their mothers are just not going to come forward and feel strong enough to face the consequences until they know several things:

(a) that there is someone definite, and well publicised, they can turn to for help;
(b) that their story will be believed;
(c) that a certain course of action will follow and that different agencies will not contradict each others' policies;
(d) that they will have a sympathetic support system to help them through each phase of their ordeal;

(e) that someone has begun trying to educate the public about incest, so they can hope for a sympathetic response from at least some in their community – instead of horror, disgrace or ostracism.

This book is a must for all those who want to establish a clearer picture of the whole subject of incest and who are ready to have their prejudices and misconceptions dislodged to make way for some clear thinking.

SisterWrite Bookshop
190 Upper Street, London N1 1RQ (Tel: 01-226 9782). This is a co-operative women's bookshop selling books which provide a penetrating feminist insight into women's issues. Monthly booklists of new titles are available on subscription, £1.75 for six months. There are numerous titles on rape, sexual abuse, and violence, seen from a woman's perspective. For further details *see* Chapter 8, 'Women Only'.

Thou Shalt Not Be Aware: Society's Betrayal of the Child by Alice Miller. Published by Pluto Press, Allison and Busby Limited, Publishers, 6a Noel Street, London W1V 3RB (Tel: 01-734 1498). Price £5.95.
In the preface, the author states that

> 'This book can be read and understood by everyone who doesn't hate the idea of having once been a child – no matter how long ago.'

Her love of children shines through her every word, and this includes seeing each child and the child in adults suffering from deprived and abused childhoods, as very real individuals in their own right. She exhibits a considerable flexibility of approach, debunking dogmatic ideologies. While paying tribute to Freud and his useful influence on her own work, she nevertheless rebuts his theory of drives, of penis envy and related concepts. She frees the child from the guilt of being responsible for adults' crimes against her, while recognising that 'guilt' wherever placed is not particularly helpful. Nevertheless, when a child has been abused, a crime has been committed – it cannot simply be called an ambivalent love. If a child is made to feel guilty, say for a father leaving the household, this may be the projection of adults. Social workers themselves may be responsible for such attitudes. A child will need to know that cruelty is cruelty.

> 'It can save the child's character. It can save his (her) judgement of what is cruel and what is human.'

Alice Miller discusses the question of infantile sexuality through her own progress in her work, which has resulted in adopting the basic principle of learning from her patients instead of trying to make them fit her theories. She writes

> 'Some, though by no means all, of the anxiety, bewilderment, and uncertainty present in every patient's childhood was of a sexual nature. But I no longer interpret such difficulties the way I was taught to – as a defence against the child's own sexual desires – but in part as reactions to adults' sexual desires, of which the child was object . . . It is quite natural for children to awaken sexual desire in the adult, because they tend to be beautiful, cuddly, affectionate, and because they admire the adults so much, probably more than anyone else does. If adults have a satisfying sex life with another adult, they have no need to act upon desires aroused by the child or to ward them off. But if they feel themselves humiliated and not taken seriously by their partner, if their needs were never allowed to unfold or mature, of if they were themselves seduced and violated as children, then these adults will show a strong tendency to impose their sexual needs on the child.'

CHAPTER 10

The Love Bugs (or Change Partners and Chance VD)

Sexually transmitted diseases (STDs) are those which are passed on by sexual contact. Only three STDs are mentioned in the Venereal Diseases Act 1917 (syphilis, gonorrhoea and soft chancre), but a wide range of diseases are now recognised as being passed on by sexual contact, as well as a number which may be passed on in a variety of ways, including sexually.

The whole subject is clouded by myth and ignorance and perhaps the first point to establish is exactly what is meant by sexual transmission. The organisms which cause the trouble rapidly perish outside the warmth of the body and it is rare for the primary STDs to be caught other than by intimate genital contact with another person. Most commonly, this means male/female sexual intercourse, in which the disease can be passed either way. But it is important to realise that transmission can also occur through oral sex or anal intercourse and in homosexual as well as heterosexual relationships. Syphilis can sometimes be transmitted mouth to mouth, or from fingering infected sexual parts, particularly if there is a break in the skin.

There are four basic problems which cause the prevalence of STDs to be much greater than they might be:

(a) the diseases can be passed on during the incubation phase;
(b) The symptoms may pass unrecognised, particularly if they are slight or (in the case of women) if they arise in a part of the body which is out of sight; or
(c) the symptoms may be noticed, but the sufferer neglects to do anything about them, either through ignorance or from feelings of shame. After quite a short time, the symptoms disappear and the person imagines (mistakenly) that the disease has cleared up of its own accord. (In fact, it has simply gone underground: the victim remains infectious and the disease wreaks havoc within the body.); or
(d) there may be no observable symptoms (this mainly applies to women).

If someone who has caught an STD neglects to seek treatment, there are several dangerous consequences: the disease takes a stronger hold; they remain infectious and may pass the disease on to others; the person from whom they caught the disease remains untraced and may similarly pass it on to others. Some of the diseases, obviously, are more damaging than others, but a number of them, if neglected, can cause irreparable harm to bodily (especially reproductive), sensory, and mental functions. Syphilis, though now uncommon in the UK, if caught by a pregnant woman and left untreated, can seriously damage her unborn child, while gonorrhoea and some other diseases can infect the eyes of the child as it leaves its mother's body.

Since the early 1950s, there has been a fourfold increase in new cases recorded in clinic returns in England and Wales. This is partly because less stigma is now felt about visiting special clinics, but, paradoxically, the major reason for this massive rise lies with the increased use of oral contraceptives. While we are now better able to guard against unwanted pregnancies, this has inevitably led to much greater sexual freedom of association and, at the same time, a reduced reliance on mechanical methods of contraception which afford some, if not full, protection against infection.

The Main Sexually Transmitted Diseases and Their Symptoms

In general, symptoms vary with particular diseases and in individuals. They may – especially in women – be so slight as to pass unnoticed, but typical signs are abnormal discharge from the vagina or penis, and sores, spots or ulcers on or around the genitals or any other area which has had genital contact. They may, of course, result from something other than an STD, but you can't be too careful.

Gonorrhoea

Popularly known as 'the clap', gonorrhoea remains one of the most common sexually transmitted diseases. It is easy to cure, but if untreated can spread throughout the body and cause serious damage. Treatment affords no immunity – it can be caught any number of times. In men, symptoms may appear anything from two to ten days after infection, when there may be discomfort in the penis, particularly when urinating. There may also be a yellowish discharge from and a reddening of the 'eye' of the penis and the glands in the groin may become swollen. Women may experience no symptoms at all or at most an unusual vaginal discharge, sometimes burning when urinating and perhaps a feeling of malaise.

One treatment is usually sufficient to effect a cure, but some strains are becoming resistant to penicillin and may require other antibiotics or more prolonged treatment. A follow-up test is essential and you must persist with treatment until you are fully cleared.

Syphilis

Syphilis is commonly known as the 'pox', formerly 'great pox' to distinguish it from small pox. Although it is still a very serious disease if neglected, the use of antibiotics has revolutionised treatment and has reduced its incidence in the UK to very low levels, so that the risk of catching it is now small. Without treatment, the disease progresses through a number of stages marked by some early symptoms, all deceptively disappearing of their own accord, but leaving the disease active and destructive, until finally it takes a dreadful toll of various bodily organs and of the central nervous system.

The symptoms are common to men and women. In the first stage, about three weeks after infection, a painless sore ('chancre') develops on or near the infected area. It may well occur inside rather than outside the body (for example, in the rectum or vagina). After this has cleared up, and if the disease remains untreated, a body rash usually appears. This may not itch and may be accompanied by a general feeling of malaise and other symptoms similar to those experienced in influenza.

Syphilis is easily detected by blood tests and a course of antibiotics will clear up the infection. Provided treatment is given before the late stage, it will prevent serious damage. Treatment does not, however, confer immunity from future infection.

Non-specific Genital Infection

This covers a group of sexually transmitted diseases, which together account for the largest number of reported STD cases requiring treatment. They are 'non-specific' in that the agent responsible for infection is not isolated and identified after laboratory tests. The most that can be said is that they are not caused by other known agents, such as the organism which causes gonorrhoea.

The most common is urethritis, affecting men as an inflammation of the tube which runs from the bladder to the tip of the penis (the urethra). Though less serious than gonorrhoea, which has similar symptoms, it can, if untreated, lead to disease of the joints and eyes. Women are more often carriers of the disease and may not experience any symptoms.

In women, similar unidentified infections are described as non-specific vaginitis and non-specific cervicitis.

Herpes Genitalis

Most of us are familiar with the effects of the herpes virus as 'cold sores' on and around the lips. When it affects the genital area it is known as herpes genitalis. Sores on the genital organs can be very uncomfortable and there may be difficulty in urinating and painful lumps in the groin. The virus lies low after an attack, but is usually only dormant. Most people suffer further attacks, but these often become progressively less severe. There is, as yet, no cure for herpes, but the symptoms can be alleviated. The natural processes of healing will usually defeat the virus in time. As well as through direct sexual contact, genital herpes can be caught from items such as lavatory seats and infected towels. The disease is now quite prevalent in the United States, and there is concern that it is on the increase in this country.

See also details of *The Herpes Association* on page 80.

Thrush (Candidiasis)

This is not strictly a sexually transmitted disease although it can be transmitted sexually. The fungus-like organism *candida albicans* is often present in the intestines, where it is perfectly benign. It can also lie dormant and harmless within the vagina, but disturbance of the natural conditions there may activate its growth. It can pass to others through sexual activity or, sometimes, from wearing infected clothing next to the genital area.

In men, the effects are mild – an irritating rash on the penis – but in women it may cause a thick vaginal discharge, with intense itching or soreness and an unpleasant odour, with pain when urinating and during intercourse. Some precautions are desirable to avoid re-infection. It is important that any male partner receives treatment, as he may be carrying the infective organism.

If intercourse takes place while he is under treatment, he should wear a sheath. The woman should avoid wearing underwear made from synthetic material or any clothing which is tight around the genital area. Anti-fungal suppositories and creams will usually clear up this irritating condition.

Trichomonas

Though the germs causing 'trich' can be carried by a man in his genital organs, the infection essentially affects women, causing a vaginal discharge, white to yellow in colour, with an unpleasant odour. The vagina and vulva become red and irritated. It provides an exception to the normal rule in that trichomonas germs can survive for some time outside the warmth of the body, so that the infection may occasionally be picked up other than by sexual activity. The condition is easy to diagnose and is readily cleared up by prescribed tablets taken by mouth.

Genital Warts

Usually, but not always, sexually transmitted warts on or near the genitals are caused by a virus. They are not serious, but can be annoying. Removal involves skilled medical techniques.

Other Infections

There are a number of other infections which can be sexually transmitted, but which occur only rarely, as well as the well-known infestations of pubic lice (crabs) and scabies mites, which can be passed on in close encounters of a certain kind.

Acquired Immune Deficiency Syndrome (AIDS), first identified as recently as 1981, already represents a major threat to human kind and is considered separately in Chapter 11.

Precautions

The Family Planning Information Service says that the risks are not quite as great if a man wears a sheath (condom, 'french letter' or protective). But he must be careful not to touch the woman's sex organs before he has put the sheath on, and must handle the sheath as little as possible after they've had sex. Washing the genital organs with soap and water before and as soon as possible after intercourse also reduces the risk somewhat.

A condom which covers both penis and scrotum is available from a number of sex aid suppliers (see Chapter 17, 'Sex Aids').

Tests and Treatment

If you suspect that you might have an STD, either because you notice symptoms or simply because you have recently put yourself at risk, you owe it to yourself and to others to seek help. If you would prefer not to talk to your own GP, you can go to a 'special clinic', so that tests can be carried out. This applies particularly to anyone who has taken a new partner or whose regular partner may have strayed. The problem affects people from all walks of life and while the dangers are obviously greater if you or your partner enjoy a lot of casual relationships, 'sleep around' or go with prostitutes, it can rarely be assumed that a new partner is 'safe'. Homosexual men who have a number of different, sometimes anonymous partners, with anal intercourse, are particularly and increasingly at risk. In all save the most stable relationships, we know too little of each other's sex lives to be totally confident that a partner is free from infection. Indeed, as we have seen, infected people may themselves be unaware that they are passing on a disease.

Nowadays, with the availability of antibiotics and notably penicillin, early treatment is simple, straightforward, quick, painless and effective. You may have to screw up your courage to go to a special clinic, but although some of them can be rather forbidding, most are welcoming and you are now far less likely to encounter censorious, disapproving attitudes. Staff will not be 'shocked' and will understand your feelings. It may be that you don't have an STD at all and even if you have you are on the way to a cure. You don't need a doctor's letter, and your GP will not be told unless you request it. Treatment is free and absolutely confidential. To protect that confidentiality, you can be identified at the clinic only by a number, but this is undesirable as they really do need to know your name and address or somewhere you can be contacted; it could be vital that the clinic be able to get in touch with you. The clinic will respect your wishes regarding confidentiality, even as between husband and wife, but they plainly need to know what sex partners you've had in recent months and whether you can find them again.

Clinics will test anyone who fears that they may have caught an STD. You should be prepared to undress and have an examination which includes your genital area, to give a sample of urine, and to have a blood test on your first visit. You need to be frank with the doctor. It is important that if you have had oral sex or anal intercourse that you overcome any natural embarrassment and bring it to notice. Sometimes, results can be advised after a short wait, but it may take a few days. In some cases several checks may be necessary to exclude the disease. It is just as important that you go back for results as that you present yourself in the first place . Inertia is a friend of the love bugs and, apart from sex itself, is the main reason for the spread of STDs.

You really cannot diagnose or treat yourself. Different infections can produce similar symptoms and specialist testing is needed to identify the cause and indicate the appropriate treatment. Everything is treatable with the minimum of inconvenience – even in the late stages of syphilis some damage can be avoided and possibly reversed.

Where to Go for Help

Special Clinics

Special clinics are located throughout the United Kingdom, and are listed in telephone directories, usually under the heading Venereal Disease or VD. In case of any difficulty, telephone your nearest general hospital or the Family Planning Information Service, 27–35 Mortimer Street, London W1N 7RJ (Tel: 01-636 7866). Local Community Health Councils will also have details of clinics in their areas. Some areas have a pre-recorded telephone message which gives information about symptoms and clinics. Clinics will normally give telephone advice to reassure you and to tell you where and when to attend. They have a variety of names. They may be called 'Special' or 'STD' clinics or 'Special Treatment Centres' or be part of Departments of Genito-Urinary (or Genital) Medicine or of Venereology. The grander titles reflect a wider function which encompasses services relating to various problems and disorders.

The Herpes Association

41 North Road, London N7 9DP (Tel Helpline: 01-609 9061)

The Association acts as an umbrella organisation to provide information and advice to those who have primary and recurrent attacks of herpes, and to liaise with doctors, co-ordinate support groups for members, respond to media coverage about herpes, and generally to promote increased public awareness about the condition.

A quarterly newsletter, *Sphere*, is circulated free to members. The newsletter keeps abreast of the latest developments in research into herpes, reports on drug trials, and gives information to members about what is happening in the Association. *Sphere* aims to provide members and professionals with the latest information in an accessible way.

Support group meetings are held monthly in five London areas and in seven other places around the country. In addition, individuals are counselled at the London office.

Women's Health Concern

Ground Floor, 17 Earl's Terrace, London W8 6LP (Tel: 01-602 6669).

WHC will answer questions about STD for women and provide private counselling. See also Chapter 8, 'Women Only'.

Selected Further Information

VD, the Facts about Sexually Transmitted Diseases. Free leaflet issued by the Family Planning Information Service (27–35 Mortimer Street, London W1N 7RJ (Tel: 01-636 7866)).

Health Education Authority (78 New Oxford Street, London WC1A 1AH) free leaflets:

Guide to a Healthy Sex Life. Explains STDs, how to avoid them and how to treat them.

Herpes. What to Do and How to Cope.

Note: at the time of writing, a change of address is possible, but we have no firm details.

Herpes, AIDS and other sexually transmitted diseases by Derek Llewellyn-Jones. Published by Faber and Faber, 1986. Price £2.95.

Sets out to explain how STDs occur, what they are, how they may be recognised, and how they should be treated.

Recent Advances in Sexually Transmitted Diseases – 2 edited by J.R.W.Harris. Published by Churchill-Livingstone, 1981. Price £23.50.

For the specialist reader.

Recent Advances in Sexually Transmitted Diseases – 3 edited by J.D.Oriel and J.R.W.Harris. Published by Churchill-Livingstone, 1986. Price £35.

For the specialist reader.

Sexually Transmitted Diseases by C.B.S.Schofield. Published by Churchill-Livingstone, 3rd edition, 1979. Price £5.95.

A medical text book.

Sexually Transmitted Diseases edited by Yehudi M.Feldman. Published by Churchill-Livingstone, 1986. Price £55.

The most recent text book providing practical, up-to-date information on the clinical management of a wide range of diseases, offering detailed advice on diagnosis and treatment. Each chapter focuses on a specific disease (including AIDS) and has been written by an expert in the management of that particular disease.

Sexually Transmitted Diseases and VD by Duncan Catterall. Published by Family Doctor, British Medical Association, BMA House, Tavistock Square, London WC1H 9JP, 1982. Price 95p plus postage.

A concise booklet explaining what the diseases are, how they are contacted, the risks if they are left untreated, and where (and how) to go for help.

CHAPTER 11

Acquired Immune Deficiency Syndrome (AIDS)

Though predominantly a sexually transmitted disease, it is appropriate to consider AIDS apart from other such diseases, not least because, unlike other sexual scourges, it is as yet incurable.

The known facts are fairly straightforward. AIDS starts with infection by one of a number of closely related human immunodeficiency viruses (HIV). The virus attaches itself to, and damages, certain lymphocyte cells, whose normal function is to promote an immune response against infection, causing their depletion in the blood and thus reducing the person's ability to resist infection. In common with other viral infections, 'antibodies' are produced, but these seem to have little if any effect in combating the virus. In the United Kingdom, not less than 30,000 and perhaps as many as 50,000 people are already carrying the HI virus, and this figure is likely to rise steeply over the years, with the number of AIDS cases doubling every six to twelve months. In the United States, an estimated three to four million persons are already infected, and globally the total is estimated at up to ten million. So far, in the UK, a relatively small proportion of those infected have progressed to full blown AIDS – 731 at the end of Febuary 1987 – but a study in *The Lancet* suggests that the number of cases is likely to reach 3,000 by the end of 1988. Dr Thomas Stuttaford, medical correspondent of *The Times*, in an article in *Midweek*, 27 November 1986, opines that 30 per cent of HIV sero-positive patients will develop AIDS within five years, and that even this figure may be 'too encouraging' (*sic*). In these cases, the disease is potentially fatal. Of the cases reported by the end of February 1987, over half had already died (377 out of 731 cases).

The effect of AIDS is to break down the body's natural defences, leaving it open to other diseases. Many such patients develop serious infections of the lungs, digestive system, central nervous system and skin. They may also develop particular forms of cancer.

Transmission

Whether or not HIV infection progresses to AIDS, most infected people will remain carriers of the disease, potentially capable of passing the virus on to others. The evidence to date suggests that the HI viruses are passed on in particular and limited circumstances:

1. Sexual activity

This is now by far the most common source of infection. HIV are not strong and cannot survive for long outside the body. But acts of penetration – vaginal, anal or oral – present a high risk. The virus can pass through the mucosa in any of these parts, either in semen or blood from a man, or in vaginal and cervical secretions or blood from a woman. The risk of infection is greater if intercourse causes bleeding, so that anal intercourse is particularly dangerous.

Though less likely, the disease can be transmitted through external cuts and abrasions, or through the eyes.

In the United Kingdom, a high proportion of cases in this sexually transmitted category have so far been homosexual and bisexual men, but there is clearly a potential for transmission in heterosexual lovemaking, and there are already indications of a significant increase of the infection among heterosexual men and women. In some African countries, where genetic factors may account for high prevalence of HIV infection, and where heterosexual activity is high, often with numerous partners, the disease is already affecting as many women as men.

2. Blood and body fluid contact apart from sex

In addition to sexual transmission, HIV can pass from body fluids to the bloodstream in a number of other ways. Until 1985, there was a special risk from blood transfusions, but all donated blood is now tested. Haemophiliacs (all male) have been particularly vulnerable. They need injections of Factor 8, a blood product which helps the blood to thicken. This is now heat-treated and screened, but not before an estimated 1,200 of the United Kingdom's 2,000 or so haemophiliacs had been infected. At the time of writing, 21 of these have been notified as having AIDS of whom 19 have died. The problem in relation to haemophiliacs is now primarily one of helping those already infected, and of trying to ensure that they do not transmit the disease to others, especially their partners.

Another significant danger arises from the use of hypodermic needles which have been in contact with the blood of an infected person. Injections by drug abusers who share syringes are particularly risky. The problem may (unwittingly) have been intensified by police discouragement of the sale of needles and syringes in their efforts to curb drug abuse. The Government has recently responded (somewhat belatedly) by recognising the overriding need for needles to be provided.

Health workers are at some risk from accidental piercing of the skin with contaminated needles. But this should not be exaggerated. There have been only two substantiated cases worldwide of health care workers who have been infected as the result of an accident at work with an infected needle causing inoculation of the blood. Several hundred other workers have had minor accidents with needles resulting in exposure to blood but none has become infected with an HI virus.

Other possible routes of infection can arise if the body fluids of a carrier – blood, semen, urine or faeces – come into contact with the bloodstream of another person through a cut, abrasion or mucous membrane, for example in giving first aid treatment, dealing with specimens, or through contact with those who cannot control their bodily secretions. But this should not occur given normal health care precautions. The Advisory Committee on Dangerous Pathogens has published *Guidelines* (June 1986) which include recommendations on general counter-infection measures and more detailed guidelines for health care and laboratory staff. Similar information and guidance, in lay terms, is provided for local authority staff in a DHSS letter LASSL(86)8 (July 1986). See 'Selected Further Information' at the end of this chapter for details of both.

3. Mother to baby

Infection can occur either through the placenta during pregnancy, or at birth, or, possibly, through breast feeding. This is a special category. Although at present very few women in the United Kingdom have been infected, there is evidence to suggest that if an infected woman becomes pregnant there is a greater risk of her progressing to AIDS. There is also a high probability that the infection will be transmitted to the foetus, and a substantial risk that the baby will develop AIDS. It is a gloomy prognosis, but one which indicates that women who know they are infected – even if the virus appears to be dormant – should avoid pregnancy. A report by Dr Anthony Pinching and Dr Donald Jeffries for the Scientific Advisory Committee of the Royal College of Obstetricians and Gynaecologists goes further, recommending that if a pregnant woman is found to be infected, whether or not there are symptoms of the disease, she should be considered for and counselled about termination.

4. Other (unlikely) circumstances

Although the virus has been found occasionally in tears and in saliva, there are no recorded instances of the infection having been transmitted by contact with these fluids. Nor is there any evidence that the infection is passed on by coughing, sneezing or spitting, by sharing cooking, eating or drinking utensils or other articles in general use, by the sharing of toilet facilities, or by routine contact with people socially, domestically or at work. While experience provides no evidence of airborne infection, nor of transmission in saliva, there have been some suggestions that there may be a risk from concentrated respiratory intake and direct contact in mouth to mouth resuscitation, but even this seems far fetched. Official advice is that, if possible, an airway should be used, but that in an emergency direct mouth to mouth resuscitation should not be denied. It would certainly be sensible to avoid using someone else's razor or toothbrush which might be contaminated with infected blood.

Safer Sex (not, please note, Safe Sex)

In the absence, as yet, of any effective cure, AIDS is a massive threat to human kind. Dr Hadjan Mahler, head of the World Health Organisation, has said that

> 'there is a risk that it will overshadow all other communicable diseases.'

It is therefore not something to be 'played down' to assuage people's fears – informed concern is entirely appropriate.

It follows that every precaution in sexual activity should be taken. Short of total abstinence, the plea is for 'safer sex': that means for those who know they are infected, or who think that they may be or may become infected, a restriction on the kinds of sexual activity they take part in and the number of partners they do it with. At the very least, if penetration (vaginal, oral or – especially – anal) is to occur, a condom (sheath) should be used with a lubricant. It isn't foolproof: latex is liable to tear, particularly during anal intercourse, though there is less chance of this if the lubricant is water-based rather than oil-based. Regrettably, however, the truth is that penetration is something to avoid, along with other practices which involve an exchange of body fluids. More detailed advice is available from the people and organisations mentioned on pages 84–87, and in a number of publications (*see* Selected Further Information starting on page 87). We felt, however, that it might be helpful to include our own risk analysis table based on a variety of views we have studied (*see* Table 11.1).

Table 11.1 Level of risk

	Low	*Some*	*Significant*	*High*	*Very high*
Any act which draws blood					★
Any act where body fluids (especially blood or semen) are able to enter a partner's bloodstream through a cut, tear, abrasion or mucous membrane					★
Intercourse:					
-vaginal with a sheath			★		
-vaginal without a sheath				★	
-anal with a sheath				★[1]	
-anal without a sheath					★[1]
Other forms of penetration:					
-dildoes, vibrators, butt plugs etc:					
-shared by others				★	
-used on only one person	★				
-'fist fucking'			★		
-'finger fucking'		★			
Oral sex:					
-cunnilingus (sucking vaginal area)		★			
-fellatio (sucking the penis):					
-without ejaculating		★			
-ejaculating in mouth			★		
-ejaculating out of mouth		★			
-anilingus ('rimming', i.e. tonguing the anus)			★		
Other:					
-urination on a partner		★[2]			
-penis contact between thighs or buttocks but without penetration		★			
-French kissing		★			
-dry kissing	★				
-masturbation with partner(s)	★				
-enemas or douches (as sex acts in their own right)		★			
-massage, hugging, rubbing with genital contact	★				

NOTES

1. *If preceded by an enema or douche, the risk of infection is probably higher; if followed by an enema or douche it may again increase the risk by carrying the virus further into the body.*
2. *The risk is increased if urine gets into the mouth, anus or eyes.*

A different approach is suggested by Dr Alex Comfort in *The Guardian* 7 November, 1986. He points out that some spermicidal contraceptives are capable of killing the HI virus, and suggests the development of a simple and effective point-of-sale prophylactic, both as a back up for barrier methods and for use by itself. Such a product, he argues, would have the added benefit of limiting the spread of other sexually transmitted diseases and, possibly, inhibit the agent of cervical cancer.

Testing

At present, tests for the HI viruses themselves are not easy, and are not routinely available. However, a simple blood test will show if you have at some time developed antibodies to an HI virus. A positive result will indicate that you have been in contact with the virus, but not whether the virus is still present and active, nor whether you will go on to develop AIDS. A negative result means that antibodies to an HI virus have not been detected. Unfortunately, however, it does not rule out the possibility that you have been infected, because it can take up to three months after infection for the test result to become positive

The antibody test is now widely available in STD clinics, through GPs, or, in the case of haemophiliacs or their partners, through Haemophilia Centres (*see* page 86). What is less straightforward is whether the information will help. It can be argued that those who know they have been in contact with the virus will be more likely to modify their sexual behaviour, and thus reduce the risk of passing on the infection. Against this is the fact that such knowledge is extremely difficult to live with, creating fear that AIDS will develop, and, if others find out, the prospect of social rejection, as well as the possibility of practical difficulties, for example in employment or in taking out life insurance. People's attitudes to AIDS are commonly misinformed and irrational, and anyone contemplating being tested would at the very least want to be satisfied that the test will be confidential. They must also consider that there is a massive psychological burden to be carried. Some people think that because 'safer sex' and other precautionary measures can be practised without checking whether sexual partners are infected (ie on the basis that either of them might be), there is little point in testing; in effect, that ignorance is bliss. To others, awareness is important; truth something which is better faced up to with fortitude and a positive response. Certainly, if you are already experiencing symptoms which may be the result of HIV infection, it could be important to be tested to assist diagnosis. Or if you are a woman who may become pregnant, and you may have been in contact with an HI virus, it could be vital to know whether there would be a danger in having children. In the end, having the test has to be a personal decision, but it may help to discuss the problem with someone else, perhaps with your own doctor or one of the organisations described in the next section. *See also* Selected Further Information starting on page 87.

Where to Go for Help or Advice

Your doctor, if you feel this to be appropriate, or any STD clinic (listed in telephone directories under Sexually Transmitted Diseases or Venereal Disease; best to telephone first).

Other organisations which can help include the following: *Terrence Higgins Trust*, BM/AIDS, London WC1N 3XX (Helpline – Tel: 01-242 1010, Mondays to Fridays 7 p.m. – 10 p.m. Saturdays and Sundays 3 p.m – 10p.m).

The Trust, established in 1982, has developed a range of services as detailed below:

A support group for people who have actually developed AIDS, through which those directly affected by the syndrome can help and support one another. It is run by a highly qualified nurse and a psychiatric social worker and meets fortnightly.

Groups for people who are HIV antibody positive, with the aim of helping them to better understand and live with their condition. They run weekly for a period of four weeks.

'Buddies' for people with AIDS, who keep in regular contact to give any help and support that may be needed – from laundry to counselling.

A telephone 'hot-line' service during the hours shown above to advise and inform on AIDS and its related conditions.

A crisis intervention service for individuals, their carers and families if they need immediate short-term help (counselling, information, accommodation, etc.). This can help with the trauma of being diagnosed with AIDS or of being found to be HIV antibody positive.

Health education, including the publication of leaflets (*see* page 89) and a workshop on safer sex which explores the idea of risk management and encourages participants to re-examine the place and meaning of sex in their lives.

A medical/scientific group and sub-groups working on AIDS-related projects, and providing advice for the Trust and its information services. They play a vital role in maintaining close links with the medical services, and have proposed several research initiatives, a number of which have been taken up by London hospitals.

A comprehensive library of books, articles and papers concerned with AIDS.

A social services group, the main responsibility of which is to inform and educate social services departments, professional organisations and schools of social work about the needs and problems of people with AIDS in the community.

A legal services group to provide legal advice to people who have AIDS or who are HIV antibody positive, and to others who are at risk.

Information for other groups in London and around the country.

Body Positive, 63 Edith Road, London W14 0TH (Telephone number changes daily; it can be obtained on any given day from either Lesbian or Gay Switchboard (*see* page 141), or The Terrence Higgins Trust (*see* page 54) or the DHSS National Advisory Service on Aids (Tel: 0800 567123).

Body Positive is an advice, information, counselling and support organisation working in the field of AIDS. It provides a daily telephone helpline, whose counsellors are themselves carriers of the HI virus. Additionally, it provides a number of regular discussion and counselling groups for anyone seeking information regarding HIV/AIDS. For people experiencing periods of illness requiring hospitalisation, Body Positive provides a hospital visiting service.

To counter the isolation which is a common part of the experience of HIV carriers, Body Positive organises numerous social events, and distributes free a fortnightly newsletter which carries details of all Body Positive activities, personal experiences, information about forms of treatment etc.

Body Positive believes that there is a great deal which individuals infected by this virus can do for themselves to protect and develop their health, and to that end arranges or offers a number of health workshops which have as their aim the reclaiming or re-acceptance of responsibility for one's own health.

New volunteers of whatever background or experience are welcome and are invited to attend a Counselling Training Weekend.

At the time of writing Body Positive is planning to open a drop-in/community centre in the Central/West London area.

College of Health, 18 Victoria Park Square, London E2 9PF.

As part of its telephone information service HEALTHLINE, the College has prepared twelve tapes on AIDS with the help of a panel of medical experts and AIDS counsellors. People who ring the HEALTHLINE number (01-980 4848) between 6 p.m. and 10 p.m. on any night of the week can have played over to them the tape of their choice. The titles are:

136 *What is AIDS?*
229 *Who is at risk of contracting AIDS: the main groups*
230 *Testing for AIDS: what test is available, what it shows and where you can have it done*
232 *Symptoms and signs of AIDS*
234 *Safer sex for heterosexuals worried about AIDS*
235 *Safer sex for gay men and bi-sexuals worried about AIDS*
236 *Safer sex for haemophiliacs worried about AIDS*
237 *Safer sex for drug users worried about AIDS*
239 *AIDS and blood transfusions*
240 *AIDS and artificial insemination*
241 *How you can help someone who has AIDS*
228 *Guide to the College of Health AIDS Information Service*

AIDS Helplines for gays

These telephone support and advisory services operate under a variety of names but fulfil a similar purpose. We list those local services of which we are aware (there may be others):

BELFAST Belfast (0232) 226117
BIRMINGHAM Birmingham (021) 622 1511
BOURNEMOUTH Bournemouth (0202) 38850
BRADFORD/W.YORKS Bradford (0274) 732939
BRIGHTON Brighton (0273) 734316
BRISTOL Bristol (0272) 273436
COLCHESTER Colchester (0206) 560225
COVENTRY Coventry (0203) 714144
ESSEX Colchester (0206) 560225
GWENT Caerleon (0633) 422 532
HAMPSHIRE Chichester (0243) 776998
LEEDS Leeds (0532) 444209
MANCHESTER Manchester (061) 228 1617
MERSEYSIDE Liverpool (051) 708 0234
NORFOLK Colchester (0206) 560225
NOTTINGHAM Nottingham (0602) 585526
OXFORD Oxford (0865) 246036
PLYMOUTH Plymouth (0752) 663609
READING Reading (0734) 503377
SCOTLAND Edinburgh (031) 558 1167
SOUTHAMPTON & SOLENT Southampton (0703) 37363
SOUTH LINCOLNSHIRE Grantham (0476) 60192
SUFFOLK Colchester (0206) 560225
SUSSEX Brighton (0273) 734316
WEST SUSSEX Chichester (0243) 776998

The Haemophilia Society, 123 Westminster Bridge Road, London SE1 7HR (Tel: 01-928 2020).

The Society is primarily concerned to promote research

into the causes, diagnosis and treatment of haemophilia and all related blood disorders, and to provide or assist with appropriate medical, surgical and pharmaceutical care and treatment, together with advice and aid (both financial and in kind) for those with haemophilia and all related disorders who are in need. AIDS was recognised as a serious threat during 1983, and it has since come to dominate the work of the Society, an ever increasing proportion of its resources of time and money being devoted to the problems associated with its apparently rapid transmission through the use of blood products in treatment.

Fortunately, the supply of blood products which have been heat treated against the HI viruses is now sufficient, so that newly-diagnosed patients are no longer at risk from AIDS as a consequence of their treatment. Many people with haemophilia have not been so lucky, and the main concern of the Society is to ensure that accurate information is made available to them and to members of the general public. Its efforts are directed towards informing people of the facts about the way in which the HI viruses are transmitted, particularly through sexual intercourse, and to combat scaremongering information.

The Society's office is open Monday to Friday, from 9 a.m. to 5 p.m., and the staff are happy to advise members by telephone. Written advice and information is also available. The Society publishes a series of regular fact sheets, *Haemofact*, designed to convey immediate, accurate information about haemophilia in general and now about AIDS in particular, including a brief guide *Advice on Safer Sex* (for details *see* 'Selected Further Information', starting on page 88).

Treatment for haemophilia must be given or be supervised by a registered Haemophilia Centre, at some of which social workers are now available to give advice and counselling on AIDS. At the time of writing, local provision is recognised as being less than adequate, but with continued government support, it is the Society's aim to improve and extend its counselling services. Centres are located as follows:

ENGLAND

London
Royal Free Hospital, Pond Street, London NW3 2QG (Tel: 01-794-0500)
St. Thomas' Hospital, London SE1 7EH (Tel: 01-928 9292 ext. 2268)

Manchester
The Royal Infirmary, Manchester M13 9WL (Tel: 061-276 1234)

Newcastle
Royal Victoria Infirmary, Newcastle upon Tyne, Tyne and Wear NE1 4LP (Tel: Newcastle (0632) 325131 ext. 773)

Oxford
Churchill Hospital, Headington, Oxford OX3 7LJ (Tel: Oxford (0865) 64841 ext. 532, 552, 569, 584)

Sheffield
Royal Hallamshire Hospital, Glossop Road, Sheffield S10 2JF (Tel: Sheffield (0742) 387253)

NORTHERN IRELAND

Belfast
Royal Victoria Hospital, Grosvenor Road, Belfast BT12 6BA (Tel: Belfast (0232) 40503)

SCOTLAND

Edinburgh
The Royal Infirmary, Edinburgh EH3 9YW (Tel: 031-229 2477 ext. 2099)

Glasgow
Royal Infirmary, Glasgow G4 0SF (Tel: 041-552 3535 ext. 203)

WALES

Cardiff
University Hospital of Wales, Heath Park, Cardiff CF4 1XW (Tel: Cardiff (0222) 755944)

In addition to these hospital-based facilities, there are local groups of the Society throughout the country. These give members an opportunity to meet and discuss mutual problems.

SCODA (Standing Conference on Drug Abuse), 1-4 Hatton Place, Hatton Garden, London EC1N 8ND (Tel: 01-430 2341/2).
SCODA publishes a national directory *Drug Problems – Where to Get Help* (price £2), a 'yellow pages' type guide to services in the UK for people with drug problems, including related AIDS infection. The organisation also produces a bi-monthly newsletter about services for people with drug problems, the law, funding, prevention, training, etc, plus articles and personal views from people working with drug users, book reviews and Parliamentary reports. As part of a range of relevant publications, SCODA has produced leaflets and booklets specifically concerned with AIDS and drug use: *Facts*

about AIDS for Drug Users, *Facts about AIDS for Drug Workers*, *Briefing for Drug Workers on AIDS*, and *Prevention Policy Options* (for details *see* 'Selected Further Information' below).

Selected Further Information

AIDS. A Family Doctor booklet published by the British Medical Association, BMA House, Tavistock Square, London WC1H 9JP, 1987. Price 95p plus postage.

AIDS – The Acquired Immune Deficiency Syndrome by Dr V.G.Daniels. Published by MTP Press Ltd, Falcon House, Queen Square, Lancaster LA1 1RN, 1985. Price £9.95.
This book sets out to explain what the causes of AIDS are thought to be, who can be affected, what the symptoms are and how they can be controlled, and offers important advice for blood donors. It is likely to be of interest primarily to those in the medical profession who may encounter patients with AIDS.

AIDS – A Guide to Survival by Peter Tatchell. Published by GMP Publishers Ltd, 1986. Price £3.50.
This book is intended as a brief and simple guide to understanding, preventing and fighting back against AIDS, and is primarily intended for those who are antibody positive or who have AIDS or AIDS-related conditions. In his first two chapters, concerned with understanding and prevention, Peter Tatchell is more or less on common ground with other authors. It is in the subsequent chapters on 'fighting back' and 'living with' AIDS that he is distinctive. He urges the view that no one need or should face the disease as a passive victim. Drawing on studies of immune-deficient cancer patients, the author puts forward a programme for strengthening the body's natural defences, through diet, exercise, sleep and relaxation techniques, and proposes techniques of meditation and mental imagery to fight AIDS, with special concern for sustaining self-worth and the will to live. Characteristically, the final chapter has a political dimension in which Peter Tatchell inveighs (with some justification) against media misrepresentation, social discrimination, and government lethargy, contrasting the comparatively swift and practical response of the gay community, and sets out an action plan for an effective programme to meet the challenge of AIDS.

AIDS Guidelines. Available from the Royal College of Nursing, UK, Publications Department, 20 Cavendish Square, London W1M 0AB. Price £3.75 including postage.
Recommended for health workers and those caring for people with AIDS.

AIDS. Health Education Video Unit, Leicestershire Health Authority, Clinical Sciences Building, Leicester Royal Infirmary, PO Box 65, Leicester LE2 7LX, 1986. Price £60.
This video programme is a 15-minute mini-documentary illustrating the history, basic science, modes of transmission and means of prevention of AIDS. It is designed for the general public, individuals at particular risk, medical and allied health personnel and students of health, general science and biology. A summary emphasising precautionary measures and listing further sources of information accompanies the cassette.

AIDS and the New Puritanism by Denis Altman. Published by Pluto Press, £4.95.

AIDS: Questions and Answers by Dr V.G.Daniels. Published by Cambridge Medical Books, Tracey Hall, Cockburn Street, Cambridge CB1 3NB (Tel: Cambridge (0223) 212423). Price £3.75 plus 25p postage.
Organised in a simple question and answer format covering the medical, social and sexual issues.

AIDS: the Reality and the Myth. Master Class educational video, 1986, 42 minutes, £17.35 (£8 to hire) from Concord Films Council, 201 Felixstowe Road, Ipswich IP3 9BJ.
A programme produced through the combined efforts of two consultant physicians based at the Regional Department of Infectious Diseases and Tropical Medicine, Mansall Hospital, Manchester, which covers AIDS from its first discovery to the present day. It details the precautions that hospital staff, dentists and others should take when dealing with patients, and how people can be carriers.

AIDS: the Story of a Disease by John Green and David Miller. Published by Grafton Books, 1986. Price £5.95.
This is the ideal book for the general reader. The authors, notwithstanding their considerable expertise, present the facts with clarity and simplicity. They manage to write as though alongside, rather than above, the reader, and are both compassionate and understanding in their approach, without ever shrinking from discussing all aspects of the subject thoroughly and objectively.

The book contains a clear account of the history, development and mechanisms of AIDS. The authors explain the workings of the immune system, the actions of viruses, and the way in which vaccines operate. Having ourselves grappled with the difficulty of describing the way in which the disease is transmitted, we particularly admire the way in which this is covered: the absolute essentials are packed into five lines (page 69), before lucid explanations are given of the various routes the virus can take, refuting the myths which have arisen in the popular imagination.

The book continues with a review of the current situation and the prospects for major risk groups, and outlines the changes in life-style and behaviour that the AIDS crisis demands.

AIDS – the Victims. Video, 1985, 30 minutes, £50 (£10 to hire), from Concord Films Council, 201 Felixstowe Road, Ipswich IP3 9BJ.
TV Eye talks to two homosexual men who are living with AIDS. They describe their feelings about living with the possibility of early death and finding themselves, at the same time, social outcasts.

AIDS. The Virus, its Clinical Features, Transmission and Prevention. Video, 1985, 30 minutes, £7 to hire, from Concord Films Council, 201 Felixstowe Road, Ipswich IP3 9BJ.
A guide for doctors and health workers by Dr Anthony Pinching of St. Mary's Hospital, London. It describes the virus and its clinical manifestation, its transmission and incidence, and the possibilities of treatment and prevention.

AIDS: What Everybody Needs to Know. Health Education Council, February 1986; free from Department A, PO Box 100, Milton Keynes, MK1 1TX or your local health education unit.
A small, but invaluable booklet providing basic information.

AIDS – What You Must Know Before You Give Blood (NBTS 1181, September 1986). A free leaflet prepared by the DHSS and the Central Office of Information for the National Blood Transfusion Service.

A Plague on You. Terrence Higgins Trust video, 1985, 30 minutes, £29 (£10 to hire) from Concord Films Council, 201 Felixstowe Road, Ipswich IP3 9BJ.
This fast moving film challenges the media's presentation of AIDS as a plague caused by homosexuality. It contrasts press and TV coverage with an explanation of the real facts by Michael Adler of the Middlesex Hospital and Richard Wells of the Royal College of Nursing.

DHSS publications. Health Publications Unit, Number 2 Site, Manchester Road, Heywood, Lancs OL10 2PZ, free:

> *Information and Guidance on AIDS for Local Authority Staff* (LASSL(86)8), July 1986. Briefly reviews what AIDS is, its impact in the UK, how it spreads, and how infection can be prevented. Most importantly it provides infection control guidelines for the community care of AIDS patients and other HIV antibody positive clients.
>
> AIDS booklets
> No.1 *General information for doctors* (CMO(85)7, May 1985)
> No.2 *Information for doctors on the introduction of the HTLV III antibody test* (CMO(85)12, October 1985)
> No.3 *Guidance for surgeons, anaesthetists and dentists and their teams in dealing with infected people* (April 1986).
>
> *Children at School and Problems related to AIDS* (CMO(86)10, June 1986). A Department of Education and Science administrative memorandum.
> *LAV/HTLVIII – the Causative Agent of AIDS and Related Conditions* (HN(86)20, June 1986 and LASSL(86)7, July 1986). Revised guidelines from the Advisory Committee on Dangerous Pathogens. Intended for the general reader; contains a wealth of information on the background to AIDS, and counter-infection measures, with guidelines for health care and laboratory staff.

The Facts about AIDS. Thames TV *Help!* programme with the Terrence Higgins Trust, March 1986, free.
A wealth of information compressed on to six A4 sides.

Haemophilia Society publications (123 Westminster Bridge Road, London SE1 7HR, Tel: 01-928 2020):

> *Advice on Safer Sex* (October 1985, free to members, donation from others) Intended for heterosexual people.
> *Haemofact: AIDS* (September 1983 onwards, free to members, donation from others). Regularly issued fact sheets containing the latest available information.

Standing Conference on Drug Abuse (SCODA) publications (1-4 Hatton Place, Hatton Garden, London EC1N 8ND, Tel: 01-430 2341/2):

> *Briefing for Drug Workers on AIDS*. A detailed briefing on infection and AIDS including sections on counselling and health and safety.
> *Facts about AIDS for Drug Users* (free up to 100 copies). Leaflet for drug users explaining AIDS and infection from the virus, what activities increase the risk of infection and how to reduce the risks.
> *Facts about AIDS for Drug Workers* (free up to five copies). Booklet for drug workers explaining what AIDS is, modes of transmission, symptoms of infection. Gives advice on testing, risk reduction and health and safety.
> *Prevention Policy Options* (free). Short guide to different prevention policy options which drug services might adopt. Includes brief monitoring questionnaire

as a means of assessing the effectiveness of the policy which is adopted.

Panic – The Story of AIDS by Robin McKie. Published by Thorsons Publishing Group, 1986. Price £1.99.
The author, science correspondent of the *Observer*, has followed the extraordinary story of AIDS from its first recognition, and, unlike many journalists, brings an informed mind to the subject. He presents an accurate and balanced (if not optimistic) account of the development of the disease on an historical canvas. The result is an immensely readable text which is particularly accessible to the general reader.

Terrence Higgins Trust publications (BM AIDS, London WC1N 3XX, all are free.):

AIDS: The Facts (6th edition, January 1986). A brief leaflet compiled with the help and advice of doctors which sets out basic facts (including the symptoms of AIDS) with great clarity.
AIDS: More Facts for Gay Men (5th edition, February 1986): a brief leaflet, but frank and very much to the point.
Facts about AIDS for Drug Users A fourteen page booklet, clearly set out, dealing positively with questions about the antibody test, the areas of risk, and ways of helping others.
AIDS and HTLVIII : HTLV Antibody – To Test or not to Test. A leaflet outlining the nature of the test, the implications of the result (negative or positive) and the points to be considered before you decide whether to be tested.
AIDS and HTLVIII : Medical Briefing (2nd edition, October 1985). A 24-page booklet written by the Trust's Medical Group, intended primarily for Trust volunteers, but invaluable for health workers, doctors and others concerned about AIDS. Like all the Trust's literature it is clearly set out, pulls no punches, and does not waste words.
You Can't Catch AIDS By . . . Royal Society of Medicine video, VHS, 1986, £23 including postage and packing (not available for hire) from the Society's Medicine Film and TV Unit, 1 Wimpole Street, London W1M 8AE.
Aimed at health and social service professionals, this video consists of short interviews with a wide range of carers both in the community and in hospitals. It attempts to address both the obvious and hidden concerns of caring professionals, and aims to encourage a calm and sensible approach by health professionals to people with AIDS.

CHAPTER 12

Sexuality and Disability

This chapter is not written with any intention of suggesting that disabled people's sexual needs are in any way different from anyone else's; this is clearly not so. Rather it is a means of drawing together information of a specialised nature where this might be helpful. Otherwise we would recommend that any readers who have a disability should quite naturally seek information to suit their requirements from all the other varied sources as described throughout the book. Some specialist services are also listed in Chapter 21, 'Guide to Local Services'.

Disability can affect our sexual activities in a number of different ways, either directly or indirectly. There is a direct effect when the spinal cord is damaged and nerves passing to the sexual organs are affected. If messages from the brain intended to stimulate sexual responsiveness are not able to travel effectively all the way down the spinal cord until they reach the sexual organs, then, depending on the severity of the damage, the functions and the feelings of those organs will be affected to a greater or lesser degree. This would affect for instance, those with spinal injuries through accidents or those with multiple sclerosis – a disease of the nervous system where the sheaths surrounding nerves in the brain and spinal cord are damaged, thus affecting the function of the nerves involved – or people with spina bifida whose spinal cord has not developed properly.

Problems which may indirectly affect sexual activity include:

Incontinence (*see* page 91).
Pain (which, if prolonged, will naturally diminish the sex drive, and is especially liable to affect people with arthritis).
Fear of further physical damage, for instance, after a hip replacement operation or after a heart attack.
Lack of body control as occurs with spasms.
Fear of inducing fits in those with epilepsy.

It is never an easy task to make available enlightened and practical services to help us with the difficulties we encounter in our sex lives. There is always a body of prejudiced opinion which is pulling in the opposite direction. Such opinion would limit discussion of this most important area in all our lives – the very basis of our human existence. Consequently, many of us feel guilty in the expression of our sexuality and disabled people have taken the full brunt of this guilt. All too often, they are expected to deny their natural feelings and to behave as if they were asexual.

Fortunately, however, there is now a growing body of opinion which accepts that sexual adjustment and fulfilment is at the very heart of successful rehabilitation. In a study conducted in Nigeria to investigate the relationship between sexuality and various areas of adjustment to disability among male paraplegics and tetraplegics, it was found that

> 'There is a close relationship between good sexual adjustment and the ability to use aids to daily living, mobility to perform role activities, high morale, relative independence and general satisfaction about life.'

('Sexual Adjustment among Upper Class Nigerian Male Paraplegics and Tetraplegics' by Vincent C. B. Nwuga, Faculty of Health Sciences, University of Ife, Nigeria in the *Journal of Tropical Medicine and Hygiene* (1982), pages 77 – 80, 85.)

Despite this reality, repression of feelings, with all its horrific emotional consequences, has been practised by otherwise seemingly 'caring' people in homes and institutions and sometimes even in loving families. We are all fragile in this area of our lives and can be easily hurt and damaged. By learning to understand our own and others' sexuality we each become a more complete person. In acts of physical loving we ordinary mortals may find a way to communicate and share a means of fulfilment which, at its best, can reach sublime heights.

For some, intercourse is rarely, or never, possible. But it can be a great mistake to see the goal of intercourse as the only reason for making love. Sadly, for many able-bodied couples it is all there is: two or three minutes of mechanical activity. They miss the delights of gentle and prolonged love making with no essential, predictable goal, centred on shared pleasuring rather than tumultuous release. Such expression is a joy in itself, and is valid whether or not it culminates in intercourse. Nor should we be put off by the stereotypes of physical love: those pictures of young bodies which can be turned any way up. We are not all sexual athletes. Hardly anybody is so disabled that they cannot find some satisfaction in sexual activity, with or without a partner. As Alex Comfort remarks in *Sexual Options for Paraplegics and Quadriplegics* (now out of print)

> 'When a disabled person is unable to enjoy sex, the greatest obstacle to enjoyment usually isn't the difficulty or impossibility of making particular movements, but the social convention that sex consists of putting the penis in the vagina and that all the rest of the rich range of human and mammalian sexual responses – oral, manual and skin stimulation – are abnormal. Human sex is widely versatile and not limited to the genitalia.'

Older men who took part in the Starr-Weiner survey (*see* discussion on sexuality for older people in Chapter 16, 'Sex in Later Life', page 131,) wrote

> 'that in spite of impotence they feel sexual and are very active, engaging in mutual masturbation, oral sex, or just kissing, stroking and cuddling'.

The report goes on,

> 'Therefore it is possible to have powerful fulfilling sexual experiences with or without an erection. It is what you feel and experience with your partner that counts, not so much what you do.'

It is now accepted that a large proportion of women do not have orgasms in intercourse without manual stimulation of the clitoris. The notion of a separate vaginal orgasm has been shown to be a myth; for most women, the action of the penis alone does not provide the stimulation necessary to bring the clitoris (the centre of a woman's joy) to climax. With this knowledge, many women are discovering the pleasure of reaching climax separately from intercourse (on their own at times), but otherwise through manual or oral stimulation by their partners. When the pressure to conform to stereotyped sexual roles is lifted, we are better able to explore a wider range of sexual options.

We all know how easily love-lives can go stale with the same old routine, and it is only by being imaginative and varied that we can ensure this does not happen to us. Finding new ways to enjoy sexual activities can be very rewarding and is marvellous for releasing inhibitions. Willingness to experiment can be a great asset for everyone and especially for anyone with limited movement. Different positions padded up with pillows, prolonged caressing and massage, oral sex, masturbation, varying the surroundings, warm shared baths and showers, gently lit beds in a cosy room with drinks at hand can all add a new dimension and be especially helpful to people whose bodies have parts which do not respond in the way they would wish.

Orgasm for some people can be elusive and sometimes physically unattainable, although we know of spinally injured people who can induce a state of high mental excitement during love-making, reaching what they describe as psychological climax even though the physical process of orgasm has been damaged or blocked altogether. One man described this clearly when he said

> 'Orgasm goes on between my ears not between my legs.'

This is only possible, of course, for those who experienced climaxes before their accident or disability and who have the imaginative ability to practise a deep recall of the excitement of their previous orgasmic experiences.

Others who have difficulty reaching climax may be affected by drugs they are taking (in this case, they would be wise to talk to their doctor to see whether the medicaments could be changed), while in other people it is the disease or condition which will not allow them to attain orgasm or, in men, stops them from having erections. It may be easier to come to terms with the difficulties and to build up alternative love-making activities if you have a full understanding of your own situation. Men will need to learn whether their lack of erections stems from permanent physical causes or from a purely psychological impotence arising after a period of ill-health, which, given suitable treatment and help from an understanding partner, may be only temporary. In addition, there are methods for having intercourse when the penis is only partly rigid and these may be learnt from psychosexual counsellors with special understanding of these problems. SPOD (*see* page 94) may be able to recommend you to a local counsellor.

Some people find the use of vibrators, either with or without partners, helpful in intensifying weaker sensations (*see* Chapter 17, 'Sex Aids'). The use of aids and erotic pictures all have their place in providing us with the stimulation which helps us to explore and enjoy our sexual feelings to the full. The sexual side of our nature, if it is not to be starved, needs as much attention and planning as we give to other areas of our life.

Incontinence

Incontinence is a condition in which there is a weakening or loss of control of the bladder or bowel or of both.

There can be any number of causes, which may be temporary or permanent. These include temporary illness, childbirth, local conditions – including infections – affecting the bladder or womb, disease or injury of the spinal cord, and diseases affecting the central nervous system, such as multiple sclerosis.

Whatever the cause of incontinence or of 'being caught short', it is the result which those who have the problem have to live with. Let's face it, such difficulties can cause havoc in our sex lives. It is hard to equate pleasure with our sex organs when they are, at the same time, causing us great inconvenience. Nevertheless, the management of incontinence is improving all the time. This is not to say it is ever easy, but a greater understanding and awareness of the individual needs of people who have these difficulties has led to the development of techniques of management and the production of more acceptable equipment. It is therefore vital for anyone who is experiencing complications in their sexual activity resulting from practical difficulties associated with the management of incontinence to seek professional help and advice. With proper diagnosis and management techniques, it has been found that only a small proportion of people need to use appliances on a long-term basis. In seeking help it is important to persist, even if the first doctor or nurse approached is not helpful. Your family doctor or consultant should be prepared to help, not only in better overall management of an incontinence problem, but also with regard to its relevance to sexual activity. It is worth noting that attached to some district general hospitals are urological assessment clinics, with sophisticated equipment for diagnosis. We describe below some basic management techniques, but the importance of seeking medical advice in this matter before adopting any particular procedure cannot be emphasised too strongly.

General Incontinence Management

1. Fluid intake.

While the overall intake of fluid must be maintained, as it is a vital means of combating infection, it is often possible to regulate this to fit in with sexual activity.

2. Control exercises.

In some cases of urinary incontinence a great deal can be done to improve the condition by the use of simple physical techniques carried out by the individual. This mostly applies in the case of 'stress' incontinence where it may be possible gradually to strengthen the appropriate muscles. Stress in this context is a purely physical condition, when a minor leakage occurs during some slight exertion, such as sneezing, laughing or coughing. The exercises are described in the book *Incontinence* – *see* page 95.

3. Emptying the bladder.

Some people are able to use what is known as the Credé method to make sure the bladder is totally empty at a particular time. This involves taking a deep breath, folding arms across the abdominal area and bending forward at the waist to increase the pressure in the lower abdominal area. Another method, known as 'percussion', is simply to bang the abdomen with palm or fist. This can be very frustrating if it does not work and is not worth the aggravation of persisting for too long.

4. Emptying the bowel.

Maintaining a regular bowel programme is the best protection against accidents; however, a degree of flexibility in routine can be achieved, where this is needed to fit in with a personal lifestyle. The frequency of bowel management varies considerably from person to person, from once a day to twice a week, with some people reporting once weekly evacuation with no ill effects. For those people using suppositories, a suppository inserter can be a great help.

5. Intermittent or self-catheterisation.

In the past few years this system of regularly emptying the bladder has gained a wider acceptance and indeed has been found preferable where retention of residual urine is a problem. Intermittent self-catheterisation is a clean, non-sterile method of introducing a catheter into the bladder to empty the bladder every two to four hours, depending on the doctor's guidance and your own individual requirements. In order to introduce the programme it would be necessary to take instruction in the procedure from a doctor or nurse who had experience of the technique.

In some cases, the catheter can be removed just before sexual intercourse and a clean one inserted afterwards. If you know the bladder is reasonably empty, you will have less to fear from accidents. For those who keep their catheter in place all the time, it is sometimes possible for a man to fold the catheter back over the penis, while using a condom, while a woman may tape the catheter to one side.

6. Cleanliness and smell

This is perhaps the biggest single problem and causes the most distress to the disabled person and their partner – however, much can be done to eliminate odour as far as possible. Since problems of odour arise as soon as urine or faeces are exposed to the air, it is essential that any wet or soiled articles are dealt with as soon as possible. A neutralising deodorant will help in this respect. One example is Nilodor. A drop or two can be used in appliances, commode pans, urinals and on protective padding, bed linen, carpets, etc. It is available from chemists. It is worth remembering that while it is necessary to avoid smell, fresh urine is in no way harmful.

Where to Go for Help with Incontinence Problems

There is a wide variety of equipment on the market. The best possible advice, combined with trial and error, should usually produce the most useful equipment for individual needs. The following organisations may prove helpful.

ASBAH (The Association for Spina Bifida and Hydrocephalus)
22 Upper Woburn Place, London WC1H 0EP (Tel: 01-388 1382).
Provides advisory and welfare services – there are also local organisations. The Disabled Living Adviser is producing fact sheets and information about incontinence for those with spina bifida and will be glad to offer advice.

Disabled Living Foundation
380-384 Harrow Road, London W9 2HU (Tel: 01-289 6111).
Has a list of incontinence aids. It also has an incontinence adviser who will answer queries. Its publication list includes books on incontinence.

Thames Valley Medical
Chatham Street, Reading RG1 7HT (Tel: Reading (0734) 595835).
A commercial organisation selling a wide range of various manufacturers' goods. It provides a free advisory service on incontinence. Telephone calls or letters are welcomed.

Where to Go for Help with Other Sex Disability Problems

We describe below organisations which provide specialist services and also some of the general organisations which have indicated they would be glad to help whenever they can. It is not possible to list all of these; for instance, some local branches of the National Marriage Guidance Council are accessible to people in wheelchairs and also have counsellors who have an understanding of special needs. It would always be worth enquiring of any organisation mentioned anywhere in the book whether they can help you in the way you need. After all, you may be the first person to approach them in this way and your encouragement could be all they require to extend their services to other people with similar needs.

We list only those disability organisations which have indicated that they are prepared to help with sexual problems. For a complete list of disability organisations, *see* the *Directory for Disabled People* (for details of this book, *see* page 9).

Action For Research into Multiple Sclerosis (ARMS)
4a Chapel Hill, Stansted, Essex CM24 8AG (Tel: Bishops Stortford (0279) 815553).
ARMS Telephone Counselling Service is available as follows:
South-East: 01-222 3123
Scotland: 041-637 2262 (restricted hours)
Birmingham: 021-476 4229.

Action for Research into Multiple Sclerosis is a self-help pressure group and charity where all the members have MS or have a close relative with MS. They run a very good 24-hour telephone counselling service, staffed by trained counsellors who know about MS from personal experience. They are there to listen to any problems concerning MS at any time of the day or night and on any day of the year, from people with MS, their families, or friends. The counsellors help callers cope with their distress, fears and anger, and try to help them find hope for the future. Some ARMS branches now employ professional face-to-face counsellors who are available to counsel couples with sexual difficulties in particular as well as anyone in general with MS in the family, in a colleague or a client.

Brook Centres
Brook Centres welcome young disabled people, but only their Centres in London, 153a East Street, London SE17 (Tel: 01-708 1234), Coventry, Gynaecological Outpatients, Coventry and Warwickshire Hospital, Stoney Stanton Road, Coventry (Tel: Coventry (0203) 412627), and Edinburgh, 2 Lower Gilmore Place, Edinburgh EH3 9NY (Tel: 031-229 5320) are accessible. For full details, *see* Chapter 3, 'Family Planning'.

DISCERN
94 Mansfield Road, Nottingham NG1 3HD (Tel: Nottingham (0602) 588043). DISCERN was set up by a group of professional people who in the course of their work had encountered many disabled people who were experiencing sexual problems. These counsellors are willing to work with individuals, couples and groups. Although DISCERN is based in Nottingham, and prefers

counselling its clients face-to-face, it is happy to provide a national telephone service. Anyone requesting the service DISCERN offers should contact any member of the team between 2.00 p.m. and 8.00 p.m. Monday to Thursday.

Gemma
BM Box 5700, London WC1N 3XX.
For full details of this organisation for disabled lesbian and bisexual women, *see* Chapter 18, 'Homosexuality'.

Muscular Dystrophy Group of Great Britain and Northern Ireland
Nattrass House, 35 Macaulay Road, London SW4 0QP (Tel: 01-720 8055).
The Group has a Patient Services Department to advise people with muscular dystrophy and their carers. This service can deal with specific welfare queries and can also provide details of the nearest genetic counselling centre. Among a variety of publications is included a useful handbook, providing a wealth of information on living with muscular dystrophy and also a leaflet: *Inheritance and the Muscular Dystrophies*, providing a brief summary of the complex genetics of these conditions.

NHS Domiciliary Family Planning Services
These operate in a number of areas. If you are seeking birth control advice and services and have difficulty in reaching a clinic, arrangements could be made for the domiciliary service to visit you. Your social worker or family doctor could advise about this or you could contact your local family planning clinic (in the telephone book under Family Planning.)

Outsiders Club
PO Box 4ZB, London W1A 4ZB (Tel: 01-741 3332).
The Club invites into membership those who feel themselves to be socially isolated, particularly handicapped people. From time to time, some of the members may find marriage partners within the Club, but the real objective is rather that members should help and encourage each other to express themselves sexually and to find loving relationships. Regular lunches and social events are arranged.

Spinal Injuries Association
76 St James's Lane, Muswell Hill, London N10 (Tel: 01-444 2121).
The SIA is run by wheelchair users and their friends for paraplegics and tetraplegics (spinal cord injured people) and their families and aims to help individuals achieve their own goals, bring about the best medical care and rehabilitation and stimulate scientific research into paraplegia.

The SIA is marvellously refreshing in avoiding patronising attitudes to its members and this is best reflected in its newsletter, which deals practically and imaginatively with all aspects of living with a disability. In contrast to many other magazines in the field of disability, it is above all else reader responsive and indeed, its readers set the tone by writing frankly and fully of their difficulties and of their achievements. Sexual matters, artificial insemination, management of incontinence and all other matters of daily living are discussed regularly and fully.

The SIA Welfare Service aims to provide friendly counselling and advice for members to help solve problems (including those of a personal and sexual nature), sometimes by putting people in touch with other individuals or organisations.

SPOD (The Association to Aid the Sexual and Personal Relationships of Disabled People)
286 Camden Road, London N7 0BJ (Tel: 01-607 8851).
SPOD was set up in 1972 by the National Fund for Research into Crippling Diseases, with the object at that time of studying and advising on sexual problems that might be experienced by disabled people. In a few years a great deal has been achieved towards changing people's attitudes by bringing discussion into the open and showing that disability doesn't rule out sexual feelings, sexual needs or, usually, sexual capabilities.

SPOD provides information on disability and sexuality, including a range of publications (*see* page 98), has a countrywide network of counsellors, and can usually put disabled people in touch with a counsellor near to their home. SPOD also arranges study days on such subjects as 'Sexuality and Disability', 'Sex Education for Physically Handicapped Young People' and 'Sex Education for Mentally Handicapped People'. A teaching pack on sex education for mentally handicapped people is also available.

For further information contact Morgan Williams, the Director.

WinVisible: Women with Visible and Invisible Disabilities
71 Tonbridge Street, Kings Cross, London WC1 (Tel: 01-837 7509).
WinVisible exists to exchange experiences and to express the views of women with all kinds of disabilities, including invisible ones such as epilepsy and cancer.

Selected Further Information

The following are books and publications specifically concerned with disability. For other publications, see the relevant chapters.

Living with Huntington's Disease by Dennis H. Phillips.

Available from the Association to Combat Huntington's Chorea, 34a Station Road, Hinckley, Leicestershire LE10 1AP (Tel: (0455) 615558). Price £1.95 plus postage.
This book aims to cover all aspects of the condition for patients and families, including reference to sexual aspects.

Directory for Disabled People, compiled by Ann Darnbrough and Derek Kinrade. Published by Woodhead-Faulkner in association with The Royal Association for Disability and Rehabilitation, fourth edition, 1985. Available from Woodhead-Faulkner, Fitzwilliam House, 32 Trumpington Street, Cambridge CB2 1QY (Tel: Cambridge (0223) 66733). Price £13.10 including postage and packing.
A comprehensive guide to services and opportunities for disabled and handicapped people. Starting with a section on state benefits and allowances, the *Directory* then covers topics such as specialised aids and equipment, the house and home, education, employment, motoring, holidays and leisure pursuits, giving in each case names and addresses of suppliers and a description of the product or service concerned. The Directory also contains a useful section on sex and personal relationships.

Drugs and Sexual Function For details of this book *see* Chapter 22, 'Selected Further Reading'.

Entitled to Love: the Sexual and Emotional Needs of the Handicapped by Dr Wendy Greengross. Available from SPOD, 286 Camden Road, London N7 0BJ (Tel: 01-607 8851). Price £3 including postage.
The author sets out to challenge at all levels the widely accepted view that people with disabilities do not, or should not, have sexual feelings. This is not a handbook on sex, but a discussion weaving understanding and concern into readable patterns. She makes the point that we all have to take emotional risks and being over-protective to people with disabilities is never kind and may often be cruel.

Dr Greengross goes on to discuss the problems of handicapped people in institutions (e.g. having little privacy), as well as the problems of staff who may find difficulty in coming to terms with the sexual needs of those in their care. She deals with sex education and the sexual problems of the adolescent, and also makes a plea that couples, where movements are restricted, should be ready to consider experimentation to widen the scope of their love-making.

Handicapped Married Couples by Michael and Ann Craft. Published by Routledge & Kegan Paul. Price £11.95.
This is an excellent and moving account of 40 mentally handicapped couples as discovered through the authors' careful analysis of a survey they carried out. Michael Craft is a consultant psychiatrist and Ann Craft is a social worker. The idea that mentally handicapped people are capable of normal sexual feelings and are entitled to express them has until recently been severely frowned upon. The authors are able to show through this book that marriage between mentally handicapped people, under the right conditions, has a high chance of success and should be encouraged rather than forbidden.

Images of Ourselves edited by Jo Campling. Published by Routledge & Kegan Paul, 1981. Price £5.50 (paperback).
Brief lives of 24 disabled women who talk very frankly about themselves. They range from adolescence to old age and their disabilities are various. We learn very clearly how these women have coped with living with their disabilities and the attitudes they have encountered. Thus, the themes of relationships, sexuality, motherhood, education, employment and the practical problems of daily life emerge in a personal and essentially real way. These women are not conventional characters, they have a determination and sense of individuality which would make their standards hard to reach. Nevertheless, many women readers will have a happy time identifying with the intimate details of coping with and enjoying life. This is a provocative and stimulating book.

Incontinence – A Guide to the Understanding and Management of a Very Common Complaint by Dorothy Mandelstam. Published for the Disabled Living Foundation by Heinemann Health Books, 1977. Available from DLF (Sales) Ltd, 45 East Hill, London SW18 2QZ. Price £4, including postage and packing.
This book presents information about a whole range of appliances and special clothing. It also describes. very briefly, 'ways of improving control' through exercises for pelvic muscles and through bladder drill. The general management of incontinence is discussed, but no special mention is made of the needs of those who are sexually active while having to cope with incontinence.

Living with a Colostomy by Margaret Schindler. Published by Thorsons Publishers Ltd, 1981. Price £5.50. including postage and packing.
This book is written to provide reassuring advice on returning to normal life after a colostomy operation. It gives guidance on diet, appliances, travel and personal relationships. The discussion of sexuality comes alive through the words of people who have themselves had colostomies. They are a source of considerable encouragement in the way they tell of their experiences.

Just one story will give the flavour – the author describes her visit to a 50-year-old patient who was very unhappy on her return home from hospital.

'I took with me for this visit a very young looking 70-year-old friend who is a colostomist as well as having a mastectomy, and blessed with a delicious sense of humour. When we arrived we found that the patient and her husband were very distressed because they had been told when they asked about their sex-life that at 50 they would have to forget all about "that kind of thing". My 70-year-old friend said "Well, I don't know about you, but twice a week is just about right for me".

Living with Paraplegia by Michael Rogers. Available from booksellers or in case of difficulty from the publisher, Faber & Faber Ltd, 3 Queen Square, London WC1N 3AU. Price £5.95. The author, who is himself paralysed, maintains that since patients treated by modern methods in specialised centres can now usually look forward to a normal lifespan, they must learn a new way of living if they are to enjoy a worthwhile existence. The author discusses with the benefit of personal experience, the information necessary and the mental adjustments to be made when returning to the community. He includes a wide range of information and has chapters on sexuality and the psychological aspects of paraplegia.

Marriage, Sex and Arthritis. Produced by the Arthritis and Rheumatism Council, 41 Eagle Street, London WC1R 4AR (Tel: 01-405 8572). Price 20p, including postage.
A short, clearly written booklet containing information on sex, family planning, pregnancy, childbirth and inheritance of arthritis.

MENCAP (The Royal Society for Mentally Handicapped Children and Adults.)
MENCAP publish several leaflets relating to sex which are available from the Bookshop, MENCAP National Centre, 123 Golden Lane, London EC1Y 0RT (Tel: 01-253 9433). Among these are the following:

Help your Child to Understand Sex by Victoria Shennan. Straightforward and helpful seven-page pamphlet written especially for parents. Price 50p.
Sex and Social Training in an Adult Training Centre by Lindsey Lowes. Price 50p.
Sex Education and the Mentally Retarded by George W. Lee, including short sections on parent involvement, programme planning objectives and curriculum. Price £1.50.
Add 25p per £1 of order.

Multiple Sclerosis: a Self-help Guide to its Management by Judy Graham. Published by Thorsons Publishers Ltd (reprinted 1982). Price £4.95 plus 55p postage and packing.

There has been very little information of a practical nature available to people with MS. The matter of diets has been dealt with in a piecemeal way, but it has always been very difficult for those with MS to get hold of facts. Now Judy Graham has brought out a complete life-style book of inestimable value to individuals who want to run their own lives and want to try regimes or diets which may not have been fully proved to defeat MS, but which have nevertheless been shown to be of benefit to many people.

Naturally, the author writes about relationships and sex, woven in as they should be in her recommendations for managing MS and for establishing a pattern for more satisfactory living. The book now also includes a chapter on childbirth.

Personal Relationships, the Handicapped and the Community. Edited by D. Lancaster-Gaye. Available from the Spastics Society, 12 Park Crescent, London W1N 4EQ. Price £1, plus postage and packing.
This book looks at residential alternatives and also covers the problems which arise in personal relationships, discussing love, sex and companionship.

Sex Education for Young People with a Physical Disability A guide for Parents and Teachers. by Mary Davies. Published by SPOD, 286 Camden Road, London N7 OBJ (Tel: 01-607 8851). Price £1.25.
This book is to help parents and teachers provide sex education for young people with a physical disability. It is written in an easy to understand style and takes a positive and practical approach.

Sex and the Handicapped Child by Dr Wendy Greengross. Published by the National Marriage Guidance Council. Available from SPOD (*see* above). Price £1, including postage and packing.

Erection, masturbation, homosexuality and contraception present particular problems to the parents of handicapped children. Yet there is very little help available. This book examines the reasons for this and suggests positive ways of helping. The book concludes with two useful lists: one of helpful reading; the other of helping organisations.

Sex and the Mentally Handicapped by Michael and Ann Craft. Published by Routledge & Kegan Paul. Available from bookshops and from SPOD (*see* above). Price £5.25 including postage and packing.
Written for professionals and parents, the authors look at many of the questions, anxieties and fears raised by the sexuality of this group. They examine myths and misconceptions and offer guidelines for those wishing to plan health and sex education programmes for mentally

handicapped youngsters and adults. They give the results of research into marriages, where one or both partners are mentally handicapped and conclude that with adequate counselling and support, a partnership can relieve much tension and loneliness and also enrich the quality of life enjoyed by handicapped people.

Sex and Young People with Spina Bifida and Cerebral Palsy. Available from the Association for Spina Bifida and Hydrocephalus, 22 Upper Woburn Place, London WC1H 0EP (Tel: 01-388 1382) and also from the Spastics *Society*. Price £1.25.

This is a wonderfully straightforward book, with sensitive line drawings by Liz McQuiston which illustrate the text perfectly. The illustrations are helpfully explicit without being too clinical. In addition, there are some delightful drawings showing the joy of loving and coupling, where the lines of the bodies merge in a manner which would be difficult to portray so gracefully in photographs.

Essentially this is a book for the young and uninitiated and for their parents. It explains carefully all those aspects of growing up which disabled youngsters may well find perplexing, cut off as they so often are from the sort of contact and communication their able-bodied peers take for granted. There are full descriptions of the bodies of men and women and their functions, including how conception takes place and how a baby grows. Worries about having a handicapped baby and genetic counselling are also discussed. There is helpful advice on menstruation and coping with incontinence in order to be able to enjoy sex. There are brief references to abortion and sterilisation and useful information about some of the methods of contraception. Masturbation is discussed and reassurance given about this very natural form of sexuality. Homosexuality is also mentioned, along with the very usual mixed-up emotions most teenagers have with regard to their feelings for their own and the opposite sex. Finally there is a useful dictionary of terms and some helpful names and addresses and a brief list of further reading.

We would warmly recommend this book to young disabled people who are seeking to understand their own sexuality. While written specifically for those with spina bifida and cerebral palsy, it would be a useful book for those with different handicaps.

Sex Therapy: a Practical Guide by Keith Hawton. In describing a treatment approach in the area of sex therapy, the author includes the treatment of sexual problems of physically disabled people. For fuller details of the book *see* page 8.

Sexual Adjustment: a Guide for the Spinal Cord Injured Published by Accent Special Publications, Box 700, Bloomington, Illinois 61702, USA. Price US $4.95, plus US $1.15 shipping.

While written mainly about sexual adjustment for the paraplegic male, this book offers useful information to individuals with other physical disabilities as well.

Sexual Aspects of Social Work by W. F. R. Stewart. Published by Woodhead-Faulkner, 1979. Available from Woodhead-Faulkner (Publishers) Ltd, Fitzwilliam House, 32 Trumpington Street, Cambridge CB2 1QY (Tel: Cambridge (0223) 66733). Price £12.95.

Many human problems have sexual aspects, and this book aims to help social workers towards a better understanding of this side of their work. A must for those social workers who wish to understand and help the 'whole' person.

Sexuality & Handicap: Problems of Motor Handicapped People edited by B.H.H. Dechesne, C. Pons and A.M.C.M. Schellen. Published by Woodhead-Faulkner, 1979. Available from Woodhead-Faulkner (Publishers) Ltd, Fitzwilliam House, 32 Trumpington Street, Cambridge CB2 1QY (Tel: Cambridge (0223) 66733). Price £19.50.

This book has been written primarily for doctors, paramedical personnel, psychologists, educators, social workers and health-care workers. It would be of interest to disabled people with a basic medical knowledge who want to gain an intimate understanding of the subject. It is split into three parts and concerns itself with the medical, psycho-social and ethical aspects of sexuality and handicap faced by motor handicapped people.

The Sexual Side of Handicap: a Guide for the Caring Professions by W. F. R. Stewart. Published by Woodhead-Faulkner, 1979. Available from Woodhead-Faulkner (Publishers) Ltd, Fitzwilliam House, 32 Trumpington Street, Cambridge CB2 1QY (Tel: Cambridge (0223) 66733). Price £12.95.

The aim of this book is to provide guidance and practical information for those working with physically or mentally handicapped people. The first section of the book examines the sexual problems experienced by many handicapped people and sets them in the context of relationships and social outlook. Sexual education, counselling, problems of the institutional setting and legal aspects of sex and disability are also discussed. In the second part of the book the author describes typical disorders and their effect on relationships, sexual capacity and parenthood.

Sexuality and Multiple Sclerosis by Michael Barrett of the MS Society of Canada. Reprinted by SPOD (286

Camden Road, London N7 0BJ (Tel: 01-607 8851)). Price 50p, plus postage and packing. (Free to people with MS.)
This booklet describes itself as

> 'an exploration of sexual possibilities, expectations and concerns and of ways to communicate them'.

As such, it has a warm and encouraging way of discussing sexuality and of helping people with MS to cope with the frustrations, tensions and fatigue which all too often characterise the condition. The author emphasises the need to discover and use imaginative ways of love-making to enhance sexual activity which may otherwise be restricted.

Sexuality and the Physically Disabled – an Introduction for Counsellors. Available from SPOD (286 Camden Road, London N7 0BJ (Tel: 01-607 8851)). Price £2, including postage and packing.
Many professionals are reluctant to consider problems in the personal and sexual relationships of disabled people as part of their concern. This can be because they do not have relevant information easily available to them.

The aim of this booklet is to provide information on various disabilities, outlining possible implications for sexual and personal relationships. Subjects considered include masturbation, sex aids, drugs and sex, incontinence and, to help the reader gain further information, a resource list and a list of helpful organisations.

So You're Paralysed by Bernadette Fallon. Available from the Spinal Injuries Association (76 St James's Lane, Muswell Hill, London N10 (Tel: 01-444 2121)). Price £4, plus 50p postage.
This book has been written for those who are newly paralysed through injury, but it would be most helpful to anyone who has a degree of paralysis, however caused. The approach is sensitive, down-to-earth, and will particularly help people who find themselves in the bewildering position where responsibility for their most intimate bodily functions seems to have been handed over to medical staff. Sex is just one of the subjects covered in this book; it takes its place, as, of course, it should, with all the other physical (and mental) functions of life.

SPOD Advisory Leaflets – a maximum of three advisory leaflets and two resource lists are available free of charge from SPOD (286 Camden Road, London N7 0BJ (Tel: 01-607 8851)).
Titles include the following:

1. *SPOD Is ....* A description of SPOD and the way it can help.
2. *Physical Handicap and Sexual Intercourse: Positions and Techniques*. We rather expect to know all about sex as a normal matter of course, but, in any case, if in doubt would be ashamed to admit our ignorance. This may be because we feel there is a very limited amount to know – the 'lights out, under the blankets, one position' routine. In fact lack of knowledge about sex can be blamed for a great deal of unhappiness among both able-bodied and disabled people. This leaflet discusses some helpful techniques.
3. *Physical Handicap and Sexual Intercourse: Methods and Techniques*. For too long, many people have felt that adventurous love-making, involving different positions and a degree of planning was somehow wrong. For disabled people, experimenting with different positions may be vital and this leaflet discusses such positions and questions the reluctance to try new ways.
4. *Aids to Sex for the Physically Handicapped*. The leaflet explains that

   > 'for those disabled people who meet with physical difficulty in their sexual relationships, a number of aids can be used. They may vary from such everyday articles as pillows or cushions to specially made appliances'.

   We are further reassured that the use of aids need not be seen as 'wrong' or 'kinky', but of value where they meet a need. A warning is given to avoid sharp suppliers who seek to con you into buying useless articles at fancy prices.
5. *Sex for the Severely Disabled*. This reassuring leaflet shows that many severely disabled people do achieve intercourse, but that where this is not possible, there are many other ways of fulfilling a loving and caring relationship.
6. *Mentally Handicapped People and Sex*. This leaflet is provided mainly for parents and others involved in the care of mentally handicapped persons, for, as we know, myths about the sexuality of mentally handicapped people abound. The leaflet discusses the fears concerning this sexuality, putting them in a proper perspective and asks not whether a mentally handicapped child or adolescent should have sex education, but how and from whom.
7. *Your Handicapped Child and Sex*. To many parents of handicapped children, the dawning realisation that their child is becoming sexually adult can come as quite a shock. Their reactions may be ones of denial and over-protection. In fact to deny young people sexual knowledge can make life very difficult for them. This leaflet broadly discusses atti-

tudes and problems and recommends seeking further advice where necessary.

8. *Your Disabled Partner and Sex*. The problems for those whose partners were already disabled when they married are different from those who became disabled after marriage. For some people there are no problems at all. This leaflet discusses the questions and the difficulties of those who find it hard to be both nurse and lover.
9. *Physically Handicapped People and Contraception*. Disability does not usually affect fertility, so disabled people who do not wish to have children or who want to plan their family need to choose a method of contraception appropriate to their state of health, life-style, physical and mental capabilities, and personal preference.
10. *Sex and the Person with an Ostomy*. Some reassuring facts, including what an ostomy is; how it affects sex, what to do if the man can't get an erection, fertility and some practical suggestions.

SPOD Information Sheets

Each Information Sheet costs 25p. Titles are as follows:

1. *Male Fertility after Spinal Injury*
2. *Resuming Sexual Activity after a Heart Attack*
3. *No title*
4. *Sex Aids*
5. *Incontinence and Sex*
6. *Sex and Arthritis*
7. *Positions for Sex for either Men or Women Suffering from Arthritis*
8. *Drugs and Sex*.

SPOD also has a range of resource lists which give details of books, papers, films, tapes, etc., on a particular subject. These are listed below and cost 25p each.

1. *Arthritic Disorders*
2. *Attitudes Towards Sex and Disabled People*
3. *Disabled People and Marriage*
4. *Elderly People*
5. *Multiple Sclerosis*
6. *Sexual Concerns of Disabled Women*
7. *Sexuality and the Heart Patient*
8. *Sexuality and Mastectomy*
9. *Sex Education for the Mentally Handicapped*
10. *Sex Education for the Physically Handicapped*
11. *No title*
12. *Spinal Injury*
13. *Sexuality and Visual Impairment*
14. *Films on Sexuality and Disability*
15. *Audio Visual Materials on Sexuality and Mental Handicap*
16. *Professional Workers' Training and Sexuality*

Toward Intimacy: Family Planning and Sexuality Concerns of Physically Disabled Women by The Task Force on Concerns of Physically Disabled Women, edited by Susan Shaul, Jane Bogle and others. Published by the Human Sciences Press, 3 Henrietta Street, London WC2E 8LU (Tel: 01-240 0856). Price £5 plus postage and packing.

The booklet is dedicated to exploring the various relationships in a disabled woman's life. It explores a woman's relationship to her body and how this image affects her personally and in her relationships with others. A major section is devoted to a thorough exploration of sexuality as it relates to specific disabilities and there is a detailed investigation of contraceptives related to these disabilities. Menstruation, masturbation and the many forms of sexually related disease are covered. Also included are discussions of the important relationships with parents and health care practitioners. The booklet contains personal statements of disabled women, discussing their own experiences, including both the joys and the frustrations of sexuality and disability. This sensitively illustrated manual acknowledges the unique concerns of disabled women and provides the reader with the comfort of sharing other disabled women's similar experiences.

Stroke! A Self-help Manual for Stroke Sufferers and their Relatives by Dr R.M. Youngson. Published by David & Charles. Price £5.95.

The information in this book will help anyone who has had a stroke to gain lost confidence and recover faster. It concentrates on the area where support is most needed – at home – and affirms the valuable role each family can play in aiding rehabilitation. The book includes helpful findings from recent research, as well as showing how the latest aids can help. Information is included on 'sex after a stroke'.

The Wheelchair Child by Philippa Russell. Available from Souvenir Press, 43 Great Russell Street, London WC1. Price £6.95 plus postage.

This book covers problems from early childhood to young adulthood. The author combines basic information on the main handicapping conditions, the medical and community services available to handicapped children, and practical advice on aids, appliances and home adaptations and financial grants, with a thoughtful consideration of the developmental, sexual and emotional problems attached to disability.

Within Reach: Providing Family Planning Services to Physically Disabled Women by The Task Force on Concerns of Physically Disabled Women, edited by Julia

Hale-Harbaugh, Ann Norman and others. Published by the Human Sciences Press, 3 Henrietta Street, London WC2E 8LU (Tel: 01-240 0856). Price £5 plus postage and packing.

The companion volume to *Toward Intimacy* (*see* above), this book examines the health services' and family planning clinics' responsibilities towards working with the physically disabled woman. Special sections include providing for in-service training of staff, counselling, administering physical examinations and providing for physical accessibility to the grounds of the clinic.

Also discussed are the medical aspects of physical disabilities, especially those which occur most frequently among women of childbearing age, including spinal cord injury, cerebral palsy, poliomyelitis, rheumatoid arthritis and multiple sclerosis. The final section delineates in chart form the many aspects of female sexuality, reproduction and special considerations for contraceptive use for each specific disability.

Films and Video-tapes

Like Other People, 16 mm, colour, 37 minutes. Available from Concord Films Council Ltd, 201 Felixstowe Road, Ipswich, Suffolk IP3 9BJ (Tel: Ipswich (0473) 76012/715754). To hire: film: £12.60 + £6 carriage + VAT, video £11 + £1.30 postage and packaging + VAT.

Made in 1972 (it doesn't seem to date) under the auspices of the Mental Health Council, this film depicts the problems of two severely disabled spastic people in a residential home. They want to establish their right to work, love and live 'like other people'. What this couple say about their need for fulfilment applies equally to people handicapped in other ways.

Why is it for Them and not for Me: Sex and Physically Handicapped People. Brook Advisory Centres have produced an 85-minute video tape, presented in four sections which are intended to be viewed separately: Maureen's story (24 minutes); John's story (15 minutes); Jim's story (25 minutes); and Elaine's story (21 minutes). The video-tape is designed to trigger discussion and is accompanied by supporting materials for the presenter. It is available from Brook Advisory Centres, Education and Publications Unit, 10 Albert Street, Birmingham B4 7UD. Tel: 021-643 1554. Prices: to buy – £35; to hire – returnable deposit £35, hire charge – £15.

CHAPTER 13

Learning about Sex

Sex should not be seen as a thing apart. It is inextricably bound up with the intensity and subtlety of our feelings about life and our appreciation of the world around us. The joy of sex is an extension of a wider perception of sensual delight : the taste of a peach, the shape of a vase, the sound of a voice, the feel of old wood, the smell of mown grass. In a chipboard society, such values decline and the importance of nurturing the potency of sensual appreciation is too often neglected.

We are convinced that people cannot begin to experience the full delights of sexual partnership without acquiring social skills and an understanding of their own and others' sexuality and feelings. A good sexual relationship, certainly in the long term, depends on perceptive self-knowledge and a consideration of the partner's needs and responses. Sexual love is as much about pleasing your partner as pleasing yourself.

You really can't talk about loving someone if you don't like them first. It requires something more than physical attraction. It takes admiration and respect, seeing your lover as a person in his or her own right, with a readiness to give companionship, support and sympathy as necessary, and with a willingness to communicate and negotiate. Then it needs a thorough knowledge of sexual techniques and an understanding of fundamental strategies – a recognition, for example, that generally speaking a woman takes longer to come to the boil than a man and that her sexual interest is set in a wider emotional context or, equally, that a man's self-image and confidence can be very fragile and can easily be destroyed.

There needs to be an acceptance that you can cuddle or sleep together naked without it necessarily leading to sex. And even more essential, an acceptance of the principle that the conception of children should be planned, responsible and mutually agreed.

Such basic ground rules as these not only serve to elevate sexual love above the mere fulfilment of an animal urge, but can enhance that fulfilment to the peaks of ecstasy and provide a basis for a relationship which can survive beyond the first flood of passion.

The Ingredients of Sex Education

We have talked about the more generalised aspects of sexual knowledge first because they are easily overlooked. Of course, a full sex education programme will have many facets and many aims. The Family Planning Association's description of these could hardly be bettered:

- 'To provide an adequate knowledge of:
  anatomy of sexual organs;
  secondary sexual characteristics;
  male and female reproductive physiology;
  intercourse, conception, gestation, birth;
  contraception;
  sexually transmitted diseases;
  varieties of sexual behaviour;
  marriage and parenting.
- To develop objective and understanding attitudes towards sex in its various manifestations.
- To help people to develop an insight into their relationship with members of both sexes.
- To provide the education and understanding that will enable individuals to use their sexuality effectively and sensitively in any role, whether as partner, parent, community member or citizen.
- To help people understand social expectations regarding sexuality and develop a responsible attitude towards their own sexuality and that of others'.

Sex Education and Young People

In recent years, there has been a substantial rise in teenage sexual activity in the UK. It is estimated that about 70 per cent of girls will have had intercourse before their 18th birthday and many of them will have had sex before reaching the legal age of consent. A fascinating survey by the magazine *19* (April/May 1982) among its (female) readers concluded that

> 'women are increasingly rejecting the idea of saving themselves for their husband, and are acquiring an amount and variety of sexual experience nearer to levels that were once the prerogative of men'.

Although the effects are often exaggerated, this burgeoning of sexual activity implies a higher risk of catching a sexually transmitted disease and has certainly resulted in some increase in unwanted pregnancies, measured in the main by a rise in the level of abortions.

There are some who see sex education as actively contributing to these trends. A small but vocal minority reinforces the fears and prejudices which have so strongly characterised British society in the past and which continue to stand in the way of enlightenment and progress. They believe that sex education gives young people 'ideas', which are further encouraged by making contraception readily available.

We are convinced, on the contrary, that the darker side of the sexual revolution points to a lack of, rather than the influence of, responsible sex education. Available data points to British young people being well down the league of sexual awareness. All too few receive even a fraction of the knowledge they need. The indications are that the great majority of youngsters are given only minimal information about sex while at school and negligible advice from their parents. Abortion and 'special' clinics are full of people who know next to nothing about birth control and sexually transmitted diseases. Whatever limited knowledge such people do have seems mostly to have been acquired from friends and 'informal' sources and is often unreliable. Indeed, it is frequently necessary later in life, when relationships have gone wrong, to expend enormous effort in helping people to unlearn misconceived behaviour patterns and family ideas about love and sex which have become ingrained and habitual. Anyone with practical experience knows that lack of sexual knowledge or incorrect learning is responsible for extensive and profound unhappiness. It can corrode self-confidence, destroy marital harmony, blight development and spill over into anti-social behaviour. It leads inevitably to unwanted pregnancies, a sorry state of affairs reflected in the continuing high level of abortions. Most teenage suicides are attributed to sexual or relationship crises.

The survey by *19* confirmed the view that while pressures on young people to be sexually active have dramatically increased, this has not been matched by the ability to cope with sexual freedom – either emotionally or on a practical level. Guilt, anxiety and dissatisfaction persist and, notwithstanding that the general educational standard of most of those who responded was above average, it was found that 12 per cent of single girls under 18 had sex without using any contraceptive method at all, while a further 12 per cent used risky withdrawal or rhythm methods.

Parents who are antagonistic to or doubtful about their offspring receiving sex education should reflect that the alternative is not an unsullied vacuum. Ignorance does not equate with innocence. Children will instead rely on the half-baked ideas of their peers and the misleading fiction of smuggled magazines. And sex will begin to be a furtive activity, a secret subject, hidden from family and associated with guilt.

Sexual intercourse, like eating, is at the most basic level an instinctive activity, but its full expression for mutual pleasure is, like cooking, a learned skill. Along with that learning, young people need to be helped to take responsibility for themselves. They should, perhaps above all, be helped to understand the importance of not going overboard too early in life, either into unplanned parenthood or a marriage for which they are not ready.

You can argue about when sex education should begin, how fast it should progress and how far it should go (and we will simply provide a range of options), but the need for adequate sex education, about values and emotions as well as biology, seems to us to be beyond any question or doubt.

Sex Education and Physically Handicapped People

Nowhere is fear and prejudice more rife than it is in relation to disabled people. There is a common feeling, sometimes shared by parents and caring staff, that disabled people are sexless – or ought to be. Thus, sex education is seen as inappropriate, even a danger, in that it might encourage sexual aspirations which cannot be fulfilled, causing harm and disappointment to disabled people themselves and disturbing the social order.

Fortunately, such ideas are losing ground. There is an increasing awareness that, while disability may impose special difficulties, handicapped people are as sexual as anyone else, with ordinary needs and desires for themselves and in their relationships with other people. In recent years, a great deal of attention has been focused upon improving the opportunities for disabled people to overcome loneliness and isolation, to relate to others, to enjoy sexual expression and to correct the effects of long-standing neglect and deprivation. The need for sex education for physically handicapped people has been recognised as urgent. As we have remarked elsewhere, disability need not and should not separate people into a category which is seen as being radically different from others. All that we have said about sex education in this chapter has application for disabled people as for anyone else. However, specific disabilities and general problems like incontinence (see page 91) do present sexual difficulties which interfere with full and free expression, and specific techniques are needed to cope with individual handicaps. Equally, sex education programmes for disabled people require a wider compass. To the aims of general sex education set out on page 101, the Family Planning Association adds the following objectives.

- 'To provide an adequate knowledge of:
  the effect of particular disabilities on sexual function;
  how to cope with menstruation;
  the varieties of possible sexual activity relevant to a particular disability;
  the considerations important in choice of contraception;
  genetic counselling and its availability;
  artificial insemination by donor or husband.
- To explore attitudes to masturbation and consider problems particular to disabled people.
- To help people come to terms with their handicap and develop a positive self-image.
- To provide an environment in which people can explore their attitudes and feelings towards sexuality in its widest sense, including their fears (which may be considerable).'

Sex Education and Mentally Handicapped People

Mentally handicapped people need to be encouraged to understand and come to terms with their feelings and needs in a way which is socially acceptable. In a definitive article, Dr Mary Davies, former Education and Training Officer of SPOD (*see* page 108), has pointed out that without sex education the stirrings of puberty and the onset of menstruation can be frightening, but that properly guided, the mentally handicapped person can cope and gain positive benefit from the knowledge that it is a normal part of growing up. Mentally handicapped people, she goes on, are usually fertile and there is, therefore, a risk of unwanted pregnancy. They need to be made aware, as far as possible, of the facts of sexual intercourse and the consequences which can follow if precautions are not taken, and to learn that expressions of sexual feelings, such as masturbation, while normal, are acceptable only in private.

It is a difficult area which poses problems both in institutional care (where staff feel that there might be legal problems if they give residents opportunities for privacy and intimacy) and in society generally, as more mentally handicapped people are living in the community rather than in hospitals. More enlightened concepts of care, however, reinforce rather than lessen the need for appropriate sex education and training.
(*See also* SPOD, page 108.)

In Conclusion

Responsible attitudes to sex and the deepest experience of sexual fulfilment depend on a sound sex education. This implies not only the provision of honest factual information, but more open attitudes within the family, in society and between partners. So long as sex remains 'something we don't talk about', we heighten the risk of it being thought of as dirty and ridden with taboos. Some people fear that enlightenment in sexual matters is a passport to promiscuity. This is rather like thinking that driving lessons encourage dangerous driving. The idea that you can protect people by shielding them from the truth is a fallacy. Essentially, it betrays a fearful approach to life which stifles healthy development and erodes sexual maturity. Attempts to protect are unrealistic and may actually turn out to be counter-productive. Sex education, like any other kind of education, aims to bring light where there is darkness, to dispel myths and to help us to set a course which avoids the tragic pitfalls which can so easily ruin the lives of the unwary. Of course it needs to be responsibly and expertly taught, with a perception of what is appropriate for different ages and groups. In the case of children there needs to be a respect and sensitivity for the views of parents (who may also need to be shown the importance of a sound sex education), and safeguards are now built into our legislation by the Education (No.2) Act 1986, section 46 to secure that pupils should be encouraged to have regard to 'moral considerations and the value of family life'. A sound sex education programme should always provide information about sex in the context of relationships and responsibility, both to other people and to oneself. It should help us to appreciate our own sexuality and feelings, to understand and have consideration for others and to take rational decisions about our own sex lives. It is a continuous process which can be relevant at any age.

Where to Go for Help

BLAT Centre for Health and Medical Education
BMA House, Tavistock Square, London WC1H 9JP (Tel: 01-388 7976). Working mainly through the medium of educational technology, defined in the broadest terms, BLAT seeks to promote further education of the medical profession and the general public in the fields of preventive medicine and health by encouraging

individuals and institutions to introduce new ideas and materials to their teaching. It has books and films on sex education, and offers a wide range of expertise and facilities, including research, graphic design, electronics, printing, teaching and the provision of information. Contact the Information Officer for further details.

The British Society for Research on Sex Education (British Rose)

BM Rose, London WC1 3XX.

Rose was formed in December 1979 at the fourth Congress of the World Association of Sexology, as it was felt that current trends of thought and development in the study of human sexuality had overlooked the needs of many parts of the world. In addition to an international committee, it was agreed to set up national sub-committees in various countries and British Rose was established in May 1980 as one of these.

The aims of the organisation lie in three directions – research, education and events.

Research is conducted with the following aims:

(a) to research the most effective methods of providing and evaluating sex education;
(b) to co-ordinate existing strands of research and training and to provide an overview of the current situation;
(c) to offer a venue for sharing ideas and resources.

Education aims to achieve the following:

(a) to generate guidelines for the content and standards of training of sex educators;
(b) to identify any particular problems of different cultures within our multi-racial society;
(c) to encourage inter-disciplinary co-operation in sex education.

Events are arranged with the following aims:

(a) to organise seminars, workshops and conferences on themes of interest to those concerned with sex education;
(b) to facilitate the exchange of information and discussion of future projects.

The annual membership subscription is £7.50, which gives an entitlement to reduced rates of admission to events organised by Rose anywhere in the world. Members receive a twice-yearly bulletin, containing up-to-date information on research and activity in the field of sex education. Together they form a committed network of people who are keen to share and to co-operate in action to further common objectives and ideals.

Brook Advisory Centres

153a East Street, London SE17 2SD (Tel: 01-708 1234/1390).

Alongside its clinic services (see Chapter 3, 'Family Planning') Brook's information and education work is rapidly expanding. Both clinic and national office staff provide advice on an individual basis in response to telephone calls, letters and personal visits. The philosophy of the organisation is perhaps best summed up in the words of one of the eminent advisers, James Hemmings, PhD:

> 'our aim should be to help young people to attain sexual maturity as a foundation for personal and marital life. We can make or mar the happiness of their lives, and the lives of their children, by the way we help or hinder their sexual development'.

Brook's Education and Publications Unit in Birmingham produces and distributes educational material about personal relationships, reproduction and birth control for young people and professionals, including a specially designed teaching programme for disabled people. Brook Advisory Centres also provide speakers for schools, youth projects etc.

Edinburgh Human Sexuality Group

Family Planning Centre, 18 Dean Terrace, Edinburgh (Tel: 031-332 7941).

The Group is an association of six centres co-ordinating teaching, training and treatment in the field of human sexuality. It provides teaching for a wide range of professional groups on most aspects of this subject, arranges training workshops and runs a three-term course of seminars to introduce health professionals to the problems of human sexuality and to develop skills in approaching them. EHSG also runs a more comprehensive 21-month training which includes development of counselling skills, weekly discussion seminars, clinical work with supervision, as well as academic teaching.

The Group has produced a film, *Breaking the Ice: Approaching Sexual Problems*, which has proved useful in helping people to learn how to discuss sexual topics with patients. A further film is envisaged.

The Family Planning Association

27–35 Mortimer Street, London W1N 7RJ (Tel: 01-636 7866).

The FPA is pre-eminent among organisations providing sex education services. One of its declared aims is

> 'to educate the public in the field of procreation, contraception and health, with particular reference to personal responsibility in sexual relationships, and to the consequences of population growth'.

Its motto, in a snappier style, would be 'Every child a wanted child', a view we would wholeheartedly endorse.

In association with the Health Education Authority, the FPA operates the Family Planning Information Service, to provide information of all kinds – including leaflets, posters and publications – and enquiry services on all aspects of family planning and personal relationships. The Service is particularly concerned to ensure that people know about and use the free National Health family planning facilities. It is run from the above address, where there is a walk-in information and reference library, as well as a telephone information service, and is where all the FPIS literature is stocked. There are also 11 regional administrators (*see* page 000), most of whom hold stocks of the FPIS leaflets. Posters, information and other services are available free of charge, as is a comprehensive range of leaflets on all aspects of family planning, methods of contraception and related subjects. Fact sheets, providing up-to-date information on specific aspects of family planning are available on request and a quarterly bulletin of family planning information and a bi-monthly classified review of family planning literature are distributed on subscription, both at £3 per annum.

The FPIS Information and Resource Centre assembles publications and information for public reference on sexuality, fertility and population. Two information officers assist with enquiries by letter or telephone on weekdays from 11 a.m. to 3 p.m..

The FPA also runs, independently, a Book Centre at the Mortimer Street address, which is open Monday to Friday from 9.30 a.m. – 5 p.m. Subjects covered include sexuality and relationships; sex education; family planning, birth control, abortion; pregnancy, birth and childcare; general health: physical and emotional; subfertility; sexually transmitted disease; psychosexual problems family planning and related issues.

There is a mail order service and a booklist is obtainable from them free on request (a stamped, self-addressed envelope is appreciated).

The FPA Education Unit provides an education and training service in the UK, to enable professionals to improve their understanding of sexuality and personal relationships. As well as providing factual information, the Unit runs a variety of courses in London and the FPA regions. These range from two- to three-day basic courses for anyone working with children and young adults, to specialist courses designed for specific professional groups or organisations. Applications and queries about regional courses should be made to the relevant regional administrator (*see* page 28). In London, contact the Course Administrator, FPA Education Unit, at the Mortimer Street address (*see* above). A free prospectus is available.

Regional Offices throughout the UK (*see* page 28) carry out a range of information and educational activities in their locality, with library and resource facilities, book centres and enquiry services. They work with a range of medical, health and community care professionals, providing education courses, speakers and exhibitions for them and for members of the public.

Fact Sheets D2: *How Do People First Learn about Sex?* and D6: *Sexual Rights of Handicapped People* are particularly helpful in summarising, respectively, study evidence and problems and resources.

Forum Magazine

The Northern and Shell Building, PO Box 381, Mill Harbour, London E14 9TW (Tel: 01-987 5090).

We have so far withheld from discussing the role of erotic books and magazines. Undoubtedly they do have an educational element, which is accessible to a very large readership, a high proportion of which would not read more serious literature. But this benefit is offset by the fact that much of the material is positively misleading, unbalanced and overtly physical, relegates women to the status of mere sex objects and, at its worst, deals in deviations and practices which might encourage people with dangerous tendencies. Its primary purpose is that of commercial profit and its purveyors are not usually guided by higher principles.

We believe, however, that there is a place for non-textbook literature which is exciting and stimulating, frank and open and honest, without being 'worthy'. The best thing we have so far is *Forum* magazine. *Forum* is an 'international journal of human relations', published in no less than six countries. The magazine reflects three basic beliefs:

(a) that because of ignorance, fear and guilt, the great majority of people in our country are today enjoying only a fraction of the potential joy and pleasure they could receive from their relationships;
(b) that by sharing the experiences of others, readers will gain a greater understanding of themselves and others through realising that no one is alone in their fears or frustrations or unique in their problems and;
(c) that when people can talk about their sexual experiences they find it easier to communicate in all areas and that many so-called sexual problems are symptoms of more basic difficulties with intimacy, closeness and love.

Forum is backed by a distinguished board of consultants which includes many of the world's leading experts in the sexual field. The magazine receives and is able to respond to a stream of letters from readers with individual sexual problems.

The UK subscription is £21 for 13 (lunar) monthly issues.

The Health Education Authority
78 New Oxford Street, London WC1A 1AH (Tel: 01-631 0930).
(Note: At the time of writing a change of address is possible but no details are yet available).

The HEA provides a wide range of resources for both specialist and general use. The Resources Centre at 71–75 New Oxford Street incorporates audio-visual and other multi-media materials, a library and an information service. There is a great deal of reference material on all aspects of human sexuality and resource lists have been prepared on the following subjects:

Health, Hygiene and Sex Education – for mentally handicapped children, adolescents and adults.
Sexually Transmitted Infections
Personal Relationships
Family Planning

Free leaflets which are available include the following:

A Self-help Guide to Thrush – what causes thrush in women, how to treat it and how to prevent further attacks
Herpes. What to Do and How to Cope
Guide to a Healthy Sex Life – explains sexually transmitted diseases, how to avoid them and how to treat them
AIDS – What Everybody Needs to Know
Cystitis – explains what it is, why it occurs and what to do about it.

The HEA is the major curriculum development agency for personal, social and health education in the UK, and, through its Young People's Programme, funds curriculum development projects for ages 4 to 19 and promotes in-service training for teachers. The Professional Development Programme is concerned with the training and development of health education staff in the Health Service and other professional groups, organising courses, conferences and workshops, and seeking to encourage the inclusion of health education in the training programmes of relevant professions. Although sex education is only a part of a much larger commitment to health education, the HEA is uniquely placed to act as a national centre of expertise and knowledge and to provide advice to statutory and voluntary bodies.
Health Education Authority funded material includes the following:

HEA Health Education in Initial Teacher Education Project – training material, with a unit on 'Relationships and Mental Health', and one on 'Sexuality'. Published 1987. Available from the HEA Health Education Unit, Department of Education, University of Southampton, Southampton SO9 5NH.
HEA 16-19 Project Material – a resource for staff working with 16-19 year olds. Published 1987. Available from the HEA Health Education Unit, as above.
Health Matters – the YTS Health Education Resource Pack. Published by the National Extension College, 1986. Price £25, including packing and postage. Includes a module entitled 'Stepping Out', to help young people with their personal relationships. Available from National Extension College, 18 Brooklands Avenue, Cambridge CB2 2HN.

The Institute for Sex Education and Research
40 School Road, Moseley, Birmingham B13 9SN (Tel: 021-449 0892).
The Institute, which is directed by Martin Cole, PhD, is a non-profit-making company set up to promote education and research in the field of human sexual behaviour and to stimulate an interest in more scientific methods of treatment (*see also* Chapter 1, 'The Helping Therapies').

It aims among other things to encourage the communication of ideas and information on all aspects of human sexuality and to promote a more effective approach to sex education. The director observes that knowledge of exactly how and when the evolving individual should receive information about sex is largely unknown to those parents, teachers and educational authorities who have responsibility for them.

The Institute has produced a number of explicit sex education films. The films, which are available for purchase or hire, include the following:

Growing Up 16 mm colour (20 minutes).
Understanding Sex slide talk.
Sexual Intercourse 16 mm colour (33 minutes).

For the Institute's films on sex therapy, *see* page 9.

Sex, it is asserted, is essentially a visual subject and the use of film is of the greatest importance in all forms of sex education. Recognising that there are those who question the necessity for using sexually explicit material, it is argued from experience that it serves three purposes:

(a) the provision of honest, scientific information in a straightforward manner;
(b) the reduction of anxiety through enlightenment, as the viewer discovers approval being given to hitherto taboo behaviour (good visual material, it is

said, can help to 'desensitise' the subject to his inhibitions, guilt and blocks in sexual response);

(c) exposure to arousal, whereby the viewer learns or is reminded that sex is not only about hormones and the 'plumbing', but about feelings as well.

Institute of Behaviour Therapy

38 Queen Anne Street, London W1 (Tel: 01-580 4972). The Centre is directed by Dr Robert Sharpe, a consultant behavioural psychologist, and provides courses on tape cassettes, which are aimed at developing 'life skills'. They provide techniques and methods which can be used both to overcome personal problems and to develop personal control and growth. In the area of sexual activity, inter-personal frictions, stress and anxiety are often responsible for unsatisfactory relationships and inadequate performance. Dr Sharpe believes that control techniques, together with mental or verbal strategy building, can transform an individual's behavioural patterns and significantly improve attitudes to sex and to other people.

The cassettes each cost £6, including postage and packing. Of particular interest is the course titled *Don't be Shy!*, which deals with the practical stages of starting and developing relationships. It covers conversational skills, dealing with rejection, entrance and exit skills for joining and leaving groups, choosing the place to meet people and developing deeper levels of intimacy in a relationship.

Dr Sharpe also runs day training courses – mostly in London – on inter-personal effectiveness, the practical skills needed to manage interaction with other people.

The tapes may also be obtained from: Lifeskills, 3 Brighton Road, London N2 8JU (Tel: 01-346 9646).

International Planned Parenthood Federation

Regent's College, Inner Circle, Regent's Park, London NW1 4NS (Tel: 01-486 0741).

Founded in 1952, the IPPF is a world-wide federation of 104 national family planning associations. From its headquarters in London, the IPPF liaises with family planning and health organisations in Europe and North America and provides financial and technical support to programmes in over 80 developing countries. The IPPF has an active library and documentation service (open to the public) and maintains a publication programme. Publications include the following:

Planned Parenthood and Women's Development: Lessons from the Field
Male Involvement in Family Planning
Family Planning Handbook for Midwives and Nurses
Community Participation and Family Planning: Issues and Examples
Family Planning Handbook for Doctors
Family Planning in Five Continents
Human Numbers, Human Needs
Islam and Family Planning
Optimum Conditions for Childbearing
Handbook on Infertility
Details of Sexually Transmitted Diseases
Sexuality and Handicapped People
Sex Education and Adolescence in Europe

All publications are available in English; selected publications are also available in French, Spanish and Arabic. A publication list is available on request.

London Institute for the Study of Human Sexuality

Langham Mansions, Earls Court Square, London SW5 9UH (Tel: 01-373 0901). Directed by Dr Michael Perring.

The Institute is a non-profit-making organisation, dedicated to the further understanding of human sexuality. It has three functions of equal importance:

(a) to provide training for sex therapists and sex educators;
(b) to provide services designed to alleviate sexual problems of all kinds;
(c) to disseminate facts and accepting attitudes about sex to the widest possible public.

The Institute regularly provides training and educational programmes and courses designed to impart knowledge of sex, both inside and outside the context of relationships. As well as catering for professionals (who can gain formal qualifications in sex education and sex therapy), there are group programmes of varying length, designed to deal with interactive problems, to extend education in human sexuality and to give sexual enrichment, both for individuals and couples seeking enhancement of their lives in this area. In carrying out its work, the Institute believes that everyone has an unqualified right to the expression of his or her own sexuality, as long as it is without harm to others.

A typical weekend workshop costs £40.

The National Marriage Guidance Council

Herbert Gray College, Little Church Street, Rugby, Warwickshire CV21 3AP (Tel: Rugby (0788) 73241).

In addition to its counselling work (*see* Chapter 15, 'Marriage Guidance'), the NMGC is involved in a variety of educational projects. Educational workers usually work with small groups of people who are interested in a whole variety of topics, such as growing up, parenthood or other aspects of family life. Workers meet with youngsters in schools and colleges, with parents in prenatal clinics and with special groups, such as prisoners, engaged couples or parents of handicapped children.

However, because of the enormous demand for this kind of work and the comparatively small number of educational workers available to undertake it, the NMGC, in some places, offers training to teachers and others in regular contact with these specialist groups to enable them to undertake this work themselves.

The Council has an excellent bookshop at its Rugby address and offers the valuable facility of a mail order service. Free booklists are available, including *A General List of Recommended Books and Booklets* and *Young People in Relationships*, a special list of recommended reading for counsellors, teachers, youth leaders, health visitors and others concerned with education in personal relationships.

The Scottish Marriage Guidance Council and the *Catholic Marriage Advisory Council* (*see* Chapter 15, 'Marriage Guidance') have similar group project and information facilities.

New Grapevine
416 St John Street, London EC1 4NJ (Tel: 01-278 9147).
The NG offers both individual counselling (*see* Chapter 21, 'Guide to Local Services') and basic sex education sessions in schools, colleges, youth clubs, etc. for young people under 25 in the London boroughs of Camden and Islington. A minimum of three or four sessions is needed to cover anatomy, contraception, sexually transmitted diseases and to build up enough trust with the young people to allow discussion of personal relationships, attitudes and expectations. A fee is charged for educational sessions, except in youth clubs, but this is kept as low as possible.

Redwood Educational Programmes
83 Fordwych Road, London NW2 3TL (Tel: 01-452 9261). Directed by Anne Dickson.
Redwood offers courses designed to promote personal development by improving self-direction and helping people become well-informed in the expression of their sexuality, in personal relationships and in professional and social commitments. The methods used emphasise self-help group co-operation and mutual support.

Courses are available in London, of varying duration, on weekday evenings and weekends. Subjects covered in previous programmes included the following:

Assertiveness Training.
Women's Sexuality.
Sexual and Emotional Competence in Men.
Personal and Relationship Problems in Gay and Bisexual People.
Psychosexual Counselling Skills (for people in the helping professions who wish to be more competent in handling the sexual problems of their clients or patients).
Co-counselling (this is a method of self-help, teaching a variety of techniques. These can be used to unlock and release feelings which, left unexpressed, can undermine our ability to enjoy intimate adult relationships. Co-counselling dispenses with the traditional pattern of the helper and the helped, training people to be both client and counsellor).

In addition to the above courses, the Redwood Women's Training Association offers courses in assertiveness and sexuality for women in various parts of the UK. A list of contacts can be obtained from the above address, as well as details of all the Redwood educational courses.

Scottish Health Education Group
Woodburn House, Canaan Lane, Edinburgh EH10 4SG (Tel: 031-447 8044).
Although independent of the Health Education Authority (*see* page 000), the SHEG fulfils a similar role in Scotland and collaborates with the HEA and FPA in the provision of information. Through involvement in the Family Planning Information Service, it provides a wide range of free leaflets and posters, including a number on family planning, sex education, sexually transmitted diseases and women's health problems. Many of these are notable for their impact, quality and clarity. The leaflet on male and female sterilisation is a model of its kind. The move towards the promotion of positive health is reflected in an excellent booklet entitled *Well Woman*.

SPOD (The Association to Aid the Sexual and Personal Relationships of People with a Disability)
286 Camden Road, London N7 0BJ (Tel: 01-607 8851).
This small, but vigorous, organisation is deeply committed to sex education. Both in scope and quality its literature is very impressive. It has pioneered the cause of handicapped people wishing to be recognised as normally sexual. Disabled youngsters are commonly sheltered from the 'facts of life', both at home and at school, and reach adulthood generally less well-informed than their able-bodied peers. They tend to be isolated and may become unable to relate to others. They are sexual 'outsiders'.

When SPOD was founded in 1972, few disabled people received any form of advice or counselling in sexual matters, although as research soon discovered, their sexual deprivation was widespread and in many cases, acute.

SPOD recognised the urgent need for sex education to be brought to disabled people and for it to be extended to become relevant to their special problems. It established links with counsellors throughout the country to offer advice and support to disabled people as individuals and to set up courses in sex education for teachers and carers of handicapped people. There is a first-rate information service, which includes response to personal enquiries by telephone or letter.

SPOD has also been in the forefront of making available a wide range of specialist literature. This is discussed in Chapter 12, 'Sexuality and Disability'. Resource lists are available of books on sex education for physically handicapped people and of books, booklets, films, filmstrips, audio tapes and charts on sex education for mentally handicapped people. (*See also* the book, *Sex Education for the Physically Handicapped* on page 111.)

Young Peoples Advisory Services

In recent years, caring workers have come to understand that young people require specialist services which are particularly geared to their needs. Drop-in centres in informal settings, with the minimum of fuss and where confidentiality can be guaranteed, provide the sort of surroundings and atmosphere in which young people are likely to feel at home. Ages usually range from about 13 to 25 years.

Such centres emphasise the dignity of the individual and treat their young people as young adults, having the right to services and information which will help them to make their own informed decisions on how to run their own lives. Young people often feel embarrassed about seeking help. Some questions are difficult to ask, especially in sexual matters when there is a risk of being thought 'improper'. There is often a fear of revealing ignorance, of appearing naive, of asking 'silly' questions. Though we are well past our teens, we can clearly remember the striving for an understanding of our sexuality, our only knowledge put together from bits of information and misinformation, mostly from people hardly more knowledgeable than ourselves. Boys have a special problem in trying to aspire to manhood without really knowing what to do. They must take the lead however inexperienced they feel. When boy meets girl, you have two unsure young people trying to cope with their own clumsiness and strength of sexual feelings, while not knowing where to turn for advice. Girls can feel especially vulnerable, wondering whether they should have sex even if they don't feel ready for it, because they believe it is expected of them. It is hard to take contraception seriously when you half believe you shouldn't be having sex anyway. Girls need a lot of help to sort out the practical problems which are all mixed up with conflicting emotions and whirlwind romances.

Young people's centres exist all over the country with staff who are well aware of these difficulties. Many provide counselling help and some will provide a variety of services to help with sexual problems, including family planning advice. Most will make available a range of information.

The NAYPCAS (National Association of Young People's Counselling and Advisory Services), 17–23 Albion Street, Leicester LE1 6GD (Tel: Leicester (0533) 558763), represents the numerous individuals and agencies providing counselling/advisory services for young people and can provide local addresses.

We have listed a few local centres in Chapter 21, 'Guide to Local Services'. Some local family planning clinics also have youth advisory services (*see* page 22). Brook Advisory Centres are primarily intended for young people and provide contraceptive, pregnancy and sexual advice (*see* page 30). If you have any difficulties, the Family Planning Information Service (*see* page 28) will give you details of the nearest service to you to help with contraceptive, pregnancy or sexual problems.

Girls may also find it useful to look at Chapter 8, 'Women Only'.

Selected Further Reading

The written word is a prime source of sexual knowledge and in recent years a number of excellent books have appeared, which are both educative and eminently readable. Some of these, where they relate to particular aspects of sexuality, are reviewed in appropriate chapters; otherwise our selection can be found in Chapter 22, 'Selected Further Reading'. Many of the organisations mentioned in this chapter produce booklists and supply books to mail order.

The following publications and resource lists will be helpful for those who work in the field of sex education and parents.

Aspects of Sexuality and Family Planning edited by John Sketchley. Published by The British Life Assurance Trust for Health Education, BMA House, Tavistock Square, London WC1H 9JP (Tel: 01-388 7976), 1985. This is a series of seven self-instructional modules intended for health professionals. An increasing number of people are presenting with sexual problems of all kinds, and many of those working in the helping professions often feel incapable of giving help, partly because they do not have the necessary information and skills, but sometimes because they are affected, like their clients, by taboos and constraints. These materials take a profound look at the attitude of the helpers, which often impede the ability to help.

Books with Care. Available from the NMGC Book Department, Herbert Gray College, Little Church Street, Rugby, Warwickshire CV21 3AP.

A National Marriage Guidance Council list of recommended reading for counsellors, teachers, youth leaders, health visitors and others concerned with education in personal relationships.

Health Education Index. Published by B. Edsall & Co. Ltd (Cambridge House, 373-375 Euston Road, London NW1 3AR (Tel: 01-388 3171). The 1987/8 edition costs £40.

A comprehensive resource list of all health education material throughout the UK. The Index contains sections on sex education, marriage, menstruation, contraception, family planning, birth control, homosexuality, venereal disease and sterility.

Health, Hygiene and Sex Education for Mentally Handicapped Children, Adolescents and Adults by Ann Craft, 1987. Available from the HEA, 78 New Oxford Street, London WC1A 1AH.

A review of audio-visual resources compiled for the Health Education Authority (*see* page 106) by Ann Craft. The material has been selected to provide theoretical background and 'revision' for parents and professionals, to indicate what might be used with a mentally handicapped audience and to suggest further publications of interest to the reader who wishes to pursue the whole subject in more depth. The resources listed include books, films, filmstrips, video-tapes, leaflets, wallcharts and articles.

Human Sexuality. Produced as part of the University of Sheffield Library's Biomedical Information Service, Sheffield S10 2TN (Tel: Sheffield (0742) 78555 Ext 6232).

Annual subscription (January to December) is £30. Back issues are available for the previous year.

A monthly bulletin of new books and articles on all aspects of human sexuality.

My Mother Said . . . The Way Young People Learned about Sex and Birth Control by Christine Farrell, in collaboration with Leonie Kellaher. Published by Routledge & Kegan Paul, 1978. Price £10.95.

Based on over 1,500 interviews with a national random sample of 16- to 19-year-olds, this book examines the sources of information encountered by young people during their early years which helped or hindered them in their acquisition of knowledge about sex and birth control.

The study explores teenage patterns of sexual behaviour and contraceptive practice and looks at the way in which learning and sexual behaviour are related. Interviews were also conducted with over 300 parents of the teenagers, their attitudes to and experiences of the provision of sex-related information being discussed and described in detail. The authors' findings suggest that although sex education from parents and in schools has improved over the past ten years, there is still considerable room for changes in attitude and education.

The Ostrich Position – Sex, Schooling and Mystification by Carol Lee. Published by Unwin Paperbacks, 1986 (first published 1983). Price £2.95.

By reputation, the ostrich buries its head in the sand. That, Carol Lee finds, is all too often the attitude adopted by parents, teachers, doctors and politicians towards sex education. Yet, as she reminds us, sex is 'one of the most intimate ways for showing affection for one another as well as the way we procreate.' Therefore, if we intend to equip young people for adulthood, 'educating them about sex is vital.' Without denying the family a role in this process, Carol Lee points out that one of the many reasons why parents are not normally allowed to keep children away from school and to educate them themselves is that many parents would not bother to educate, others would not have the necessary skills and knowledge and others would give dangerously biased information. Often it would be – indeed it is – a case of the blind leading the blind.

Miss Lee, herself an experienced sex educator, firmly believes that sex education must not only give information and increase understanding, but also promote responsible behaviour, combat exploitation, cultivate the ability to make informed decisions and develop educational skills for future parents and child carers. But you have to begin where children are and use appropriate language. Teenagers, in particular, and despite appearances to the contrary, often display a 'pathetic ignorance'. Carol Lee explains, from her own experience, the strategies by which young people can be encouraged to reach decisions from a position of intelligence, rather than ignorance, as well as describing the things – and the negative moral attitudes – which get in the way. Again and again she hits the nail on the head, as when she tells us, 'My own criticism of Soho is not that it is an area of heaving sexuality, but that it is not.'

Enlightenment and understanding are the antidotes to prejudice and fear, and this book will go a long way to taking the blinkers off (and the sand out of) the eyes of open minded people. Motes may take a little longer, but Miss Lee takes us irresistibly forward. She concludes

> 'At the moment, fulfilling relationships are lost to thousands of young people through lack of example and through their failure to express themselves. Rather than shying away from our responsibilities to educate as fully as possible – to educate

for life and living – I think we should be moving firmly and rapidly towards them.'

Sex Education for Mentally Handicapped People – a Teaching Aid for Parents and Teachers by Mary Davies, illustrated by Mick Devine. Produced by and available from SPOD (286 Camden Road, London N7 0BJ, Tel: 01-607 8851). Price £10.
Mentally handicapped people are often treated as 'Peter Pans' – children who never grow up. However, they do grow up and develop physically into men and women; the women have to cope with menstruation and the men with erection and wet dreams. Their life-style can be improved if they are to take responsibility for their behaviour, including their sexual behaviour.

A programme of sex education can bring considerable benefits to mentally handicapped people. Fear and anxiety can be reduced when they know that menstruation and wet dreams are normal body functions. Acceptable social behaviour is important if they are to be a part of our society. This is particularly important as far as sexual behaviour is concerned and mentally handicapped people can be taught that normal expressions of sexual feelings, including masturbation, are only acceptable in private.

Mentally handicapped people are vulnerable to sexual exploitation. This risk can be minimised by information and training, for example, on how to respond to strangers.

The teaching pack consists of a set of visual aids on plastic laminated cards. These are clear and explicit and are accompanied by a booklet of notes and suggestions on how to use the visual aids.

Sex Education for the Physically Handicapped. Produced by and available from The Disabilities Study Unit, 'Wildhanger', Amberley, Arundel, West Sussex BN18 9NR. Price £3.50, including UK postage.
This is the report of an important survey of the sex education currently provided for physically handicapped children in England and Wales, carried out by W.F.R. Stewart, a leading expert on the sexuality of disabled people.

It establishes that deficiencies in sex education for handicapped young people currently result in a level of sexual knowledge which is generally far below that of their able-bodied peers, with ideas about sex and sexual relationships which can be dangerously naïve. It claims that disabled children need to be taught all that other children are taught, with additional advice as to the likely effect of disability upon their own sexual function and relationships.

Sex Education in Perspective. Available from the NMGC Book Department, Herbert Gray College, Little Church Street, Rugby, Warwickshire CV21 3AP. Price £1.25 (paperback).
A symposium of current work which is 'invaluable to teachers and counsellors.' (The NMGC).

Sex Education – Some Guidelines for Teachers by Dilys Went. Published by Bell & Hyman, 37–39 Queen Elizabeth Street, London SE1 2QB, 1985. Price £6.95 (paperback), £12.95 (hardback).
This book gives the background to the development of sex education, and the rationale behind it, outlines the many factors involved, and gives suggestions for possible approaches to each age level, from pre-school children to adolescents.

Sex Education for Young Disabled People by Mary Davies. Available from SPOD, 286 Camden Road, London N7 0BJ (Tel: 01-607 8851/2). Price £1.25.
Outlines why young people with a physical disability have a particular need for sex education. Considers what sex education is appropriate, and the role of the professional worker.

Taught Not Caught – Strategies for Sex Education by The Clarity Collective (Helen Myles, Wendy Gale, Tricia Szirom, Deborah Davison and Sue Dyson). British edition edited by Hilary Dixon and Gill Mullinar. Published by Learning Development Aids, 32 Bridge Street, Cambridge CB2 1UJ, Tel: Cambridge (0223) 65445. Price £9.95 plus 99p postage and packing.
First published in Australia, this book offers a range of practical teaching strategies accompanied by step-by-step instructions. It examines values and attitudes to sex, exploring areas such as communication, roles and relationships, sexual decision making, self-esteem and body image. It also provides relevant information on puberty, menstruation, contraception and sterilisation, pregnancy, birth and bonding, and sexually transmitted diseases. There is a valuable final section devoted to resources – books, films, videos and other teaching materials, with names and addresses of useful agencies and groups concerned with sex education.

CHAPTER 14

Finding a Mate – or a Date

Many of us at some time in our lives may be without, but wanting, a partner, yet unable for one reason or another to find one. We may be lonely, yet too shy to make contact in a natural way. Perhaps we find ourselves somehow out of the social swim, a 'non-runner' in the mating game. Or perhaps we simply want a change or to enlarge our circle of friends. It isn't an unusual situation. There are thousands of others similarly placed and the trick is to find one of them who is right for you.

Bureaux

One possibility is to use a commercial service – either a marriage bureau if you are absolutely certain you want to marry or a dating and introduction agency if you just want a friend, perhaps with marriage as a possibility, but not as a goal.

Here we must strike a note of caution. Marriage bureaux and dating agencies have been the subject of two searching studies by the Office of Fair Trading in 1977 and 1981. These showed clearly that unrealistic expectations were raised by many bureaux in their advertisements and publicity, and that there has been widespread concern, both as to the number and suitability of introductions provided. A 40-year-old divorcee told the OFT that she paid £99 to an apparently reputable bureau and was assured, after an interview, that there were many suitable men in the bureau's membership to whom she would be introduced. After nine months, having received only two introductions, she asked for a refund. In the absence of any reply, she continued to write. Eventually, six months after her original complaint, the bureau answered, claiming that it had fulfilled entirely its side of the bargain.

In another case, a Lancashire widower in his fifties hoped that a marriage bureau could help him find a wife to save him from loneliness. The bureau said that they had a number of suitable ladies looking for someone in his position and that there should be no problem. After six months, he had been given only one contact and she did not reply to his letter. The experience made him feel more lonely than ever, and also cheated, in view of the confident terms in which the bureau advertised and the promise that was made to him when he joined.

There were further complaints of poor service, of supplying names of contacts who could not be traced or who had already asked to be taken off the bureau's lists, of mismatching and of offering contacts in the wrong areas.

In July 1981, the Director General of Fair Trading urged the setting-up of a trade association and offered guidelines for a code of good practice. In response, a number of bureaux have formed the Association of British Introduction Agencies, based at 29 Manchester Street, London W1. Membership is governed by an agreement to adhere to a code of practice, based on the principles suggested by the OFT. The main purpose of the code is to safeguard customers from exploitation and to outlaw the practice (at least among Association members) of raising false hopes. It is essentially dishonest to take a client's money unless there is a realistic prospect of finding a partner from a reasonable selection of potentially suitable people. Older women, in particular, may have to be told that their position is likely to be 'difficult', given that there are approximately six times as many single women over 55 as there are men, and that those men who do remain often want younger women. Any client is entitled to be fully informed about how an agency operates before agreeing to go on its books – to know, for instance, the duration of membership covered by the fee and roughly how many introductions can be anticipated.

A list of Association members appears on page 114. Perhaps the best known and the biggest is Dateline, famous for its specialised matching techniques and computer searching. Dateline was in the forefront of the moves to establish the ABIA.

It does not follow, of course, that non-members of the

Association are necessarily disreputable and we would certainly not wish to imply that this is the case! Bureaux vary widely, ranging from one-person businesses with no more than a few dozen clients to those relatively few bureaux with membership numbered in thousands. Some are locally based and attract their clientele from small-ads in the local press. Others offer a nationwide service advertised in national newspapers and magazines. Some cater solely for particular religious or ethnic groups or for people of a distinct kind, such as single parents or upper-middle-class professionals. While the agency best suited to your needs will depend on what those needs are, there are some general guidelines which are largely a matter of common sense. It is very important to consider whether the agency has the facilities to give you the best and most appropriate service and chance of success. The size of its membership is very important; only a company with a large number of members can hope to provide you with a reasonable choice of partners. You should also consider the quality and integrity of the company offering the service. How long has it been established, will it respect your privacy and provide value for money? If you can, it is a good idea to visit the agency. Dingy rooms up the backstairs do not inspire confidence. You need to be careful before you commit yourself.

Be Honest

Whatever your reason for seeking a partner, it is important that you, as a client, should try to be honest when giving details about yourself. You should be clear about the kind of partner you are seeking and straightforward about whether you are looking for marriage or a long-term or short-term relationship. This will influence both the kind of agency appropriate to your needs and your chances of finding a suitable match. Compatibility is not necessarily a simple matter of two people having similar interests and characteristics; for many couples it is more important that their needs and interests complement each other's. It can be a mistake to set out to look for an 'ideal partner', as one whose interests and personality are a carbon copy of your own. Rather, it is important to consider and to outline your 'requirements' in terms of the kind of person you like to be with, identifying a potential partner in reasonably broad terms and in the light of the kind of relationship you are seeking. It calls for a positive rather than a negative approach. If selection within a small geographical area is based largely on excluding people for various reasons, the chances of finding a partner are likely to be decidedly limited, particularly for those who are no longer young.

Self-selection

A number of agencies do little more than circulate lists of their members, with sparse self-supplied details, and leave you to make your own selection. There is, naturally, an excitement in putting forward your name and particulars and awaiting results, but you do have to be prepared for some unwelcome responses. Another disadvantage of this system is that the lists will cover a wide spread of ages and locations, so that finding someone potentially suitable may be a laborious process. Unless the lists are regularly updated and contain sufficient numbers of people of the right sex and age within your own area, your search may well be unproductive. The whole process can tend to the superficial. One advertisement before us offers 'instant' friendship/marriage lists and extends the invitation, 'meet your ideal partner NOW, through these delightful lists'. Clients are asked to provide 'brief details' about themselves. Well, you could be lucky!

One organisation using this method is worthy of special mention. This is the Outsiders Club, PO Box 4ZB, London W1A 4ZB (Tel: 01-741 3332). Its fees are exceptionally modest and it invites into membership those who feel themselves to be socially isolated, particularly handicapped people. From time to time, some of the members may find marriage partners within the club, but the real objective is rather that members should help and encourage each other to express themselves sexually and to find loving relationships. Regular lunches and social events are arranged. Outsiders may well also be able to suggest other agencies that you can try. (For further details *see* Chapter 12).

Small-ads

Unlikely as it may seem, seeking a partner through the small-ads can sometimes be very successful. There are literally thousands of lonely people in similar need who read newspapers and magazines. The wording of the advertisement is all important. It must appeal to the kind of person you are looking for. The Outsiders Club recommends that someone else writes the advertisement, preferably someone who is of the same sex as the person you are looking for. If you have any significant handicaps it is best that they are candidly stated – and remember that giving the area in which you live is almost as important as indicating your sex! There is merit in frankness. Even if it puts some people off, you will have cleared the ground for those who do reply.

Of course, contact advertising is not without its dangers. Whereas the partners suggested by a commercial agency will at least be people who have gone so far as to pay fees and who are thus likely to be of serious intent, classified advertisements are open to all and sundry: Tom, Dick and dirty-Harry. You may get responses you would rather be without and for obvious reasons it is best always to use a box number. There is some risk of exploitation too, particularly of older women.

There are also pitfalls for those who respond to contact ads. Quite a number of them are inserted by agencies as a 'come-on', some are bogus and others, in a certain kind of magazine, are thinly veiled offers of 'professional' services. If you want to play it as safely as possible, choose a magazine or journal of some repute. You may like to try a specialist publication like Singles (Singles Scene Ltd, 23 Abingdon Road, London W8), in which the charge at the time of writing is £12 for 20 words, plus 40p for each extra word (box number a further £1). It may be worth while using a special interest magazine in the hope of catching the eye of someone with broadly similar interests to your own. Older people might find it advantageous to advertise in a journal catering for their own age group. The readership may be relatively small, but it is more likely to be relevant to your needs.

In Conclusion

Our last word must be a warning against expecting too much from agencies and advertising. There are bound to be disappointments when a meeting is contrived with the sole purpose of striking up a relationship between strangers, both under some stress. We believe that, wherever possible, it is still preferable to meet other 'available' people through activities such as sport, further education, dancing, special interest classes and so on. All that may be needed is that you acquire some social skills, make yourself more attractive and be bolder and more positive in 'breaking the ice'. If a personality or sexual problem is standing in your way, we mention in other parts of this book organisations, courses, counsellors and therapists who may be able to help you. A friendship which starts naturally and casually out of some common interest can develop easily if there is a good match. Don't be too intense. It's a good idea to practice having 'dates', gaining confidence and finding out from experience who is really right for you.

List of Members of The Association of British Introduction Agencies

The Association of British Introduction Agencies
29 Manchester Street, London W1.
According to the Association, its purpose is to disseminate information about its members to the public and to assist the consumer with any problems he or she may experience with a member company. It must be stressed, however, that any problems a consumer may have with a member agency must first be brought to the attention of that member agency. The Association offers to deal with queries from members of the public, but asks that an SAE should be enclosed.
Note: all members of ABIA introduce men to women, and vice versa, for the purposes of marriage and/or friendship. The ways in which they achieve this are indicated after the name below as follows:

1. Personal introductions effected by either the Principal or member(s) of staff;
2. Computer comparison of clients;
3. Lists (*see* page 113)

ENGLAND

AVON

Paulton
Janus Introduction Bureau (1)
Crossways, Bath Road, Paulton.
Services offered: Unlimited number of introductions with quoted minimum numbers. Special facilities for expatriate British nationals.
Areas covered: National.
Age range: Adults only.
Fees: Standard register £40/£55; executive register £50/£70.
Length of membership: 6 or 12 months.

BEDFORDSHIRE

Bedford
Disdate (1)
56 Devizes Avenue, Bedford (Tel: Bedford (0234) 40643).
Services offered: Caters for disabled people. Will write to clients if they are in need. Three names and addresses guaranteed, more if required.
Areas covered: Nationwide.
Age range: 18 years plus.
Fees: £12.
Length of membership: unlimited.

Henlow
Choose Partners (1)
The Maltings, Henlow, Bedfordshire (Tel: Hitchin (0462) 815801).
Services offered: Unlimited introductions, subject to suitability. Introductions mainly by telephone.

Areas covered: Bedfordshire/ Hertfordshire/ Buckinghamshire/ Northamptonshire.
Age range: 18 to 55 years.
Fees: £50 (with reductions for young women and older men).
Length of membership: one year.

CHESHIRE

Chester
The Friendship Bureau (1 and 3)
Chester (0244) 679188.
Areas covered: Cheshire, Merseyside, South Lancashire, Staffordshire, North and Mid Wales, Shropshire.
Age range: 18 to 75 years.
Fees: Service A (personal introductions) £38; service B (lists) £25.
Length of membership: one year.

Knutsford
Janus Introduction Bureau (1)
8 Gaskell Avenue, Knutsford, Cheshire WA16 0DA (Tel: Knutsford (0565) 52516.
Services offered: Unlimited number of introductions with quoted minimum numbers. Special facilities for expatriate British nationals.
Areas covered: National.
Age range: Adults only.
Fees: Standard register £40/55; executive register £50/70.
Length of membership: 6 or 12 months.

CLEVELAND

Middlesbrough
Kate's Intro Bureau (1)
304 Linthorpe Road, Middlesbrough TS1 3QX (Tel: Middlesbrough (0642) 240249).
Services offered: Unlimited introductions (five initially).
Areas covered: North of England.
Age range: 18 to 70 years.
Fees: £45.
Length of membership: one year.

DEVON

Plymouth
Cheek to Cheek Introduction Consultants (3)
8 Masefield Gardens, Honicknowle, Plymouth PL5 3HU (Tel: Plymouth (0752) 707947).
Services offered: Personal contact and assistance maintained throughout enrolment. Professional/business register at no additional charge.
Areas covered: Devon and Cornwall.
Age range: 18 to 75 years.
Fees: Standard service £32; combined service £42; special service £62.50 (substantial discount for women 18 to 29 years and men 50 plus).
Length of membership: one year.

The Friendship Bureau (1 & 3)
163 Citadel Road, The Hoe, Plymouth PL1 2HU (Tel: Plymouth (0752) 672171 or Taunton (0823) 77809). Also in Chester.
Areas covered: Devon, Cornwall, Somerset and West Dorset.
Age range: 18 to 75 years.
Fees: Service A (personal introductions) £38; Service B (listing service) £25.
Length of membership: one year.

ESSEX

See also Greater London (Havering).

Colchester
Kathleen Kent Bureau (1, 2 & 3)
11a Eld Lane, Colchester (Tel: Colchester (0206) 67111).
Services offered: Unlimited introductions; everyone interviewed by Principal.
Area covered: Greater East Anglia.
Age range: 18 to 80 years.
Fees: £75 for full service; £45 for limited introduction service; £20 for self-selection service.
Length of membership: one year.

GREATER LONDON

Bromley
Caroline James Introductions (1)
9 Broadlands Road, Bromley, Kent BR1 5DE (Tel: 01-851 7758).
Service offered: All applicants interviewed. Personal contact maintained throughout membership period.
Areas covered: South London and North Kent.
Age range: 18 to 60 years.
Fees: £55.
Length of membership: one year.

Camden
Hedi Fisher Marriage and Friendship Consultants (1)
45 – 46 Chalk Farm Road, London NW1 (Tel: 01-267 6066 or 01- 485 2916).
Services offered: 40 per cent of clients are Jewish.
Areas covered: All UK and international.
Age range: 18 to 80 years.

Fees: UK clients £75 plus £10 for personal interview; overseas clients between £80 and £150.
Length of membership: one year.

Ealing
Suman Marriage Bureau (1)
83 South Road, Southall, Middlesex UB1 1SQ (Tel: 01-574 4867 or 01-571 5145 (day), 01-579 2732 (evenings Monday to Friday)).
Services offered: Asian introductions, but also Europeans/Asians and vice versa; unlimited introductions.
Areas covered: UK and overseas.
Fees: UK residents £75; overseas and visitors £85; marriage settlement fee £95.
Length of membership: one year.

Havering
Advance Introduction Services (1)
139 Hornchurch Road, Hornchurch, Essex (Tel: Hornchurch (040 24) 71721/2 and 52396/7/8).
Areas covered: East London, all of Essex, some central London.
Age range: 18 to 70 years.
Fees: women under 25 years £22.75; women over 25 £27.75; all men £29.75; £10 refund if no one introduced within first six months.
Length of membership: one year.

Kensington and Chelsea
Dateline International Limited (2)
23 Abingdon Road, London W8 6AH (Tel: 01-938 1011).
Services offered: Unlimited introductions (up to six names on each computer run, with subsequent re-runs costing £2 each).
Areas covered: Nationwide.
Age range: 18 to 70 years.
Fees: £75.
Length of membership: one year.

Westminster
Select Friends (1)
58 Maddox Street, London W1R 9PA (Tel: 01-493 9937).
Services offered: Register aimed at professional/executive market. Guaranteed minimum of five introductions. Principal offers personal consultation throughout membership.
Areas covered: London and home counties.
Age range: 18 to 70 years.
Fees: £50 for initial interview and compilation of personal profile. £100 membership.
Length of membership: one year.

GREATER MANCHESTER

Manchester
Needa Frend (3)
4 St Ann's Square, Manchester M2 7HF (Tel: 061-834 5482).
Areas covered: North-west England (Lancashire, Cheshire and Derbyshire).
Age range: 18 years upwards.
Fees: Service A £28; service B £36.00; professional and executive register £56.
Length of membership: life.

HAMPSHIRE

Fareham
Dream Friendship Agency (1)
14 Chantrell Walk, Fareham (Tel: Fareham (0329) 239810).
Services offered: social events organised.
Areas covered: South of England.
Age range: 18 years upwards.
Fees: standard service £35 plus VAT; professional register £55 plus VAT.
Length of membership: one year.

HUMBERSIDE

Grimsby
Orion Introductions (1)
4 Rosedale, Waltham, Grimsby DN37 0UJ (Tel: Grimsby (0472) 824085).
Areas covered: All UK, but mainly England.
Age range: 16 to 80 years.
Fees: Service A (two year's enrolment, unlimited introductions) £58; service B (one year's enrolment, unlimited introductions) £40; service C (one year's enrolment, one introduction) £28 plus £4.50 for each subsequent introduction.
Length of membership: as above.

Hull
Humberside Friendship/Marriage Bureau (1)
Princes Dock Office, Princes Dock Side, Hull HU1 2LF (Tel: Kingston-upon-Hull (0482) 223000).
Areas covered: Humberside (outer limits: Lincoln, York, Scarborough).
Age range: 24 to 75 years.
Fees: £35 for one year's membership; £50 for two year's membership; £20 combined fee on marriage.
Length of membership: as above.

Margaret Moody Bureau (1)
40 Canada Drive, Cottingham, nr. Hull HU16 5EJ, (Tel: Kingston-upon-Hull (0482) 840539).
Services offered: Unlimited introductions.
Areas covered: Yorkshire and countrywide.
Age range: 20 to 75 years.
Fees: £36.
Length of membership: one year.

KENT

See Greater London (under Bromley).

MIDDLESEX

See Greater London (under Ealing).

NORFOLK

Norwich Partners and Company (1)
The Glass House, 9-13 Wensum Street, Norwich NR3 1LA (Tel: Norwich (0603) 615200 ext. 238)
Services offered: Initial consultation (compulsory); socials as an optional extra; seminars on 'single' life as an optional extra.
Areas covered: East Anglia.
Age range: 18 years upwards.
Fees: £55.
Length of membership: one year.

NORTH YORKSHIRE

York
White Rose Agency (1)
10 Sycamore Terrace, Bootham, York YO3 7DN (Tel: York (0904) 22696).
Services offered: First two introductions on receipt of fee; further introductions on request.
Areas covered: mainly Yorkshire.
Age range: 18 to 75 years.
Fees: £30.
Length of membership: one year.

SUFFOLK

Beccles
Anglia Friendship Bureau (3)
The Cottage, Smallgate, Beccles (Tel: Beccles (0502) 715374).
Areas covered: Nationwide, with particular emphasis on East Anglia and surrounding area.
Age range: 18 to 70 years.
Fees: £42, which covers a list of four to five possible introductions and personal box number. Further introductions on request, with fee to cover administration (at present £2).
Length of membership: one year.

SUSSEX

Brighton
Jane Scott (3)
3 North Street Quadrant, Brighton BN1 3GJ (Tel: Brighton (0273) 26610).
Area covered: Nationwide.
Age range: 16 to 80 years
Fees: Male, £21.50 – £24.50. Female, £17.50 – £19.50, after six months further listings at nominal cost.
Length of membership: four to six months.

WEST YORKSHIRE

Halifax
Brontë Consultants (1)
25 Bradshaw Lane, Bradshaw, Halifax HX2 9XB (Tel: Halifax (0422) 240580).
Services offered: Depending on applicant's requirements, a minimum of two introductions per month.
Areas covered: Yorkshire only.
Age range: 18 years upwards.
Fees: enrolment fee £12, three months' subscription £15, six months £18, one year £25.
Length of membership: as above.

YORKSHIRE

See North Yorkshire and West Yorkshire.

SCOTLAND

GRAMPIAN

Aberdeen
Data-Link (Scotland) Ltd (2)
35a Union Street, Aberdeen AB1 2BN (Tel: Aberdeen (0224) 580287, Edinburgh 031-557 2586, Glasgow 041-332 3016).
Area covered: Scotland.
Age range: 17 to 70 years.
Fees: £54 – £60 plus VAT for up to four introductions, then £2 for further computer runs.
Length of membership: one year.

CHAPTER 15

Marriage Guidance

Much misunderstanding, pain and despair stem from the fact that we tend to see our sexual problems and those of a partner in intensely personal terms, attaching guilt, shame and resentment when, in reality, our difficulties are commonplace and mostly not in the least worthy of blame. On the one hand, we are constrained by acquired inhibitions and on the other, we judge ourselves, our partner and our performance against a largely fictional ideal, rather than in the light of reality. Many of our sexual scars are self-inflicted. A counsellor can help to bring a truer insight and perspective.

The trouble with marriage guidance is that people, on the whole, seek it only as a last resort, when their difficulties seem overwhelming. By then, functional problems may have become deep-rooted and discords in the relationship hardened, polarised and locked. The task of the counsellor is far more difficult if help is not sought early. Guidance is something better taken before you start out and as you progress, rather than when you are completely lost.

Not all marriage guidance counsellors are trained as sex therapists, but comparatively few people need intensive sexual therapy anyway. All National Marriage Guidance Council (NMGC) counsellors, however, are trained to offer help with the sexual problems which present as part of relationship difficulties. If they do think that more extensive and specialist help is needed, they will refer these clients to the nearest marriage guidance sex therapist working in a local Marriage Guidance Council.

Some Causes of Marital Problems

Problems often arise from marrying young. Statistically, the chances of a young bride being divorced are twice as great as for others. Divorce rates are about twice as high for girls who married before their twentieth birthday as for those aged 20 to 24 at marriage. Very often if a girl marries young, she is very much the junior member of the partnership and the man will make the major decisions. He may, for example, dictate where they live because of his job, and how the house is run. The woman, therefore, is not negotiating on the sort of terms which are going to give her a happy and fulfilled marriage. Later on, perhaps, as she matures and grows up within her own setting, she may come to dislike and resent this system, but by this time it has become a regime and negotiation is virtually impossible. She is living in the shadow of her husband's life and not enjoying it.

It is commonly the same story in bed. The man may have been encouraged to think that he is entitled by marriage to use her for his own ends and because his needs are more obvious this is what happens; he fails to realise the pleasure to be gained from working together with his partner to mutual satisfaction. Neither partner understands all the various ways of making love and in a very short time the situation becomes stereotyped and boring.

This fairly typical pattern of male domination isn't necessarily the man's fault. He has been taught all his life that he is going to have to look after a family, to 'take charge', to 'be the head of the household'; the same order tends to apply in sexual matters, because in the first instance a man has to be more positive: he has a course of action which starts with getting an erection. Women often don't at first realise that they can play a more positive role and he therefore takes the lead and takes charge of her sexually. This can leave her feeling inadequate, so that she becomes a passive object, a status which sooner or later she comes to resent. She may find ways to repel her partner's advances, so that now he too becomes resentful and the symptoms of estrangement set in. Either partner, or both, may look for 'consolation' elsewhere. Negotiation and communication, if they were ever satisfactory, now dry up completely and the marriage drifts inexorably towards the rocks.

Some people marry without any period of living

together and therefore without any depth of experience of interaction under testing conditions. They fail to negotiate their respective needs and limitations and come together as man and wife with expectations rather than genuine insight. What they expect often falls short of what they get and disillusionment replaces euphoria.

Some people marry from a vague social pressure that it is the 'thing to do', rather than from inner conviction. They settle on a partner as a means to an end, often on the basis of a superficial attraction; if they foresee any relationship difficulties at all, they imagine that they will be able to mould their partner to their wishes and iron out any differences. In practice, this doesn't happen. Discord tends to become more rather than less profound and this is quickly followed by disappointment and loss of regard. Their assumptions about how they should live turn out to be contradictory and they can soon find themselves either heading in opposite directions or in a way which suits one partner and not the other. Nowadays, these problems of incompatability are heightened by the fact that women's aspirations and expectations of marriage are generally much greater than they used to be. All too often they find that in reality marriage is a hindrance rather than a help to their self-fulfilment.

Another common problem is that women, especially those who have had a repressed upbringing, may think that sex is really not very ladylike, but must be tolerated for the sake of their husbands. They put up with it, just about, but certainly don't want to learn more about it – it could become nasty, dirty, disgusting. Sometimes women will find reasons for rejecting every possible form of contraception; the fact of the matter is that they don't want sexual intercourse at all and they don't want the sort of help which would seek to make them more receptive. If they must live with their husbands, they would prefer to do so at arms' length.

Conversely, a sexually active woman may find that her partner is disinterested or impotent or both, or has withdrawn his love after a breakdown in the relationship. She wants a loving relationship, but is frustrated. She gives vent to petulance or may belittle her partner. The rift is aggrevated and there is a spiral of disharmony.

There are, of course, many other ways in which a relationship may break down and not all of them are sexual in origin. If the problems are long-standing, estrangement and bitterness may be so strong and the imbalance between the partners so great, that one or both does not have the will to find a solution. There are very real difficulties in helping married couples in such circumstances – in the simplest terms, what he wants may not be what she wants or *vice versa*. There are limitations as to what is acceptable to one partner or the other and there are relationship patterns and barriers which have become firmly established. Real sexual growth, which may be needed to overcome a functional problem, is inhibited by the well-established boundaries, habits and strategies of the relationship. Thus, for example, if there is a problem of premature ejaculation which has persisted for a long time and the woman has consistently failed to reach orgasm, she is likely to feel such resentment that she won't have the patience, concern or clinical interest to help. Dealing with this kind of intransigence and shifting the balance permanently, where one partner is seeking help, while the other is simply not interested, can be very difficult.

This does not mean that nothing can be done. Marriage guidance is not synonymous with sex therapy. Many marriages can survive and be rescued, in spite of sexual problems. A survival plan can sometimes be drawn up which leaves the sexual difficulties unresolved. Wise counselling may help an individual to overcome those problems which can be overcome and to be more reconciled to those that can't, so that the relationship is somewhat improved. Sometimes, even a bad relationship is worth preserving in preference, say, to breaking up a home or facing years of loneliness. Some people, having been helped to evaluate their position and weighing up the depth of their unhappiness, may yet prefer to 'soldier on'. Or, they may come to terms with the fact that the relationship is dead and that separation or divorce is the best course. Even in this situation, couples can be helped to avoid the long-drawn-out bitterness that so many suffer and which can cause such pain to their children. There are no circumstances so dire that sensitive marriage guidance cannot be of positive benefit. It can reveal how and why the relationship has gone wrong and show that it is not simply a matter of personal inadequacy (as many people think). It can propose ways in which the situation might be improved, if not solved. It can lead on to more specialist help, including sex therapy. And, having appraised the status of the relationship and the nature of the problems, it can present and develop alternative strategies for the future. A counsellor would not wish to impose decisions on the best way forward, but can certainly chart the course.

A final word of caution, however. Such is the current rate of marital breakdown that in many places marriage guidance organisations are working under great pressure. There is often a waiting list, which in an emergency situation can be very disturbing. May we, therefore, once again recommend that help is sought sooner rather than later and well before problems have deteriorated to the point of crisis. Various options are discussed in Chapter 1, 'The Helping Therapies'. Women, including those who suffer assault from their partner, may find appropriate help from one of the organisations described in Chapter 8, 'Women Only' or Chapter 9, 'Sexual Abuse'.

Where to Go for Help

Marriage Guidance Services

The National Marriage Guidance Council (NMGC)
Herbert Gray College, Little Church Street, Rugby, Warwickshire CV21 3AP (Tel: Rugby (0788) 7321).
The first thing to be said about the NMGC is that, despite its title, its services are available to all, of any age, of either sex, in any circumstances, who are worried about personal relationships, regardless of whether they are married or not. It can be a couple or a man and woman alone. The Council urges that it is never too soon to seek help; as we have pointed out in our preamble, problems can fester and grow if they are not tackled.

NMGC counsellors are carefully selected and trained. They are equipped to deal with all kinds of emotional problems and will not take a 'moral' or judgemental stance. They will, however, have their own ethical and moral views and will not assent to attitudes or behaviour which exploits or damages another person. They will certainly believe that committed relationships are of fundamental social and psychological importance and as they explore with clients the consequences of their choices, they will be aiming, wherever possible, to strengthen those relationships.

Counselling normally takes place in the NMGC premises and not at home. Sessions are usually arranged weekly to last for an hour, free from interruption, for as long as is necessary for clients to talk through their problems. The NMGC approach is to 'help people work out their own solutions' by creating an atmosphere in which clients can come to share their troubles and anxieties and helping them 'to listen to themselves'. Counsellors will, of course, vary in their exact approach and the intensity at which they work, but they will seek to guide and not to recommend solutions or impose remedies. There can be a problem here, because people in distress find it difficult to think straight and if their difficulties are long-standing, they will have mentally gone over the ground again and again. At first, at least, clients may need to be 'guided' in a fairly positive way. Of course, if the problem is a straightforward or practical one, a counsellor can offer advice and give information. Inter-personal relationships are complex and highly individual; their exploration can be painful and stressful, but little by little and with expert help, clients can come to see their situation more clearly, to recognise the underlying causes of conflict and, hopefully, to consider the potential for future action.

If there is a sexual problem, as distinct from purely a relationship problem, it may be appropriate, with the client's agreement, to seek the help of one of the NMGCs Sexual Therapy Clinics (*see* page 5). Here, specially trained counsellors can attempt to find a solution to functional difficulties, using techniques similar to those pioneered by Masters and Johnson in the United States (*see* page 7). If necessary, counsellors have access to other kinds of specialist help, should they and their clients decide that it is necessary.

There is no obligatory charge for counselling help, but naturally the NMGC, as a voluntary organisation, hopes that clients will contribute to the cost of the work and this is something the counsellor will discuss with you.

The NMGC operates in England, Wales and Northern Ireland. It is independent and is not attached to any sectarian, denominational or cultural institution. There are now over 500 counselling centres throughout the country, with a total complement of more than 1,900 counsellors.

To make an appointment, telephone, write or call in to your local MGC. Telephone numbers and addresses for MGCs are listed in the following pages (for Scottish Marriage Guidance Councils *see* page 128).

Marriage Guidance Councils (except Scotland)
Some appointment centres are only open part time. If you have difficulty contacting a local MGC, try the local telephone directory or the headquarters.

ENGLAND

AVON

Bath
3rd floor, 14 New Bond Street, Bath BA1 1BE (Tel: Bath (0225) 65593).

Bristol
19–21 Merchant Street, Bristol BS1 3EH (Tel: Bristol (0272) 214248).

North Avon Centre, South View Farm, Latteridge, Iron Acton, Bristol.

Weston-super-Mare
Roselawn, Walliscote, Grove Road, Weston-super-Mare BS23 1UT (Tel: Weston-super-Mare (0934) 27206).

BEDFORDSHIRE

Bedford
6 St Paul's Square, Bedford MK40 1SQ (Tel: Bedford (0234) 56350).

Luton
1st Floor, 85–87 George Street, Luton LU1 2AT (Tel: Luton (0582) 20664).

BERKSHIRE

Bracknell
Brooke House, 54 High Street, Bracknell RG12 1LL (Tel: Bracknell (0344) 51160).

Maidenhead
Redcote, Holmanlease, Maidenhead SL8 8AW (Tel: Maidenhead (0628) 25320 (for urgent calls)).

Newbury
The Town Hall, Market Place, Newbury, RG14 5AA (Tel: Newbury (0635) 33979.

Reading
20 Prospect Street, Reading RG1 7YG (Tel: Reading (0734) 507283).

BUCKINGHAMSHIRE

Aylesbury
23a Walton Street, Aylesbury HP20 1UB (Tel: Aylesbury (0296) 27973).

Chesham
12 Townsend Road, Chesham HP5 2AA (Tel: Chesham (0494) 785980).

Milton Keynes
The Quaker Centre, Fairford Crescent, Downhead Park, Milton Keynes MK15 9AE (Tel: Milton Keynes (0908) 660100).

CAMBRIDGESHIRE

Cambridge
8 Market Passage, Cambridge CB2 3PF (Tel: Cambridge (0223) 357424).

Peterborough
17 Manor House Street, Peterborough PE1 2TL (Tel: Peterborough (0733) 68551).

CHESHIRE

Chester
83 Watergate Street, Chester CH1 2LF (Tel: Chester (0244) 42747).

Crewe
50 Victoria Street, Crewe CW1 2JD (Tel: Crewe (0270) 213139).

Hooton
7 Vernon Avenue, Hooton, South Wirral L66 6AL (Tel: 051-327 1845).

Macclesfield
42a Sunderland Street, Macclesfield SK11 6JL, Cheshire (Tel: Macclesfield (0625) 611887).

Northwich
43 Chester Street, Castle, Northwich CW8 1HA (Tel: Northwich (0606) 783502).

Warrington
21a Wilson Patten Street, Warrington WA1 1PG,(Tel: Warrington (0925) 30124).

CLEVELAND

Middlesbrough
1 Albert Terrace, Middlesbrough TS1 3PA (Tel: Middlesbrough (0642) 246051).

CORNWALL

St Austell
Cornish Unit Building, rear of 14 High Cross Street, St Austell PL25 4AN (Tel: St Austell (0726) 74128).

CUMBRIA

Barrow-in-Furness
52 Paradise Street, Barrow-in-Furness LA14 1JG (Tel: Barrow-in-Furness (0229) 24074).

Carlisle
14 Spencer Street, Carlisle CA1 BQ, (Tel: Carlisle (0228) 25950).

Kendal
134a Highgate, Kendal LA9 4HW (Tel: Kendal (0539) 23944).

Penrith
Brent House, Fell Lane, Penrith CA11 8AQ (Tel: Carlisle (0228) 25950).

Workington
Vulcans Lane, Workington (Tel: Workington (0900) 5398).

DERBYSHIRE

Chesterfield
12 Saltergate, Chesterfield S40 1UT (Tel: Chesterfield (0246) 31010).

Derby
62 Friar Gate, Derby DE1 1DJ (Tel: Derby (0332) 49177).

DEVON

Barnstaple
30 Joy Street, Barnstaple EX31 1BP (Tel: Barnstaple (0271) 45268).

Exeter
3 Wynards, Magdalen Street, Exeter EX2 4HX (Tel: Exeter (0392) 217632).

Plymouth
Higher Lane House, Higher Lane, Plymouth PL1 2AN (Tel: Plymouth (0752) 665708).

Torquay
20 St George's Road, Babbacombe, Torquay TW1 3QY (Tel: Torquay (0803) 27854).

DORSET

Bournemouth
2 Alma Road, Winton, Bournemouth BH9 1AA (Tel: Bournemouth (0202) 514630).

Dorchester
57 High West Street, Dorchester DT1 1UT (Tel: Dorchester (0305) 62285).

CO. DURHAM

Darlington
West Lodge, West Crescent, Darlington DL3 7PS (Tel: Darlington (0325) 461500).

Durham
31 Old Elvet, Durham City DH1 3JA (Tel: Durham (0385) 41198).

EAST SUSSEX

Brighton
58 Preston Road, Brighton BN1 4QF (Tel: Brighton (0273) 697997).

Eastbourne
35 Old Orchard Road, Eastbourne BN21 3JA (Tel: Eastbourne (0323) 288828).

ESSEX

Basildon
4 Cherrydown West, Basildon SS16 5AT (Tel: Basildon (0268) 286888).

Chelmsford
79 Springfield Road, Chelmsford CM2 6JG (Tel: Chelmsford (0245) 58680).

Colchester
64a High Street, Colchester CO1 1DN (Tel: Colchester (0206) 578948).

Harlow
Bentham House, Hampstel Road, Harlow CM20 1EP (Tel: Harlow (0279) 23655).

Southend
29 Harcourt Avenue, Southend on Sea SS2 9HT (Tel: Southend (0702) 342901).

GLOUCESTERSHIRE

Cheltenham
24 Cambray Place, Cheltenham GL50 1JD (Tel: Cheltenham (0242) 523215).

Gloucester
27 Park Road, Gloucester GL1 1LH (Tel: Gloucester (0452) 22071).

GREATER LONDON

Barnet
5 Woodhouse Road, Tally Ho Corner, Finchley, London N12 9EN (Tel: 01-445 8522/9549).

Bromley
83 Tweedy Road, Bromley, Kent BR1 1RG (Tel: 01-460 6832).

Croydon
9 Ramsey Court, Church Street, Croydon CR0 1RF (Tel: 01-680 1944).

Enfield
Southgate Town Hall, Green Lanes, London N13 4XD (Tel: 01-886 1615).

Harrow
Terrapin No.1, Civic Centre Complex, Station Road, Wealdstone, Harrow HA1 2UL (Tel: 01-427 8694).

Havering
'Langtons', Billet Lane, Hornchurch, Essex RM11 1XL (Tel: Hornchurch (040 24) 41722).

Kingston-upon-Thames
41 Fife Road, Kingston-upon-Thames, Surrey KT1 1SF (Tel: 01-549 3318).

Merton
The Guild House, 30–32 Worple Road, Wimbledon, London SW19 4EF (Tel: 01-946 1788).

Purley
103 Brighton Road, Purley, Surrey CR2 4HD (Tel: 01-660 6492).

Richmond
51 Sheen Road, Richmond, Surrey TW9 1YQ (Tel: 01-940 8578).

Sutton
Mint House, 6 Stanley Park Road, Wallington SM6 0EU (Tel: 01-647 8826).

Waltham Forest
Waltham Forest Council Offices, Sidmouth Road, Leyton, London E10 5RA (Tel: 01-539 2939).

Westminster
76a New Cavendish Street, Harley Street, London W1M 7LB (Tel: 01-580 1087).

GREATER MANCHESTER

Bolton
Queen Street Mission Building, Central Street, Bolton (Tel: Bolton (0204) 28302).

Bury
3 Crompton Street, Bury BL9 0AD (Tel: 061-764 4113).

Cheadle Hulme
Flat 7, Manor Lodge, 1 Park Road, Cheadle Hulme, Cheadle SK8 7DA.

Leigh
14 Walmesley Road, Leigh WN7 1YE (Tel: Leigh (0942) 679170).

Manchester
346 Chester Road, Cornbrook, Manchester M16 9EA (Tel: 061-872 0303).

Oldham
14 Waterloo Street, Oldham OL1 1SQ (Tel: 061-872 0303).

Rochdale
Champness Hall, Drake Street, Rochdale OL16 1PB (Tel: Rochdale (0706) 33834).

Salford
1 Cumbria Walk, off London Street, Salford 6 (Tel: 061-737 1400).

Wigan
1 Parsons Walk, Wigan WN1 1RU (Tel: Wigan (0942) 41294).

HAMPSHIRE

Aldershot
12 Arthur Street, Aldershot GU11 1HL (Tel: Aldershot (0252) 24679).

Basingstoke
Chute House, Church Street, Basingstoke RG21 1QT (Tel: Basingstoke (0256) 24364).

Portsmouth
Training Centre Building, Dugald Drummond Street, Portsmouth PO1 2BB (Tel: Portsmouth (0705) 82706).

Southampton
3 Kings Park Road, Southampton SO1 2AS (Tel: Southampton (0703) 229861).

Winchester
Litton Lodge, 13a Clifton Road, Winchester SO22 5BS (Tel: Winchester (0962) 61336).

HEREFORD AND WORCESTER

Hereford
6a St Owen Street, Hereford HR1 2PH (Tel: Hereford (0432) 276023).

Worcester
7 Castle Street, Worcester WR1 3AD (Tel: Worcester (0905) 28051).

HERTFORDSHIRE

Cheshunt
96 Turners Hill, Cheshunt EN8 8LQ (Tel: Hertford (0992) 37161).

Hemel Hempstead
19 Hillfield Road, Hemel Hempstead HP2 4AA (Tel: Hemel Hempstead (0442) 62618).

Letchworth
Old Grammar School, Broadway, Letchworth SG6 3PS (Tel: Letchworth (046 26) 79139).

St Albans
19 Victoria Street, St Albans AL1 3JJ (Tel: St Albans (0727) 58126).

Watford
Watford Advice Centre, 149 The Parade, High Street, Watford WD1 1NA (Tel: Watford (0923) 41803).

Welwyn Garden City
The Health Centre, Parkway, Welwyn Garden City, AL8 6JD (Tel: Welwyn Garden (0707) 325040).

HUMBERSIDE

Bridlington
92 Quay Street, Bridlington (Tel: Bridlington (0262) 602922).

Grimsby
10 Town Hall Street, Grimsby DN31 1HN (Tel: Grimsby (0472) 54392).

Hull
21a Albion Street, Hull HU1 3TG (Tel: Hull (0482) 29621).

Scunthorpe
48 Oswald Road, Scunthorpe DN15 7PQ (Tel: Scunthorpe (0724) 861889).

ISLE OF WIGHT

Newport
31 Quay Street, Newport PO30 5BA (Tel: Newport (0983) 524402).

KENT

Broadstairs
97 High Street, Broadstairs CT10 1NQ (Tel: Thanet (0843) 61228).

Canterbury
21 Palace Street, Canterbury CT1 2DZ (Tel: Canterbury (0227) 66094).

Chatham
The White House, Riverside, Chatham ME4 4SL (Tel: Chatham (0634) 46914).

Dartford
Hubert House, Knights Manor Estate, St Vincent's, Templehill, Dartford DA1 5HU (Tel: Dartford (0322) 75691).

Folkestone
9 West Cliff Gardens, Folkestone CT20 1SP (Tel: Folkestone (0303) 52798).

Maidstone
60 Marsham Street, Maidstone ME14 1EU (Tel: Maidstone (0622) 677065).

Sittingbourne
The White House, 5 Brenchley Community Centre, Roman Square, Sittingbourne ME10 4BJ (Tel: Sittingbourne (0795) 77770).

Tunbridge Wells
10a High Street, Tunbridge Wells TN1 1UX (Tel: Tunbridge Wells (0892) 29927).

LANCASHIRE

Blackburn
37 Limbrick, Blackburn BB1 8AB (Tel: Blackburn (0254) 52827).

Blackpool
20 Deansgate, Blackpool FY1 1BN (Tel: Blackpool (0253) 21877)

Burnley
1 Cow Lane, Burnley BB11 1LT (Tel: Burnley (0282) 26915).

Lancaster
87 King Street, Lancaster LA1 1RH (Tel: Lancaster (0524) 66428).

Preston
160 Garstang Road, Fulwood, Preston PR2 4NB (Tel: Preston (0772) 717597).

Skelmersdale
79 Westgate, Sandy Lane Centre, Firbeck, Birch Green, Skelmersdale WN8 6PW (Tel: Skelmersdale (0695) 25900).

LEICESTERSHIRE

Leicester
94 London Road, Leicester LE2 0QS (Tel: Leicester (0533) 543011).

LINCOLNSHIRE

Boston
Health Clinic, Lincoln Lane, Boston (Tel: Boston (0205) 65533).

Lincoln
16 St Martins Lane, Lincoln LN2 1HY (Tel: Lincoln (0522) 24922).

LONDON

See Greater London.

MANCHESTER

See Greater Manchester.

MERSEYSIDE

Liverpool
7 Copperas Hill, Liverpool L3 5LB (Tel: 051-709 2058).

St Helens
22 Vincent Street, St Helens WA10 1LF (Tel: St Helens (0744) 27118).

NORFOLK

Great Yarmouth
6 School Road, Martham, Great Yarmouth NR29 4PX (Tel: Norwich (0603) 625333).

Kings Lynn
22 Queen Street, Kings Lynn PE30 1HT (Tel: Kings Lynn (0553) 773813).

Norwich
6 Kingsley Road, Norwich NR1 3RB (Tel: Norwich (0603) 625333).

NORTHAMPTONSHIRE

Northampton
24 Hazelwood Road, Northampton NN1 1LN (Tel: Northampton (0604) 34400).

NORTH YORKSHIRE

Harrogate
1 Haywra Street, Harrogate HG1 5BJ (Tel: Harrogate (0423) 502173).

Scarborough
5 West Parade Road, Scarborough YO12 5ED (Tel: Scarborough (0723) 369858).

York
10 Priory Street, York YO1 1EZ (Tel: York (0904) 25971).

NOTTINGHAMSHIRE

Mansfield
84 Nottingham Road, Mansfield NG18 1BP (Tel: Mansfield (0623) 36553).

Nottingham
84 Mansfield Road, Nottingham NG1 3HD (Tel: Nottingham (0602) 507836).

OXFORDSHIRE

Oxford
33 Iffley Road, Oxford OX4 1AE (Tel: Oxford (0865) 242960).

SHROPSHIRE

Shrewsbury
7 Barker Street, Shrewsbury SY1 1QJ (Tel: Shrewsbury (0743) 4010).

Telford
The Old Vicarage, Church Street, Madeley, Telford TF7 5BN (Tel: Shrewsbury (0743) 4010).

SOMERSET

Bridgwater
5a Court Street, off Fore Street, Bridgwater (Tel: Bridgwater (0278) 428155).

Queen Camel
The Tithe Barn, Queen Camel (Tel: Marston Magna (0935) 850999).

Taunton
3 Upper High Street, Taunton TA1 3PX (Tel: Taunton (0823) 75983).

Wells
16 Market Place, Wells BA5 2RB (Tel: Wells (0749) 77920).

SOUTH YORKSHIRE

Barnsley
8a Eastgate, Barnsley S70 2EX (Tel: Barnsley (0226) 206834).

Doncaster
52 Christchurch Road, Doncaster DN1 2QR (Tel: Doncaster (0302) 67805).

Rotherham
8 Percy Street, Rotherham S65 1ED (Tel: Rotherham (0709) 377644).

Sheffield
Voluntary Service House, 69 Division Street, Sheffield S1 4GE (Tel: Sheffield (0742) 20778).

STAFFORDSHIRE

Burton-on-Trent
Orchard House, Orchard Street, Burton-on-Trent DE14 3SJ (Tel: Burton-on-Trent (0283) 61697).

Cannock
33 Park Road, Cannock WS11 1JN (Tel: Cannock (054 35) 77281).

Lichfield
29 Levetts Field, Lichfield WS13 6EE (Tel: Lichfield (054 32) 52760).

Newcastle under Lyme
The Arts Centre, Brampton, Newcastle under Lyme ST5 0QP (Tel: Newcastle (0782) 619541).

Stafford
SDVS Building, Chell Road, Stafford ST16 2QA (Tel: Stafford (0785) 42779).

Tamworth
8 Albert Road, Tamworth B79 7JN (Tel: Tamworth (0827) 57010).

SUFFOLK

Bury St Edmunds
67a St Andrews Street North, Bury St Edmunds IP33 1TZ (Tel: Bury St Edmunds (0284) 67305).

Ipswich
19 Tower Street, Ipswich IP1 3BE (Tel: Ipswich (0473) 54118).

Lowestoft
88 Alexandra Road, Lowestoft NR33 1PL (Tel: Lowestoft (0502) 63733).

SURREY

Epsom
The Cedars, Church Street, Epsom KT17 4BQ (Tel: Epsom (037 27) 22976).

Esher
Esher Lodge Annexe, High Street, Esher KT10 9SE (Tel: Esher (0372) 62111 ext. 141).

Guildford
3a Leapale Road, Guildford GU1 4JX (Tel: Guildford (0483) 66254).

Reigate
1a Park Lane, Reigate RH2 8JU (Tel: Reigate (073 72) 45212).

Woking
14 York Road, Woking GU22 7XH (Tel: Woking (048 62) 5285).

TYNE AND WEAR

Newcastle upon Tyne
Mea House, Ellison Place, Newcastle upon Tyne NE1 8XS (Tel: Newcastle upon Tyne (0632) 329109).

Sunderland
4 Toward Road, Sunderland SR1 2QF (Tel: Sunderland (0783) 658353).

WARWICKSHIRE

Leamington Spa
35 Regent Grove, Leamington Spa CV32 4NN (Tel: Leamington Spa (0926) 24899).

Rugby
11 Little Church Street, Rugby CV21 3AW (Tel: Rugby (0788) 65675).

Welford-on-Avon
Castle House, Milcote Road, Welford on Avon CV37 8JX (Tel: Stratford-upon-Avon (0789) 750165).

WEST MIDLANDS

Birmingham
74 Broad Street, Birmingham B15 1AQ (Tel: 021-643 1638).

Coventry
11 Bayley Lane, Coventry CV1 5RN (Tel: Coventry (0203) 25863).

Dudley
16a Stone Street, Dudley DY1 1NS (Tel: Dudley (0384) 57392).

Sandwell
Oldbury Municipal Buildings, Freeth Street, Oldbury, Warley B69 3DB (Tel: 021-544 7088).

Walsall
132 Lichfield Street, Walsall WS1 1SL (Tel: Walsall (0922) 26004).

Wolverhampton
183 Stafford Street, Wolverhampton WV1 1ND (Tel: Wolverhampton (0902) 25082).

WEST SUSSEX

Chichester
Bell House, 6 Theatre Lane, Chichester PO19 1SR (Tel: Chichester (0243) 788935).

Crawley
3 Station Road, Crawley RH10 1HY (Tel: Crawley (0293) 517925).

Worthing
5 North Street, Worthing (Tel: Worthing (0903) 202512).
45 South Street, Tarring, Worthing BN14 7LU (Tel: Worthing (0903) 202512).

WEST YORKSHIRE

Bradford
19 Piccadilly, Bradford BD1 3NQ (Tel: Bradford (0274) 726096).

Halifax
38 Clare Road, Halifax HX1 2HX (Tel: Halifax (0422) 63845).

Huddersfield
23 John William Street, Huddersfield HD1 8BL (Tel: Huddersfield (0484) 28212).

Keighley
Voluntary Services Centre, Spring Gardens Lane, Keighley BD20 6LB (Tel: Keighley (0535) 605047).

Leeds
Rutland House, 38 Call Lane, Leeds LS1 6DT (Tel: Leeds (0532) 452595).

Wakefield
41 George Street, Wakefield WF1 1LW (Tel: Wakefield (0924) 372494).

WILTSHIRE

Salisbury
24 St Edmund's, Church Street, Salisbury SP1 1EF (Tel: Salisbury (0722) 336763).

Swindon
Friends' Meeting House, 79 Eastcott Hill, Swindon SN1 3JF (Tel: Swindon (0793) 27664).

Trowbridge
24a Church Street, Trowbridge BA14 8DY (Tel: Trowbridge (022 14) 65310).

WALES

CLWYD

Colwyn Bay
28 Rivieres Avenue, Colwyn Bay LL29 7DP (Tel: Colwyn Bay (0492) 33919).

Wrexham
2 Grosvenor Road, Wrexham LL11 1BW (Tel: Wrexham (0978) 265028).

DYFED

Carmarthen
71 Penlan Road, Carmarthen SA31 1DN (Tel: Carmarthen (0267) 4644). For appointments you can also phone: Cardigan (0239) 613297 Llanelli (055 42) 56307 Pembroke (0646) 3949.

GWENT

Newport
41 Stow Hill, Newport, Gwent NP9 1JH (Tel: Newport (0633) 53982).

MID GLAMORGAN

Merthyr Tydfil
Probation Service, The Law Courts, Glebeland Place, Merthyr Tydfil (Tel: Merthyr Tydfil (0685) 71131).

POWYS

Newtown
NFU Building, 17 High Street, Newtown SY16 2NQ (Tel: Newtown (0686) 27285).

SOUTH GLAMORGAN

Cardiff
26 High Street, Cardiff CF1 2BZ (Tel: Cardiff (0222) 29850).

WEST GLAMORGAN

Swansea
2 De Le Beche Street, Swansea SA1 3EY (Tel: Swansea (0792) 55960).

NORTHERN IRELAND

BELFAST

76 Dublin Road, Belfast BT2 7HP (Tel: Belfast (0232) 223454).

ISLE OF MAN

Onchan (near Douglas)
'Mannin Veen', 3 Hollydene Avenue, Birchill Onchan (Tel: Douglas (0624) 23902).

The Scottish Marriage Guidance Council
26 Frederick Street, Edinburgh EH2 2JR (Tel: 031-225 5006).
The SMGC is constitutionally separate from the National Marriage Guidance Council (*see* page 107), but close working links are maintained. It operates in a similar way and has virtually the same objectives. Like the NMGC, it aims to foster the success and stability of marriage as the foundation of family life and of the well being of society. Similarly, too, they will not tell you what to do, nor even say 'If I were you. . . ', but believe that it is better to 'help you to decide what's best for yourself'. In addition, sex therapy is available in Aberdeen, Edinburgh, Glasgow, Jedburgh and Stirling.

Booklists, leaflets (very imaginative) and other information about the work of the Marriage Guidance Councils may be obtained from any local MGC (or from the national office) and appointments can be made by telephone, in writing, or by calling in.

For the SMGCs role in sex education *see* Chapter 13, 'Learning About Sex'.

Scottish Marriage Guidance Council Secretaries

BORDERS

Mrs A. Veitch, Honeyfield, Honeyfield Road, Jedburgh TD8 6JN (Tel: Jedburgh (0835) 62811).

CENTRAL

Mrs M. Sutton, 19 Randolph Road, Stirling (Tel: Stirling (0786) 72031).

DUMFRIES AND GALLOWAY

Mrs S. Wilson, 12 Norfolk Avenue, Glencaple, Dumfries DG1 4RX (Tel: Dumfries (0387) 77455).

FIFE

Mrs Maureen Ramsay, 38c St Clair Street, Kirkcaldy, (Tel: Kirkcaldy (0592) 266271).

GRAMPIAN

Mrs Doris Meston, 10 Belmont Street, Aberdeen (Tel: Aberdeen (0224) 648412).

ORKNEY

Mrs J. Ridgway, Old Schoolhouse, Kirbirster, Orphir, Orkney (Tel: Orphir (085 681) 202).

HIGHLANDS

No Secretary at time of writing.

LOTHIAN

Mrs D. Bett, Lothian Marriage Counselling Service, 9a Dundas Street, Edinburgh EH3 6QG (Tel: 031-556 1527).

STRATHCLYDE

Ayrshire
Mrs J. Connelly, 37 Pemberton Valley, Alloway, Ayr KA7 4UH (Tel: Ayr (0292) 43744).

Dumbarton & District
Mrs B.Robertson, 7 McGregor Drive, Dumbarton G82 1LL (Tel: Dumbarton (0389) 63378).

Glasgow
Mrs M. Hamilton, 27 Sandyford Place, Glasgow G3 7NG (Tel: 041-248 5249).

Inverclyde
Mrs Morag Struthers, 78 Newton Street, Greenock (Tel: Greenock (0475) 20786).

Lanarkshire
Mrs R. Milligan, 5 John Murray Court, Motherwell (Tel: Motherwell (0698) 282828 ext. 6138).

Oban
Mrs M. Harris, Roroyare, Taynuilt, Argyll (Tel: Taynuilt (086 62) 249).

TAYSIDE

Mrs Ann Noltie, 14 Victoria Chambers, Victoria Road, Dundee (Tel: Dundee (0382) 26459).

Other Helpful Organisations

The Association of Sexual and Marital Therapists
PO Box 62, Sheffield S10 3TL.
Will provide details of therapists in a given local area. Your local therapist will provide the special help you need. An SAE is essential for a reply.

The Catholic Marriage Advisory Council
15 Lansdowne Road, London W11 3AJ (Tel: 01-727 0141).
The work of the CMAC is naturally influenced by its particular religious beliefs, but having said that, its aims and functional arrangements are not dissimilar from those of the National Marriage Guidance Council. It

> 'regards the family unit as the major influence for individual growth and social stability, and is therefore committed to helping people to initiate, sustain and enrich the marriage relationship'.

A service of trained counsellors is available to help people who are encountering marital difficulties to

> 'a better understanding of their problems so that they can cope with them'.

They point out that the role of the counsellor

> 'is not that of an adviser, not merely to listen, diagnose the trouble and indicate a remedy, but rather to enable the person in trouble to understand the situation himself, to see the possible remedies and to act accordingly'.

The counselling service is backed up by a medical service for those cases where the root cause of marital disharmony is a medical one or where stress from family troubles gives rise to medical symptoms. The medical advisers help in a large range of cases: difficulties of consummation of marriage, aversion to marital relationships, frigidity, impotence, suspected sterility, fear of pregnancy, pathological conditions making childbirth a real or imagined risk, rapid repetition of pregnancies, genetic problems and the various neuroses and psychoses. Help is given with the regulation of birth by 'natural methods', within the context of Roman Catholic belief.

There are now 81 CMAC centres throughout the UK which offer a free service and where training is provided in natural family planning methods (CMAC teaches the sympto-thermal method). The Book Room at Lansdowne Road keeps stocks of selected books on marriage and family life, and a booklist is available.

Divorce Conciliation and Advisory Service
38 Ebury Street, London SW1 0LU (Tel: 01-730 2422).
The DCAS is a registered charity which offers a private,

confidential service for people with practical or emotional problems – at any stage in the divorce process – before starting, during proceedings or in their aftermath.

The Service is staffed by experienced counsellors who help clients to appraise their individual needs. As appropriate, they will:

(a) assist in clarifying confusion – both practical and external – when contemplating or experiencing divorce;
(b) offer conciliation to couples;
(c) offer professional casework help to divorcees in the post-divorce situation.

Legal advice is not given, but clients can be referred to a suitable solicitor. Essentially, the DCAS is complementary to legal help for those who want more time to consider the consequences than a solicitor's time permits. One of the most valuable aspects of the service is the opportunity for couples to reach agreement; disputes which might be fought interminably through solicitors at great expense, can be worked through face to face. It may not be painless, say the DCAS, but there is less risk of unresolved conflicts being left to fester.

Even when both parties will not agree to discuss their differences, helping one of them to adapt can be significant. Failed relationships tend to undermine self-respect and confidence and the DCAS can help clients to restructure their lives in a positive way.

A contribution of £20 is requested for anything up to one and a half hours, but this charge can be reduced if there are financial difficulties.

The Service is open Monday to Thursday 10 a.m. – 5 p.m. and Friday 10 a.m. – 1 p.m. Appointments can be arranged by telephoning Hilary Halpin or Patricia Harris at the number given above.

Institute of Marital Studies
Tavistock Centre, Belsize Lane, London NW3 5BA (Tel: 01-435 7111).
This is a specialist organisation, a unit of the Tavistock Institute of Medical Psychology, which is a registered charity.

A therapeutic service is offered to both partners of married, engaged, co-habiting or separating couples, who have relationship problems. An initial consultation is offered to establish whether on-going treatment is appropriate and, if it is, both partners are expected to attend weekly interviews with two therapists. The couples are seen together or separately according to need. Advice cannot be given by telephone.

The service covers the whole range of psychological difficulties experienced by partners in their relationships. These include problems in communication; emotional and physical intimacy; psychiatric symptoms; and the basic question of whether to remain together or to part.

The fee is negotiable according to income. It varies from £1 to £33 (the actual cost of the service) per person per session. For appointments and further information, ask for the Appointments Secretary, who is available on weekdays between 9.30 a.m. and 5.30 p.m.

Selected Further Reading

Although, for the sake of clarity, we have discussed 'Marriage Guidance' in a separate chapter, it will be apparent that people with sexual/relationship problems will undoubtedly find other parts of this book relevant to their needs. Associated with many of these chapters is a wide range of selected further reading which may be of great benefit to those who are experiencing difficulties in their partnership. A number of organisations, notably the Family Planning Association (27–35 Mortimer Street, London W1N 7RJ (Tel: 01-636 7866)) and the National Marriage Guidance Council (Herbert Gray College, Little Church Street, Rugby, Warwickshire CV21 3AP (Tel: Rugby (0788) 73241)) make available free booklists, and books and literature can be obtained by mail order.

Marriage guidance all too often does not achieve reconciliation, and the partners are faced with divorce or separation, an experience which can be traumatic even though it may be the only way out of an unhappy relationship. In such circumstances, the following book may be helpful:
Divorce by Dr Caroline Shreeve. Published by Thorsons Publishing Group, 1986. Price £3.95.
The author, who has had many years' involvement in marital and sexual counselling and has personally experienced divorce, has provided a guide to coping both emotionally and practically with this major life crisis. She outlines some of the commonest causes of divorce (with hints on how to avoid them), suggests sources of advice, and discusses the alternative routes of divorce and separation if the choice has to be made; the effects on children; coping with the aftermath; and moving forward to a new life.

Marital Therapy in Britain Edited by Windy Dryden: for details *see* Chapter 1, 'The Helping Therapies'.

CHAPTER 16

Sex in Later Life

Older people, like everyone else, are greatly affected by society's attitudes, particularly in such a delicate area of sensibility as sex. And the popular view seems to be that they are really not supposed to be interested in sex at all. This denial of sexuality in older people by younger generations is appropriately described by Sally Greengross, Assistant Director of Age Concern, in a paper presented to a conference as

> 'one of the most pernicious forms of discrimination against old people which persists in today's society. For all of us' she continues, 'a part of our identity and personality as human beings is derived from our sexuality and this is with us from birth until we die.'

Sally Greengross goes on to say that to deny our sexuality is to deny an essential part of our personality. Older people are sadly aware that freedom of sexual expression seems to be reserved for the young with their beautiful body images. As a result many older people are likely to feel inhibited when their bodies no longer conform to the accepted image of sexual beauty. This attitude is most likely to affect older women who were brought up to conform to a particular stereotype which dictates that pleasing and attracting men must be their prime aim in life. When youthful beauty fades they may feel undermined as people and may also feel their sexuality is no longer of any worth. Sally Greengross says,

> 'To a great many women, the only power which they ever experience is the power which they can hold over men by attracting them sexually . . . Therefore sexuality to many women represents the only power they will ever have, and when it goes, or is perceived to disappear, their hopes will disappear with it.'

But it need not be like that. In *World Medicine* (April 1982) Ivor Felstein told a lovely story of indomitable sexuality in the face of advancing years of a woman just turned 70 whose fourth husband could not match her sexual expectations of intercourse at least three times a week. She requested he seek advice to overcome his failing erectile function, since she had no intention of accepting that 'they were too old for that sort of thing'. After a certain amount of psychotherapy for them both and medical attention for the husband (she learning to step down her desires a little, he learning to cope better), matters improved, each gaining insight into the other's needs. After that there seemed to be no further problems. The husband died some seven years later, followed by the indomitable lady, apparently in her early 80s, shortly after. However after her death her relatives dug out her birth certificate. It appeared that when she died she was, in fact, over 90 years old! We can't help feeling that women, at least, can gain great encouragement from that story.

Many other older people are giving the lie to the notion that they are not interested in sex. There is also ample evidence that for many people in the mature years interest is accompanied by vigorous action. Far from being 'past it', they have been shown to be leading active and imaginative sex lives. The signs, if we care to be perceptive, are all around us.

Positive evidence is available in a survey conducted by Bernard Starr and Marcella Weiner into sexuality and the over-60s in the United States. In this survey, 800 adults between the ages of 60 and 91 answered questions about their sexual lives and generally registered very positive attitudes to enjoying and using their sexuality – a great comfort and encouragement to all of us who might be concerned at the prospect of waning powers in our later years.

Starr and Weiner were able to show that many people responding to their questionnaire had kept pace with modern views, adjusting their attitudes accordingly, despite the generally unpermissive age in which they had been brought up – most having had no sex education at all. The one taboo that most persisted from earlier days concerned masturbation. This was found to still to have a grip on many people coming from a generation when even doctors referred to the practice as 'self-defilement' and warned against the horrible dangers those who 'abused' themselves would suffer. Starr and Weiner felt it a matter of some regret that

> 'older men and women should cast their sights back to the repressive values of another generation (in this particular matter) when so much more freedom and fulfilment should rightfully be theirs'.

They felt this was particularly true for those left on their own who were denying themselves a natural and convenient outlet for their sexual feelings. It is, of course, easier said than done to release ourselves from inhibitions which have been firmly embedded by the strictures of early teaching, however irrational.

A number of men in the Starr/Weiner survey wrote that in spite of impotence they

> 'felt sexual and were very active, engaging in mutual oral sex or just kissing, stroking and cuddling. . . Therefore, it is possible to have powerful, fulfilling sexual experiences with or without an erection.'

Some respondents reported that their love-making had improved with a reduction of the urgency of desire and the fears of pregnancy removed. One 72- year-old woman explained,

> 'Your sex is much more relaxed, I know my body better and we know each other better. Sex is unhurried and the best in our lives.'

Another woman, aged 69, said,

> 'Sex is much more enjoyable and satisfying now. It used to be more frequent, and while pleasurable it has now become less frequent, but each time lasts longer and has much greater sensory impact during climax for both of us.'

A woman of 68 said,

> 'Now it is necessary to stimulate my clitoris during coitus to reach orgasm. However, climax is much more intense and prolonged and contractions much stronger.'

Starr and Weiner remark,

> 'Far from sitting on the side-lines or giving up their sexual selves these older adults have achieved higher levels of sexual fulfilment. Their comments give power to the belief that the human mind is the most potent sex organ. Sex is better for those respondents because of greater understanding, increased self-awareness, less worries and greater appreciation and meaning of the sexual experience – showing a state of mind that can enhance and even transcend biology.'

Certainly, many people objected to being seen as uninterested in sex. One man said,

> 'I was a widower for five years. Six months ago I remarried and everyone said to me, 'It's good that you married again because you need companionship.' Everyone tells me about companionship. It gets me mad. Sure I want companionship, but I also got married for sex. I always had an active sex life and still do and I am 82 years old.'

A woman of 63 asked why she should be considered different now than when she was younger,

> 'Only my outer shell has changed.'

Starr and Weiner themselves say

> 'Our fear that our sexuality – alive and well in our 20s, 30s, and 40s – should suddenly atrophy and die as we move into the later decades, makes no more sense than the notion that our ability to enjoy food or smells or conversation will disappear. Many such functions do change as we age, but there is no reason to assume that the potential for sexual pleasure should fall off any more rapidly than other capacities; yet we persist in assuming that this is what happens . . . Despite what society has conditioned us to believe, our data clearly show that the need to be touched, stroked, cuddled and caressed is a lifelong one. Physical contact is a basic human need, and that need is as powerful in the 60s, 70s and 80s as it is in infancy, childhood and early adulthood.'

One thing that is made apparent in a number of writings is that those people, barring accident or illness or the loss of a partner, who have led active sex lives throughout their earlier years are more able to take this drive and ability into old age. Those who have suffered from sexual hang-ups all their lives, perhaps as a result of early family pressures, are more likely to use old age as an excuse or explanation for opting out of sexual activity. It will be more likely to be the hang-ups rather than the process of ageing which accounts for their lack of sexual interest. However, it is encouraging to learn that if sexuality is kept cultivated and alive there is no reason, unless poor health intervenes, why it cannot be a lifelong experience for both sexes.

People of each sex may experience difficulties from time to time. Men may sometimes be unable to get an erection, they may take longer coming to climax and they may not be able to erect so often. On the other hand, older men when they do get an erection, are very often able to maintain it for longer before ejaculation than a younger man could. This can be a distinct advantage for a partner who thus has more time to reach her own climax. Such a skill can even make an older man a far better lover than in his earlier years.

Masters and Johnson (*see Human Sexual Response*, page 7) reported,

> 'The ageing male's sexual capacity and performance varies from individual to individual and from time to time in a particular individual . . . The most important factor in the

> maintenance of effective sexuality for the ageing male is consistency of active sexual expression.'

They go on to say that a man who has been constantly sexually stimulated is likely to be able to maintain his performance in later years. However, they also encouragingly say that a potent man whose sexual responsive ability has lain dormant for physical or social reasons, may be restimulated if he

> 'wishes to return to active sexual practices and has a partner interested in sexual performance'.

Masters and Johnson describe the dangers that healthy older men face if they allow themselves to be too easily put off by temporary periods of impotence. In their words,

> 'There is no way to overemphasise the importance that the factor fear of failure plays in the ageing male's withdrawal from sexual performance!'

They stress the need to recognise the temporary nature of the difficulty and the need to continue to maintain regular sexual activity and perhaps to take longer over the caressing and cuddling and 'setting the scene', for it is this that will help to restore powers which may lapse from time to time.

Apart from ill health, which may seriously affect our sex lives, we do not always realise the effect drugs can have in this respect. Tranquillisers and other drugs may cause a loss of sexual desire. It would be important to discuss this matter with your doctor. Perhaps some drugs may be reduced, while others may be changed and yet others may be dropped altogether. People sometimes continue to take drugs long after they are needed.

We have discussed briefly the problems men may have. Women may also slow down, with their orgasms coming less often. Encouragingly though, there is plenty of evidence to show that there is no real loss of sensitivity with ageing, and ability to climax continues right through into old age. Lubrication may be slower to respond or at times may be absent. Should there be a difficulty, lubricating creams (K-Y Jelly can be bought in any chemist's shop) can be used or of course a lover's saliva can be a pleasant replacement. In some cases hormone therapy may be prescribed (*see* Chapter 7, 'Menstruation, Pre-menstrual Tension and Menopause').

On the whole it has been found that if individuals are happy with their partners, they can adjust to problems as they arise and in any case may take positive enjoyment in accepting that intercourse does not always have to be an essential part of love-making for satisfaction to be gained. Aiming for a goal every time can cause an unnecessary sense of failure if that goal is not achieved. Such a sense of failure may discourage a couple from enjoying love-making for itself in all its varied aspects.

We would recommend that readers of this chapter, when confronted with particular problems related to sexuality, should seek appropriate help as described in other chapters. Each chapter has information useful to older people and help may be sought from the various organisations described. In Chapter 21, 'Guide to Local Services', we have shown where special help for older people is available, but if none is mentioned where you live, other agencies would usually be glad to help. Women may find special help in Chapter 8, 'Women Only'.

Selected Further Reading

Ageing for Beginners by Mary Stott. Published by Blackwell, 1981.
We have not had the pleasure of reading this book, but having heard a number of good reports of it we felt it should be included and we repeat below a review given by Mary Davies, former Education and Training Officer of SPOD (*see* page 94) with her permission.

> 'Mary Stott, herself in her eighth decade, points out that the usual images of elderly people do not often fit the reality since they are often healthy, happy and attractive people. She considers in a very practical way suitable places to live and the need everyone has for other people. She reminds us that "desire can be as fierce in the autumn as in the spring".
>
> After pointing out that it can be even more painful, since the odds are so heavily stacked against it being satisfied, she suggests that it would be helpful to encourage lonely people, both men and women, to accept the idea of masturbation without embarrassment or disgust.
>
> Other chapters include preparation for retirement, pleasures, pursuits and politics, with information on the organisation Age Concern. The last chapter is entitled 'Doorway' and is a moving and interesting discussion about death, ending with the idea that death might be a doorway.
>
> A lovely book for anyone concerned with ageing, their own or anyone else's.'

Sexuality in Later Life Edited by Cynthia Wyld. Published by the University of Keele in association with the Health Education Authority and the British Association for Service to the Elderly. Price £2 + 70p postage and packing.
This is the fourth contribution to the Health Education Authority's *Working Papers on the Health of Older People.* In this booklet, Mary Davies, Sally Greengross and Mervyn Eastman put forward some challenging arguments about the issue of sexuality in later life. Men and

women, they argue, retain their sexual identities throughout their lives. However, it is common practice for families and professional carers to ignore the fact that older people have a sexual life and sexual needs. The authors explore some of the myths and stereotypes in this area and make some recommendations for change.

On Sex and Sexuality in the Mature Years by Bernard D. Starr, PhD, and Marcella B. Weiner, EdD. Published by W. H. Allen, 1981.

This book, written as a result of a survey of older people's views on sex in the United States, is unfortunately out of print.

CHAPTER 17

Sex Aids

In this country, sex aids have a bad image. Sold in sleazy sex shops and tastelessly advertised in erotic magazines, they have come to be closely identified with the 'porn' trade, the exploitative, male-orientated, sex for sale merchants. Many people shrink from crossing the threshold of a 'sex shop' and still more would be shocked by most of the sex aid catalogues and the context in which they are presented. They reinforce the view that sex aids are somehow immoral and improper. While all kinds of aids are accepted in every other aspect of daily living, there is a widespread reticence about the use of things artificial in sexual activities.

There are, of course, dangers in an over-mechanistic approach to sex in an emotional vacuum: using aids for kicks can be carried too far. But within reason, and provided inhibitions can be overcome, an introduction to the use of sex aids can enhance people's relationships. Quite apart from their potential for harmless fun in bed, many such aids can be positively helpful in overcoming sexual problems and have a special place where disability has adversely affected sexual function and sensation.

Some Common Sex Aids

Dildoes

Perhaps the most commonly used and certainly the oldest sex aid is the dildo, known to have been used in Greek and Roman civilisations as early as the fifth century BC. The dildo is simply an artificial penis and is used as a penis substitute. Some are hand held, some can be strapped on to the body and there is even a double dildo which allows lesbian lovers to achieve penetration at the same time. The development of soft latex has revolutionised the form, flexibility and feel of dildoes and many are now remarkably realistic. They come in various sizes, from the more or less standard to the huge. More sophisticated versions are provided with an ejaculatory device.

Vibrators

The widely used vibrator is, of course, a modern development of the dildo. At first coyly advertised as body massagers, they now seem to be generally accepted as sex aids for masturbation or stimulation of the erogenous zones (of either sex). We think that all the vibrators at present marketed specifically for sexual purposes, at least in this country, are battery operated, and this is indeed one of their major drawbacks for they tend to lose power quite quickly (though a mains operated vibrator might produce a different kind of sensation if not adequately earthed!).

Product quality is of the utmost importance, and hygiene is, of course, absolutely essential. The vibrator is largely a means of achieving or heightening sexual excitement, but it can also be positively beneficial in helping women to overcome sexual problems, especially vaginismus (see Chapter 2, 'Some Common Problems') and in generally learning to develop or revitalise sexual response and orgasm.

Versions are available which both thrust and vibrate, and latex sleeves and so-called 'happy tops' can be fitted to provide, it is claimed, additional sensation. We think we should repeat Dr David Delvin's warning (*The Book of Love*, *see* Chapter 22, 'Selected Further Reading') against rectal vibrators which can disappear up the anus and whose removal may require surgery.

Male Sleeves

For men, the equivalent of the dildo-vibrator is provided by vibrating latex sleeves which are available in various styles, mostly simulating the vagina, but sometimes in inflatable dolls, offering other orifices. They are inherently less realistic than the dildo, both visually and, we are told, in use (notwithstanding in one model 'wettable spongy lining, bulb pump, and variable tightness'!), but given a certain amount of imagination, they can offer pleasure and solace for those denied a partner. We would be less than honest, however, if we did not admit to misgivings about the dolls. They carry with them the idea that a woman is something to be used, while those decapitated heads offering oral sex are surely offensive even to (or perhaps especially to) the sexually liberated.

Chinese Balls

Known by various names, these balls, or 'love eggs', are intended to provide pleasure through bodily movement when placed in the vagina. They can be used by therapists where women find difficulty with intercourse, by helping them to focus attention on the vagina and to get used to containment and use of the vaginal muscles.

Clitoral Stimulators

One of the misfortunes of the human anatomy is that the female clitoris is seldom situated to receive much by way of direct stimulation during sexual intercourse. It has long been fashionable among certain races to adorn the penis in an attempt to redress this imbalance between the sexes. Nowadays, clitoral stimulators, moulded in soft material, can be worn around the base of the penis. There are numerous designs, but the common principle is to bring flexible protuberances into contact with the clitoris at full penetration. It sounds like a good idea in theory and plainly individual techniques and responses may make them helpful and pleasurable in some cases, but our enquiries suggest that the stimulation of the clitoris is not sufficently intense and consistent to play a major part in prompting orgasm.

A more sophisticated clitoral stimulator consists of a small vibratory unit that fits over the base of the penis and which is said to provide highly erotic sensations when brought into contact with the clitoris, while simultaneously affording pleasant sensations to the wearer.

French Ticklers

These are non-contraceptive latex condoms with bumps, reminiscent at times of some kinds of cacti. The idea is that the soft protusions heighten sensation for the woman. We doubt that their effect will be felt to be significant, except in terms of reduced sensation for the man, but it may be fun to try. Similar products are available for use on the fingers or to adorn the penis head.

Extension Sheaths

These are fitted over the penis head to augment length. Again it is somewhat doubtful if this provides any greater satisfaction to the female. The vagina will normally closely accommodate the male organ whatever its size and mere length cannot enhance sensation in the critical area of the clitoris.

Pharmacological Products

Numerous proprietary sprays, pills, potions, creams and unctions are on sale with claims of some sexual potency. We have yet to find anyone with expert knowledge who has a good word to say about them. If they work at all, we are told they do so through faith or irritation of tissue and some can be damaging. Creams and sprays against premature ejaculation may have some effect, but only at the expense of a loss of sensation.

Aids for Men with Erection Problems

The simplest device, dating back hundreds of years, is the penis ring. It is used to help sustain an erection. Many versions are available, sometimes combining clitoral/vaginal stimulators, but the primary purpose is the rudimentary one of impeding the flow of blood out of the erect penis to prevent an untimely return to its flaccid state.

Blakoe Ltd (*see* later in this chapter) market a rectangular ebonite ring which has small metal plates inlaid on opposite inner surfaces. It has a swivel opening and is fitted by the user to encircle the neck of the scrotum and the base of the penis. The plates in contact with the skin give off a minute electric current. Blakoe claim that 'marked improvements' in erection ability are derived from wearing the ring routinely during the day.

For more serious erection problems, a penile support can be used (available from Harmony (Bulkcourt Ltd) listed on page 137). This is a latex cylinder, incorporating plastic stiffeners and worn around the penis, so as to leave the glans and head exposed. It is designed to facilitate vaginal penetration when the penis is only partially erect.

Alternatively, if the female partner is emotionally able to accept it, a hollow prosthetic penis can be worn, secured by a strap harness (one sex therapist was able to quote to us two cases from his own experience where marriages had been saved by the use of this device). Some models combine a vibratory motor.

Where to Go for Help

Though it is possible that sex aids are provided in some clinics, the only one we know of is the Psychosexual

Clinic at the Eccles Health Centre, Manchester (*see* Chapter 21, 'Guide to Local Services').

Sex shops carry comprehensive stocks, and a personal visit (if you don't find it too objectionable or embarrassing) has the merit of allowing examination of the product. Of the various chains, the Ann Summers shops (Lydcare Ltd) are perhaps the least offensive to those of tender susceptibilities.

Otherwise, there are a number of mail order suppliers, including:

Blakoe Ltd, 229 Putney Bridge Road, London SW15 2PY (Tel: 01-870 0971).

Blakoe's range of aids and their presentation is orientated towards therapeutic use (which they call 'mechanotherapy'). They produce a very useful booklet on sexual dysfunction which contains details of the aids available. The literature is the least likely to offend.

Harmony (Bulkcourt Ltd), 41 Cross Street, Manchester 2 (Tel: 061-834 2934).

This company is also sensitive to people with sexual problems and supplies prosthetics to the National Health Service and various medical groups. Its catalogues, though explicit, offer useful explanations. Discounts are available to disabled customers.

Selected Further Reading

Sex Aids. A leaflet from SPOD (The Association to Aid the Sexual and Personal Relationships of People with a Disability), 286 Camden Road London N7 0BJ (Tel: 01-607 8851). Price 10p (free to disabled people).

CHAPTER 18

Homosexuality

An estimated one person in 20 is exclusively or predominantly homosexual. That is to say they are erotically and emotionally attracted to others of their own sex. What causes this sexual orientation is not entirely clear, but it is none the less real and for the individuals concerned, natural. Society at large commonly takes a different view. Given that the majority of people are attracted to the opposite sex and that the 'hetero' sex act is closely identified with procreation and this in turn with the natural order, homosexuality is widely regarded as aberrant, a perversion and immoral. This view is reinforced by society's conventional image of male and female gender roles. To be gay is seen as a betrayal of the sexual stereotypes, whether male or female.

It is a well-known, if primitive, characteristic of group behaviour to disparage and ostracise those who differ significantly from orthodox models or who fail to conform to accepted norms. So it is that homosexual people commonly find themselves isolated, ridiculed and the victims of discrimination in areas such as employment, housing, and even, alas, the law. It is not surprising that the reproving attitudes of society tend to rub off onto many homosexuals, inducing feelings of shame and guilt which fortify loneliness and rejection from within.

The danger which arises in this situation is that it is all too easy for the individual to *see* homosexuality itself as a problem; if she or he is then perceived as needing counselling and support and so on, her or his fears and introspection can be aggravated. Simply being gay is not of itself a medical or psychological problem, any more than being heterosexual is. Difficulties can arise, certainly, particularly when people realise they are gay only after marrying, but it is important to recognise the essentially external nature of such relationship conflicts and indeed of the distress which arises from social disapproval.

Many homosexuals have found that the best approach to their particular situation is to 'come out' – to stop hiding the fact that they are gay and instead to be glad of it. By doing so, not only do they throw off the tensions of keeping their sexual identity a guarded secret, but they present a positively asserted challenge to the myths and prejudices by which they are circumscribed. Not everyone, by any means, will wish to be a part of the 'swinging' gay scene, but there are by now a wide variety of self-help organisations and groups which act out of a personal understanding, do not perceive homosexuality as something to be 'cured' and which can offer help at every level and in total confidence.

Where to Go for Help

We offer in the following pages details of some of the main organisations providing advice to homosexual people – those at least who have responded to our questionnaire. Apart from these and outside the scope of this Directory, a large number of groups exist, linking homosexuals within existing political, religious, professional and special interest sectors or which meet mainly for social activities. An excellent guide to such groups throughout Britain and Ireland is provided in *Gay Times* (*see* page 42).

Campaign for Homosexual Equality (CHE)
Room 221, 38 Mount Pleasant, London WC1X 0AP.
This is a political pressure group campaigning for changes in criminal and civil law and social practice so as to eliminate discrimination and prejudice against lesbians and gay men. The organisation cannot and does not undertake personal casework, but will refer callers to a group appropriate to their needs; however, where the problem is one caused by discrimination – e.g. lesbian mothers with divorce/custody problems; people in trouble with the police; lesbians/gays who have been evicted, refused housing, unfairly sacked, or organisations refused premises, meeting facilities or publicity – CHE may be able to help. (Legal advice and help is available from GLAD, *see* page 139).

CHE is, however, essentially concerned in the purely

campaigning, educational and 'activist' sphere and publishes a wide range of books, leaflets and a tape-slide kit suitable for school and youth club use.

Friend

Friend is an affiliate network of groups providing information, advice, befriending and counselling around the issues of homosexuality. Services are provided through telephone helplines, social/support groups, individual face to face meetings and by letter. Information on local services can be obtained by writing to: BM Friend, London WC1N 3XX, or ringing London Lesbian and Gay Switchboard on 01-837 7324 (24 hour service).

London Friend can be contacted at 33A Seven Sisters Road, London N7 6AX. For Helpline telephone 01-359 7371, 7.30pm – 10pm every night of the year.

Gaydaid

Trevor Thomas, 36 Pembroke Street, Bedford MK40 3RH (Tel: Bedford (0234) 58879). If writing, please enclose a stamped, self-addressed envelope.

A service to help disabled gays, primarily men, (*see* Gemma (see below) for women) who, because of disability, have special sexual problems or who are concerned about AIDS. Commonly those seeking help are housebound or tied to their families and cannot go out alone. They find difficulty in expressing their sexuality and may experience isolation and personal worries in an acute form. Concerns over intimate sexual problems are often bottled up, with no one to whom they feel they can turn. Trevor Thomas offers a listening ear and the benefit of friendly, understanding advice. He cannot and does not operate as a contact or dating agency, but can provide concerned and supportive guidance from a long and involved personal experience.

Gay Legal Advice (GLAD)

London Lesbian & Gay Centre, 69 Cowcross Street, London EC1 (Tel: 01-253 2043). Advice 7 p.m. – 10 p.m. weekdays.

An organisation formed to provide basic legal advice to gays experiencing legal problems arising from their sexual orientation. GLAD will provide free legal advice on a wide variety of legal problems, including sexual offences, court procedure, housing, custody and divorce, property, wills, employment, immigration etc.

Gay Liberation Front Information Service

5 Caledonian Road, London N1.

This service, which operates only by post, is basically concerned to fight prejudice against homosexuality and to help gays to cope with this prejudice. A range of inexpensive literature is made available to homosexual men and women or to any person or group with an interest in the subject. Speakers can also be supplied.

Gay's the Word

66 Marchmont Street, London WC1N 1AB (Tel: 01-278 7654).

A gay community bookshop catering specifically for the lesbian, gay and feminist market, selling books, periodicals, cards, records, badges etc. Open Monday to Saturday 11 a.m. – 7 p.m. and Sunday 2 p.m. – 6 p.m. Customers are welcome to browse and there is a small coffee/tea area. A mail order service is available (subscription to the newsletter is £2.50 per year – six issues) and libraries are supplied (enquiries from librarians welcome at the shop).

Gemma

BM Box 5700, London WC1N 3XX.

This is a group for disabled/able-bodied lesbian and bisexual women of all ages, aiming to lessen the isolation of those whose disability hinders appropriate relationships and access to homosexually-orientated literature. The group stresses that it is not a dating agency, nor a ghetto of disabled lesbians, nor even a counselling service – it is simply a group of friends with some understanding through personal experience, providing a bridge into a wider friendship circle.

Gemma's quarterly newsletter (in print or on tape) costs £2 a year and includes friendship listings and advertisements (free to members). London members meet on the second Sunday in each month in accessible premises; two members can do amateur signing and finger-spelling. Occasionally, meetings are held in Brighton, Dorset, Bury St Edmunds and Liverpool. Help is available with transport for disabled members.

Gemma members offer to be pen-, tape- and phone-friends, and seek to enable each other to contact local lesbian/gay groups and to attend their events and meetings.

There are now 250 Gemmas in 35 English counties, Wales, Scotland and Ireland. Enquiries can be made by letter (please enclose SAE), on tape or in Braille.

A tape recording of the GLC Charter of Lesbian and Gay Rights '*Changing the World*' (or a shortened version in Braille) is available from Gemma.

Identity

Beauchamp Lodge, 2 Warwick Crescent, London W2 6NE (Tel: 01-289 6175).

This organisation provides a range of confidential counselling services for those struggling with relationships, loneliness, loss, depression or uncertainty. It is for men and women of all ages for whom self-expression and/or sexual orientation pose problems, with a particular concern for people in sexual minorities including homosexual men and women, bisexuals, transvestites and transsexuals. Identity can arrange ongoing help with a trained counsellor or will encourage contact with a specialist agency if appropriate, e.g. for medical or legal matters. The service is run by trained and qualified counsellors who maintain links with the helping professions: social workers, clinics, doctors, and pyschotherapists. Fees are negotiable, but help does not depend on one's ability to pay.

Lesbian Custody Movement
See Chapter 20, 'Sex Law', page 163.

Lesbian and Gay Youth Movement
BM/GYM, London WC1N 3XX (Tel: 01-317 9690) A national organisation of lesbians, gays and bisexuals under 26 (with no lower age limit). It has self-run sections of young lesbians, under-17s, and black gays.
The Movement:

- runs a phoneline, a penfriend scheme and a London drop-in;
- organises lesbian and gay youth events, camps and weekends;
- publishes 'Lesbian and Gay Youth' magazine and other literature;
- gives advice on sex and health, the law, and housing; supports young lesbians and gays dealing with social workers, psychiatrists, police and courts.

Lesbian Line
This is a telephone 'help' service for women who require information about the lesbian scene or who want to talk about their feelings about being lesbian (or indeed doubts about their sexual direction) or about relationship experiences and any connected matters. Most questions are about 'coming out' – acknowledging and being prepared to be seen as homosexual. Some 'Lines' arrange social activities and will give talks to interested groups. The service operates in various parts of the country and the lines listed below are known. The list is correct at the time of writing, but in case of difficulty, we suggest that readers contact Lesbian Line or Lesbian and Gay Switchboard (*see* page 141) at their London telephone numbers.

ENGLAND

CAMBRIDGESHIRE

Cambridge
Tel: Cambridge (0223) 311753.
Hours: Friday 6 p.m. – 10 p.m.

ESSEX

Colchester
Tel: Colchester (0206) 870051.
Hours: Last Tuesday of month 7 p.m. – 9.30 p.m.

GREATER LONDON

Tel: 01-251 6911, or write BM Box 1514, London WC1N 3XX.
Hours: Monday and Friday 2 p.m. – 10 p.m.; Tuesday, Wednesday, Thursday 7 p.m. – 10 p.m.

GREATER MANCHESTER

Tel: 061-236 6205.
Hours: Monday to Friday 7 p.m. – 10 p.m.

LANCASHIRE

Lancaster
Tel: Lancaster (0524) 63021.
Hours: Wednesday 6 p.m. – 8 p.m.

MERSEYSIDE

Liverpool
Tel: 051-708 0234.
Hours: Tuesday and Thursday 7 p.m. – 10 p.m.

NOTTINGHAMSHIRE

Nottingham
Tel: Nottingham (0602) 410652.
Hours: Monday 7 p.m. – 9 p.m.

OXFORDSHIRE

Oxford
Tel: Oxford (0865) 242333.
Hours: Wednesday 7 p.m. – 10 p.m.

WEST MIDLANDS

Birmingham
Tel: 021-359 3192.
Hours: Wednesday and Friday 7.30 p.m. – 9.30 p.m., Tuesday 4 p.m. – 6 p.m.

WEST YORKSHIRE

Bradford
Tel: Bradford (0274) 305525.
Hours: Thursday 7 p.m. – 9 p.m.

Leeds
Tel: Leeds (0532) 453588.
Hours: Tuesday 6.30 p.m. – 9.30 p.m.

WALES

SOUTH GLAMORGAN

Cardiff
Tel: Cardiff (0222) 374051.
Hours: Thursday 8 p.m. – 10 p.m.

WEST GLAMORGAN

Swansea
Tel: Swansea (0792) 467365.
Hours: Friday 7 p.m. – 10 p.m.

SCOTLAND

STRATHCLYDE

Glasgow
Tel: 041-248 4596, or write GLL, PO Box 57, Glasgow.
Hours: Wednesday 7 p.m. – 10 p.m.

Manchester Gay Information Centre
61a Bloom Street, Manchester 1. Postal address: PO Box 153, Manchester M60 1LP.
The Centre houses two advice and information phonelines, various support and social groups and a weekend coffee bar. Users are primarily gay men. The Centre also aims to educate people about the problems facing gays and is happy to provide speakers to talk about their work. For more information, contact Terry Waller, Liaison Officer, on 061-228 3554 (office hours) or for specific services phone any of the following:

Gay Information (Tel: 061-236 5986).
Hours: Daily 4 p.m. – 10 p.m.
Friend (Tel: 061-236 6283).
Hours: Monday to Saturday 7 p.m. – 10 p.m..
Gay Youth Group (Tel: for contact numbers ring Gay Information (above) or leave a message for the youth worker, Nigel Leach, on 061-228 3554).
Open to both sexes under 21, but mainly used by gay men. Hours Saturday 3 p.m. – 7 p.m.
Manchester Parents Group (Tel: 061-678 6884 – Joyce)
A support group for parents of lesbians and gay men.

Gay and Lesbian Switchboards
These telephone helplines operate in many parts of the country and are listed in *Gay Times* (*see* page 142). Their activities, although broadly similar, vary according to local needs and the availability of relevant services; some may be heavily involved in counselling, others in information and some in support group activities. Most encompass the range of offering help, information and advice on all aspects of homosexuality, and in recent years on AIDS related problems.

The London Switchboard (01-837 7324) now handles 200,000 calls a year, and has experienced a huge increase in enquiries on medical problems, mostly AIDS related. It has shown a positive commitment to discussing safer sex with all relevant callers, and has provided appropriate training to its volunteers.

National Union of Students
Nelson Mandela House, 461 Holloway Road, London N7 6LJ (Tel: 01-272 8900).
Although obviously not primarily concerned with homosexual issues, the NUS makes regular gay liberation campaign mailings to all college groups and to any students' unions who want to receive them. Its Student Welfare and Information Service produces papers which clarify in a straightforward way the nature of homosexuality and the arguments for change in social attitudes and legislation.

Sigma
BM Sigma, London WC1N 3XX (Tel: 01-837 7324 – most evenings).
A self-help and support group for those people with a gay or bisexual partner. Counselling is available if requested. Membership subscription is £5 per annum.

Selected Further Information

Gays and the Law by Paul Crane. Published by Pluto Press Ltd, Unit 10, Spencer Court, 7 Chalcot Road, London NW1 8LH, 1982. Price £4.95 (paperback).

The first major account of the law on homosexuality. The publishers say that it

> 'shows the impact of prejudice about gender and sexuality and the widespread effects of the law on personal life in housing, the care of children, property and bereavement'.

The author also considers civil rights issues: police powers, political freedom, immigration, and the treatment of gay people in the armed forces.

Gay Times. A monthly magazine published by Bulletrose Ltd, PO Box 626, London NW1 6HN, price £1.
Attractive and well presented, its pages carry reports, news, articles, reviews, letters and personal ads which give fresh and lively information on all aspects of gay living. Its 'Round Britain Gay Guide' contains an unrivalled and constantly updated guide to the gay scene: national organisations, counselling and information services, professional and special interest groups, clubs and societies in London and throughout the UK.

Lesbian Mothers – Breaking the Silence. Video film, 65 minutes, colour, available from Concord Films Council, 201 Felixstowe Road, Ipswich, Suffolk, IP3 9BJ (Tel: Ipswich (0473) 76012), price £75 (to hire £10).
Explores some of the relevant facts about custody practices, the personal struggles within the family, and how some lesbians are becoming mothers by means other than heterosexual intercourse. The production was shown on Channel 4 in 1985, and demonstrated the extreme prejudice such women face, and the strength and courage they show.

Rocking the Cradle: Lesbian Mothers – a Challenge in Family Living by Gillian E. Hanscombe and Jackie Forster. Published by Sheba Feminist Publishers, 1982. Price £3.50 (paperback).
This is not just a book for lesbians. It also reaches out to anyone who has never seriously considered the basis of lesbian sexuality and the right of lesbians to parenthood. It counters prejudice with reason and logic and challenges the conventional image of lesbians and the associated idea that they are perverted people who are unfitted for motherhood.

The authors argue cogently that in matters of sex

> 'what is natural. . . is what comes naturally'

and contest the view that the heterosexual, nuclear family is necessarily the best environment for bringing up children. Though lesbians, like non-lesbians, differ in all manner of ways from each other, there are no grounds for perceiving a fundamental disparity in maternal characteristics in either group or for thinking that the children of lesbians suffer psychological damage or exhibit unusual characteristics. Indeed, the authors assert,

> 'lesbian sexuality is a way of feeling and behaving that is dormant in every woman',

while

> 'motherhood is a peculiarly feminine phenomenon which has no natural dependence on a heterosexual lifestyle'.

Drawing on a series of interviews collected during the summer of 1978 on a tour of England and Wales, this important book looks at the various ways in which lesbian mothers conceive (including a good chapter on AID) and bring up their children in a largely hostile society, finally looking to a more generous future in which

> 'relations between the sexes will be based on friendship, co-operation and equality'

and in which

> 'individual human people, of all ages and of each sex, may live together in all manner of different ways'.

SisterWrite Bookshop

190 Upper Street, London N1 1RQ (Tel: 01-226 9782).
This is a co-operative women's bookshop, selling books which provide a penetrating feminist insight into women's issues, including numerous titles concerning lesbian literature. Monthly booklists of new titles available on subscription: £1.75 for six months. For further details, *see* Chapter 8, 'Women Only'.

We're Here by Angela Stewart-Park and Jules Cassidy. Published by Quartet Books, 1977. Price £1.95.
The title itself invites you to add 'because we're here' and that would probably be a fair reflection of the authors' views. Certainly the book doesn't set out to prove anything about lesbians, much less to justify their sexual orientation, but in presenting frank conversations with 11 lesbians of various ages and backgrounds it helps to sort out reality from myth and presents an open and honest account of 'ordinary' lesbians.

The short introduction is particularly powerful in clearing the ground, and faces honestly the dilemma of choice between hiding one's sexuality as though it was something of which to be ashamed and 'coming out', with its attendant risks of rejection and discrimination. All the contributors have faced their own problems and made their own decisions in the real world; here they speak for themselves, but in many ways offer a testimony for all those who believe, with the authors, that men are not indispensible.

We Speak for Ourselves by Jack Babuscio. Available from the SPCK, Holy Trinity Church, Marylebone Road, London NW1 4DU, 1976. Price £4.50.
First published in 1976, this remains an extraordinarily

helpful book. Though written primarily for those who wish to counsel others, its almost conversational style is immediately accessible to anyone who needs guidance or reassurance about their homosexual orientation.

It draws extensively on the stories and views of real people, expressed in their own words, with whose problems it is very easy to identify. The author looks in turn at the problems of identity, the stigma which is often attached to homosexuality and the human consequences of social pressures. He explores what it is to be 'different' (concluding that

> 'an exclusive pattern of sexuality can never be permanently denied by conversion')

and the temptation to conceal one's homosexuality in the face of oppressive social systems. There are chapters on interactions within marriage and the church and finally on the process of 'coming out', declaring oneself as gay and readjusting to a new basis of relationships and perhaps a new circle of friends, given the opportunities for 'coming together' with people of similar sexual orientation within the 'gay scene'.

CHAPTER 19

Transvestism and Transsexuality

Transvestism

Transvestites are people who sometimes feel a compulsion to dress and behave as members of the opposite sex. When they do so they experience an intense emotional release which allows them to return to their normal lives refreshed. This desire can vary among individuals from a need to use a single item of clothing to a compulsion to achieve a complete imitation of the opposite sex in clothing, appearance and behaviour.

While it is possible that a few women may describe themselves as transvestites, the term usually applies to men. Perhaps this is because women can dress as they please anyway, expressing themselves in a wide variety of styles from 'mannish' to 'ultra feminine' with individual styles of dress, while not necessarily attracting very much comment from friends and family. Our discussion, therefore, tends to concentrate attention on male transvestites, who are likely to be heterosexual, but where applicable we hope that females may also find the information useful.

Others who sometimes wear women's clothes, but who may not be described as transvestites, may include a minority of homosexuals who wear 'drag' in order to attract a homosexual partner and masochists who may use women's clothing to play the role of the 'weaker' sex in order to be dominated by another person. A transsexual also may choose to appear as a transvestite, having decided to retain his male role for family or employment reasons while cross-dressing (wearing the opposite sex's clothes) only at intervals. Nevertheless, a transsexual is not happy in his body's form and function and usually seeks to change it, while a transvestite is unlikely to want to change his body, but thinks of his personality as alternating between masculine and feminine or being a mixture of both. A male transsexual's inclination would be to dress and behave as female all the time.

What Makes a Person a Transvestite

The compulsive desire of male transvestites to dress up in women's clothing and to make themselves appear as feminine as possible has proved difficult to understand – not least for the men themselves. Each person will tend to dress very differently to express individual preferences, some choosing glamour in a consciously exhibitionistic style, while others prefer the quiet and retiring role.

The obsession is likely to have started early on in life and may have developed in a number of different ways. There may be a fetishistic attachment (*see* Chapter 2, 'Some Common Problems' for a definition of this term) to certain items of women's clothing (worn for masturbation purposes) or a man may have been dressed as a girl by his mother, who at the time was expressing a preference for a daughter. A man may also be affected by a deep psychological preference to be identified with the female rather than always with the male role. Many transvestites think of their personalities as alternating between masculine and feminine or being a mixture of both.

While transvestism plainly has sexual implications, this is only part of the experience, since men do not necessarily cross-dress to have sex or depend on cross-dressing to gain orgasm.

The compulsion can rarely be removed, though some sexual therapists have been able to help those who have sought help by seeking to intensify other pleasurable sensations which are also available to that particular individual and so diminishing the need for this type of gratification. One thing is certain, the urge to cross-dress is overpowering, an extraordinarily deep-rooted compulsion which is virtually impossible to deny. Treatments aimed at removing or 'curing' what is essentially part of an individual's psychological orientation may end up creating more problems than can be solved.

One man describes, in the *Beaumont Bulletin* (*see* page 147) how he learned at age ten that he liked girls' clothing after a 'dressing-up' session with a friend. He goes on to describe how, several years later, 'the old feeling' (no more clearly defined than that) returned when he tried on a silky and slinky evening dress. Some years on again, his wife's clothes one day proved to be irresistible and the 'old feeling' increased in intensity. Now he has a collection of women's clothes of his own and he says,

> 'Choice indeed. But no choice at all as to whether I wear them or not.'

Should Transvestites get Married?

Many heterosexual transvestites are married, but their transvestite inclinations can be devastating for such a relationship, where male and female roles are usually clearly defined. It is difficult for a wife to understand why the man in her life should wish to give so much time and effort to indulging in periods of female living when she needs and admires him as a regular, full-time and complementary male. She may feel very undermined and quite unable to cope with this sexual disorientation. Some men, fearing this reaction, will try to keep their periods of cross-dressing secret and may suffer a good deal of stress in coping with the double living this entails and the furtive arrangements for changing over. On the other hand, some wives accept the situation and will even help their partners to choose their clothes.

Obviously. however painful, it is important for the transvestite to discuss the matter with his partner before marriage to try to gain her understanding of his condition. The chances of him being able to keep his obsession secret are slender. His strange absences, when he disappears to his 'female' life, whatever this entails, will be likely to breed all kinds of suspicions, while a sudden discovery could prove a shattering blow to the marriage from which neither partner may ever fully recover. It is never wise for a transvestite to marry in the hope of a 'cure'. This is unlikely to happen; after a short period of apparent success, he is likely to find his desires returning, as strongly as before.

Sharing the Problems

A male transvestite is likely to be greatly helped in coming to terms with this facet of his personality if he is able to meet with others having similar wishes and problems. Wives and girl friends may also find encouragement from sharing circumstances which seem out of step from the generally accepted 'norm'. Transvestites can help each other immeasurably by providing social occasions where they can find an outlet for their compulsion and gain confidence in their female role with others who share similar problems and needs. The swapping of tips and information on friendly clothing shops and hairdressers, a constant source of concern to transvestites, can be very encouraging.

Cross-dressing in isolation and secrecy, as many transvestites do, can be a lonely and, in the end, an unfulfilling and frustrating experience. By mixing with others in a similar situation, expertise in dressing and confidence in the female role can be strengthened sufficiently to make it possible to appear publicly, perhaps with a friendly escort, without the fear of being discovered or 'read' as the saying goes. Many transvestites will say that one of their main pleasures is walking out in this way.

We give, starting on page 146, details of self-help and support groups which have an interest in gender identity problems. Counselling may help a transvestite and any female partner to reconcile themselves to this deep-rooted compulsion.

Transsexuality

A transsexual is a person who feels an overwhelming need to live and function in the opposite gender role to that of his or her biological sex. In most cases, this belief is so strong that the person will go to great lengths to obtain the 'right' body. A transsexual is usually heterosexual, but may be partly or fully homosexual or bisexual.

The cause of transsexuality is not known; it is possible that a genetic factor is responsible. Alternatively, hormonal imbalance before or during infancy may account for the condition. Environmental influence may also play a part.

It is not known how many transsexuals there are in Britain; estimates vary from 10,000 to 20,000, of whom less than a quarter are women (wishing to be men).

Sex Change Treatments

The desire to change sex, as transexuals affirm, is overpoweringly compulsive, and attempts to 'treat' or change the condition through therapy or drugs seem inevitably doomed to failure and may well have disastrous results. A committed transsexual has only one 'cure' and that is to live wholly and fully as a member of the chosen sex.

This can be achieved only through medical treatment and surgical intervention, which will involve major operations to make the external sexual characteristics conform to the individual's innate view of him/herself.

Hormonal treatment will be necessary. A man will aim to enlarge his breasts, to develop a more rounded shape through increased fat deposits, and to reduce the rate of growth of facial and body hair; a woman will look for her voice to 'break' and for there to be a growth of facial hair.

Unfortunately, hormones will not help a man to heighten his voice once it has broken. The best he can do is to have speech therapy to help him to modulate and soften his tone. Nor will hormones significantly inhibit existing beard growth. Only extended and expensive electrolysis can eventually achieve this. Surgery will be necessary to remove, as appropriate, breasts, vulva, penis, testicles, and replace them with more personally acceptable organs, although as yet it seems to have proved impossible to produce a completely satisfactory penis.

Medically speaking, there can be no such thing as a 'sex- change', since biological sex in the medical sense is determined by an individual's chromosomes, and cannot be changed. So the term used is 'gender reassignment', meaning a social, hormonal and surgical reassignment. Such surgery may be performed under the NHS. Private surgery is likely to cost in the region of two to three thousand pounds, and the number of experienced surgeons, private or NHS, willing to carry out the full major operation required is extremely limited and certainly insufficient to respond to all those demanding such an operation.

Legally, a British birth certificate cannot be altered to reflect a gender reassignment (*see* page 160).

It is obvious that the greatest thought has to be given to the possibility of gender reassignment. There are practical, social, physical and psychological considerations to be given due weight before the decision is made to approach a surgeon, who will, in any case, require that the person lives for at least one year totally in the desired gender role before any consideration will be given to irreversible surgery on healthy organs. *A Handbook for Male to Female Transsexuals* (*see* page 146) describes very well the many aspects to be considered before committing yourself to seeking surgery and treatment. The authors stress how important it is to seek counselling help, preferably with someone who has previous experience of the problems transsexuals face. Both Shaft (*see* page 147) and the Beaumont Society (*see* page 146) will be glad to put you in touch with a suitably qualified counsellor in your area or as near as possible.

Information on Gender Identity Clinics is hard to come by; however, a few are listed in the Shaft *Handbook* (*see* page 147). In the first place your family doctor might be prepared to refer you to a psychiatrist with an interest in and experience of transsexuals. Organisations like Shaft and the Beaumont Society can often suggest suitable psychiatrists in many parts of the country. Some organisations in Chapter 21, 'Guide to Local Services', may also be able to help.

The Right to Marry

Unfortunately, British transsexuals are still denied the right to marry. Unlike a number of other countries the UK will not countenance a change of gender on a transsexual's birth certificate, despite there having been surgical intervention. It is still against the law to alter a birth certificate in this way. For further details *see* Chapter 20, 'Sex Law'.

Where to Go for Help

Many of the organisations in Chapter 18, 'Homosexuality', will help transsexuals and transvestites and have special meetings for them.

The Beaumont Society
BM Box 3084, London WC1N 3XX.
(Tel: 01-730 7453 Tuesdays 7 p.m. – 11 p.m.; 061-256 2521 for wives and partners, Wednesdays 7 p.m. – 10 p.m.). An organisation run by and for heterosexual transvestites and their families. Regular meetings and social occasions are held in London and in various other parts of the country. The Society seeks to provide members with a means of self-acceptance, peace of mind and understanding, to replace the feelings of loneliness, fear and self-condemnation so many isolated transvestites are likely to experience. In addition, it seeks to gather and disseminate information to interested people in medical, legal and social agencies.

The arranging of social occasions allows transvestites the chance to cross-dress from time to time and meet in social surroundings, thereby reducing tension. At the same time they and their partners can discuss problems with others in a relaxed atmosphere.

The Beaumont Society also, as far as possible, tries to help transsexuals, but it is unable to undertake to find surgeons who are willing to perform 'sex-change' operations (*see* Shaft, page 147).

Complete confidentiality is maintained at all times throughout the Society. Members usually adopt a 'femme' name (a woman's name used by a transvestite) which is used when they are cross-dressing and as a code name when members are referred to as individuals in Society publications. Names and addresses are never divulged to anyone, including other members. A clever contact system is used to put members in touch with each other. The Beaumont Society is at pains to point out that 'no other person will get your address unless you give it to them'.

Membership involves a £5 processing fee and costs £13 for an annual subscription. Members receive the magazine, *Beaumont Bulletin*, every two months, which mainly consists of members' contributions, news from the regions, details of meetings and social occasions around the country, personal advertisements, and advertisements for clothing, wigs, electrolysis, etc. Regional groups also often publish their own newsletters.

Literature available: *The Beaumont Society – Some Questions and Answers*, also 'question and answer' booklets on transvestism and transsexuality (*see* page 148). The Society also intends to produce a leaflet, highlighting the problems of the disabled transgenderist.

The Beaumont Trust
BM Charity, London WC1N 3XX (Tel: Beaumont Trustline 01-730 7453 Tuesdays 7 p.m. – 11 p.m; 061-256 2521 for wives and partners Wednesdays 7 p.m. – 10 p.m.).
The Trust is an independent charitable organisation, separate from the Beaumont Society, while liaising closely with it. The Trust plays an educative and informative role to help caring organisations better understand the needs of heterosexual transvestites and to a lesser extent, transsexuals. Counsellors also might find it useful to contact the Trust for information and guidance.

Identity
Beauchamp Lodge, 2 Warwick Crescent, London W2 6NE (Tel: 01-289 6175).
This organisation provides a range of counselling services to meet sexual, personal and relationship problems with a particular concern for those in sexual minorities including gays, bi-sexuals, transvestites and transsexuals.

TV and TS Group
2 – 4 French Place, (off Bateman's Row), Shoreditch, London E1 6JD. (Tel: 01-729 1466 – Helpline, Friday, Saturday, Sunday 7.30 p.m. – 10 p.m.; other nights: 01-359 7371 (7.30 p.m. – 10 p.m.).
Formed in 1976, this self-help group provides information and advice to transvestites, transsexuals, and all concerned with them such as families, spouses, and employers. They operate via a nationwide telephone helpline, correspondence and face to face interview without charge, apart from that for the booklets they publish and the supportive meetings they hold; strict confidentiality is, of course, maintained and no personal details of clients are sought. The Group has close links with the medical profession specialising in the field (and is used as a source of information by the medical profession and statutory agencies).
The *Glad Rag* is the journal of The TV/TS Group and is available by postal subscription. The Helpline (01-359 4868) is open every Friday, Saturday and Sunday night from 8 p.m. until 10 p.m. An answerphone is available at other times.

Shaft (Self-help Association for Transsexuals)
46 Liddell Way, Ascot, Berkshire SL5 9UX (Tel: Ascot (0990) 27916).
The aims of Shaft include making available to transsexuals details of the medical, professional and counselling help available; to provide friendship and contacts within the Association; and to help the families of transsexuals who need and ask for help.

The membership subscription costs £15 per annum. Members receive newsletters every two months, which act as a link between members and include information on medical and surgical treatment available, both NHS and private, accounts by members of their medical, surgical and life experiences when these are in some way exceptional, general articles and book reviews.

Introductory information is available including *The Reality of Transsexualism*. See also *A Handbook For Male to Female Transsexuals*, details below.

Selected Further Information

A Handbook for Male to Female and Female to Male Transsexuals. A Shaft publication (46 Liddell Way, Ascot, Berkshire SL5 9UX (Tel: Ascot (0990) 27916)). Price £1.50 to members, £2 to non-members.
A very useful booklet, with just the right blend of hard facts and encouragement, plus a warning of the dangers and strain involved in seeking to change gender roles. To quote:

> 'The course of gender reassignment is a slow and complex one, fraught with difficulties, involving many emotional, social and physical readjustments, requiring much patience and enormous motivation. It is a sensitive continuing process, of which surgery, whilst it is the culmination, is but one of the many essential elements of a successful tranformation.'

Each chapter goes into the various aspects of transsexuality in some depth, discussing sensitively such subjects as 'passing' successfully, electrolysis, social reassignment, younger transsexuals and their parents, the married transsexual, employment, Gender Identity Clinics (describing and listing GICs), hormones, surgery (reassignment and cosmetic) and the legal situation.

In conclusion, the book makes no bones about the problems of 'changing over'. We can do no better than give you a final quote,

> 'It is an extraordinarily difficult thing to accomplish successfully, requiring utter determination, huge sacrifices and more than average common sense, stability and patience. The years of change-over are very testing and the price of failure high. It may require more courage to accept that one has made a mistake and go back, than to press on. All who venture to try should clearly understand this.'

SisterWrite Bookshop
190 Upper Street, London N1 1RQ. (Tel: 01-226 9782).
A co-operative women's bookshop that is well worth a visit. The stock includes subjects of special interest to women. The section on 'Sexuality and Psychology' has a number of books on gender identity and on androgyny (when the characteristics of both sexes are present in one individual).

The Transsexual Empire: The Making of the She-male by Janice Raymond. Published by The Women's Press, 34 Great Sutton Street, London EC1 ODX (Tel: 01-251 3007). Price: £4.50 +60p postage and packaging.
Unfortunately, we have not had the opportunity to read this book so we will simply quote from the cover:

> 'Ostensibly, the transsexers (from psychologists to urologists) are curing a disease, actually they engage in the religious and political shaping and controlling of "masculine" and "feminine" behaviour'.

The book is described in the Women's Press catalogue as

> 'an exposure of the "business" of "changing" gender identity by surgical means, which is really the making and controlling of gender stereotypes.'

Transsexualism – Some Questions and Answers. A Beaumont Society publication (BM Box 3084, London WC1N 3XX).
An easy and clear presentation of information relating to the more obvious questions with which transsexuals are particularly concerned. A brief discussion of treatment is included.

Transvestism – Some Questions and Answers. A Beaumont Society publication (BM Box 3084, London WC1N 3XX).
A very helpful little booklet which answers briefly some of the more obvious questions which transvestites and their families worry about regarding the law, marriage, morality, discrimination, whether to tell children, information about the Beaumont Society and so on.

CHAPTER 20

Sex Law

What follows is a brief *resumé* of the principal legislation relating to sex as it applies, except where otherwise stated, to England and Wales. By removing a lot of detail we hope that the general import of the law will be clearer to the ordinary reader. Thus, for example, we omit information about rules of evidence, corroboration, mode of trial (except where it affects the penalty) and those instances where prosecution can be brought only by or with the consent of the Director of Public Prosecutions or the Attorney-General. In particular cases, of course, such matters can be of vital importance, and our summary should not be read as a complete statement of the law, nor as a substitute for professional legal advice.

The law in Scotland is similar, but there are some significant variations. Readers are referred to the Sexual Offences (Scotland) Act 1976 and the Incest and Related Offences (Scotland) Act 1986.

Preliminary Definitions

1. *Sexual intercourse* means penetration by the male penis into the female vagina, however slight the penetration and whether or not there is an 'emission of seed'. It does not cover oral or anal penetration (but, *see* Buggery (page 153) in the latter case), nor penetration with objects such as bottles.
2. *Man* can include a boy, but it has been held that a boy under 14 should not be charged with any offence which would involve regarding him as capable of sexual intercourse.
3. *Woman*, similarly, can include a girl.

Abortion

It should be clearly understood that action to procure a miscarriage remains a criminal offence, except in certain carefully defined circumstances. Under Section 58 of the Offences Against the Person Act 1861, the use of drugs or any instrument with intent to procure a miscarriage, either by a pregnant woman on herself or by any person on a woman, whether or not she is actually pregnant, is an offence punishable by penal servitude for life.

Further, the Infant Life (Preservation) Act 1929 (aimed at protecting the life of a viable foetus) provides the same penalty for any person who with wilful intent to destroy the life of a child capable of being born alive, by any wilful act causes a child to die before it has an existence independent of its mother, unless it is proved that the act which caused the death of the child was done in good faith for the sole purpose of preserving the life of the mother. For the purposes of this Act, evidence that at the material time the mother had been pregnant for 28 weeks or more is taken to be *prima facie* proof that she was at that time pregnant of a child capable of being born alive.

The Abortion Act 1967

The 1929 Act is not affected by subsequent legislation, but some easement of the 1861 Act is provided by the Abortion Act 1967. This provides that a person shall not be guilty of an offence under the law relating to abortion when a pregnancy is terminated under regulations made by the Secretary of State (Statutory Instrument (SI) 1968 No. 390 as amended by SI 1969 No. 636 and SI 1976 No. 15) by a registered medical practioner, if two registered medical practioners (but see the *Note* below) are of the opinion, formed in good faith:

(a) that the continuance of the pregnancy would involve
(i) risk to the life of the pregnant woman, or
(ii) injury to the physical or mental health of the pregnant woman or any existing children of her family, greater than if the pregnancy were terminated. (In determining (ii) account may be taken of

the pregnant woman's actual or reasonably forseeable environment); or

(b) that there is a substantial risk that if the child were born it would suffer from such physical or mental abnormalities as to be seriously handicapped.

Treatment must be carried out in an NHS hospital or a place specially approved by the Secretary of State (except as in the *Note* below).

Except in circumstances set out in the *Note* below, no one is placed under a duty by the Act to take part in treatment to terminate a pregnancy if they have a conscientious objection.

Note: The requirement of having two registered medical practioners and of carrying out treatment only in an approved place, and the allowance for conscientious objection do not apply when a registered medical practitioner forms the opinion in good faith that termination of pregnancy is *immediately* necessary either to save life of or to prevent grave permanent injury to the physical or mental health of the pregnant woman.

Although the law allows for medical termination of pregnancy up to the twenty-eighth week of pregnancy, in practice, abortions are rarely performed after 20 weeks. The BMA's *Handbook of Medical Ethics* advises

> 'The doctor should recommend or perform termination after 20 weeks only if he is convinced that the health of the woman is seriously threatened, or if the child will be seriously handicapped.'

Doctors are naturally concerned to avoid an abortion which offends against the Infant Life (Preservation) Act 1929, resulting from an error in calculating the length of the pregnancy.

The Family Law Reform Act 1969, Section 8, affords young people aged 16 or more the right to consent to surgical and medical treatment without parental consent (*see* page 152), and it is a matter of medical ethics and confidentiality should be respected.

The case of *Paton* v. *Paton* (1978) established a precedent that a husband has no right to overrule his wife's desire to have an abortion.

The Abortion Act 1967 covers only England, Wales and Scotland. In Northern Ireland there is legislation dating from 1938 which permits abortion in hospital on strong medical grounds or if the woman is mentally handicapped, if she has been in contact with rubella or if the foetus is likely to be genetically handicapped.

Children and Young People

The sexual abuse of children is particularly offensive, involving as it does a breach of trust or the expoitation of weakness, obedience and naïvety. It is also notoriously difficult to combat. Many such offences occur within the family; if they are apprehended and met with the full severity of the law, as the facts may well merit, one likely consequence is the disintegration of the family, with a strong possibility that the abused child will paradoxically feel a dreadful burden of blame. Moreover, in such cases, unless there is a guilty plea, the young victim will almost certainly have to go through the ordeal of giving evidence in person.

Age of Consent

See Intercourse with a girl, page 151.

Age of Majority

By the Family Law Reform Act 1969, the age at which young people can vote and marry without parental consent is 18. In Scotland, the Age of Majority Act 1969 reduced the voting age to 18, but did not refer to marriage because young people have always been able to marry by common law at 16 without parental consent. In Northern Ireland, the age of majority is 18, but by the Age of Marriage (Northern Ireland) Act 1951, the legal minimum age for marriage is 16 and by the Marriages Act 1954 (as amended), parental consent is required up to age 18.

Custody

It is unusual for lesbians to be granted custody of children in divorce proceedings. In a case in which custody was, exceptionally, so granted, Lord Justice Watkins, in the Court of Appeal, is reported to have said that he was 'uneasy' over the case and that while it was neither the 'time nor the place to moralise or philosophise' about sexual deviance, the possible effects of homosexuality on children living in close proximity to those practising it were a matter of public concern. He indicated that the courts should countenance allowing children to live in such a household only when they were driven to the conclusion that it was in the interests of the child and that there was no other acceptable form of custody. (*Guardian*, 22 July 1982). *'Lesbian Mothers' Legal Handbook'* published by The Women's Press, 34 Great Sutton Street, London EC1V ODX (Tel: 01-251 3007), 1986, price £3.95 plus 60p postage, offers guidance to lesbians on what precautions to take if they want to keep charge of their children, and what to do in the event of a custody dispute.

See also Lesbian Custody Project, page 163.

Evidence

In October 1986, the Home Secretary announced that legislation would be enacted to allow, with the judge's agreement, children who have been sexually attacked to give evidence and be cross-examined on closed-circuit television, thus avoiding the distress of a court appearance.

Illegitimacy

A child born of parents who do not marry is illegitimate unless legitimated by adoption. This includes children born by artificial insemination by donor (*see* Chapter 6, 'Infertility').

The Attorney General announced on 22 April 1986 that the Government would introduce legislation at 'the earliest opportunity' to remove legal disadvantages suffered by illegitimate children. This has been reinforced by a Report of the Law Commission (No.157, following an earlier Report No.118 of 1982) recommending a Bill to remove the description 'illegitimate' or any such word entirely, and to rule that children hitherto so-called will automatically be included in references to children (or other relationships) in future legislation or in legal documents, unless, exceptionally, the contrary needs to be stated. The proposals envisage, eventually, like treatment under the law for all children, even though differences in parental relationships will remain.

Incest

Incest with children is an offence under the Sexual Offences Act 1956 (*see* Incest, page 154). It is also an offence (under the Criminal Law Act 1977, Section 54) for a man (*see* definition 2 on page 149) to incite a girl under 16 to have sexual intercourse with him, when he knows her to be his grand-daughter, daughter or sister (including half-sister). Such a relationship may be proved to apply, notwithstanding that it is not traced through lawful wedlock.

Maximum penalties:

summary – six months' imprisonment or a £2,000 fine or both;
indictment – two years' imprisonment.

The law on incest extends to illegitimate children, but not to adopted or step-children, though other legislation (intercourse with a girl, indecent assault) may well apply where the child is not within the prohibited relationships.

Indecent Photographs

Under the Protection of Children Act 1978, it is an offence to take or permit to be taken any indecent photograph of a child (for the purposes of this Act, under 16) or to deal in such photographs, i.e. to distribute or show, or to have possession with a view to their being distributed or shown, or to publish or cause to be published any advertisement likely to be understood as conveying that the advertiser distributes or shows such indecent photographs, or intends to do so.

The word 'indecent' is not defined and would be a matter for magistrates or jury (in the light of other legislation and case law).

'Photograph' includes films (including video films), copies and both negatives and positives.

Maximum penalties:

summary – six months' imprisonment or a £1,000 fine or both;
indictment – three years' imprisonment or an unspecified fine or both.

Intercourse With a Girl

It is an offence under the Sexual Offences Act 1956, Section 6 (as amended) for a man (*see* definition 2 on page 149) to have unlawful sexual intercourse (*see* definition 1 on page 149) with a girl under the age of 16. Consent is immaterial, but there are two important exceptions:

(a) where, though the marriage is in fact invalid (because the wife is under 16) the husband has sexual intercourse with her reasonably believing her to be his wife; and
(b) where the man is under 24, has not previously been charged with a like offence (including any attempt) and believes the girl to be 16 or more and has reasonable cause for the belief.

Apart from these exceptions, maximum penalties are as follows:

Maximum penalties:

summary – six months' imprisonment or a £2,000 fine or both;
indictment – two years' imprisonment.

An attempt to commit the offence carries the same penalty.

Note: By a majority in the Gillick case, the Appellate Committee of the House of Lords held that a doctor, in prescribing a contraceptive for a child under the age of 16, would not generally become an accessory to the man's offence of unlawful sexual intercourse with her. (For a full discussion, see *'New Law Journal'*, 22 and 29 November, 1985).

If the girl is under the age of 13, Section 5 of the Sexual Offences Act applies. Under this Section, it is an offence for a man (*see* definition 2 on page 149) to have unlawful sexual intercourse (*see* definition 1 on page 149) with a girl under the age of 13, irrespective of consent or whether the accused believed her not to be under 13.

Maximum penalty:

life imprisonment.

An attempt to commit this offence carries a maximum penalty of seven years' imprisonment.

In Northern Ireland the age of consent is 17 and the law distinguishes between offences against girls under 14 (maximum penalty, life imprisonment) and from 14 up to the age of 17 (maximum penalty, two years). Also in Northern Ireland there is no defence that the man believed her to be 17 or more, whatever her true age.

Indecent Conduct Towards a Young Girl

It is an offence under the Indecency with Children Act 1960 for anyone to commit an act of gross indecency (not defined) with or towards a child under 14 or to incite a child under that age to such an act with himself or another.

Maximum penalties:

summary – six months or a £2,000 fine or both;
indictment – two years' imprisonment.

Marriage

Under the Marriage Act 1949, Section 2, and the Matrimonial Causes Act 1973, Section 11, a marriage between persons either of whom is under 16 is void. For young people aged 16 or more, but under 18, parental or equivalent consent is normally required (*see* Section 3 and Schedule 2 of the 1949 Act, as amended by the Family Law Reform Act 1969, Section 2(1)(a)). Where consent is refused, application can be made to a magistrates' court, county court or high court for permission and the court may overrule the parents' decision.

See also Age of Majority on page 150.

Medical Treatment

It is clear from the Law Lords ruling in the Gillick case that consent can be given by a minor under 16 to medical treatment, including contraception, when he or she 'reaches a sufficient understanding and intelligence to be capable of making up his own mind on the matter requiring decision' (Lord Scarman, House of Lords, 1985).

In practice, doctors advising and treating minors are likely to differ on this issue. Normally it is considered good practice to involve parents, but in cases where this is unacceptable, advice and treatment may be given without parental involvement.

In cases where surgical treatment is required, it is extremely unlikely that a doctor or anaethetist would be prepared to perform an operation without involving the next of kin, but parental consent may not be an absolute requirement.

Prostitution

It is an offence for anyone having custody, charge or care of a child who has attained the age of four and is under 16 to allow the child to reside in or to frequent a brothel (Children and Young Persons Act 1933, Section 3).

Maximum penalty:

summary – six months' imprisonment or a £100 fine or both.

See also Prostitution, page 158.

Female Circumcision

The Prohibition of Female Circumcision Act 1985, Section 1 makes it an offence for any person:

(a) to excise, infibulate or otherwise mutilate the whole or any part of the labia majora or labia minora or clitoris of another person; or
(b) to aid, abet, counsel or procure the performance by another person of any of those acts on that other person's own body.

Maximum penalties:

summary – £2,000 fine or six months' imprisonment or both;
indictment – unspecified fine or five years' imprisonment or both.

There are exceptions for necessary surgical operations, but this takes no account of any belief that the operation is required as a matter of custom or ritual.

Homosexuality

Buggery

By the Sexual Offences Acts of 1956 and 1967, it is an offence to commit an act of buggery, either with another person or with an animal. Except as specifically allowed by Section 1 of the 1967 Act (*see* 'Consenting Adults' below) consent does not afford a defence and the consenting party offends along with the principal to the act. The law covers anal intercourse with a man or a woman (including a man with his wife) or with an animal, and vaginal intercourse man/animal or animal/woman.

Maximum penalties:

with a boy under 16, a woman or an animal, life imprisonment;
with another man of 16 or more, unless the other man consented, ten years' imprisonment;
with a consenting man of 16 or more, but under 21, by a man aged 21 or more, five years' imprisonment;
otherwise, with a consenting man of 16 or more, two years' imprisonment.

Attempted buggery with a boy under 16, or with a woman, or an animal carries a maximum penalty of ten years' imprisonment. An assault on a person with intent to commit buggery is an offence under Section 16 of the 1956 Act and carries a maximum penalty of ten years' imprisonment. Procuring another man to commit with a third man an act of buggery which by the 1967 Act, Section 1 (*see* 'Consenting Adults' below) is not itself an offence, nevertheless carries a maximum penalty of two years' imprisonment or on summary conviction, six months' imprisonment or a £2,000 fine or both.

Consenting Adults

Under the Sexual Offences Act 1967, Section 1, a homosexual act in which a man commits buggery with another man or commits an act of 'gross indecency' with another man or is a party to the commission by a man of such an act ceased to be an offence provided that the parties concerned consented to the act and were both aged 21 or more

There remain, however, a number of exceptions to this relaxation.

1. An act which, notwithstanding privacy, is done when more than two persons take part or are present or which takes place in a public lavatory or involves a man suffering from a severe subnormality within the meaning of the Mental Health Act 1959. (Such a person cannot, in law, 'consent'. It is, however, a defence if the person charged can prove that he did not know and had no reason to suspect the subnormality.)
2. An act which notwithstanding being between two consenting adults in private, takes place on a UK merchant ship, wherever it may be, by a man who is a member of the crew of that ship with another man who is a member of the same crew or of any other UK merchant ship ('crew' includes the Master and apprentices).

In addition to these exceptions an act, notwithstanding being between two consenting adults in private, is not precluded from being an offence under legislation relating to the armed forces (Army Act 1955, Air Force Act 1955, Naval Discipline Act 1957).

Homosexual Brothels

The legislation against brothels in the Sexual Offences Act 1956, Sections 33/35 is extended, by the Sexual Offences Act 1967, Section 6, to premises resorted to for 'lewd homosexual practices' where the circumstances are such that, if the lewd practices had been heterosexual, they would have led to the premises being treated as a brothel.

Indecency Between Men

Except as provided by the Sexual Offences Act 1967 (*see* 'Consenting Adults' above) it is an offence under the Sexual Offences Act 1956, Section 13, for a man (*see* definition 2 on page 149) to commit an act of 'gross indecency' with another man (*see* definition 2 on page 149) or to be a party to such an offence. (*See also* 'Indecent Behaviour', page 157.)

Maximum penalties:

summary – six months' imprisonment or a £2,000 fine or both;
indictment – if by a man of 21 or over with a man under 21, five years' imprisonment;
otherwise, two years' imprisonment.

Procuring an act of 'gross indecency' between men is also an offence, except (by the Sexual Offences Act 1967, Section 4(3)) where the procuration is to commit the act with the procurer himself and the act is not itself an offence by reason of Section 1 of the Sexual Offences Act 1967 (*see* 'Consenting Adults', above).

Maximum penalties:

If by a man of 21 or over to procure a man under 21 to commit an act of 'gross indecency' with another man, five years' imprisonment;
otherwise, two years' imprisonment.

Lesbian Relationships

There is no legal restriction on homosexual acts between women over 16 who both consent.

Living on Earnings of Male Prostitution

A man or woman who knowingly lives wholly or in part on the earnings of male prostitution commits an offence under the Sexual Offences Act 1967, Section 5.

Maximum penalties:

summary – six months' imprisonment or a £2,000 fine;
indictment – seven years' imprisonment.

Incest

It is an offence under the Sexual Offences Act 1956, Section 10, for a man (*see* definition 2 on page 149) to have sexual intercourse (*see* definition 1 on page 149) with a woman (*see* definition 3 on page 149) whom he knows to be his grand-daughter, daughter, sister (including half-sister) or mother.

Maximum penalties:

If with a girl under 13, life imprisonment;
otherwise, seven years' imprisonment.

The jury may alternatively find the accused guilty under the Sexual Offences Act 1956, Section 5 or Section 6 (*see* 'Intercourse with a Girl', page 151).

Attempted incest by a man carries the following maximum penalties (as amended by the Indecency with Children Act 1960):

Maximum penalties:

If with a girl under 13, seven years' imprisonment;
otherwise, two years' imprisonment.

It is an offence under Section 11 of the Sexual Offences Act 1956 for a woman of 16 or more to permit a man (*see* definition 2 on page 149) whom she knows to be her grandfather, father, brother (including half-brother) or son to have sexual intercourse (*see* definition 1 on page 149) with her by her consent.

Maximum penalties:

seven years' imprisonment;
for an attempt to commit the offence, two years' imprisonment.

(*See also* Children and Young People, page 150.)
Note: buggery is not incest.

Indecent Assault

Indecent Assault on a Woman

It is an offence under the Sexual Offences Act 1956, Section 14, indecently to assault a woman (*see* definition 3 on page 149). Consent can constitute a defence if the woman is 16 or more, but cannot be offered if the assault is alleged on a girl under 16, except in the case of a husband on his wife, where although the marriage is invalid by reason of the wife being under 16, the husband believes her to be his wife and has reasonable cause for that belief.

Maximum penalties:

summary – six months or a £2,000 fine or both;
indictment – ten years' imprisonment (by the Sexual Offences Act 1985).

Indecent Assault on a Man

This is an offence under the Sexual Offences Act 1956, Section 15. Again, consent can be offered in defence, but not if the assault is on a boy under 16. *See* definition 2 on page 149.

Maximum penalties:

summary – six months' imprisonment or a £2,000 fine or both;
indictment – ten years' imprisonment.

Marriage

By the Matrimonial Causes Act 1973, Section 11, there are a number of grounds which render a marriage celebrated after July 1971 void, including:

(a) (i) the parties are within prohibited degrees of relationship (for which *see* Marriage Act 1949, Section 1(1) and Schedule 1, Part 1, as amended by the Marriage (Prohibited Degrees of Relationship) Act 1986),
(ii) either party is under the age of 16,
(iii) the parties have intermarried in disregard of certain requirements as to the formation of marriage;

(b) at the time of the marriage either party was already lawfully married;
(c) the parties are not respectively male and female (in the case of *Corbett* v. *Corbett (Ashley)* (1970) it was held that the 'marriage' of a male with an operated male transsexual was invalid).

By Section 12 of the same Act, a marriage celebrated after 31 July 1971 is voidable on a number of grounds, including:

(a) non-consummation, owing to the incapacity of either party or the wilful refusal of the respondent;
(b) at the time of the marriage the respondent was suffering from a venereal disease in a communicable form or was pregnant by some person other than the petitioner (on either of these grounds proceedings would need to be instituted within three years of the date of the marriage and the court would need to be satisfied that the petitioner was at the time of the marriage ignorant of the facts alleged).

In the case of voidable marriages, a decree of nullity will not be granted if the respondent satisfies the court:

(a) that the petitioner, having knowledge open to him to have the marriage avoided, so behaved towards the respondent as reasonably to lead the respondent to believe that he/she would not seek to do so; and
(b) that it would be unjust to the respondent to grant the decree.

For marriages prior to 1 August 1971, *see Rayden on Divorce*, thirteenth edition, published by Butterworths, 1979, pages 185–188.

Mentally Handicapped People

Current legislation, designed to protect severely mentally handicapped people from exploitation, effectively prohibits them as adults from entering into sexual relationships even if they wish to do so.

Describing such people as 'defectives', the law provides for criminal charges as follows:

(a) causing or encouraging prostitution – *see* Sexual Offences Act 1956, Section 29 (maximum penalty: two years' imprisonment);
(b) indecent assault *see* Sexual Offences Act 1956, Sections 14/15 (for penalties, *see* 'Indecent Assault', page 154);
(c) procurement of a severely mentally handicapped woman *see* Sexual Offences Act 1956, Section 9 (maximum penalty: two years' imprisonment);
(d) unlawful intercourse with a severely mentally handicapped woman – *see* Sexual Offences Act 1956, Section 7 (maximum penalty: two years' imprisonment);
(e) buggery or gross indecency by a man with a severely mentally handicapped man – *see* Sexual Offences Act 1956, Sections 12 and 13 and Sexual Offences Act 1967, Section 1(3) (for penalties *see* under 'Homosexuality', page 153);
(f) unlawful intercourse (i.e. outside marriage) between a male member of staff with a woman who is receiving treatment for a mental disorder in the hospital (this applies equally to guardians) *see* Mental Health Act 1959, Section 128 (maximum penalty: two years' imprisonment).

Note: where consent affords a defence, it is held that a person suffering from a severe mental handicap cannot in law give any such consent. But in such circumstances a person would not be convicted if able to prove that he/she did not know and had no reason to suspect that the other party was suffering from severe subnormality.

In its Working Paper on Sexual Offences, the Criminal Law Revision Committee canvassed a new scheme to replace the existing prohibition on unlawful sexual intercourse and homosexual relations with severely mentally handicapped people. It was proposed (provisionally) that a person responsible for a severely mentally handicapped person, male or female, should be able to apply to a county court for a non-molestation order which would in effect prohibit a named man or woman from associating with the mentally handicapped person.

In a booklet *Getting Together* (1982), the National Assocation for Mental Health calls for a reform of the law so as to allow the test of consent to be applied as with non-handicapped people and thus to permit consensual sexual relationships between mentally handicapped people. It also calls for clarification of the position of staff in hospitals and residential units in the civil law, with guidelines from the DHSS to remove the inhibitions of staff who fear the legal consequences of encouraging the development of sexual relationships.

Obscenity and Indecency

Cable Programmes

By the Cable and Broadcasting Act 1984, Section 25 (which Section does not extend to Scotland), a person providing a cable programme service is guilty of an offence if:

(a) the inclusion of a programme in the service involves the publication of 'an obscene article'; or
(b) a programme included in such a service is such that,

if any matter included in it were recorded, the inclusion of the programme would involve the publication of an obscene article.

There is an exclusion for a service involving the reception and immediate transmission of a broadcast made by a broadcasting authority, and a defence to prove that the inclusion of the programme was justified as being for the public good on the ground that it was in the interests of drama, opera, ballet or any other art, or of literature or learning.

Maximum penalties:

(summary) £2,000 fine or six months' imprisonment;
indictment – unspecified fine or three years imprisonment or both.

Proceedings under Section 2 of the Obscene Publications Act 1959 are correspondingly restricted.

Displays

The Indecent Displays (Control) Act 1981 aims to remove indecent material from public view. It is an offence under the Act to display or to cause or permit to be displayed 'indecent matter' so as to be visible from a 'public place'.

'Indecent' is not defined in the Act and would be a question for magistrates or jury (in the light of other legislation and case law). 'Matter' means anything capable of being displayed, except an actual human body or any of its parts (which may, however, offend common law). 'Public place' means any place to which the public has or is permitted to have access – whether by payment or not – while the indecent material is being displayed. Any part of the matter which is not exposed must be disregarded.

There are, however, two important exceptions which are effective, provided that persons under 18 are not admitted:

(a) a place to which the public is permitted to have access only on payment which is or includes payment for that display; or
(b) a shop or any part of a shop to which the public can only gain access by passing beyond an adequate warning notice (specified in Section 1(6)).

Section 1(4) excepts television broadcasts by the BBC, IBA or a cable broadcast which is or does not need to be licensed, plays within the meaning of the Theatres Act 1968, film exhibitions as defined in the Cinemas Act 1985, museums and art galleries and authorised Crown and local authority displays on their own premises.

Maximum penalties:

summary – a £2,000 fine;
indictment – two years' imprisonment or an unspecified fine or both.

Films

By the Cinemas Act 1985, exhibitions of moving pictures (including video films), other than the simultaneous reception and exhibition of programmes transmitted by the BBC, IBA or included in a cable programme service which is or does not need to be licensed under Section 4 of the Cable and Broadcasting Act 1984, may be given only in premises licensed by the local authority. There is, of course, power to withhold licences or to impose conditions (including the power to allow only films certified by the British Board of Film Censors).

There are some exceptions to licensing control. These include:

(a) film shows in private dwellings (Section 5);
(b) film shows to which the public are not admitted or are admitted without payment, or which are given by certain excepted organisations under prescribed conditions (Section 6).

These exceptions are intended for the benefit of film shows on domestic occasions or by bona-fide film societies, etc. They do not apply to film shows promoted for private gain, which are under licensing control, and thus effectively under censorship.

Maximum penalties:

use of any premises in respect of which a licence under Section 1 is not in force for an exhibition requiring such a licence: £20,000 fine;
other offences, e.g. breach of regulations/conditions: £2,000 fine.

The penalties apply to the following:

(a) any person concerned in the organisation or management of the exhibition;
(b) the licence holder (where a licence is in force);
(c) any other person who, knowing or having reasonable cause to suspect that the premises would be illegally used either
(i) allowed the premises to be so used or
(ii) let the premises or otherwise made them available, to any person by whom an offence in connection with that use of the premises has been committed.

There are also powers of entry and seizure.

Film shows are also subject to the Obscene Publications Act 1959 (*see* page 158) and this applies to film clubs. However, there appears to be some reluctance to prosecute where the viewing takes place in restricted circumstances.

Importation of Indecent or Obscene Matter

Section 42 of the Customs Consolidation Act 1876 has survived a great deal of amending and reorganising legislation and prohibits the importation of

> 'indecent or obscene prints, paintings, photographs, books, cards, lithographic and engravings, or any other indecent or obscene articles'.

By the Customs and Excise Management Act 1979, Section 50, anyone who, with intent to evade the prohibition, imports or is concerned in importing prohibited goods (whether or not the goods are unloaded) or who unships, unloads, lands or removes them or assists or is otherwise concerned with any of these actions commits an offence.

Moreover, by Section 170 of the 1979 Act there are similar provisions against anyone who knowingly acquires possession of such prohibited goods or who is in any way knowingly concerned in carrying, removing, depositing, harbouring, keeping or concealing or in any manner dealing with them, with intent to evade the prohibition.

Maximum penalties:

summary – a fine of £1,000 or three times the value of the goods (whichever is the greater) or six months' imprisonment or both;
indictment – an unlimited fine or two years' imprisonment or both.
In addition the goods are liable to forfeiture under Section 49 of the 1979 Act.

Note: Although this legislation remains on the statute book, the Government has made it clear that in future Customs will apply the prohibition in line with relevant domestic legislation. Officers will, in practice, have to test the publication against the Obscene Publications Act 1959, which has more stringent tests of obscenity and indecency and greater scope for defence. This follows an EEC ruling on the importation of inflatable sex dolls, as well as the abortive prosecution of Gay's the Word bookshop.

Indecent behaviour

Section 5 of the Public Order Act 1936 has sometimes been used to prosecute alleged indecent behaviour. This provides, among other things, that 'insulting' behaviour in a public place which is likely to occasion a breach of the peace is an offence.

Maximum penalties:

summary – six months' imprisonment or a £2,000 fine or both.

It seems to us, however, that behaviour of a sexually indecent nature will seldom come within this legislation. *R.* v. *Howell* (1981) clarified a breach of the peace as an act or threat of an act which either harmed a person (or in his presence his property) or was likely to cause such harm or which put someone in fear of such harm being done. More recently, in *Parkin* v. *Norman* (1982), a case involving homosexual activity in a public lavatory, it was held by the Court of Appeal that Section 5 would 'more often than not' be an inappropriate charge against such behaviour.

Indecent Exposure

Depending on the circumstances, there may be an offence under the Town Police Clauses Act 1847, Section 28, of 'wilfully and indecently' exposing the person in a 'street' to the annoyance of the residents or under the Vagrancy Act 1824, Section 4, for 'wilfully, openly, lewdly and obscenely exposing' the person 'with intent to insult any female'.

Maximum penalties:

under the 1847 Act – a £400 fine or 14 days' imprisonment and
under the 1824 Act – three months' imprisonment.

Obscene Telephone Calls

By the Telecommunications Act 1984, Section 43, it is an offence to send 'by means of a public telecommunication system' a message or other matter that is 'grossly offensive or of an indecent, obscene or menacing character'.

Maximum penalty:

a £400 fine.

Plays

By the Theatres Act 1968 it is an offence to give a performance of an 'obscene' play, whether in public or private and whether or not for gain. A play is regarded as obscene if when taken as a whole, its effect is such as to tend to deprave and corrupt those likely to attend.

It is a defence to prove that the performance was justified as being 'for the public good on the ground that it was in the interests of drama, opera, ballet or any other art, or of literature or learning'. The Act does not apply to performances on a domestic occasion in a private dwelling, nor to performances given solely or primarily for rehearsal or to enable a recording or cinematograph film to be made, for broadcasting or for transmission to subscribers of a diffusion service.

Maximum penalties:

summary – a £2,000 fine or six months' imprisonment;
indictment – an unspecified fine or three years' imprisonment or both.

Postal Restrictions

The Post Office Act 1953, Section 11, prohibits sending or attempting to send or procuring to be sent, a postal packet which encloses 'any indecent or obscene print, painting, photograph, lithograph, engraving, cinematograph film, book, card or written communication, or any indecent or obscene article whether similar to the above or not' or which has on the packet or on its cover 'any words, marks or designs which are grossly offensive or of an indecent or obscene character'.

Maximum penalties:

summary – a £2,000 fine;
indictment – 12 months' imprisonment.

Publishing

By the Obscene Publications Acts 1959 and 1964 (as amended by the Criminal Law Act 1977, Section 53) it is an offence to 'publish' an 'obscene article' (whether or not for gain) or to have an 'obscene article' (including anything which is intended for use in the reproduction of obscene articles, e.g. film negatives) in ownership, possession or control, with a view to publication for gain (either for the person having the article or for another).

An 'article' may be anything which contains or incorporates matter to be read or looked at or both and any sound record and any film or other record of a picture or pictures. The test of obscenity is whether the matter tends to deprave and corrupt those who are likely to read, see or hear it.

'Publish' covers distribution, sale, circulation, letting on hire, giving, lending or offering for sale or hire; or (in case of matter to be looked at or of a record) showing, playing or projecting (there is, however, an exception in favour of anything done in the course of television or sound broadcasting. A further exception in favour of film shows was removed by the Criminal Law Act 1977 Section 53.)

Under Section 4 of the Act, there is a defence that a person shall not be convicted if it is proved that publication is justified as being 'for the public good on the ground that it is in the interests of science, literature, art or learning [this has been held to mean a product of scholarship] or other objects of general concern', except in the case of a 'moving picture film or soundtrack' where it is necesssary to prove that its publication is justified as being for the public good, as being in the interests of drama, opera, ballet or any other art or of literature or learning.

Maximum penalties:

summary – a £2,000 fine or six months' imprisonment;
indictment – an unspecified fine or three years' imprisonment or both.

There are also powers of search, seizure and forfeiture.

Sending Unsolicited Sexually Explicit Printed Matter

By the Unsolicited Goods and Services Act 1971, Section 4 it is an offence for anyone to send or cause to be sent to another person any book, magazine or leaflet (or advertising material for any such publication) which he knows or ought reasonably to know is unsolicited and which describes or illustrates human sexual techniques.

This Section applies to relevant advertising material even if it does not itself describe or illustrate human sexual techniques.

Maximum penalties:

summary only – a £2,000 fine.

Prostitution

While prostitution as such is not unlawful, there are a number of associated offences, mostly under the Sexual Offences Act 1956, including the procuring of a woman (*see* definition 3 on page 149) to become a prostitute or causing or encouraging the prostitution of a girl under 16 or a 'defective'. There are severe penalties for those who live on the earnings of prostitution ('pimps') and for women who exercise control over prostitutes for gain. Other sections of the 1956 Act legislate against letting or permitting premises to be used for prostitution.

A 'common prostitute' who loiters or solicits in a street or public place for the purposes of prostitution commits an offence under the Street Offences Act 1959, while a man who solicits offends against the 1956 Act. In neither of these cases does the display of a notice advertising 'services' constitute soliciting, but this could offend against the Indecent Displays (Control) Act 1981 or against common law. (*See* 'Soliciting' as to penalties).
Note: The Report of the Criminal Law Revision Committee (1985 Cmnd 9688) recommends the repeal of Section 30 of the Sexual Offences act 1956 (the offence of living on immoral earnings), and the enactment of three new offences: organising prostitution, directing or controlling the activities of a prostitute, and assisting a person to meet a prostitute.

Rape

See Unlawful Sexual Intercourse, page 161.

Sex 'Establishments'

The Local Government (Miscellaneous Provisions) Act 1982 contains legislation for the control of sex establishments, *viz.* sex shops and sex cinemas. The terms 'sex shop' and 'sex cinema' will be colloquially understood, but for anyone needing a precise definition, the Act provides explicit detail.

Part II of the Act provides that a local authority may resolve that from a stipulated date (not less than one month after the resolution) and after due notice, Schedule 3 to the Act is to apply to its area. Schedule 3 provides for a system of licensing of sex establishments and prescribes offences for unlicensed use, etc. Paragraph 6 of the Schedule provides that no person may use any premises, vehicle, vessel or stall as a sex establishment, except under and in accordance with the terms of a licence. There is an exclusion in favour of articles made primarily for use in, or which primarily relate to, birth control, and provision in paragraph 7 for formal application for the licensing requirements to be waived. The local authority can allow such an application if it considers that to require a licence would be unreasonable or inappropriate.

Applications for a licence must contain prescribed details (paragraph 10) and there are requirements about giving public notice. Objections can be lodged within 28 days of any application (the name and address of the objector being confidential to the authority) and the police also have a right to submit observations. Before refusing to grant, renew or transfer a licence, the authority must give the applicant (and in the case of a transfer the intended beneficiary) an opportunity of being heard by a committee appointed for the purpose. The applicant is also entitled, if he or she so requires, to a written explanation of any refusal.

Grounds for refusal of a grant or renewal are as follows:

(a) the applicant is unsuitable (having been convicted of an offence or for any other reason); or
(b) the business is to be managed or carried on for the benefit of someone other than the applicant who would be refused if he were to apply; or
(c) the number of sex establishments in the relevant locality is equal to or greater than that number which the authority considers appropriate to that locality (which may be nil); or
(d) the grant or renewal of the licence would be inappropriate, having regard
(i) to the character of the relevant locality, or
(ii) to the use to which any premises in the vicinity are put, or
(iii) to the layout, character or condition of the establishment in respect of which the application is made.

Note: (a) and (b) above are also grounds for refusing a transfer or for revoking a licence.
Licences will not be granted to the following (or having been granted they may be revoked):

(a) person under 18;
(b) a person disqualified under paragraph 17(3) (which provides that where a licence is revoked, its holder shall be disqualified from holding or obtaining a licence in the area of the appropriate authority for 12 months)
(c) a non-UK resident;
(d) a body corporate not incorporated in the UK;
(e) a person who has, in the previous 12 months, been refused the grant or renewal of a licence for the establishment in question.

Local authorities are empowered to make regulations prescribing standard conditions applicable to licences, i.e. terms, conditions and restrictions, for example, concerning:

(a) hours of opening/closing;
(b) displays or advertisements on or in the establishment;
(c) visibility of the interior;
(d) change of use from sex shop to sex cinema or vice versa.

A person commits an offence who:

(a) knowingly uses, causes or permits the use of a sex establishment contrary to paragraph 6 (see above); (*Note*: the prosecution must prove that the defendant knew both that the premises were used as a sex establishment and that they were being used without a licence).
(b) knowingly makes a false statement in connection with an application for a grant, renewal or transfer of a licence.

A person, being a licence holder, commits an offence who:

(a) employs a person he knows to be disqualified from holding a licence in the business of a sex establishment;
(b) without reasonable excuse, knowingly contravenes or permits the contravention of licence conditions (this offence also applies to a servant or agent of the licence holder);
(c) knowingly permits a person under 18 to enter the sex establishment, or employs such a person.

Maximum penalties:

Each of the above offences carries a maximum penalty on summary conviction of £20,000. Failure to exhibit a licence carries a maximum penalty of £400.

Surrogate Motherhood

A 'surrogate mother' is a woman who 'carries' a child with a view to it being handed over to, and the parental rights being exercised (so far as practicable) by, another person or persons. Such an arrangement is a 'surrogacy arrangement'.

The Surrogacy Arrangements Act 1985 aims to prevent third parties deriving financial benefit from surrogacy arrangements. By Section 2, it is an offence for any person, other than prospective surrogate mothers or those who intend a surrogate mother to carry a child for them, to do any of the following acts on a commercial basis:

(a) initiate or take part in any negotiations with a view to the making of a surrogacy arrangement,
(b) offer or agree to negotiate the making of a surrogacy arrangement, or
(c) compile any information with a view to its use in making, or negotiating the making of, surrogacy arrangements, or
(d) to knowingly cause another to do any of those acts on a commercial basis (the term 'commercial basis' is closely defined).

There is also an offence relating to an organisation ('body') which as an activity negotiates or facilitates the making of surrogacy arrangements, when someone acting on its behalf takes any part in negotiating or facilitating the making of a surrogacy arrangement in the United Kingdom for which payment is received either from or on behalf of a woman who carries a child in pursuance of the arrangement, the person or persons for whom she carries it, or anyone connected with the surrogate mother or the person(s) for whom she carries the child.

Any person who in the United Kingdom takes part in the management or control of such a body or in any of its activities also commits an offence.

Section 3 establishes further offences in relation to advertisements about surrogacy.

Maximum penalties:

summary Section 2 – a fine of £2,000 or three months imprisonment, or both
Section 3 – a fine of £2,000.

Note: a more detailed explanation of the Act (which extends to Northern Ireland) appeared in the *New Law Journal*, October 4, 1985.

Transsexuals

In the UK the consensus of medical opinion is that an actual change of definite physical sex cannot occur, and this view is accepted by the courts. A 'sex-change' operation is not seen as a true reversal of sex and is not so treated in law; someone who has undergone medical or surgical treatment of this kind is regarded as assuming the role, but not the gender identity, of the opposite sex. It may be possible for documents of current identity to be altered to agree with the chosen role, but this would not apply to the person's birth certificate. Apart from a provision allowing the correction of errors, a birth certificate is regarded as an immutable historical record of the facts, including sex, at the time of birth. Alteration of the birth register would, in British law, be treated as a falsification.

Note: in October 1986, the European Court of Human Rights upheld the United Kingdom Government's contention that birth certificates are an unchangeable record of events, whatever may happen subsequently.

A number of significant consequences follow this understanding, for example:

(a) a marriage between a normal male and a post-operative male to female transsexual is void, as the parties are not respectively male and female (*see* Marriage, page 154);
(b) a post-operative male to female transsexual does not

qualify for retirement pension until the age appropriate for men (currently 65, whereas women qualify at 60);

(c) transsexuals who are imprisoned or hospitalised are normally placed with members of their original biological sex;

(d) the fact that there is no legal provision for a new or amended birth certificate can cause difficulties and embarrassment when, for example, applying for employment.

Unlawful Sexual Intercourse

Administering Drugs

It is an offence under the Sexual Offences Act 1956, Section 4, to

> 'apply or administer to, or cause to be taken by, a woman [*see* definition 3 on page 149] any drug, matter or thing with intent to stupefy or overpower her'

in order to enable any man to have unlawful sexual intercourse (*see* definition 1 on page 149) with her.

Maximum penalties:

two years' imprisonment.

Buggery

Buggery does not fall under the heading of Unlawful Sexual Intercourse. *See* Homosexuality, page 153.

Heterosexual Anal Intercourse

Heterosexual anal intercourse is unlawful, irrespective of consent, in public or in private and even between man and wife. *See* Buggery, page 153.

Intercourse With a Girl Under 16

See Children and Young People, page 150.

Procurement

It is an offence under the Sexual Offences Act 1956 to procure a woman to have unlawful sexual intercourse in any part of the world with the procurer or another either by threats or intimidation (including an attempt) (Section 2) or by false pretences (Section 3). In the case of a female person under 21, procurement to have unlawful sexual intercourse with a third person is an offence whether or not there are threats, intimidation or false pretences (Section 23).

All these offences carry the same maximum penalty.

Maximum penalty:

two years' imprisonment.

See also Prostitution, page 158.

Rape

By the Sexual Offences Acts 1956 to 1976, it is unlawful for a man (*see* definition 2 on page 149) to rape a woman (*see* definition 3 on page 149). This includes a man who induces a married woman to have sexual intercourse with him by impersonating her husband.

A man commits rape if:

(a) he has unlawful sexual intercourse with a woman who at the time of the intercourse does not consent to it; and

(b) at the time he knows that she does not consent to the intercourse or he is reckless as to whether she consents to it.

This reflects the ruling of the Law Lords in *DPP* v. *Morgan* (1975) which said that if a man genuinely believed that a woman consented, no matter how unreasonable that belief, he was exonerated and should be acquitted. However, where it is offered in defence that the woman was consenting, then the presence or absence of reasonable grounds for such a belief is something which the jury is specifically enjoined to take into account in considering whether the defendant is genuine in his defence.

As the law is presently interpreted, marriage is taken to imply consent, and a husband cannot therefore commit rape upon his wife, unless it is provided in a separation order or by agreement, that the wife is not bound to cohabit with her husband. (The Criminal Law Revision Committee has recommended that a husband should be liable for the charge of rape against his wife. At present, except as above, intercourse with his wife against her will is open only to a charge of assault.)

Note: it should be noted that force is not a necessary element in the commission of rape (though it may aggravate the crime) and submission is not equal to consent. As to what has been called 'contributory negligence', the words of Lord Hailsham are worth recording:

> 'Contributory negligence does not, of course, constitute any defence in rape nor, in my view, in the absence of sexual provocation, should imprudence operate as a factor of mitigation in reduction of sentence.'

Maximum penalty

life imprisonment.

The jury may alternatively find the accused guilty of

procurement of a woman by threats (Sexual Offences Act 1956, Section 2) or by false pretences (Sexual Offences Act 1956, Section 3) or of administering drugs to obtain or facilitate intercourse (Sexual Offences Act 1956, Section 4).

Attempted rape carries a maximum penalty of life imprisonment (by the Sexual Offences Act 1985). It is also an offence to aid or abet rape and unlike the principal offence, the law extends to a husband who aids or abets a rape on his wife and to women, girls and boys.

Evidence and cross examination: By Section 2 of the Sexual Offences (Amendment) Act 1976, when a 'rape offence' (i.e. any of the following: rape, attempted rape, aiding, abetting, counselling and procuring rape or attempted rape, and incitement to rape) is contested, the defence may not adduce evidence or ask questions about any sexual experience by a complainant with a person other than the accused without the leave of the judge. A judge may only give such leave on application (in the absence of the jury) if he is satisfied that the evidence or cross examination relates to matters of such relevance to the issues under trial that it would be unfair to the defendant to exclude them.

Note: this Section aims to preclude evidence and questions simply aimed at blackening the character of the complainant; but it has been held that such questions can be allowed if they might reasonably lead the court to take a different view of her evidence. In practice, it appears that where an application is made it is more often than not granted, and that women can still be disadvantaged by unfair cross-examination and by subjective and prejudiced attitudes. For a brief but penetrating review of this subject, we recommend an article by Dr Susan S.M. Edwards in the *New Law Journal*, 28 March 1986 which also has a useful bibliography.

For a note on children required to give evidence, *see* Children, page 151.

Anonymity: Sections 4 and 6 of the 1976 Act restrict the publication, except in limited specified circumstances, of particulars identifying the complainant and defendant in 'rape offences'. As far as the defendant is concerned such restriction is removed upon conviction.

Soliciting

By Section 1 of the Sexual Offences Act 1985 (which extends only to England and Wales) it is an offence for a man (*see* definition 2 on page 149) to solicit a woman or women (*see* definition 3 on page 149) to obtain her services as a prostitute in a street or public place, either from a motor vehicle (popularly known as kerb-crawling) or in its immediate vicinity having just left it. The soliciting must, however, be persistent or (in those cases in which prosecution requires the assent of the Director of Public Prosecutions) done in such a way or in circumstances such as to be likely to cause annoyance to the woman or any of the women, or nuisance to other people in the neighbourhood.

Section 2 of the Act creates a separate offence of persistent soliciting of a woman or women for prostitution (ie to obtain her/their services as a prostitute) in a street or public place, without the conditions set out in Section 1 above.

Maximum penalty
summary – a fine of £400.

By Section 32 of the Sexual Offences Act 1956, it is an offence for a man persistently to solicit or importune in a public place for immoral purposes.

Maximum penalty
summary – six months' imprisonment or a fine of £2,000, or both;
indictment – two years' imprisonment.

By Section 1 of the Street Offences Act 1959, it is an offence for a 'common prostitute' (whose gender is not specified) to loiter or solicit in a street or public place.

Maximum penalty
a fine of £100; £400 for a second like conviction.

Video Recordings – Classification and Supply

By the Video Recordings Act 1984, most English language videos must be classified and labelled according to their suitability for viewing by people of specified groups.

Classification is decided by the British Board of Film Classification, and labelling requirements are set out in Statutory Instrument 1985 No.911. There is an exception for films registered with the Department of Trade and Industry since 1940 for cinema release.

The categories are:

<table>
<tr><td>Uc</td><td>Universal; particularly suitable for children</td><td rowspan="3">may be supplied to persons of any age</td></tr>
<tr><td>U</td><td>Universal; suitable for all</td></tr>
<tr><td>PG</td><td>Parental Guidance; for general viewing but some scenes may be unsuitable for young children</td></tr>
</table>

15 Suitable only for persons aged 15 years or over; not to be supplied to any person below that age

18 Suitable only for persons of 18 years and over; not to be supplied to any person below that age

Restricted 18 Restricted; to be supplied only in licensed sex shops to persons of not less than 18 years.

Maximum penalties:
(all relate to video recordings)

Supply or offer of unclassified work:	a fine of £20,000
Possession for supply of unclassified work:	a fine of £20,000
Supply or offer in breach of classification:	a fine of £2,000
Supply or offer in Restricted 18 category other than in a licensed sex shop:	a fine of £2,000
Supply or offer not complying with the labelling requirements:	a fine of £2,000
Supply or offer with false indication of classification:	a fine of £2,000

Where to Go for Help

In addition to normal professional legal services, some solicitors offer general advice in special sessions at Legal Advice Centres and Law Centres. Legal Advice Centres are staffed by volunteer lawyers and have limited opening hours, but offer a free service. Law centres operate normal hours with lawyers and ancillary staff; they will handle a client's case in the ordinary way, but normally also offer a free advice service.

Assistance can also be sought from any solicitor operating under the legal aid scheme, which, if allowed by the courts, is available either free of charge or against a contribution, depending on financial circumstances. Lists of solicitors willing to accept legal aid cases can be seen in public libraries, Citizens' Advice Bureaux, law centres, magistrates' and county courts, town hall information centres, housing advice centres or consumer advice centres.

Free leaflets on legal aid have been prepared jointly by the Central Office of Information, the Law Society and the Lord Chancellor's Department. These are widely available, for example, at Citizens' Advice Bureaux.

Additionally, most solicitors throughout the country operate a 'fixed fee interview' scheme whereby a person may have an initial 'diagnostic' interview at a modest charge.

There are also a number of specialist services:

Gay Legal Advice (GLAD)
London Lesbian and Gay Centre, 69 Cowcross Street, London EC1 (Tel: 01-253 2043). Advice 7 p.m. – 10 p.m. weekdays.
An organisation formed to provide basic legal advice to gays experiencing legal problems arising from their sexual orientation. GLAD will provide free legal advice on a wide variety of legal problems, including sexual offences, court procedure, property, wills, employment, immigration etc.

Legal Action for Women
King's Cross Women's Centre, 71 Tonbridge Street, London WC1H 9DZ (Tel: 01-837 7509).
This service is for women by women. Solicitors will give confidential legal advice and help on a wide range of problems, including child custody, loitering, soliciting, brothel keeping and other prostitution charges, divorce, rape, battering, sexual assault, and legal aid. Phone during office hours for advice and, where necessary, an appointment with a solicitor.

The Lesbian Custody Project
52 – 54 Featherstone Street, London EC1Y 8RT (tel: 01-251 6576) Started in 1982 to campaign for the right of lesbian mothers to have custody of their children. The group is made up of such mothers and legal workers.
The work of the group includes:

(a) provision of information and advice about custody cases to individual lesbian mothers;
(b) building up a referral list of solicitors who are knowledgeable and experienced in fighting custody cases where lesbianism is an issue;
(c) talking to social workers, court welfare officers, colleges and schools to confront and change prejudicial attitudes and practices towards lesbians with children;
(d) running workshops for legal workers about to fight custody cases where lesbianism may be used as grounds for denying a woman custody;
(e) working with lesbian mothers' groups to create a strong support network;
(f) help in contact with groups;
(g) campaigning for changes in social policy and the law.

The group has published *Lesbian Mothers on Trial. A Report on Lesbian Mothers and Child Custody*, price £2.50

including postage and packing, from the above address. *See also* the legal guide mentioned under 'Children', page 150.

London Gay Switchboard (Tel: 01-837 7324) maintains a list of solicitors sympathetic to homosexual men and lesbians on a nationwide basis.

CHAPTER 21

Guide to Local Services

This section of the book provides details of clinics, organisations and individuals who provide local services.

The list is not comprehensive. We have excluded clinics which provide only family planning services. These are very numerous and they are easily found through local telephone directories. Details of national family planning organisations providing services throughout the UK are described in Chapter 3, 'Family Planning'. Details of clinics providing infertility services are described in Chapter 6, 'Infertility'. For the rest, we have included only those services which responded to our questionnaire, the details of which could be verified at source prior to publication.

Entries appear in geographical order by county. National organisations are described in their respective chapters, for example the Family Planning Association in Chapter 3, 'Family Planning'. These organisations should be able to give you information about their own local provision. The Family Planning Information Service will provide local information on a wide range of services, including psychosexual counselling, family planning and infertility. The FPA Regional Offices will provide details of facilities in their areas. Details of these Regional Offices appear in this chapter in their appropriate geographical position.

If you have any difficulty at all in locating a particular service, please consult the Index. We hope you find what you need.

All entries have been inserted free of charge. None should be taken as implying any recommendation, nor construed as an advertisement.

Where to Go for Help

ENGLAND

AVON

Family Planning Association Regional Office
For details see the FPA Regional Office (South-west England) in Exeter, Devon.

Bath

Marital Sexual Therapy Service
Bath and District Marriage Guidance Council, 3rd Floor, 14 New Bond Street, Bath BA1 1BE (Tel: Bath (0225) 65593).
See also Chapter 15, 'Marriage Guidance'.

British Pregnancy Advisory Service
(Tel: (022 17) 3321).
Services offered: Pregnancy testing; pregnancy counselling; female sterilisation counselling; vasectomy counselling; female sterilisation reversal counselling; vasectomy reversal counselling; sub-fertility counselling; artificial insemination counselling.
Is professional referral required? No.
Fees: for details *see* BPAS in Chapter 3, 'Family Planning'.
For further details of BPAS services, *see* Chapter 3.

Bristol

Avon Sex Clinic (Bristol)
Muriel Russell (Organising Secretary), Third Floor, 14 New Bond Street, Bath BA1 1BE (Tel: Bath (0225) 65593).
Services offered: Treatment programmes based on Masters and Johnson techniques to people who are experiencing sexual difficulties.

Problems dealt with: Male – primary and secondary impotence, ejaculatory incompetence; female – vaginismus, dyspareunia, orgasmic dysfunction; loss of libido/interest.
Is professional referral required? Preferable.
Hours: Normal working hours and some evenings.
Fees: Maximum £10 per session. Individual financial circumstances will be taken sympathetically into consideration.

Brook Advisory Centre
25 Denmark Street, Bristol BS1 5DQ (Tel: Bristol (0272) 292136).
Services offered: As well as family planning services, this Centre also provides psychosexual counselling.
Is professional referral required? No.
Hours: Monday to Friday 9 a.m. – 4.30 p.m. and 6 p.m. – 8 p.m.; first and third Saturdays in the month 10 a.m. – 12 noon.
Fees: These vary.
For further details of Brook services *see* Chapter 3, 'Family Planning'.

BUPA Medical Centre
4 Priory Road, Clifton, Bristol BS8 1TY (Tel: Bristol (0272) 731433). For details *see* Greater London (Camden).

Marital Therapy Clinic
Gloucester House, Southmead Hospital, Bristol (Tel: Bristol (0272) 743846).
Services offered: Full range of help for personal and sexual difficulties; counselling for disabled people and advice on achieving ejaculation for paraplegics.
Problems dealt with: Psychosexual and marital problems; sexual dysfunction.
Is professional referral required? Yes.
Hours: By appointment.
Fees: None (but patients can also be seen privately).

Marriage Sexual Therapy Service
Bristol Marriage Guidance Council, 19–21 Merchant Street, Bristol BS1 3EH (Tel: Bristol (0272) 214248).
See also Chapter 15, 'Marriage Guidance'.

BEDFORDSHIRE

Family Planning Association Regional Office
For details, see the FPA Regional Office (North of the Thames) in Bedford.

Bedford

British Pregnancy Advisory Service
(Tel: Bedford (0234) 46574).
Services offered: Pregnancy testing; pregnancy counselling; female sterilisation counselling; vasectomy counselling.
Is professional referral required? No.
Fees: *See* BPAS in Chapter 3.
For further details of BPAS services *see* Chapter 3.

Psychosexual Counselling Clinic
c/o Dr. J. Harrison, Rogers Court, Cauldwell Street, Bedford MK42 9AD (Tel: Bedford (0234) 45111 ext. 47).
Services offered: Counselling (joint FP doctor/ clinical psychologist).
Problems dealt with: any functional problem.
Is professional referral required? Normally.
Hours: five sessions a month (Tuesday mornings).
Fees: none.

The Family Planning Association (North of the Thames Regional Office)
27 St Peter's Street, Bedford MK40 2PN (Tel: Bedford (0234) 62436).
See also Chapter 3, 'Family Planning'.
Services offered: Information on FP services within the region; resource centre–leaflets, books and films; telephone information service; vasectomy clinics in Luton, St Albans and High Wycombe.
Problems dealt with: Menopause advice. *See* above.
Is professional referral required? No.
Hours: Monday to Friday 9.30 a.m. – 4.30 p.m. (make appointments by telephone).
Fees: Phone for details.

Luton

British Pregnancy Advisory Service
(Tel: Luton (0582) 26287). Services offered: pregnancy testing; pregnancy counselling; abortion counselling; contraception; morning after birth control.
Enquiries about: infertililty problems; artificial insemination.
Is professional referral required? No.
Hours: Monday to Friday 9 a.m. – 5 p.m.
Fees: *See* BPAS in Chapter 3.
For further details about BPAS services *see* Chapter 3.

Psychosexual Clinic
Liverpool Road Health Centre, 9 Mersey Place, Liverpool Road, Luton LU1 1HH. (Tel: Luton (0582) 424133). Services offered: treatment of sexual dysfunction, sexual counselling.
Problems dealt with: all sexual problems related to heterosexual relationships. Counselling for any other sexual problems and referral where appropriate.
Is professional referral required? Yes, although sometimes a self-referral is accepted.
Hours: 9.30 a.m.– 12 noon each Friday.
Fees: None.

BERKSHIRE

Family Planning Association Regional Office
For details, *see* the FPA Regional Office (North of the Thames) in Bedford, Bedfordshire.

Maidenhead

Marital Sexual Therapy Service
Middle Thames Marriage Guidance Council, Redcote, Holmanleas, Maidenhead. (Tel: Maidenhead (0628) 25320). *See* Chapter 15, 'Marriage Guidance'.

BUCKINGHAMSHIRE

Family Planning Association Regional Office
For details see the FPA Regional Office (North of the Thames) in Bedford, Bedfordshire.

Aylesbury

Marital Sexual Therapy Service
Aylesbury Vale Marriage Guidance Council, 23a Walton Street, Aylesbury HP20 1TZ (Tel: Aylesbury (0296) 27973). *See also* Chapter 15, 'Marriage Guidance'.

High Wycombe

Family Planning Association
6 Harlow Road, High Wycombe, Buckinghamshire (Tel: High Wycombe (0494) 26666). (The FPA Regional Office is in Bedford.) *See also* Chapter 3, 'Family Planning'.
Services offered: All methods of family planning; pregnancy testing; Well Woman Clinic, including menopause and pre-menstrual tension advice; vasectomy clinic; resource centre with books and literature; telephone advisory service.
Problems dealt with: Family planning and related subjects, including psychosexual problems.
Is professional referral required? No.
Hours: Monday, Thursday, Friday 9.30 a.m. – 4.30 p.m. (all appointments by telephone); Tuesday and Wednesday 9.30 a.m. – 4.30 p.m. and 6.30 p.m. – 8.30 p.m.
Fees: Variable, dependent upon services requested.

Milton Keynes

British Pregnancy Advisory Service
Eaglestone Health Centre, Standing Way, Milton Keynes, MK6 5AZ. (Tel: Bedford (0234) 46574).
Services offered: Pregnancy testing; pregnancy counselling; abortion assessment; contraception; morning-after birth control. Enquiries about: infertility problems; artificial insemination.
Hours: Monday, Tuesday and Thursday 6.30 p.m. – 8.30 p.m.
Fees: *See* BPAS in Chapter 3.
For further details of BPAS services *see* Chapter 3.

Outpatient Clinic Milton Keynes General Hospital
Milton Keynes (Tel: Milton Keynes (0908) 660033).
Services offered: Psychosexual therapy.
Problems dealt with: Psychosexual and marital relationship problems.
Is professional referral required? Yes.
Hours: Sessional.
Fees: None.

CAMBRIDGESHIRE

Family Planning Association Regional Office
For details, *see* the FPA Regional Office (Eastern England) in Norwich, Norfolk.

Cambridge

Clinic 6 (Psychosexual Counselling)
Addenbrooke's Hospital, Hills Road, Cambridge CB2 2QS (No telephone messages taken.)
Services offered: Psychosexual counselling.
Problems dealt with: All problems related to sexual dysfunction – in men and women.
Is professional referral required? Yes, only general practitioner or consultant referral accepted.
Hours: By appointment on Monday 9 a.m. – 1 p.m; Wednesday 2 p.m. – 5 p.m.
Fees: None.

Family Planning Association Information Service
4a Gonville Place, Cambridge CB1 1LY (Tel: Cambridge (0223) 62143).
This is an extension of the Norwich FPA Regional Office and Information Centre – *see* Chapter 3, 'Family Planning'.
Services offered: Free information on contraception, birth control, pregnancy testing, women's health and related areas. Referral to other support services where required. Books for sale on a wide range of women's and family health; lending library.
Problems dealt with: As above.
Is professional referral required? No.
Hours: Monday to Friday 9.30 a.m. – 4.30 p.m.
Fees: None.

Marital Sexual Therapy Services
Cambridge Marriage Guidance Council, 8 Market Passage, Cambridge CB2 3PF. (Tel: Cambridge (0223) 357424).
See also Chapter 15, 'Marriage Guidance'.

Huntingdon

Nursery Road Clinic
Nursery Road, Huntingdon PE18 6RJ (Tel: Huntingdon (0480) 53398).
Services offered: sexual counselling
Is professional referral required? No.
Hours: Wednesdays 6.30 p.m. – 9 p.m.
Fees: None

Bible Orchard Clinic (also known as Ramsey Road Clinic)
Ramsey Road, St. Ives, Huntingdon, PE17 4RA. (Tel: (0480) 62622).
Services offered: Sexual counselling
Is professional referral required? No.
Hours: Mondays 9.30 a.m. – 12 noon.
Fees: None.

Almond Road Clinic
Almond Road, St. Neots, Huntingdon PE19 1DZ. (Tel: (0480) 72261).
Services offered: Sexual counselling.
Is professional referral required? No
Hours: Tuesdays 6.30 p.m. – 9 p.m; alternate Thursdays 9.30 a.m. – 12 noon.
Fees: None.

CHESHIRE

Family Planning Association Regional Office
For details, *see* the FPA Regional Office (North-west England) in Liverpool, Merseyside.

Chester

British Pregnancy Advisory Service
98a Foregate Street, Chester CH1 1HB (Tel: Chester (0244) 27113).
Services offered: Pregnancy testing; pregnancy counselling; abortion assessment; contraception; morning-after birth control.
Enquiries about: Infertililty problems; artificial insemination.
Hours: Tuesday and Thursday 9 a.m. – 1 p.m; 7 p.m. – 8.30 p.m.
Fees: *See* BPAS in Chapter 3.
For further details of BPAS services, *see* Chapter 3, 'Family Planning'.

St. Martin's House
Princess Street, Chester. (Tel: Chester (0244) 315321 ext. 243).
Services offered: Psychosexual counselling.
Is professional referral required? Yes.
Hours: 2 p.m. – 4.30 p.m. (appointments only).
Fees: None.

Macclesfield

Marital Sexual Therapy Services
Macclesfield/Wilmslow Marriage Guidance Council, 42a Sunderland Street, Macclesfield SK11 6JL (Tel: Macclesfield (0625) 611887). *See also* Chapter 15, 'Marriage Guidance'.

Northwich

Marital Sexual Therapy Services
Vale Royal Marriage Guidance Council, 43 Chester Road, Castle Northwich, CW8 1HA. (Tel: Northwich (0606) 783502).
See also Chapter 15, 'Marriage Guidance'.

Runcorn

Psychosexual Team
Halton General Hospital, nr. Shopping City, Runcorn, Cheshire. (Tel: Runcorn (0928) 714567 ext. 3240).
Services offered: counselling by multidisciplinary team members.

Problems dealt with: Psychosexual.
Is professional referral required? Yes.
Hours: Thursdays 11.30 a.m. – 2.30 p.m.
Fees: None.

Warrington

Marital Sexual Therapy Services
Warrington and Halton Marriage Guidance Council, 21a Wilson Patten Street, Warrington WA1 1PG. (Tel: Warrington (0925) 30124). *See also* Chapter 15, 'Marriage Guidance'.

Grappenhall Clinic
Springfield Avenue, Warrington. (Tel: Warrington (0925) 61488).
Services offered: Psychosexual counselling.
Problems dealt with: Psychosexual.
Is professional referral required? No.
Hours: Three hourly sessions when necessary.
Fees: None.

CLEVELAND

Family Planning Association Regional Office
For details, *see* the FPA Regional Office (Yorkshire and North-east England) in Sheffield, South Yorkshire.

Middlesbrough

Marital Sexual Therapy Services
Cleveland Marriage Guidance Council, 1 Albert Terrace, Middlesbrough, Cleveland TS1 3PA (Tel: Middlesbrough (0642) 246051). *See also* Chapter 15, 'Marriage Guidance'.

Psychological Service
Woodlands Road Clinic, Middlesbrough (Tel: Middlesbrough (0642) 247311).
Services offered: Counselling, sexual therapy, psychotherapy.
Problems dealt with: Wide range of sexual and relationship difficulties.
Is professional referral required? No, though the GP is usually contacted when therapy is offered.
Hours: Daytime.
Fees: None.

Thornaby

Cleveland Family Planning Service, Psychosexual Clinic,
Thornaby Health Centre, Trenchard Avenue, Thornaby, Cleveland (Tel: Stockton (0642) 766047).
Services offered: In addition to the usual family planning services, counselling for couples with sexual difficulties of desire or performance is offered. A telephone information service is operated, but counselling by telephone is not possible.
Is professional referral required? Preferred.
Hours: Monday to Friday by appointment (daytime only).
Fees: This is an NHS provision. No fee is charged.

CORNWALL

Family Planning Association Regional Office
For details, *see* the FPA Regional Office (South-west England) in Exeter, Devon.

St Austell

Marital Sexual Therapy Services
Cornwall Marriage and Family Guidance Council, Cornish Unit, Rear of 14 High Cross Street, St Austell, Cornwall PL25 4AN (Tel: St Austell (0726) 74128).
see also Chapter 15, 'Marriage Guidance'.

Truro

Psychosexual Counselling Clinic
Family Planning Department, Cornwall and Isles of Scilly Health Authority, St. Clement Vean, Tregolls Road, Truro TR1 1NR. (Tel: Truro (0872) 74242).
Services offered: psychosexual counselling.
Is professional referral required? Yes.
Hours: 1st and 3rd Mondays 6.30 p.m. – 8.30 p.m.
Fees: None.

CUMBRIA

Family Planning Association Regional Office
For details, *see* the FPA Regional Office (North-west England) in Liverpool, Merseyside.

Barrow-in-Furness

Family Planning Clinic
Atkinson Health Centre, Market Street, Barrow-in-Furness, Cumbria LA14 2LR (Tel: Barrow-in-Furness (0229) 27212).
Services offered: Psychosexual counselling; youth advisory clinic; facililties for disabled people.
Problems dealt with: Any psychosexual problem.
Is professional referral required? No.
Hours: By appointment (except for youth advisory clinic which is 2nd and 4th Tuesday 4 p.m. – 6 p.m.
Fees: None.

CARLISLE

Marital Sexual Therapy Services
Carlisle and Eden Valley Marriage Guidance Council, 14 Spencer Street, Carlisle CA1 1BG (Tel: Carlisle (0228) 25950).
see also Chapter 15, 'Marriage Guidance'.

Whitehaven

Family Planning Clinic
Flatt Walks, Whitehaven, Cumbria (Tel: Whitehaven (0946) 5551). (Contact should be made by letter.)
Services offered: Vasectomy counselling; abortion counselling; female sterilisation counselling and psychosexual counselling (limited); pregnancy testing; young people's clinics – advice and counselling as well as contraception.
Problems dealt with: Frigidity, premature ejaculation, general loss of libido.
Is professional referral required? No.
Hours: Monday 6 p.m. – 7.30 p.m.
Fees: None.

Workington

Family Planning Clinic
Ann Burrow Thomas Health Centre, South William Street, Workington (Tel: Workington (0900) 2244). (Contact should be made by letter.)
Services offered: Pregnancy testing; abortion counselling; sterilisation (female) and vasectomy counselling; limited psychosexual counselling; young people's clinics – advice and counselling as well as contraception.
Problems dealt with: As above.
Is professional referral required? No.
Hours: Wednesday 6 p.m. – 7.30 p.m.
Fees: None.

DERBYSHIRE

Family Planning Association Regional Office
For details, *see* the FPA Regional Office (Yorkshire and North-east England) in Sheffield, South Yorkshire.

Chesterfield

Marital Sexual Therapy Services
Chesterfield and North-east Derbyshire Marriage Guidance Council, 12 Saltergate, Chesterfield S40 1UT (Tel: Chesterfield (0246) 31010).
see also Chapter 15, 'Marriage Guidance'.

Derby

Marital Sexual Therapy Services
Derby and District Marriage Guidance Council, 62 Friar Gate, Derby DE1 1DJ (Tel: Derby (0332) 49177).
see also Chapter 15, 'Marriage Guidance'.

Kingsmead Clinic
Kedleston Street, Derby. (Tel: Derby (0332) 47680).
Services offered: Sexual counselling.
Problems dealt with: General erectile failure, ejaculatory problems, non-consummation, vaginismus.
Is professional referral required? Yes.
Hours: 1st and 3rd Wednesday evenings 6.30 p.m. – 8.30 p.m.
Fees: None.

DEVON

Family Planning Association Regional Office
For details, *see* the FPA Regional Office (South-west England) in Exeter.

Barnstaple

North Devon District Hospital
Barnstaple, Devon EX31 4JB (Tel: Barnstaple (0271) 72577 Ext 586).
Services offered: Infertility, abortion, sex counselling; vasectomy, sterilisation. There is also a telephone advisory service.
Problems dealt with: All female psychosexual problems; family planning; unplanned pregnancies.
Is professional referral required? Yes.
Hours: Hospital says services available at all times.
Fees: None (but clients may be seen privately if they wish; a charge would then be made of £40 maximum for one hour).

Marital Difficulties Clinic
The Health Centre, Vicarage Street, Barnstaple (Tel: Barnstaple (0271) 71761
Services offered: Help with marital difficulties.
Is professional referral required? Yes.
Hours: Two sessions per month.
Fees: None.

Exeter

Family Planning Association (South-west England Regional Office)
4 Barnfield Hill, Exeter, EX1 1SR (Tel: Exeter (0392) 56711).

See also Chapter 3, 'Family Planning'.
Services offered: Information on family planning services within the south-west region. A book centre carrying a wide range of specialist books on family planning and related topics. Educational resources – speakers, displays, films, courses, etc. Mail order for books and non-medical contraceptives.
Problems dealt with: All family planning problems.

Marital Sexual Therapy Services
Exeter and District Marriage Guidance Council, 3 Wynards, Magdalen Street, Exeter EX2 4HX. (Tel: Exeter (0392) 75681). *see also* Chapter 15, 'Marriage Guidance'.

SPOD-Devon (Association to Aid the Sexual and Personal Relationships of People with Disabilities)
Millbrook Lane, Exeter EX2 6ES. (Tel: Exeter (0392) 219774 ext. 21).
Services provided: counselling; study days; courses and workshops. *see* Chapter 12, 'Sexuality and Disability'.

Ivybridge

District Department of Psychology
Moorhaven Hospital, Bittaford, Ivybridge PL21 0EX. (Tel: Plymouth (0752) 892411).
Services offered: Therapy for routine sexual dysfunctions; problems of deviance and orientation, counselling for disabled people; AIDS counselling.
Problems dealt with: Classic sexual dysfunctions; homosexuality; transsexualism; sexual difficulties for disabled people; VD and AIDS related problems.
Is professional referral required? Yes.
Hours: Normal working.
Fees: None.

Plymouth

Seventrees Clinic
Baring Street, Greenbank, Plymouth PL4 8NF (Tel: Plymouth (0752) 260071).
Services offered: A counselling service for patients with psychosexual problems. Patients are seen individually or as a couple.
Problems dealt with: Non-consummation, dyspareunia, loss of libido, anorgasmia, problems with erection and ejaculation.
Is professional referral required? Preferred – usually from general practitioners, hospital departments, health visitors, family planning services. Self-referrals should write directly to the clinic at the above address.
Hours: Monday and Friday mornings.
Fees: None – this is an NHS clinic, but arrangements can be made for private consultations outside this service if they are required.

Behaviour Therapy Nursing Service
Scott Hospital, Beacon Park Road, Plymouth (Tel: Plymouth (0752) 268011)
Services offered: Full range of psychosexual counselling and sexual therapies based on behavioural, and cognitive-behavioural, psychotherapeutic strategies.
Problems dealt with: Sexual dysfunctions in hetero- (and homo-) sexual individuals and couples. Unconventional sexual behaviour problems; psychosexual fears; marital dysfunctions; AIDS counselling.
Is professional referral required? Yes, from GP, Consultant or STD clinic.
Hours: Monday to Friday 9 a.m. – 5 p.m.
Fees: None

Psychosexual Clinic
Nuffield Clinic, Lipson Road, Plymouth PL4 8NQ. (Tel: Plymouth (0752) 660281).
Services offered: sexual counselling with conjoint behavioural treatment.
Problems dealt with: all sexual dysfunctions.
Is professional referral required? No.
Hours: Thursdays 10 a.m. – 5 p.m; Fridays 10.30 a.m. – 12.30 p.m.
Fees: None.

Marital Sexual Therapy Services
Plymouth Marriage Guidance Council, Higher Lane House, Higher Lane, Plymouth PL1 2AN (Tel: Plymouth (0752) 665708). *See also* Chapter 15, 'Marriage Guidance'.

Torquay

Marital and Sexual Therapy Services
Torbay and District Marriage Guidance Council, 302a Higher Union Street, Torquay (Tel: Torquay (0803) 27854). *See also* Chapter 15, 'Marriage Guidance'.

Psychosexual Clinic
Out-patient Department, Torbay Hospital, Lawes Bridge, Torquay TQ2 7AA (Tel: Torquay (0803) 64567 ext. 5801).
Services offered: Psychosexual counselling. Patients are seen individually or as a couple.
Is professional referral required? Preferred – usually from general practitioners, hospital departments, health visitors, family planning services.

Hours: Alternate Wednesdays 9.30 a.m. – 1 p.m.
Fees: None.

Torbay

Sexual Therapy Clinic
The Laurels, 9 Powderham Road, Newton Abbot, Devon TQ12 1EU. (Tel: Newton Abbot (0626) 51925).
Services offered: An NHS clinic, offering therapy for most sexual problems. A total of ten trained counsellors, working in a co-therapy (male/female) format. At present couples only treated.
Problems dealt with: All sexual problems.
Is professional referral required? No, but preferred.
Hours: Thursday evening 5 p.m. – 8.30 p.m. By appointment.

DORSET

Family Planning Association Regional Office
For details, *see* the FPA Regional Office (South-west England) in Exeter, Devon.

Bournemouth

British Pregnancy Advisory Service
23 Ophir Road, Bournemouth BH8 8LS (Tel: Bournemouth (0202) 28762).
Services offered: pregnancy testing; pregnancy counselling; abortion assessment; morning-after birth control.
Enquiries about: infertility problems; artificial insemination.
Is professional referral required? No.
Hours: Monday 9.30 a.m. – 1 p.m; and 4.30 – 9.30 p.m; Tuesday and Thursday 9.30 a.m. – 9.30 p.m; Wednesday 9.30 a.m. – 1 p.m.
Fees: *See* BPAS in Chapter 3.
For further details of BPAS services *see* Chapter 3, 'Family Planning'.

Marital Sexual Therapy Services
Bournemouth, Poole and Christchurch, Marriage Guidance Council, 2 Alma Road, Winton BH9 1AA (Tel: Bournemouth (0202) 514630). *See also* Chapter 15, 'Marriage Guidance'.

Dorchester

West Dorset Health Authority Psychology Services
10 Cornwall Road, Dorchester, Dorset DT1 1RT.
Services offered: Psychological assessments and psychological help of most kinds.
Problems dealt with: All kinds of psychological and medico-psychological problems.
Is professional referral required? Preferred (by a GP).
Hours: Usual Health Service hours for out-patient services.
Fees: None.

Marital Sexual Therapy Services
Dorset Marriage Guidance Council, 57 High West Street, Dorchester DT1 1UT. (Tel: Dorchester (0305) 62285). *See also* Chapter 15, 'Marriage Guidance'.

CO. DURHAM

Family Planning Association Regional Office
For details, *see* the FPA Regional Office (Yorkshire and North-east England) in Sheffield, South Yorkshire.

Consett

Psychosexual Clinic
Department of Obstetrics and Gynaecology, Shotley Bridge General Hospital, Shotley Bridge, Consett, Co. Durham DH8 0ND (Tel: Consett (0207) 503456).
Services offered: Treatment of psychosexual problems. The medical staff comprises a consultant gynaecologist, a medical assistant and principal clinical psychologist.
Problems dealt with: All psychosexual and related problems.
Is professional referral required? No.
Hours: Monday to Friday by appointment (office hours). Private appointments outside office hours.
Fees: None (unless private consultation requested – Private fees: £20 initial consultation, variable thereafter).

Marital Sexual Therapy Services
Durham Marriage Guidance Council, 31 Old Elvet, Durham DH1 3JA (Tel: Durham (0385) 41198). *See also* Chapter 15, 'Marriage Guidance'.

EAST SUSSEX

Family Planning Association Regional Office
For details, *see* the FPA Regional Office (South-east England) in Hove.

Brighton

British Pregnancy Advisory Service
Wistons Site, Chatsworth Road, Brighton BN1 5PA (Tel: Brighton (0273) 509726).
Services offered: pregnancy testing; pregnancy counsell-

ing; abortion assessment; contraception; morning-after birth control.
Is professional referral required? No.
Hours: Monday to Friday 9 a.m. – 5 p.m; Saturday 9 a.m. – 1 p.m.
Fees: *See* BPAS in Chapter 3.
For further details of BPAS services *see* Chapter 3, 'Family Planning'.

Marital Sexual Therapy Services
Brighton, Hove and District Marriage Guidance Council, 58 Preston Road, Brighton BN1 4QF (Tel: Brighton (0273) 697997).
See also Chapter 15, 'Marriage Guidance'.

Eastbourne

Family Planning Association Clinic
Avenue House, The Avenue, Eastbourne, East Sussex (Tel: Eastbourne (0323) 37121 (during clinic hours: Monday 2 p.m. – 4.30 p.m.; Tuesday 5.30 p.m. – 7 p.m.; Thursday 2 p.m. – 4.30 p.m. and 5.30–7 p.m.)).
Services offered: Contraception and sub-fertility.
Problems dealt with: Youth advisory (Tuesday 5.30 p.m. – 7 p.m.); unplanned pregnancy, counselling for sterilisation (male and female), psychosexual clinic (alternate Thursdays 9.30 a.m. – 12.30 p.m.). Fees: None.

Psychosexual Clinic
c/o The Family Planning Clinic, Avenue House, The Avenue, Eastbourne, East Sussex (Tel: Eastbourne (0323) 27121 preferably before 9 a.m. or 1 p.m. – 2 p.m., or (0323) 37121 during clinic hours).
Problems dealt with: Psychosexual problems.
Is professional referral required? No.
Hours: By appointment – alternate Thursday mornings. Private arrangements occasionally made.
Fees: None for Thursday mornings.

Hailsham

Department of Clinical Psychology
Hillingly Hospital, Hailsham BN27 4ER (Tel: Hailsham (0323) 844391 ext. 2326).
Services offered: Marital and sexual therapy.
Problems dealt with: All forms of sexual dysfunction.
Is professional referral required? Yes.
Hours: Working week.
Fees: None.

Hastings

Department of Clinical Psychology
1st Floor, Furness Mount, 4 Holmesdale Gardens, Hastings TN34 1LY. (Tel: Hastings (0424) 435066).
Services offered: sexual therapy/dysfunction.
Problems dealt with: full range of sexual problems with a psychological base.
Is professional referral required? Yes.
Hours: 9 a.m. – 5 p.m.

Hove

Family Planning Association (South-east Regional Office)
13a Western Road, Hove, BN3 1AE (Tel: Brighton (0273) 774075).
See also Chapter 3, 'Family Planning'.
Services offered: Information on family planning within the region. Women's health information centre, women's health clinic, sex education courses, pregnancy testing, menopause advice. Telephone advisory service.
Problems dealt with: Contraception choices and where available, menopause, pre-menstrual tension and all female health problems. Women's health clinic: medical information, breast examinations, cervical smears, urine tests, blood pressure, pregnancy testing. Male sexual help advisory service.
Is professional referral required? No.
Hours: Family planning and sex education in office hours. Women's health information centre, Fridays 10 a.m. – 4 p.m. Women's health clinic and men's advisory service. Various sessions by appointment only.
Fees: Only for the women's health clinic, £18 per visit.

ESSEX (*See also* Greater London).

Family Planning Association Regional Office
For details, *see* the FPA Regional Office (Eastern England) in Norwich, Norfolk.

BRENTWOOD

BUPA Medical Centre
Hartswood Hospital, Warley Road, Brentwood CM13 3HR (Tel: Brentwood (0277) 232525). For details *see* Greater London (Camden).

Colchester

BUPA Medical Centre
Colchester Nursing Home, Oaks Drive, Colchester CO3 3PT (Tel: Colchester (0206) 545462). For details *see* Greater London (Camden).

Harlow

Marital Sexual Therapy Services
Harlow and District Marriage Guidance Council, Bentham House, Hamstel Road, Harlow CM20 1EP (Tel: Harlow (0279) 23655). *See also* Chapter 15, 'Marriage Guidance'.

GLOUCESTERSHIRE

Family Planning Association Regional Office
For details, *see* the FPA Regional Office (South-west England) in Exeter, Devon.

Cheltenham

Cheltenham Maternity Hospital.
Services offered: Psychosexual counselling.
Problems dealt with: As above.
Is professional referral required? Yes.
Hours: Wednesday afternoons and Thursday mornings.
Fees: None.

Marital Sexual Therapy Services
Cheltenham and Cotswold Marriage Guidance Council, 24 Cambray Place, Cheltenham GL50 1JN. (Tel: Cheltenham (0242) 523215). *See also* Chapter 15, 'Marriage Guidance'.

Gloucester

Marital Sexual Therapy Services
Gloucester Marriage Guidance Council, 27 Park Road, Gloucester GL1 1LH. (Tel: Gloucester (0452) 22071). *See also* Chapter 15, 'Marriage Guidance'.

GREATER LONDON

Family Planning Association Regional Office
For details *see* the FPA Regional Office (London) under Hammersmith.

Brook Centres
See under Camden, Hackney, Islington, Lambeth, Newham, Southwark, Westminster.

British Pregnancy Advisory Service
For details *see* under Westminster.

For further details on each of these Centres, *see* Chapter 3, 'Family Planning'.

Barnet

Barnet Health Authority
Clinics in Barnet, Colindale, Edgware, Finchley, Golders Green and Hendon (Tel: 01-449 8711).
Services offered: Psychosexual counselling.
Problems dealt with: Psychosexual.
Is professional referral required? No.
Hours: Please telephone for an appointment.
Fees: None.

Department of Psychiatry
Dr Kevin Gournay (Behaviour Therapist), Barnet General Hospital, Barnet, Hertfordshire (Tel: 01-440 5111 ext. 603).
Services offered: Behaviour therapy. General range of anxiety-based problems, spectrum of sexual problems, marital problems. Special interests: agoraphobia and sex dysfunction.
Problems dealt with: All sexual problems, dysfunctions and deviations.
Is professional referral required? Preferred.
Hours: Monday to Friday 9 a.m. – 5 p.m.
Fees: None, but Dr Gournay also runs a private service offering evening or weekend treatment and will arrange home visits if necessary at £30 per session.
Comment: There is a full psychiatric/social work back-up service within the hospital.

Dr Rena D. Sampson
27 Oakleigh Park South, Whetstone, London N2O 9JS (Tel: 01-445 6272).
Services offered: Psychosexual counselling.
Hours: By appointment.
Fees: By arrangement.

Torrington Park Health Centre
Torrington Park, London N12. Services offered: psychosexual counselling.
Hours: By appointment.
Fees: None.

Dr Dorothea Holmquist
33 Lyndhurst Avenue, Mill Hill, London NW7 2AD. (Tel: 01-959 1466).
Services offered: Family planning and psychosexual counselling.
Hours: By appointment.
Fees: By arrangement.

Marital Sexual Therapy Services
Barnet, Haringey, Hartmere Marriage Guidance Council, 5 Woodhouse Road, Tally Ho Corner, Finchley,

London N12 9EN. (Tel: 01-445 9549 or 8522). *See also* Chapter 15, 'Marriage Guidance'.

Brent

ACCEPT
Contact ACCEPT Hammersmith for details of services in connection with alcohol and prescribed drugs problems.

Marriage Research Centre
Central Middlesex Hospital, Acton Lane, London NW10 7NS (Tel: 01-965 2367).
Services offered: Counselling services for marital and sexual problems referred from the Boroughs of Brent and Harrow.
Problems dealt with: Marital and sexual problems.
Is professional referral required? Yes.
Hours: Tuesday to Friday 9.30 a.m. – 5 p.m.
Fees: None.

Psychosexual Medicine Clinic
Pound Lane Clinic, Pound Lane, Willesden, London (Tel: 01-459 5116).
Services offered: Psychosexual counselling.
Problems dealt with: Psychosexual problems only.
Is professional referral required? Yes.
Hours: Tuesdays 7 p.m. – 9.30 p.m.
Fees: None.

The Walm Lane Clinic (Private)
146 Walm Lane, London NW2 4RU (Tel: 01-452 1973/958 7738).
Services offered: Infertility (AID, AIH and investigation); contraception; venereal disease diagnosis and treatment; vasectomy; semen banking; sexual problems of the elderly; abortion counselling; termination of pregnancy.
Problems dealt with: Problems relating to the above services.
Is professional referral required? No.
Hours: By appointment, Monday to Friday 9.30 a.m. – 5 p.m.
Fees: On application.

Bromley

Psychosexual Problems Clinic
c/o Family Planning Clinic, Beckenham Hospital, Croydon Road, BR3 3QL (Tel: 01-650 0125 Monday or Thursday 7 p.m – 9 p.m. for appointment).
Services offered: counselling and examination – men and women.
Problems dealt with: Psychosexual, menopausal.
Is professional referral required? No, but preferred.
Hours: Monday and Thursday 7 p.m. – 9 p.m.
Fees: None.

Camden

Brook Advisory Centre
233 Tottenham Court Road, London W1P 9AE. (Tel: 01-323 1522). Services offered: As well as the usual contraception service this Centre also provides psychosexual counselling. Hours: Monday to Thursday 9.30 a.m. – 7.30 p.m; Friday 9.30 a.m. – 4 p.m.
Fees: the contraceptive service is free. All other services are charged at various fees which are frequently waived or reduced in cases of financial hardship.
For further details of Brook services *see* Chapter 3, 'Family Planning'.

BUPA Medical Centre
Battle Bridge House, 300 Gray's Inn Road, London WC1X 8DU (Tel: 01-837 6484).
Services offered: Health screening for men and women, plus special clinics including: breast disease, menopause, pre-menstrual tension, marital and psychosexual counselling.
Problems dealt with: See above.
Is professional referral required? Yes.
Hours: Clinic times vary. Telephone for an appointment.
Fees: These vary with the service used. Please contact the Centre for details.
Comment: Anyone may use the Centre, but there are reduced fees for persons having health screening who are either covered by the BUPA health insurance or are members of the Institute of Directors. Fees for the specialist clinics may be fully recovered under the terms of any health insurance carried by the patient.

Marie Stopes House
The Well Woman Centre, 108 Whitfield Street, London W1P 6BE (Tel: 01-388 0662/2585).
Services offered: At this attractive, welcoming old house the emphasis is on an informal approach in friendly surroundings, offering family planning services (including 'morning after' birth control–the pill or IUCD); Well Woman screening; walk-in pregnancy testing; premenstrual tension advice and help; counselling and referral for unwanted pregnancies; vasectomy and female sterilisation on an out-patient basis; psychosexual counselling.
Problems dealt with: See above.
Is professional referral required? No.
Hours: Switchboard is open Monday to Thursday 9.30 a.m. – 7.30 p.m.; Friday 9.30 a.m. – 5 p.m.;

Saturday 9.30 a.m. – 1 p.m. Hours to see clients vary according to service, but evenings and Saturdays are usually available.
Fees: Routine visit – £12; pre-menstrual syndrome clinic – £28 (first visit), £12 (re-visit); psychosexual counselling – £20 (first visit), revisit charge as arranged by the counsellor; vasectomy – £77; female sterilisation – £140 (local anaesthetic), £160 (general anaesthetic).
Comment: Stopes also offers helpful leaflets and very full explanations of vasectomy and sterilisation operations.

New Grapevine
416 St John Street, London EC1 (Tel: (Helpline) 01-278 9147; (office) 01-278 9157).
Services offered: Advice and counselling to the under-25s on sex and relationship problems, contraception and VD. Educational work in schools, youth clubs and other informal educational units. Counselling is available by appointment. A telephone advisory service is also available. New Grapevine serves the London Boroughs of Camden and Islington.
Problems dealt with: Advice and counselling on sex and relationship problems.
Is professional referral required? No.
Hours: Tuesday 10 a.m. – 6 p.m; Wednesday 2 p.m. – 6 p.m.
Fees: Fees are charged for education sessions except in youth clubs. No fees for counselling.

The Psycho-sexual Therapy Clinic
Elizabeth Garrett Anderson Hospital (Women), Euston Road, London NW1 2AP (Tel: 01-387 2501 ext. 212).
Services offered: Therapy for marital difficulties and sexual dysfunctions, normally for women, but will include regular partners in treatment sessions.
Problems dealt with: Vaginismus, loss of libido, orgasmic dysfunctions, marital disharmony. Also the usual range of counselling for sterilisation, termination of pregnancy, menopausal symptoms. Cytology and family planning.
Is professional referral required? No.
Hours: Tuesday 1 p.m. – 4 p.m. by appointment.
Fees: None.

Women's Sexuality Workshop
Under the direction of Anne Hooper, 58 The Pryors, East Heath Road, London NW3 (Tel: 01-794 2838).
Services offered: Pre-orgasmic group for all women, four-week courses held three times a year.
Problems dealt with: Lack of orgasm, sexual ignorance, etc.
Is professional referral required? No.
Hours: The four-week courses are held on Tuesday evenings in May, October and February, 7.30 p.m. – 10.30 p.m.
Fees: £30 for the course, reductions for students, pensioners, people on social security.
Comment: Anne Hooper is the author of *The Body Electric*, published by Unwin. Price £2.50.

Croydon

BUPA Medical Centre
54 Coombe Road, Croydon CRO 5SG. (Tel: 01-680 9880). For details *see* Greater London (Camden).

Dr Brian Glaister and Mrs Heinke Glaister
(Psychologist and sociologist in private practice)
135 Foxley Lane, Purley, Surrey CR2 3HR (Tel: 01-660 7465).
Services offered: Psychosexual therapy with male and female co-therapists.
Problems dealt with: Psychological arousal and orgasm problems in men and women. When there is a partner, partner is required to attend.
Is professional referral required? No.
Hours: Evenings and Saturdays.
Fees: £28 per session.

Marital Sexual Therapy Services
Croydon and District Marriage Guidance Council, 9 Ramsey Court, Church Street, Croydon CR0 1RF (Tel: 01-680 1944).
See also Chapter 15, 'Marriage Guidance'.

Psychosexual Clinic
Woodcote House, Mayday Hospital, Mayday Road, Thornton Heath (Tel: Upper Warlingham (088 32) 2101 – all appointments to be made through Mrs Butler at Warlingham Park Hospital).
Services offered: All types of psychosexual problems.
Is professional referral required? Yes.
Hours: Friday 2.15 p.m. – 5 p.m.
Fees: None.

Ealing

Ealing Hospital
Uxbridge Road, Southall (Tel: 01-574 2481) (Women's services direct line 9 a.m. – 2 p.m. for appointment).
Services offered: Sexual counselling.
Is professional referral required? No.
Hours: Wednesday 9.30 a.m. – 12 noon.
Fees: None.

Enfield

Marital Sexual Therapy Service
Enfield Marriage Guidance Council, Southgate Town Hall, Green Lane, Palmers Green. London N13 4XD (Tel: 01-886 1615). *See also* Chapter 15, 'Marriage Guidance'.

Psychosexual Clinic
Moorfield Road Health Clinic, Moorfield Road, Enfield, Middlesex (junction of Carterhatch Lane and Hertford Road) (Tel: 01-805 5500 – this number is only available to make appointments, Monday 1.30 p.m. – 4.30 p.m.; Wednesday 9.15 a.m. – 11 a.m. and 6.15 p.m. – 8 p.m))
Services offered: Psychosexual counselling.
Problems dealt with: Any sexual problem.
Is professional referral required? No.
Hours: Monday 1.30 p.m. – 4.30 p.m.
Fees: None.

Rosemary Avenue Clinic
Rosemary Avenue, Enfield
Services offered: Psychosexual counselling.
Problems dealt with: Psychosexual.
Is professional referral required? No.
Hours: Two sessions, two and a half hours each.
Fees: None.

Psychosexual Clinic
North Middlesex Hospital, Sterling Way, London N18 Tel: 01-808 1000 Ext 1259).
Services offered: Psychosexual counselling.
Problems dealt with: Sexual dysfunction.
Is professional referral required? No.
Hours: 9.30 a.m. – 1.00 p.m.
Fees: None.

Hackney

Brook Advisory Centre
Shoreditch Brook, 210 Kingsland Road, London E2 8EB. (Telephone Tottenham Court Road Brook centre for an appointment: 01-580 2991/323 1522).
Hours: Monday 4.30 p.m. – 7 p.m.
Fees: The contraceptive service is free. All other services are charged at various fees which are frequently waived or reduced in cases of financial hardship.
For further details of Brook services *see* Chapter 3, 'Family Planning'.

Hammersmith and Fulham

ACCEPT National Services (Alcoholism Community Centres for Education, Prevention and Treatment)
ACCEPT Clinic, 200 Seagrave Road, London SW6 1RQ (Tel: 01-381 3155). (Other centres in Greater London Area.)
Services offered: Information, advice and counselling on problems related to alcohol, tranquillisers and prescribed drugs for problem and dependent drinkers, tranquilliser misusers and their families. A telephone advisory service, and walk-in/self-help service are available. (Sex and marriage problems are very often alcohol-related).
Is professional referral required? No, but ACCEPT works closely with general practitioners, with client's consent.
Hours: Monday to Friday 9.30 a.m. – 5 p.m.; Saturday and Sunday 12 noon – 4 p.m. (by appointment).
Fees: None, but donations are encouraged.
Comment: A variety of useful literature is available.

Martha and Luke Clinic
West London Hospital, Hammersmith Road, London W6 7DQ (Tel: 01-748 3441).
Services offered: Treatment of loss of libido, problems of arousal, dysparenuia, vaginismus, erectile difficulties, premature ejaculation.
Is professional referral required? Yes.
Hours: Monday to Friday 9.30 a.m. – 12.30 p.m; 2 p.m. – 5 p.m.
Fees: None.

The Family Planning Association (London Regional Office)
160 Shepherd's Bush Road, London W6 7PB (Tel: 01-602 2723 – clinic service; 01-602 3804 – information service).
See also Chapter 3, 'Family Planning'.
Services offered: In addition to family planning: pregnancy tests while you wait; vasectomy counselling; psychosexual counselling. Information on family planning services in London – or contact the Family Planning Information Service (*see* Chapter 3, 'Family Planning').
Is professional referral required? No.
Hours: Information service (Tel: 01-602 2723) daily 9.30 a.m. – 5 p.m. Pregnancy testing daily. Clinic sessions Wednesday 9.30 a.m. – 8 p.m. and Saturday mornings.
Fees: None.

Haringey Crisis Centre
Arbours, 41 Weston Park, London N8 (Tel: 01-340 8125).

Services offered: Individual psychotherapy; crisis centre; three long-stay therapeutic communities; therapy training programme.
Problems dealt with: Everything relating to emotional distress.
Is professional referral required? No.
Hours: Office: Monday to Friday 9.30 a.m. – 1.30 p.m.
Fees: Individual psychotherapy – initial interview £8, fees then vary from £3 to £20 per session. Crisis centre – £85 per day, Communities £145 per week.

Psychosexual Clinic
Wood Green Clinic, The Health Centre, Stuart Crescent, London N22 (Tel: 01-889 4311 – this number is only available to make appointments Tuesday morning 9.30 a.m. – 12 noon).
Services offered: Psychosexual counselling.
Problems dealt with: Any sexual problem.
Is professional referral required? No.
Hours: Tuesday morning 9.30 a.m. – 12 noon.
Fees: None.

Harrow

ACCEPT Harrow
See ACCEPT Hammersmith for details of services dealing with prescribed drugs and alcohol problems.

Caryl Thomas Clinic
Headstone Drive, Wealdstone, Middlesex.(Tel: 01-863 7004 for appointment ring between 9.30 a.m. – 4.30 p.m.).
Services offered: Psychosexual counselling (preferably for clients who live in the district).
Problems dealt with: Any psychosexual problems.
Is professional referral required? No.
Hours: Monday 7 p.m. – 10 p.m; Wednesday 9 p.m. – 12 midnight;
Fees: None.

Marital Sexual Therapy Services
Central Middlesex Marriage Guidance Council, Terrapin no. 1, Civic Centre Complex, Station Road, Harrow HA1 2UL Tel: 01-427 8694).
See also Chapter 15, 'Marriage Guidance'.

Havering

Romford
Main Road, Romford, Essex. (Tel: Romford (0708) 44702).
Services offered: Psychosexual counselling.
Is professional referral required? Yes.
Hours: Wednesday p.m.
Fees: None.

Hillingdon

Sexual Dysfunction Clinic
Hillingdon Hospital (attached to the FPA clinic) Pield Heath Road, Hillingdon, Uxbridge, Middlesex (Tel: Uxbridge (0895) 38282 ext. 652).
Services offered: Sexual dysfunction.
Is professional referral required? No.
Hours: Monday 6.15 p.m. – 9 p.m; Thursday 9.15 p.m. – 12 midnight
Fees: None.

Sexual Counselling
Psychology Department, Hillingdon Hospital, Pield Heath Road, Hillingdon, Uxbridge, Middlesex (Tel: Uxbridge (0895) 38282 ext. 652).
Services offered: Sexual counselling.
Is professional referral required? Yes.
Hours: By appointment.
Fees: None.

Northwood

Psychosexual Clinic
Mount Vernon Hospital, Out-patients Department No. 4, Northwood, Middlesex (Tel: Northwood (092 74) 26111; for appointments: 01-868 4400).
Services offered: Psychosexual clinic.
Problems dealt with: All marital and sexual problems (for example, non-consummation, loss of libido, vaginismus, impotence, ejaculatory problems).
Is professional referral required? Preferred.
Hours: Friday 1.30 p.m. – 4 p.m.
Fees: None.
Comment: Further details may be obtained from the Health Services Department, Keeler House, 146 Field End Road, Eastcote, Pinner, Middlesex HA5 1SB (Tel: 01-868 4400).

Hounslow

Brentford Family Planning Clinic
Health Centre, Albany Road, Brentford, Middlesex (Tel: 01-570 2805).
Services offered: Psychosexual counselling.
Is professional referral required? No.
Hours: Alternate Fridays.
Fees: None.

District Department of Clinical Psychiatry
West Middlesex Hospital, Isleworth. (Tel: 01-560 2121 for appointments 01-570 2805).
Services offered: Psychosexual counselling.
Is professional referral required? No.
Hours: By appointment.
Fees: None.

Islington

Brook Advisory Centre
Islington Brook, Manor Gardens Centre, 6 Manor Gardens, Holloway Road, London N7 6LA. (Tel: 01-272 5599).
Hours: Tuesday 1 p.m. – 3.30 p.m; Thursday 4.30 – 7 p.m.
Fees: The contraceptive service is free, all other services are charged at various fees which are frequently waived or reduced in cases of financial hardship.
For further details of Brook services *see* Chapter 3, 'Family Planning'.

Brook Advisory Centre
Barnsbury Centre, Barnsbury Clinic, Carnegie Street, London N1 9QW. (Tel: Tottenham Court Road Brook Centre for appointment 01-580 2991/323 1522).
Fees: The contraceptive service is free, all other services are charged at various fees which are frequently waived or reduced in cases of financial hardship.
For further details of Brook services *see* Chapter 3, 'Family Planning'.

BUPA Medical Centre
Webb House, 210 Pentonville Road, London N1 9TA. (Tel: 01-837 7055). For details *see* Greater London – (Camden).

Family Planning Clinic
Gynaecological Department, St Mary's Wing, Whittington Hospital London N19 5NF (Tel: 01-272 3070).
Services offered: In addition to family planning: psychosexual counselling.
Problems dealt with: Any sexual problem.
Is professional referral required? Preferable.
Hours: Friday mornings.
Fees: None.

Kensington and Chelsea

London Institute for the Study of Human Sexuality
Directed by Dr Michael Perring, 10 Warwick Road, London SW5 9UH (Tel: 01-373 0901).
Services offered: Medical evaluation, general and sexual counselling, group therapy (family planning, pregnancy counselling, etc., also available).
Problems dealt with: Psychosexual and relationship problems (both heterosexual and homosexual), including those related to disability and ageing. Problems and concerns related to pre-menstrual tension, menopause, incest or rape, unplanned pregnancies.
Is professional referral required? No.
Hours: Monday to Friday 9.30 a.m. – 5.30 p.m.
Fees: £25 per hour (but reduced for hardship). Group therapy £15.
Comment: Also active in training and sex education. *See* Chapter 13, 'Learning about Sex'.

John Hunter Clinic
St Stephens Hospital, Fulham Road, London SW10 (Tel: 01-352 8161).
Services offered: Sexual dysfunction; sexual therapy; sexual counselling or other specialist services relating to sexual matters.
Hours: Monday to Friday 9.30 a.m. – 12.30 p.m; 2 p.m. – 5 p.m.
Fees: None.

Menopause Clinic
Chelsea Hospital for Women Dovehouse Street, London SW3 6LT (Tel: 01-352 6446).
Services offered: Advice and treatment of climacteric and post-menopausal symptoms, including long-term patient management.
Problems dealt with: Hot flushes/night sweats; symptoms of lower genital tract atrophy; prevention of osteoporosis when there is a loss of bony tissue and bones become brittle.
Is professional referral required? Yes.
Hours: Monday to Friday 9 a.m. – 5 p.m.
Fees: None.

Raymede Clinic
Telford Road, London W10 (Tel: 01- 960 0942).
Services offered: Psychotherapeutic counselling.
Problems dealt with: Psychosexual problems both male and female.
Is professional referral required? No.
Hours: Monday and Thursday from 1.30 p.m.
Fees: None.

Kingston-upon-Thames

Hampton Wick
20 Seymour Road, Hampton Wick, Kingston upon Thames. (Tel: 01-977 6552)
Services offered: Psychosexual counselling.

Problems dealt with: Non-consummation, loss of libido, impotence, orgasmic dysfunction, premature or retarded ejaculation.
Is professional referral required? No.
Hours: Wednesday 6.30 p.m. – 8.30 p.m.
Fees: None.

Lambeth

Alcohol Counselling Service
34 Electric Lane, Brixton, London SW9 8JT (Tel: 01-737 3570). (Serves Lambeth, Lewisham, Southwark.)
Services offered: Advice, information and counselling for problem drinkers and/or their relatives or friends. The Service aims to help primarily those people who are not chronically damaged by prolonged alcohol abuse. The Service is committed to flexible goals, particularly as far as drinking is concerned, so does not work only with people who agree to total abstinence. Mainly one-to-one counselling. Will advise people as to the most suitable service for their needs.
Problems dealt with: In addition to drinking, there is a very wide range of problems presented. With each case a decision is made whether to deal with these or refer on. As far as resources allow, the Service tries to match clients to counsellors who have special understanding of their needs – for instance, quite a few referrals are received from Gay Switchboard.
Is professional referral required? No.
Hours: Monday to Friday 10 a.m. – 5 p.m. at main office (above), plus evening sessions in other venues in Lambeth and Lewisham (by appointment through above number).
Fees: None.

Brook Advisory Centres
Stockwell Brook, Rose McAndrew Clinic, Beale House, Lingham Street, London SW9 9HF. (Tel: Walworth Brook for an appointment – 01-703 9660/7880).
Services offered: as well as contraception services, this centre also provides psychosexual counselling.
Hours: Monday to Thursday 9.30 a.m. – 7.30 p.m; Friday 9.30 a.m. – 2.30 p.m; Saturday 9.30 a.m. – 12 noon.
Fees: The contraception service is free, all other services are charged at various fees which are frequently waived or reduced in cases of financial hardship.

Kennington Brook, Moffat Health Centre, 65 Sancroft Street, (off Kennington Road), London SE11 5NG. (Tel: Walworth Brook for an appointment – 01-703 9660/7880).
Hours: Wednesday 4.30 – 7 p.m; Saturday 9.30 a.m. – 11.30 a.m.
Fees: the contraceptive service is free, all other services are charged at various fees which are frequently waived or reduced in cases of financial hardship.

Brixton Brook 53 Acre Lane, London SW2 5TN. (Tel: 01-274 4995) Hours: Monday 11.30 a.m. – 1.30 p.m. and 3.30 p.m. – 6.30 p.m; Wednesday 9.30 a.m. – 2.30 p.m; Friday 3.30 p.m. – 6.30 p.m.
Fees: The contraceptive service is free, all other services are charged at various fees which are frequently waived or reduced in cases of financial hardship.
For further details of Brook services *see* Chapter 3, 'Family Planning'.

Helen Brook Department of Family Planning
5th Floor, New Ward Block, King's College Hospital, Denmark Hill, London SE5 8RX (Tel: 01-274 6222 Ext 2349 – Wednesday evening only 5.30 p.m.– 8 p.m.).
Services offered: Broad approach, including sexual counselling, behaviour therapy, psychotherapy.
Problems dealt with: Loss of libido, vaginismus, non-consummation, dyspareunia, impotence, premature ejaculation, retarded ejaculation, etc.
Is professional referral required? No.
Hours: Wednesday evening 5.30 p.m. – 8 p.m.
Fees: None.

Menopause Clinic
Department of Obstetrics and Gynaecology, King's College Hospital Medical School, Denmark Hill, London SE5 8RX (Tel: 01-274 6222 ext. 2710).
Services offered: Advice and treatment of climacteric and post-menopausal symptoms, including long-term patient management.
Problems dealt with: Hot flushes/night sweats; symptoms of lower genital tract atrophy; prevention of osteoporosis when there is a loss of bony tissue and bones become brittle.
Is professional referral required? No – but preferred.
Hours: Monday to Friday 9 a.m. – 5 p.m.
Fees: Only if patients wish private appointments – as recommended by the BMA.

Lewisham

Brook Advisory Centre
Lewisham Hospital, Ante-natal Department, Lewisham High Street, London SE13 6LH. (Tel: Walworth Brook for an appointment – 01-703 9660/7880).
Hours: Tuesday 5.30 p.m. – 8 p.m.

Fees: The contraceptive service is free, all other services are charged at various fees which are frequently waived or reduced in cases of financial hardship.
For further details of Brook services *see* Chapter 3, 'Family planning'.

Sexual Problems Clinic
Sydenham Green Health Centre, 26 Holmshaw Close, London SE26 (Tel: 01-639 2050).
Services offered: Help with sexual problems.
Hours: Wednesday 1 p.m. – 3 p.m.
Fees: None.

Merton

Marital Sexual Therapy Service
Merton Marriage Guidance Council, The Guild House, 30 – 32 Worple Street, Wimbledon SW19 4EF (Tel: 01-946 1788).
See also Chapter 15, 'Marriage Guidance,.

Patrick Doody Clinic
Pelham Road, Wimbledon SW19 (Tel: 01-640 3333).
Services offered: psychotherapeutic counselling.
Problems dealt with: psychosexual problems, both male and female.
Is professional referral required? No.
Hours: Alternate Fridays 2 p.m. – 4 p.m.
Fees: None.

Newham

Brook Advisory Centre
Newham Centre, West Ham Lane Clinic, 84 West Ham Lane, London E15 4PT (Tel: Tottenham Court Road Brook for appointment – 01-580 2991/323 1522).
Fees: The contraceptive service is free, all other services are charged at various fees which are frequently waived or reduced in cases of financial hardship.
For further details of Brook services *see* Chapter 3, 'Family Planning'.

Department of Genito-Urinary Medicine
Newham Hospital, Prince Regent Lane, London E13 (Tel: 01-476 1400 ext. 306).
Services offered: Diagnosis, treatment and counselling.
Problems dealt with: Genital disorders and sexual problems.
Is professional referral required? No.
Hours: Monday to Friday.
Fees: None.

Redbridge

Psychology Department
Goodmayes Hospital, Barley Lane, Ilford, Essex IG3 8XJ. (Tel: 01-590 6060 ext. 46).
Services offered: (only to those clients living within the hospital catchment area of Redbridge). Sex therapy for individuals or couples; marital therapy; advice and counselling in sexual problems including homosexuality; relationship problems, etc. Usually once a week or once a fortnight – session from 30 minutes to one hour in the department.
Problems dealt with: Any type of sexual, marital or emotional problem.
Is professional referral required? No, though it is more usual.
Hours: Monday to Friday 9.30 a.m. – 5 p.m.
Fees: None.

Richmond-upon-Thames

ACCEPT
(Tel: 01-940 7542). Services offered: help with alcohol and prescribed drugs problems. *See* ACCEPT, Hammersmith, for details of services.

Independent Professional Psychological Services
Bryan Tully, 6 Castelnau Gardens, Arundel Terrace, London SW13 9DU (Tel: 01-748 0815).
Services offered: Behavioural psychotherapy; clinical hypnosis; assessment of intellectual abilities/impairments; counselling. (Other psychological services are offered, but these are not appropriate to this *Directory*.)
Problems dealt with: Marital and relationship problems, sexual deviancy and sexual dysfunction. A special interest in gender identity/reassignment and transvestism.
Is professional referral required? No.
Hours: Monday to Friday 9 a.m. – 5 p.m.
Fees: Negotiable.
Comment: Bryan Tully is a clinical and research psychologist with a hospital and university background in England and abroad.

Marital and Sexual Therapy Services Richmond and Hounslow Marriage Guidance Council
51 Sheen Road, Richmond, Surrey TW9 1YQ (Tel: 01-940 8578). *See also* Chapter 15, 'Marriage Guidance'.

Pregnancy Advisory Service
The Cottage, 17 Rosslyn Road, East Twickenham, Middlesex. (Tel: 01-891 6833).
Services offered: A.I.D. (Artificial Insemination by Donor); sterilisation; vasectomy; cervical smears.
Is professional referral required? No.
Hours: Telephone for details.
Fees: Pregnancy test – £4 for urine test, £8 for blood test for very early pregnancy; termination of pregnancy – 19–22 weeks £255; morning after contraception – £10 (or £20 for IUD); sterilisation – £20 consultation, £170 operation; vasectomy – £20 consultation, £50 operation; cervical smear – £20.

Sheen Lane Health Clinic
Sheen Lane, London SW14 (Tel: 01-878 7561).
Services offered: psychosexual counselling.
Problems dealt with: non-consummation, loss of libido, impotence, orgasmic dysfunction, premature or retarded ejaculation.
Is professional referral required? No.
Hours: Thursday mornings.
Fees: None.

Southwark

Brook Advisory Centre
Walworth Brook, 153a East Street, Walworth, London SE17 2SD. (Tel: 01-703 0660/7880).
Services offered: As well as contraception services this Centre also provides psychosexual counselling.
Hours: Monday to Thursday 9.30 a.m. – 7.30 p.m; Friday 9.30 a.m. – 2.30 p.m; Saturday 9.30 a.m. – 12 noon.
Fees: The contraceptive service is free, all other services are charged at various fees which are frequently waived or reduced in cases of financial hardship.
For further details of Brook services *see* Chapter 3, 'Family Planning'.

Department of Psychological Medicine
York Clinic, Guy's Hospital, St Thomas Street, London SE1 9RT (Tel : 01-407 7600 Ext 3425).
Services offered: Psychosexual counselling, mainly for couples, but individuals without partners may also be seen.
Problems dealt with: The full range of heterosexual sexual problems, including loss of libido, impotence, premature ejaculation, vaginismus, dyspareunia.
Is professional referral required? Preferred.
Hours: Tuesday 1 p.m. – 5.30 p.m.
Fees: None.

Sexual Dysfunction Clinic
The Maudsley Hospital, Denmark Hill, London SE5 8AZ (Tel: 01-703 6333 ext. 281).
Services offered: Sexual dysfunction clinic, mostly catering for couples. Multi-disciplinary team of therapists. Some group therapy for singles with problems.
Problems dealt with: Impotence, premature ejaculation, failure to ejaculate, vaginismus, anorgasmia, low sex drive, marital problems.
Is professional referral required? Preferred.
Hours: Thursday 1.30 p.m. – 6 p.m.
Fees: None.

Sexual Problems Clinic
Munro Clinic, Guy's Hospital, Snowsfields, London SE1 (Tel: 01-639 2050).
Services offered: Help with sexual problems.
Is professional referral required? No.
Hours: Tuesday 2 p.m. – 4 p.m.
Fees: None.

Alexandra Clinic
St Giles Hospital, St Giles Road, London SE5. (Tel: 01-703 0898). Services offered: psychosexual counselling; sex therapy.
Problems dealt with: Sexual dysfunction, dissatisfaction.
Is professional referral required? No.
Hours: Monday, Wednesday and Friday 9 a.m. – 5 p.m; Tuesday and Thursday 9 a.m. – 6.30 p.m.
Fees: None.

Tower Hamlets

Psychosexual Counselling Clinic
4th Floor, London Hospital, Whitechapel, London E1 1BB (Tel: 01-377 7044).
Services offered: Psychosexual counselling.
Problems dealt with: Sexual dysfunction.
Is professional referral required? Yes.
Hours : Tuesday mornings.
Fees: None.

Waltham Forest

ACCEPT
(Tel: 01-531 2120).
Problems dealt with: alcohol and prescribed drugs problems.
For further details *see* ACCEPT Hammersmith.

Marital Sexual Therapy Services
Metropolitan Essex Marriage Guidance Council, Council Offices, Sidmouth Road, London E10 5RA. (Tel: 01-539 2939).
See also Chapter 15, 'Marriage Guidance'.

Wandsworth

Brook Advisory Centre
Wandsworth Centre, St Christopher's Health Centre, Wheeler Court, Plough Road, London SW11 2AY (Tel: Walworth Brook for appointment: 01-703 9660/7880).
Services offered: *see* Chapter 3, 'Family Planning'.
Fees: The contraceptive service is free, all other services are charged at various fees which are frequently waived or reduced in cases of financial hardship.

Sexual Dysfunction Clinic
St George's Hospital, Clare House, Cranmer Terrace, Blackshaw Road, London SW17 0RE (Tel: 01-672 1024 ext. 25).
Services offered: Treatment of impotence, orgasm and ejaculatory difficulties, alteration in libido, vaginismus and non-consummation.
Is professional referral required? Yes.
Hours: By appointment.
Fees: None.

Psychosexual Clinic
Bridge Lane Health Centre, 20 Bridge Lane, Battersea, London SW11. (Tel: 01-223 4211).
Services offered: Psychosexual counselling.
Is professional referral required? Yes.
Hours: Monday to Friday 9.30 a.m. – 5.15 p.m.
Fees: None.

Westminster, City of

Albany Trust
24 Chester Square, London SW1 (Tel: 01-730 5871).
Services offered: Individual, couple or group counselling/psychotherapy.
Problems dealt with: Any problems experienced by marriage partners, homosexuals, lesbians, transsexuals, transvestites; tension in any relationships; psychosexual problems.
Is professional referral required? No.
Hours: Monday to Friday, all day. Evenings by arrangement.
Fees: On application.No person will be refused counselling because of financial hardship. In case of financial difficulties you are invited to discuss the possibility of a reduced fee with the counsellor.

British Pregnancy Advisory Service
7 Belgrave Road, Victoria, London SW1V 1QB. (Tel: 01-222 0985).
Services offered: Pregnancy testing; pregnancy counselling; abortion assessment; contraception; morning-after birth control. Counselling and assessment for: infertility problems; artificial insemination.
Is professional referral required? No.
Hours: Monday to Friday 9 a.m. – 5 p.m. For further details of BPAS services *see* Chapter 3, 'Family Planning'.

British Hypnotherapy Association
67 Upper Berkeley Street, London W1 (Tel: 01-723 4443).
Services offered: The Association maintains a register of practitioners who are trained in sexology, psychodynamics, nervous conditions, psychogenic problems, psychotherapy, hypnotherapy, and counselling. Treatment enquirers must write stating their name, address, age and problem, enclosing £1. They are then sent a 16-page pamphlet answering basic questions, plus details of the nearest recommended practitioners.
Problems dealt with: Psychosexual problems, relationship difficulties, emotional problems, anxieties, fears, guilts, problems which have emotional causes.
Is professional referral required? No.
Fees: Each practitioner charges set fees approved by the Association.
Comment: The Association also provides talks and specialist publications and distributes a quarterly journal, *You*.

Genito-Urinary Department
Westminster Hospital (OP6), Dean Ryle Street, Horseferry Road, London SW1P 2AP (Tel: 01-828 9811).
Services offered: Psychosexual problems developing or present in patients attending with genito-urinary conditions are dealt with as far as possible within the department.
Problems dealt with: *See* above.
Is professional referral required? Yes.
Hours: Monday to Friday 10.30 a.m. – 5.30 p.m., by appointment.
Fees: None.

Dr Patricia Gillan (Private)
7 Upper Harley Street, London NW1 (Tel: 01-486 1348).
Services offered: Individual and conjoint therapy with the possibility of group psychotherapy.
Problems dealt with: Sexual phobias; low sex drive; anorgasmia; vaginismus; erectile impotence; premature and delayed ejaculation; relationship difficulties.

Is professional referral required? No.
Hours: Wednesday 9.30 a.m. – 12.30 p.m. and 2 p.m. – 5 p.m. or by appointment.
Fees: £50.

Identity
Beauchamp Lodge, 2 Warwick Crescent, London W2 6NE (Tel: 01-289 6175).
Services offered: A range of counselling services, from supportive or short-term crisis work to long-term work with individuals, couples or with groups to meet sexual, personal and relationship problems, with particular concern for people in sexual minorities including homosexual men and women, bi-sexuals, transvestites, and transsexuals.
Is professional referral required? No.
Hours: By arrangement.
Fees: By negotiation with each counsellor, though help is not dependent on ability to pay.

Institute of Behaviour Therapy
Under the direction of Dr Robert Sharpe, 38 Queen Anne Street, London W1. (Tel: 01-580 4972).
Services offered: Behaviour therapy treatment of all types of problems. Deals with shyness and being able to make relationships, marital therapy and directive treatment of sexual dysfunctions.
Problems dealt with: Premature ejaculation, impotence, ejaculatory incompetence, lack of orgasm in the female, painful intercourse, marital inter-personal problems and shyness, emotional difficulties.
Is professional referral required? No.
Hours: Monday to Friday 9 a.m. – 7 p.m.
Fees: £60 per consultation (approximately one hour).
Comment: for details of courses *see* Chapter 13, 'Learning About Sex'. Can carry out penile tumescence tests for impotence sufferers at a hospital unit either as day patient or on overnight stay. Cost: £100 – £300 depending on extent of testing.

Margaret Pyke Centre
15 Bateman's Buildings, Soho Square, London W1V 5TW. (Tel: 01-734 9351).
Services offered: In addition to family planning: psychosexual counselling; sub-fertility, vasectomy, female sterilisation; post-coital contraception; pregnancy testing – only available to existing patients of the Centre, who must take a sample of their urine first thing in the morning before 11 a.m. and must return after mid-day and before 3.30 p.m. for the result.
Is professional referral required? GP referral required for sub-fertility, vasectomy, and female sterilisation.
Hours: Clinic open Monday to Friday 9 a.m. – 6.30 p.m. Appointments may be made for family planning services between 9.30 a.m. and 6.15 p.m.
Fees: None.

Marital Sexual Therapy Services
London Marriage Guidance Council, 76a New Cavendish Street, Harley Street, London W1M 7LB (Tel: 01-580 1087). *See also* Chapter 15, 'Marriage Guidance'.

Pregnancy Advisory Service
13 Charlotte Street, London W1P 1HD (Tel: 01-637 8962).
Services offered: Pregnancy testing on the spot. Pregnancy counselling service – the counsellor is there to help you reach your own decision, she will be glad to discuss the alternatives, tell you what an abortion involves and answer questions. 'Morning after' contraception is available if you are treated within 72 hours. A.I.D. (Artificial Insemination by Donor), sterilisation, vasectomy, cervical smears. A telephone advisory service is available.
Is professional referral required? No.
Hours: Monday, Tuesday, Wednesday, Friday 9.30 a.m. – 5.30 p.m; Thursday 9.30 a.m. – 7.30 p.m; Saturday 9.30 a.m. – 12.30 p.m.
Fees: Pregnancy test, £4. Counselling and medical consultation for unwanted pregnancy, £25. Termination of pregnancy, £140, under 14 weeks; £170, 14 to 18 weeks; £255, 19 to 22 weeks. Morning after £10. A.I.D. £60 consultation. Sterilisation £20 consultation, £170 operation. Vasectomy £20 consultation, £50 operation. Cervical smear £20.

Pregnancy and Gynaecological Advisory Service
26 Fouberts Place, London W1V 1HG (Tel: 01-437 7125).
Services offered: Pregnancy testing and advice about abortion, sterilisation and birth control. Telephone advisory service.
Problems dealt with: People with unwanted pregnancy seeking abortion.
Is professional referral required? No.
Hours: Telephone for appointment. Monday to Friday telephones manned 9 a.m. – 7.30 p.m. and Saturday morning 9 a.m. – 1 p.m.
Fees: Abortion advice and referral is free. Birth control and general gynaecology, subject to annual fees.

GREATER MANCHESTER

Family Planning Association Regional Office
For details, *see* the FPA Regional Office (North-west England) in Liverpool, Merseyside.

Bolton

Dr Eric Curless
Beaumont Hospital, Old Hall Clough, Chorley New Road, Lostock, Bolton (Tel: Bolton (0204) 494211).
Services offered: Consultant physician in genito-urinary medicine covering sexually transmitted diseases, family planning and contraception services, sex therapy (co-therapist available if needed), Well Woman screening clinics, AIDS screening, blood test and diagnosis; AIDS information and counselling.
Problems dealt with: Psychosexual problems, family planning and sexually transmitted diseases.
Is professional referral required? No.
Hours: By appointment only.
Fees: Yes, on the BUPA scale.

Deansgate Health Centre
Queen Street, Deansgate, Bolton. (Tel: Bolton (0204) 26511 Monday, Tuesday, Thursday 7 p.m. – 8 p.m.).
Services offered: Psychosexual counselling.
Problems dealt with: Marital problems.
Is professional referral required? No.
Hours: Tuesday 7 p.m. – 8 p.m.
Fees: None.

Marital Sexual Therapy Services
Bolton Marriage Guidance Council, Queen Street, Central Street, Bolton (Tel: Bolton (0204) 28302). *See also* Chapter 15, 'Marriage Guidance'.

Hazel Grove
Outpost of Manchester Marriage Guidance Council, 1 Hatherlow Lane, Hazel Grove. *See* below.

Manchester

British Pregnancy Advisory Service
Fourways House, 57 Hilton Street, Manchester M1 2EJ (Tel: 061-236 7777).
Services offered: Pregnancy testing; pregnancy counselling; abortion assessment; contraception; morning-after birth control. Enquiries about: infertility problems; artificial insemination.
Is professional referral required? No.
Hours: Monday, Wednesday, Thursday and Friday 9 a.m. – 5 p.m; Tuesday 9 a.m. – 8 p.m.
Fees: *See* BPAS in Chapter 3, 'Family Planning'. For details of services, *see* Chapter 3.

BUPA Medical Centre
9 St John Street, Manchester M3 4DW (Tel: (061) 833 9362).
For details *see* Greater London (Camden).

Clayton Health Centre
(Tel: 061-231 1151).
Services offered: Psychosexual therapy; education and marriage guidance.
Problems dealt with: Sexual dysfunction; inter-personal relationship.
Is professional referral required? No.
Hours: Tuesday 8.30 a.m. – 11.30 a.m.
Fees: None.

Macartney Day Department, North Manchester Hospital.
(Tel: 061-795 4567 ext. 2729).
Services offered: Psychosexual therapy; education and marriage guidance.
Problems dealt with: Sexual dysfunction; inter-personal relationships.
Is professional referral required? Yes.
Hours: Monday, Wednesday and Thursday.
Fees: None.

Marital Sexual Therapy Services
Manchester Marriage Guidance Council, Cornbrook, 346 Chester Road, Manchester M16 9EA (Tel: 061-872 0303) *See also* Chapter 15, 'Marriage Guidance'.

Pregnancy Advisory Service
50 Newton Street, Manchester M1 2EA (Tel: 061-228 1887).
Services offered: Pregnancy testing; abortion advice; 'morning-after' pill; smear tests; contraception; menopausal problems; pre-menstrual tension and related problems.
Problems dealt with: All pregnancy problems. Problems peculiar to women, for example, menopausal, pre-menstrual tension, contraception advice.
Is professional referral required? No.
Hours: Monday to Friday 9 a.m. – 5 p.m.
Fees: Abortion counselling and referral, £30. Menopause clinic, £25. Pre-menstrual tension, £15. Pregnancy tests, £5 and £6.

Psychiatric Department
Withington Hospital, Nell Lane, Manchester M20 8LR (Tel: 061-445 8111).
Services offered: Psychosexual counselling.
Problems dealt with: All types of sexual dysfunction.
Is professional referral required? Usually.
Hours: Wednesday.
Fees: None.

Psychosexual Clinic
Eccles Health Centre, Corporation Road, Eccles, Manchester M30 0EQ (Tel: 061-707 5560).

Services offered: Counselling and therapy of all groups, for example, married couples or people in a relationship, transsexuals, homosexuals and handicapped people. Provision of sex aids where relevant.
Problems dealt with: Psychosexual and gender identity problems.
Hours: Wednesday afternoons.
Fees: None (but private treatment is available with Dr Goodman).

The Sister Rose Private Clinic and Pregnancy Advisory Centre
(Head office) 2 St John Street, Manchester 3 (Tel: 061-834 0440/0400.
Services offered: Counselling for sexual problems; examination and assessment for termination of pregnancy; pregnancy tests – both on the premises and also via postal pack; assessment and examination for female sterilisation, which can be performed as a day-care operation; vasectomy counselling and operations; routine smear testing; well-woman checks; menopausal clinics; contraceptive advice; morning-after pill; IUD fitting.
Is professional referral required? No, but a general practitioner's referral is preferred.
Hours: Phone for details.
Fees: Counselling, consultation and post-operative check in respect of termination of pregnancy – £30; operation fee – £107 (up to and including 13 weeks of pregnancy); £239 for prostaglandin termination (up to and including 20 weeks of pregnancy); sterilisation – £25 for counselling and £145 for day-care. Information available on postal or telephone request. Postal pregnancy tests also available.

Trees Street Clinic
(Tel: 061-720 7808).
Services offered: Psychosexual therapy; education and marriage guidance.
Problems dealt with: Sexual dysfunction; inter-personal relationships.
Is professional referral required? No.
Hours: Wednesday 6 p.m. – 8.30 p.m.
Fees: None.

Ramsbottom

Psychosexual Counselling Clinic
Ramsbottom Health Centre, Carr Street, Ramsbottom BL0 9DD (Tel: Ramsbottom (070682) 4294).
Services offered: Psychosexual counselling.
Is professional referral required? Yes.
Hours: In the evenings, by appointment.
Fees: None.

Rochdale

Baillie Street Health Centre
Baillie Street, Rochdale (Tel: Rochdale (0706) 755031).
Services offered: Psychosexual counselling.
Is professional referral required? No.
Hours: Wednesday morning. Thursday afternoons at Taylor Street, Heywood.
Fees: None.

Salford

Marital Sexual Therapy Services
Salford Counselling Centre, 1 Cumbria Walk, off Broughton Road, Salford M6 6RG (Tel: (061) 737 1400). *See also* Chapter 15, 'Marriage Guidance,.

Shaw

Independent Professional Psychological Services
Ian Rickard, 3 Brookfield, High Crompton, Shaw OL2 7QQ. (Tel: Shaw (0706) 848885).
Services offered: Psychological.
Is professional referral required? No.
Hours: Phone for appointment.
Fees: Negotiable.

HAMPSHIRE

Family Planning Association Regional Office
For details, *see* the FPA Regional Office (South-east England) in Hove, East Sussex.

Aldershot

Marital Sexual Therapy Services
Farnborough and Fleet Marriage Guidance Council, 12 Arthur Street, Aldershot (Tel: Aldershot (0252) 24679). *See also* Chapter 15, 'Marriage Guidance'.

Psychosexual Counselling – Marital Difficulties
Aldershot Health Centre, Aldershot. (Tel: Camberley (0276) 681636 for appointments).
Services offered: Psychosexual counselling.
Is professional referral required? No.
Fees: None.

Basingstoke

Family Planning Association (Basingstoke Clinic)
8 Fairfields Road, Basingstoke, Hampshire (Tel: Basingstoke (0256) 26980). (The FPA Regional Office is in Hove, East Sussex.) *See also* Chapter 3, 'Family Planning'.

Services offered: Birth control; Well Woman checks; menopause counselling; psychosexual counselling; vasectomy; pregnancy testing – counselling; youth advisory clinics; education service. Telephone advisory service, including referrals to relevant agencies.
Problems dealt with: *See* above.
Is professional referral required? No.
Hours: Clinics are two mornings, two afternoons and four evenings per week. Reception every day 9 a.m. – 3 p.m.
Fees: Phone for details.

British Pregnancy Advisory Service
Church Grange Health Centre, Bramleys Drive, Basingstoke RG21 1QN (Tel: Basingstoke (0256) 59720). Telephone answering service: Basingstoke (0256) 465425 Wednesday 6 p.m. – 8 p.m.
Services offered: Pregnancy testing; pregnancy counselling; abortion assessment. Enquiries about: infertility problems; artificial insemination.
Is professional referral required? No.
Fees: For details *see* Chapter 3, 'Family Planning'. For details of BPAS services *see* Chapter 3.

Marital Sexual Therapy Services
Basingstoke and District Marriage Guidance Council, Shute House, Church Street, Basingstoke (Tel: Basingstoke (0256) 24364). *See also* Chapter 15, 'Marriage Guidance'.

Portsmouth

BUPA Medical Centre
BUPA Hospital, Bartons Road, Havant PO9 5NP (Tel: Portsmouth (0705) 454511). For details of services *see* Greater London (Camden).

Ella Gordon Centre
St Mary's Hospital, Portsmouth PO3 6AF (Tel: Portsmouth (0705) 866301).
Services offered: Psychosexual counselling and sex therapy, involving a multi-disciplinary team of therapists. A telephone advisory service is available.
Problems dealt with: Psychosexual problems.
Is professional referral required? Preferred.
Hours: Telephone – Monday to Friday 9 a.m. – 5 p.m. Sessions – Monday afternoon and Wednesday evening.

Marital Sexual Therapy Services
Portsmouth and District Marriage Guidance Council, Training Centre Building, Dugald Drummond Street, Portsmouth PO1 2BB (Tel: Portsmouth (0705) 827026). *See also* Chapter 15, 'Marriage Guidance'.

Southampton

Marital Sexual Therapy Services
Southampton and District Marriage Guidance Council, 3 Kings Park Road, Southampton SO1 2AS (Tel: Southampton (0703) 229761).
See also Chapter 15, 'Marriage Guidance'.

Central Health Clinic
East Park Terrace, Southampton SO9 4WN (Tel: Southampton (0703) 34321).
Services offered: Counselling for sexual problems of able-bodied and disabled people, for individuals and/or partners.
Problems dealt with: Any sexual problems (for example, dysfunctions, deviance, gender identity problems), including those related to physical disabilities.
Is professional referral required? No.
Hours: Weekdays by appointment.
Fees: None.

Winchester

Family Planning Clinic
Winchester Health Authority, Kings Walk, Silver Hill, Winchester, Hampshire.
Services offered: Psychosexual counselling sessions with a doctor (in association with family planning clinics).
Problems dealt with: Psychosexual problems – male and female.
Is professional referral required? No.
Hours: By appointment.
Fees: None.

Marital Sexual Therapy Services
Winchester and District Marriage Guidance Council, Litton Lodge, 13a Clifton Road, Winchester SO22 5BS. (Tel: Winchester (0962) 61336). *See also* Chapter 15, 'Marriage Guidance'.

HEREFORD AND WORCESTER

Family Planning Association Regional Office
For details, *see* the FPA Regional Office (Midlands) in Birmingham, West Midlands.

Bromsgrove

Marital Sexual Therapy Services
Outpost of Bromsgrove Marriage Guidance Council, 47 Worcester Road, Bromsgrove. *See also* Chapter 15, 'Marriage Guidance'.

Hereford

Marital Sexual Therapy Services
Herefordshire Marriage Guidance Council, Top Floor, 6a St Owen Street, Hereford (Tel: Hereford (0432) 276023). *See also* Chapter 15, 'Marriage Guidance'.

Worcester

BUPA Medical Centre
South Bank Hospital, 139 Bath Road, Worcester WR5 3AG. (Tel: Worcester (0905) 350003). For details of services *see* Greater London (Camden).

Marital Sexual Therapy Services
Worcester Marriage Guidance Council, 7 Castle Street, Worcester (Tel: Worcester (0905) 28051). *See also* Chapter 15, 'Marriage Guidance'.

Moor Street Clinic
Moor Street, Worcester WR1 3DB (Tel: Worcester (0905) 21075).
Services offered: Fully comprehensive family planning service. Psychosexual clinic once a week. Vasectomy counselling clinic once a week. Four vasectomy operations are carried out weekly.
Problems dealt with: Problems relating to the above services.
Is professional referral required? Only for vasectomy counselling.
Hours: By appointment.
Fees: None.
Comment: The special services at this clinic are additional to a comprehensive family planning service in Worcestershire based at Worcester, Malvern, Evesham and Droitwich. A special young people's clinic operates at Moor Street, Tuesday evenings 6.30 p.m. – 9 p.m. (Tel: Worcester (0905) 23236).

HERTFORDSHIRE

Family Planning Association Regional Office
For details, *see* the FPA Regional Office (North of the Thames) in Bedford, Bedfordshire.

Bushey

BUPA Medical Centre
BUPA Hospital, Heathbourne Road, Bushey, Watford WD2 1RD. (Tel: 01-950 9090).
For details of services *see* Greater London (Camden).

Hoddesdon

ACCEPT
(Tel: Potters Bar (0707) 332157).
Services offered: Help with alcohol and prescribed drugs problems. *See* ACCEPT Hammersmith for details of services.

Potters Bar

Sylvia Knight
93 Byng Drive, Potters Bar, Hertfordshire (Tel: Potters Bar (0707) 58636).
Services offered: Private counselling and therapy. Small groups – evenings and occasional weekends. Therapy available in London and Potters Bar.
Problems dealt with: Relationship difficulties, psychosexual problems (premature ejaculation, orgasmic inhibition, etc.), homosexuality, transsexual and transvestite support counselling. Interested in reducing ignorance, fear and aggression between the sexes by frank discussion and group activities, and in promoting greater understanding, trust and openness. Creative use of dreams, guided fantasy, poetry and drawing may be used to expose blocks and to free the imaginative and erotic elements of sexuality.
Is professional referral required? No, but welcomed.
Hours: 4.30 p.m. – 10 p.m. or by arrangement.
Fees: Privately, £12 – £18 per session (one hour plus). Groupwork, £5 – £7 an evening; £15 – £18 whole day. Reductions gladly arranged for unwaged and certain referred others.

Watford

Clinical Psychology Department
Northwick Park Hospital, Watford.
Services offered: Assessment and treatment for sexual problems in general.
Is professional referral required? Yes.
Hours: 9 a.m. – 5.30 p.m.
Fees: None.

Marital Sexual Therapy Services
Watford and Three Rivers Marriage Guidance Council, Watford Advice Centre, 149 The Parade, High Street, Watford (Tel: Watford (0923) 41803). *See also* Chapter 15, 'Marriage Guidance'.

Welwyn

ACCEPT
Welwyn and Hatfield (Tel: Potters Bar (0707) 332157).

Services offered: help with alcohol and prescribed drugs problems. *See* ACCEPT Hammersmith for details of services (Greater London).

HUMBERSIDE

Family Planning Association Regional Office
For details, *see* the FPA Regional Office (Yorkshire and North-east England) in Sheffield, South Yorkshire.

Grimsby

Marital Sexual Therapy Services
South Humberside Marriage Guidance Council, 10 Town Hall Street, Grimsby DN31 1HN (Tel: Grimsby (0472) 54392). *See also* Chapter 15, 'Marriage Guidance'.

Hull

British Pregnancy Advisory Service
32 Beverley Road, (entrance North Street), Hull HU3 1YF. (Tel: Hull (0482) 223944 telephone answering service Keyingham (09644) 6431 Wednesday 6 p.m. – 8 p.m.).
Services offered: Pregnancy testing; pregnancy counselling; abortion assessment; contraception; morning-after birth control. Enquiries about: infertility problems; artificial insemination.
Is professional referral required? No.
Hours: Monday and Friday 11 a.m. – 2 p.m; Tuesday 10 a.m. – 4 p.m.
For further details of BPAS services and fees *see* Chapter 3.

Family Planning Association
Kingston-upon-Hull FPA Clinic, 82 Spring Bank, Hull HU3 1AB. (Tel: Hull (0482) 29360).
See Chapter 3, 'Family Planning', for further details.
Services offered: Birth control, Well Woman checks, menopausal advice and information service.
Problems dealt with: Same as above.
Is professional referral required? No.
Hours: Monday to Thursday 9 a.m. – 2 p.m.
Fees: Fees are charged for clinic services.

The Sister Rose Pregnancy Advisory Centres
139 Beverley Road, Hull (Tel: Hull (0482) 20100).
Services offered: Examination and assessment for termination of pregnancy; pregnancy tests: both on the premises and also via a postal pack; assessment and examination for female sterilisation which can be performed as a day-care operation; counselling and vasectomy operations; routine smear examinations; Well-Woman checks; menopausal clinics; contraceptive advice; morning-after pill; IUD fittings.
Is professional referral required? No, but a general practitioner's referral preferred.
Hours: Monday to Friday 9 a.m. – 5 p.m.
Fees: Counselling, consultation and post-operative check in respect of termination of pregnancy £30. Operation fee £107 (up to and including 13 weeks of pregnancy) and £239 for prostaglandin termination (up to and including 20 weeks of pregnancy). Sterilisation £25 for counselling and £145 for day-care.
Comment: Brochures giving brief outlines of treatment available on postal or telephone request.

Scunthorpe

Family Planning Clinic
Comforts Avenue, Scunthorpe, DN15 6PW (Tel: Scunthorpe (0724) 843481).
Services offered: In addition to family planning psychosexual counselling.
Is professional referral required? Yes for psychosexual counselling.
Hours: By appointment.
Fees: None.

Marital Sexual Therapy Services
Scunthorpe and District Marriage and Personal Counselling Service, 48 Oswold Road, Scunthorpe DN15 7PQ (Tel: Scunthorpe (0724) 861889). *See also* Chapter 15, 'Marriage Guidance'.

ISLE OF WIGHT

Family Planning Association Regional Office
For details, *see* the FPA Regional Office (South-east England) in Hove, East Sussex.

KENT (*see also* Greater London)

Family Planning Association Regional Office
For details, *see* the FPA Regional Office (South-east England) in Hove, East Sussex.

Broadstairs

Marital Sexual Therapy Services
Thanet Marriage Guidance Council, 97 High Street, Broadstairs CT10 1NQ (Tel: Broadstairs (0843) 61228). *See also* Chapter 15, 'Marriage Guidance'.

Canterbury

Psychology Service and Research Centre
St Augustine's Hospital, Chartham, Canterbury, Kent (Tel: Chartham (0227) 738382 ext. 201 or 371). (Clinics at many centres in East Kent. For details and times of these, please contact the Chartham number.)
Services offered: A psychological clinic dealing with a wide variety of problems, including sexual and marital problems.
Problems dealt with: Impotence, orgasmic dysfunction, vaginismus, premature ejaculation, problems of sexual desire, etc. More general relationship problems.
Is professional referral required? Yes (unless someone particularly wants to be seen privately).
Hours: Clinics are held during working hours and in the evenings by appointment.
Fees: None (unless someone particularly wants to be seen privately).

Chatham

Medway District Psychology Service
Psychology Department, All Saints' Hospital, Chatham ME4 5NG. (Tel: Medway (0634) 407311 Ext 251).
Services offered: Comprehensive treatment of psychosexual problems as part of general clinical psychology service (no special clinics), dealing with behavioural and emotional problems of all sorts. Individual, couple, family and group treatments provided. Age range covered includes childhood to old age.
Problems dealt with: Psychosexual problems.
Is professional referral required? Yes (consultant or general practitioner).
Hours: Monday to Friday 9 a.m. – 5 p.m. (occasional late appointments).
Fees: None.

Folkestone

Sexual Dysfunction Clinic
1 Radnor Park Road, Folkestone. (Tel: Folkestone (0303) 57311).
Services offered: Sexual counselling for couples in a stable relationship; some individual work undertaken.
Problems dealt with: Impaired arousal in females; erectile problems in males; orgasmic problems in both sexes; vaginismus, dyspareunia, etc.
Is professional referral required? Preferred.
Hours: Wednesday and Friday afternoon.
Fees: None.

Gillingham

Family Planning Clinic
Balmoral Gardens, Gillingham, Kent (Tel: Medway (0634) 595626).
Services offered: Family planning – pill, barrier, IUCD and referral for sterilisation or vasectomy counselling if appropriate. Occasionally psychosexual counselling and abortion counselling, but usually for existing family planning patients, rather than new patients seeking only psychosexual advice.
Problems dealt with: Family planning mainly – *see* above.
Is professional referral required? No.
Hours: Monday 9.30 a.m. – 11 a.m; 5.30 p.m. – 7 p.m; Tuesday 5.30 p.m. – 7 p.m; Wednesday 9.30 a.m. – 11 a.m; Thursday 5.30 p.m. – 7 p.m.
Fees: None.

Maidstone

Family Planning Clinic
Foster Street, Maidstone.(Tel: Maidstone (0622) 51509).
Services offered: Psychosexual and marital counselling.
Problems dealt with: Marital problems for men and women.
Hours: Clinic usually open twice a month, telephone for an appointment.
Fees: None.

Marital Sexual Therapy Services
Maidstone and District Marriage Guidance Council, 60 Marsham Street, Maidstone ME14 1EW (Tel: Maidstone (0622) 677065). *See also* Chapter 15, 'Marriage Guidance'.

Tonbridge

Baltic Road Clinic
Baltic Road, Tonbridge, Kent (Tel: Tonbridge (0732) 352015).
Services offered: In addition to family planning, psychosexual counselling.
Problems dealt with: Problems relating to the above services.
Is professional referral required? No.
Hours: 6.30 p.m. – 8.30 p.m., by appointment.
Fees: None.

Tunbridge Wells

The Family Planning Association
21 Dudley Road, Tunbridge Wells, Kent (Tel: Tunbridge Wells (0892) 30002). (The FPA Regional Office is at Hove, East Sussex.)

See also Chapter 3, 'Family Planning'.
Services offered: Birth control – all methods; Well Woman clinics; youth advisory service; menopause advisory service; vasectomy counselling and operation; psychosexual counselling.
Problems dealt with: *See* above.
Is professional referral required? No.
Hours: Monday 12.25 p.m. – 2 p.m. and 4.30 p.m. – 6 p.m.; Tuesday 5 p.m. – 7.30 p.m.; Wednesday 1 p.m. – 3.30 p.m.; Thursday 9.30 a.m. – 11 a.m. and 6 p.m. – 7.30 p.m. No appointments on Friday.
Fees: Phone for details.

Marital Sexual Therapy Services
West Kent Marriage Guidance Council, 10a High Street, Tunbridge Wells TN1 1UX (Tel: Tunbridge Wells (0892) 29927). *See also* Chapter 15, 'Marriage Guidance'.

LANCASHIRE

Family Planning Association Regional Office
For details, *see* the FPA Regional Office (North-west England) in Liverpool, Merseyside.

Blackburn

Larkhill Health Centre
Mount Pleasant, Blackburn (Tel: Blackburn (0254) 63611.
Services offered: Psychosexual counselling.
Is professional referral required? No.
Hours: Tuesday 7 p.m. – 9.30 p.m.
Fees: None.

Marital Sexual Therapy Services
Blackburn Marriage Guidance Council, 37 Limbrick, Blackburn BB1 8AB. (Tel: Blackburn (0254) 52827) *See also* Chapter 15, 'Marriage Guidance'.

Blackpool

Pregnancy Advisory Service
93 Abingdon Street, Blackpool (Tel: Blackpool (0253) 293096).
Services offered: Pregnancy testing; abortion advice; 'morning after' pill; smear tests; contraception; menopausal problems; pre-menstrual tension and related problems.
Problems dealt with: All pregnancy problems; menopausal problems; pre-menstrual tension; contraception advice.
Is professional referral required? No.
Hours: Monday to Friday 9 a.m. – 5 p.m.; Saturday 10 a.m. – 1 p.m.
Fees: Abortion counselling and referral, £30; menopause clinic, £25; pre-menstrual tension, £15; pregnancy tests, £5 and £6.

Psychology (Clinical)
Health Centre, 156 Whitegate Drive, Blackpool (Tel: Blackpool (0253) 63232 ext. 255).
Services offered: Psychosexual therapy.
Is professional referral required? Yes.
Hours: By appointment.
Fees: None.

Sister Rose Pregnancy Advisory Centres
Stanley Buildings, 3 Caunce Street, Blackpool (Tel: Blackpool (0253) 23009).
Services offered: Examination and assessment for termination of pregnancy; pregnancy tests, both on the premises and also via a postal pack; assessment and examination for female sterilisation which can be performed as a day-care operation; routine smear testing; well-woman checks; menopausal clinics; contraceptive advice; morning-after pill, IUD fittings, etc.
Is professional referral required? No.
Hours: Phone for details.
Fees: Counselling, consultation and post-operative check in respect of termination of pregnancy £30. Operation £107 (up to and including 13 weeks of pregnancy) and £239 for prostaglandin termination (up to and including 20 weeks of pregnancy. Sterilisation – £25 for counselling, £145 for day-care.

Burnley

Brook Advisory Centre
N.E. Lancs Brook, 79 Church Street, Burnley. (Tel: Burnley (0282) 416596).
For details of services *see* Chapter 3, 'Family Planning'.

Clitheroe

Clitheroe Health Centre
Railway View Road, Clitheroe. (Tel: Clitheroe (0200) 24171).
Services offered: Psychosexual counselling.
Is professional referral required? No.
Hours: Tuesday 9 a.m. – 11.30 a.m.
Fees: None

Lancaster

Department of Clinical Psychology
Hillside, Lancaster Moor Hospital, Lancaster LA1 3JR (Tel: Lancaster (0524) 65241 ext. 209).

Services offered: Psychological approaches to all types of personal and psychological (including psychosexual) problems; individual and group therapy.
Problems dealt with: All psychosexual/psychological difficulties. Marital and relationship problems.
Is professional referral required? Yes, usually, although self-referrals possible, in which case the general practitioner may be contacted for agreement.
Fees: None.
Comment: Similar facilities exist at Queen Victoria Hospital, Royal Lancaster Infirmary and Ridge Lea Hospital.

Preston

British Pregnancy Advisory Service
For details of services, *see* Chapter 3, 'Family Planning'.

Geoffrey Street Health Centre
Geoffrey Street, off New Hall Lane, Preston PR1 5NE (Tel: Preston (0772) 794236).
Services offered: Psychosexual counselling.
Is professional referral required? Yes.
Hours: Monday 10 a.m. – 12 p.m.; Tuesday 2 p.m. – 5 p.m.
Fees: None.
Comment: These special sessions are additional to comprehensive family planning and related services in Lancashire.

Well Women Centre
2 Hardwicke Street, Preston (Tel: Preston (0772) 555813).
Services offered: Psychosexual counselling by women.
Is professional referral required? No.
Hours: Tuesday, Wednesday, Thursday 10 a.m. – 4 p.m; Friday 10 a.m. – 1 p.m.
Fees: none.

LEICESTERSHIRE

Family Planning Association Regional Office
For details, *see* the FPA Regional Office (Midlands) in Birmingham, West Midlands.

Leicester

District Psychological Service
Hadley House, Leicester General Hospital, Gwendolen Road, Leicester LE5 4PW (Tel: Leicester (0533) 730222 ext. 610).
Services offered: Psychosexual counselling for couples along broadly behavioural lines.
Problems dealt with: All kinds of sexual dysfunction.
Is professional referral required? Yes, must come through a medical source.
Hours: Tuesday evening 5 p.m. – 8.30 p.m. Some daytime appointments.
Fees: None.
Comment: There is a waiting list and it can take several months to get an appointment. Due to lack of funding only limited areas of Leicestershire can be covered by this service.

Family Planning Clinic
St Peter's Health Centre, Sparkenhoe Street, Leicester LE2 02A (Tel: Leicester (0533) 25162).
Services offered: Psychosexual clinics (female doctors); vasectomy counselling and operations; sub-fertility clinic; pregnancy counselling; family planning and contraception services, including morning-after contraception and domiciliary family planning service. A telephone advisory service is available with a nursing sister.
Problems dealt with: Various – problems are then referred to appropriate clinics.
Is professional referral required? No.
Hours: Monday and Friday 9 a.m. – 5 p.m.; Tuesday, Wednesday and Thursday 9 a.m. – 7 p.m.
Fees: None.

Medical Aid Department, British Red Cross Society
76 Clarendon Park Road, Leicester LE2 3AD (Tel: Leicester (0533) 700747).
Services offered: Counselling service for disabled people with sexual problems and a display of a range of sex aids. A telephone advisory service is available.
Is professional referral required? No.
Hours: Referrals taken through DIAL – Disability Information Advice Line (Tel: Leicester (0533) 700666) 10 a.m. – 4 p.m. daily.
Fees: None.

Narborough

Psychosexual Clinic
Woodland Day Hospital, Narborough LE9 5EQ.(Tel: Leicester (0533) 863265).
Services offered: Treatment of sexual dysfunctions.
Problems dealt with: All problems related to sexual dysfunction.
Is professional referral required? Yes.
Fees: None for NHS services, but private treatment may be arranged with fees of between £30 and £40 per session.

Family Planning Association (Eastern England Regional Office)
20A Bridewell Alley, Norwich NR2 1SY (Tel: Norwich (0603) 628704).
See also Chapter 3, 'Family Planning'.
Services offered: Free literature from the Family Planning Information Service. Information on: contraception, birth control, pregnancy testing within the region. Referral to other support services where required. Books can be purchased on childbirth, family planning, sex education, family relationships, women's health, family health. A telephone information service is available.
Problems dealt with: As above.
Is professional referral required? No.
Hours: Monday to Friday 9 a.m. – 5 p.m., normally.
Fees: Only speaker's and tutor's fees.

Marital Sexual Therapy Services
Norfolk and Norwich Marriage Guidance Council, 6 Kingsley Road, Norwich NR1 3RB. (Tel: Norwich (0603) 25333).
See also Chapter 15, 'Marriage Guidance'.

Thetford

Family Planning Clinic
Thetford Cottage Hospital, Thetford (Tel: Thetford (0842) 2499).
Services offered: Psychosexual counselling.
Is professional referral required? Yes.
Hours: 6.30 p.m. – 8.30 p.m.
Fees: None.

NORTHAMPTONSHIRE

Family Planning Association Regional Office
For details, *see* the FPA Regional Office (North of the Thames) in Bedford, Bedfordshire.

Northampton

Marital Sexual Therapy Services
Northamptonshire Marriage Guidance Council, 24 Hazelwood Road, Northampton NN1 1LN (Tel: Northampton (0604) 34400).
See also Chapter 15, 'Marriage Guidance'.

NORTHUMBERLAND

Family Planning Association Regional Office
For details, *see* the FPA Regional Office (Yorkshire and North-east England) in Sheffield, South Yorkshire.

Morpeth

Psychosexual Problems Clinic
The Cottage Hospital, Morpeth. (Tel: Morpeth (0670) 514523).
Services offered: Counselling.
Problems dealt with: Psychosexual.
Is professional referral required? Yes.
Hours: By appointment.
Fees: None.

NORTH YORKSHIRE

Family Planning Association Regional Office
For details, *see* the FPA Regional Office (Yorkshire and North east England) in Sheffield, South Yorkshire.

Harrogate

Marital Sexual Therapy Services
Harrogate Marriage Guidance Council, 1 Hywra Street, Harrogate (Tel: Harrogate (0423) 502173). *See also* Chapter 15, 'Marriage Guidance'.

York

Marital Sexual Therapy Services
York Marriage Guidance Council, 10 Priory Street, York YO1 1EZ (Tel: York (0904) 25971). *See also* Chapter 15, 'Marriage Guidance'.

York Psychosexual Dysfunction Clinic
Clifton Hospital, York YO3 6RD (Tel: York (0904) 36661).
Services offered: Psychosexual counselling.
Problems dealt with: All sexual and marital problems.
Is professional referral required? Yes.
Hours: Wednesday 10 a.m. – 1 p.m.; Friday 2 p.m. – 5 p.m.
Fees: None. Private clinic held in York on Thursday afternoons: appointment only. £30 for 50 minutes.

NOTTINGHAMSHIRE

Family Planning Association Regional Office
For details, *see* the FPA Regional Office (Yorkshire and North-east England) in Sheffield, South Yorkshire.

Mansfield

Psychosexual Counselling Clinic
Oak Tree Lane Health Centre, Jubilee Way, Mansfield. (Tel: Mansfield (0623) 651261).

LINCOLNSHIRE

Family Planning Association Regional Office
For details, *see* the FPA Regional Office (Eastern England), in Norwich, Norfolk.

Boston

Marital Sexual Therapy Services
Boston, Spalding and District Marriage Guidance Council, Boston Health Centre, Lincoln Lane, Boston. (Tel: Boston (0205) 65533). *See also* Chapter 15, 'Marriage Guidance'.

LONDON

See Greater London.

MANCHESTER

See Greater Manchester.

MERSEYSIDE

Family Planning Association Regional Office
For details, *see* the FPA Regional Office (North-west England) in Liverpool.

Billinge

District Psychological Services
Department of Psychology, Billinge Hospital, Billinge, nr. Wigan (Tel: 0695 62 6181).
Services offered: Behaviour therapy with sexual disorders.
Is professional referral required? Yes.
Hours: By appointment.
Fees: None.

Liverpool

British Pregnancy Advisory Service
20 Rodney Street, Liverpool L1 2TQ (Tel: 051 709 1558).
Services offered: Pregnancy testing; pregnancy counselling; abortion assessment; contraception; morning-after birth control. Counselling and assessment for: infertility problems; artificial insemination.
Is professional referral required? No.
Hours: Monday to Friday 9 a.m. – 5 p.m; Saturday 9 a.m. – 1 p.m.
Fees: *see* BPAS Chapter 3, 'Family Planning'.
For further details of BPAS services *see* Chapter 3.

Brook Advisory Centre
Brook Look-in, 9 Gambier Terrace, Liverpool L1 7BG (Tel: 051-709 4558.)
Hours: Monday to Saturday – phone for details.
For further details, *see* Chapter 3, 'Family Planning'.

Family Planning Association (North-west England Regional Office)
104 Bold Street, Liverpool L1 4HY (Tel: 051-709 1938).
See also Chapter 3, 'Family Planning'.
Services offered: Counselling for vasectomy; information on family planning services and methods; women's health.
Is professional referral required? No.

Marital Sexual Therapy Services
Merseyside Marriage Guidance Council, 7 Copperas Hill, Liverpool L3 5LB (Tel: 051-709 2058).
See also Chapter 15, 'Marriage Guidance'.

Vauxhall Health Centre
Limekiln Lane, Liverpool 5. (Tel: (051) 207 5571).
Services offered: Psychosexual counselling.
Is professional referral required? Yes.
Hours: Thursday 9 a.m. – 12 noon. by appointment.
Fees: None.

Seacombe

Psychosexual Counselling Clinic
Under Fives Centre, St Paul's Road, Seacombe. (Tel: Bebington Health Centre (Dr Linda Egdell) 051-645 7661).
Services offered: Psychosexual counselling.
Is professional referral required? No.
Hours: Mondays.
Fees: None.

NORFOLK

Family Planning Association Regional Office
For details, *see* the FPA Regional Office (Eastern England) in Norwich.

Norwich

BUPA Medical Centre
Old Watton Road, Colney, Norwich NR4 7TA. (Tel: Norwich (0603) 505011). For details of services *see* BUPA Greater London (Camden).

Services offered: Psychosexual counselling.
Is professional referral required? Yes.

Hours: Alternate Wednesdays 2 p.m. – 6 p.m.
Fees: None.

Nottingham

BUPA Medical Centre
Clawson Lodge, 403 Mansfield Road, Nottingham NG5 2DP (Tel: Nottingham (0602) 622826). For details of BUPA services *see* Greater London (Camden).

Family Planning Association
Nottingham FPA Clinic, 14 Regent Street, Nottingham (Tel: Nottingham (0602) 470431).
For further details, *see* Chapter 3, 'Family Planning'.
Services offered: Birth control; Well Woman checks; pregnancy testing; vasectomy counselling; female sterilisation under local anaesthetic.
Is professional referral required? No.
Hours: Office open for enquiries, general information or to pick up items which have been prescribed, Monday to Friday 9.30 a.m. – 4.30 p.m. Appointments for clinics may also be made at these times: Monday 1 p.m. – 2.30 p.m.; Tuesday 9.30 a.m. – 11 a.m., 12 noon – 2.30 p.m., 7 p.m. – 9 p.m.; Wednesday 12 noon – 2 p.m., 6 p.m. – 8 p.m.; Thursday 12 noon – 2.30 p.m., 6 p.m. – 8 p.m.; Friday 12 noon – 2 p.m.
Fees: Phone for details.

Marital Sexual Therapy Services
Nottingham Marriage Guidance Council, 84 Nottingham Road, Mansfield, Nottingham NG1 3HD (Tel: Nottingham (0602) 507836).
See also Chapter 15, 'Marriage Guidance'.

Worksop

Psychiatric Clinic
Bassetlaw District General Hospital, Blyth Road, Worksop. (Tel: Worksop (0909) 472831 ext. 306).
Services offered: Psychosexual counselling.
Is professional referral required? Preferred but not essential.
Hours: By appointment.
Fees: None.

OXFORDSHIRE

Family Planning Association Regional Office
For details, *see* the FPA Regional Office (North of the Thames) in Bedford, Bedfordshire.

Banbury

Marital Sexual Therapy Services
Oxfordshire Marriage Guidance Council, Castle House, Cornhill, Banbury (Tel: Banbury (0295) 58141). *See also* Chapter 15, 'Marriage Guidance'.

Oxford

Marital Sexual Therapy Services
Oxfordshire Marriage Guidance Council, 33 Iffley Road, Oxford OX4 1AE (Tel: Oxford (0865) 242960).
See also Chapter 15, 'Marriage Guidance'.

The Oxford SPOD Clinic
Rivermead Rehabilitation Centre, Abingdon Road, Oxford OX1 4XD. (Tel: Oxford (0865) 240321).
Services offered: Counselling and advice on sexual problems of disabled people derived from their disability. Clinic has close contact with other specialist departments of the Oxford hospitals, for example, departments of genetics, psychiatry, obstetrics and gynaecology, and further referral or specialist advice is easily obtained.
Problems dealt with: Problems which chiefly derive from diminished or absent sexual drive, potency or expression, and the effects which these have on patient and sexual partner.
Is professional referral required? Yes.
Hours: Wednesday afternoon.
Fees: None.

Dr Peter Lewis
c/o Dr G. Duncan, Family Planning Department, Community Health Offices, Radcliffe Infirmary, Oxford OX2 6HE.
Services offered: Psychosexual.
Is professional referral required? Yes, through family planning clinics only.
Hours: By appointment.
Fees: None.

SHROPSHIRE

Family Planning Association Regional Office
For details, *see* the FPA Regional Office (Midlands), in Birmingham, West Midlands.

Telford

Wellington Health Centre
Chapel Lane, Wellington, Telford, Shropshire (Tel: Telford (0952) 55531).

Services offered: Advice on all psychosexual problems.
Problems dealt with: Psychosexual problems.
Is professional referral required? Yes.
Hours: Clinics are held every Monday morning 9 a.m. – 12 noon, by appointment.
Fees: None.

SOMERSET

Family Planning Association Regional Office
For details, *see* the FPA Regional Office (South-west England) in Exeter, Devon.

Bridgwater

Family Planning Clinic (Psychosexual Counselling)
Bridgwater General Hospital, Bridgwater, Somerset (Tel: Bridgwater (0278) 451 501 9 a.m. – 10 a.m. for appointments).
Services offered: Psychosexual counselling.
Problems dealt with: Marital and sexual problems.
Is professional referral required? No.
Hours: By appointment.
Fees: None.

Glastonbury

Glastonbury Family Planning Clinic
Health Centre, 1 Wells Road, Glastonbury. (Tel: Glastonbury (0458) 35411).
Services offered: General psychosexual counselling.
Problems dealt with: Non-consummation, impotence, etc.
Is professional referral required? Yes.
Hours: Monday 7 p.m.
Fees: None.

Taunton

Family Planning Clinic (Psychosexual Counselling)
Ante-natal Clinic, Musgrove Park Hospital, Taunton (Tel: Taunton (0823) 73444, 7 p.m. – 8 p.m. Tuesday to Thursday for appointments).
Services offered: Psychosexual counselling.
Problems dealt with: Sexual and marital problems.
Is professional referral required? No.
Hours: By appointment.
Fees: None.

Marital Sexual Therapy Services
Taunton Deane District, 3 Upper High Street, Taunton, Somerset (Tel: Taunton (0823) 75983).
See also Chapter 15, 'Marriage Guidance'.

Yeovil

Marital Sexual Therapy Services
Yeovil District Marriage Guidance Council, Secretary: Mrs W. Farr, 2 The Tithe Barn, Queen Camel, Nr Yeovil (Tel: Marston Magna (0935) 850999).
See also Chapter 15, 'Marriage Guidance'.

Yeovil Family Planning Clinic
Outpatients Department, Yeovil District Hospital, Higher Kingston, Yeovil (Tel: Yeovil (0935) 75122).
Services offered: General psychosexual counselling.
Problems dealt with: Non-consummation, impotence, etc.
Is professional referral required: Yes.
Hours: Wednesday 6 p.m.
Fees: None.

SOUTH YORKSHIRE

Family Planning Association Regional Office
For details, *see* the FPA Regional Office (Yorkshire and North-east England) in Sheffield.

Barnsley

Psychosexual Medical Clinic
29/31 Queens Road, Barnsley, S71 1AN (Tel: Barnsley (0226) 286122. For doctors to make appointments on behalf of patients tel: (0742) 434343 ext. 4052).
Services offered: Psychosexual counselling.
Is professional referral required? Yes.
Hours: By appointment.
Fees: None, but private appointments are possible. (Tel: Hope Valley (0433) 50502, Dr Bramley).

SPIDA
Dr M.A. Hossain, Rheumatology Department, Barnsley District General Hospital, Gawber Road, Barnsley (Tel: Barnsley (0226) 286122 ext. 2387).
Services offered: Psychosexual counselling for people with physical and mental disabililties.
Is professional referral required? No.
Hours: By appointment.
Fees: None.

Doncaster

Marital Sexual Therapy Services
Doncaster and District Marriage Guidance Council, 52 Christchurch Road, Doncaster DN1 2QR (Tel: Doncaster (0302) 67805).
See also Chapter 15, 'Marriage Guidance'.

British Pregnancy Advisory Service
The Bungalow, 1a Avenue Road, Doncaster DN2 4AH. (Tel: Doncaster (0302) 344893).
Services offered: Pregnancy testing; pregnancy counselling; abortion assessment; contraception, morning-after birth control. Counselling and assessment for: infertility problems; artificial insemination.
Is professional referral required? No.
Hours: Monday 11 a.m. – 12.30 p.m; Tuesday 9 a.m. – 4.30 p.m; Wednesday 9 a.m. – 12 p.m; Friday 11.30 a.m. – 1 p.m.
Fees: *see*, BPAS Chapter 3, 'Family Planning'.
For further details of BPAS services *see* Chapter 3.

Rotherham

Marital Sexual Therapy Services
Rotherham Marriage Guidance Council, 24 Percy Street, Rotherham S65 1ED (Tel: Rotherham (0709) 377644).
See also Chapter 15, 'Marriage Guidance'.

Marital and Sexual Clinic
Rotherham District General Hospital, Moorgate Road, Rotherham (Tel: Rotherham (0709) 362222).
Services offered: Sexual and marital therapy counselling.
Is professional referral required? Yes.
Hours: By appointment.
Fees: None.

Sheffield

British Pregnancy Advisory Service
160 Charles Street, Sheffield S1 2NE (Tel: Sheffield (0742) 738326; telephone answering service: Sheffield (0742) 685646 Tuesday and Thursday 9 a.m. – 12 noon.).
Services offered: Pregnancy testing; pregnancy counselling; abortion assessment; contraception; morning-after birth control.
Is professional referral required? No.
Hours: Monday, Wednesday and Friday 9 a.m. – 3 p.m.
Fees: *See* BPAS, Chapter 3, 'Family Planning'. For further details of BPAS services *see* Chapter 3.

Family Planning Association (Yorkshire and North-east England Regional Office)
17 North Church Street, Sheffield S1 2DH. (Tel: Sheffield (0742) 21191).
Services offered: Menopause, PMS and sub-fertility services. Information on family planning services within the FPA Region.
Problems dealt with: As above.
Is professional referral required? No.
Hours: Telephone for appointment.

408 Consultation Centre (Registered Charity)
408 Ecclesall Road, Sheffield S11 8PJ (Tel: Sheffield (0742) 662341).
Services offered: Contraception; abortion counselling; sterilisation counselling; psychosexual counselling; emotional and psychiatric counselling.
Is professional referral required? No.
Hours: Monday to Friday, appointments 9 a.m. – 12 noon. Clinics every evening except Monday, open lunchtimes most days.
Fees: None for local residents. If not resident in Sheffield or Derbyshire, service costs £3 per year and the cost of contraceptives.

The Marital and Sexual Difficulties Clinic
Whiteley Wood Clinic, Woofindon Road, Sheffield 10 (Tel: Sheffield (0742) 303901).
Services offered: Advice, counselling and treatment for marital and sexual problems and difficulties (provides psychotherapy, behavioural therapy and/or counselling to suit individual needs).
Problems dealt with: Marital problems, sexual problems and difficulties.
Is professional referral required? Yes.
Hours: Monday to Friday 9 a.m. – 5 p.m.
Fees: None.

Marital Sexual Therapy Services
Sheffield Marriage Guidance Council, Voluntary Service House, 69 Division Street, Sheffield S1 4GE (Tel: Sheffield (0742) 20778).
See also Chapter 15, 'Marriage Guidance'.

Sheffield Health Authority
General enquiries to: Central Health Clinic, 1 Mulberry Street, Sheffield S1 2PJ (Tel: Sheffield (0742) 768885).
Services offered: Psychosexual counselling.
Is professional referral required? No.
Hours: Wednesday 9.30 a.m. – 12 noon.
Fees: None.

STAFFORDSHIRE

Family Planning Association Regional Office
For details, *see* the FPA Regional Office (Midlands) in Birmingham, West Midlands.

Burton-upon-Trent

Marital Sexual Therapy Services
Burton-upon-Trent Marriage Guidance Council, 27 Orchard Street, Burton-upon-Trent DE14 3SJ (Tel: Burton-upon-Trent (0283) 61697).
See also Chapter 15, 'Marriage Guidance'.

Cannock

Marital Sexual Therapy Services
Cannock Marriage Guidance Council, 33 Park Road, Cannock. (Tel: Cannock (054 35) 77281). *See also* Chapter 15, 'Marriage Guidance'.

Hanley

Hanley Health Centre
Upper Huntbach Street, Hanley, Stoke-on-Trent ST1 2BN. (Tel: Stoke-on-Trent (0782) 280491).
Services offered: Psychosexual, infertility, menopausal, PMT.
Is professional referral required? No.
Hours: Week one – Monday morning, Friday afternoon; week two – Friday morning, Friday afternoon.
Fees: None.

Lichfield

Marital Sexual Therapy Services
Lichfield Marriage Guidance Council, 29 Levetts Fields, Lichfield WS13 6EE (Tel: Lichfield (0543) 252760). *See also* Chapter 15, 'Marriage Guidance'.

Stafford

Psychosexual Clinic
Mid Staffs Central Health Clinic, North Walls, Stafford (Tel: Stafford (0785) 211900).
Services offered: Psychosexual.
Is professional referral required? Yes.
Hours: Friday morning by appointment.
Fees: None.

District Psychological Services
St George's Hospital, Stafford (Tel: Stafford (0785) 57888).
Services offered: Behavioural therapy (behavioural and cognitive approaches), counselling, sex therapy, family therapy, and cognitive restructuring programmes.
Problems dealt with: Sexual dysfunction, sexual deviation, specifically incest and child sexual abuse (various forms of child molesting).
Is professional referral required? Yes.
Hours: By appointment.
Fees: None, except for certain consultations for incestuous families and child molesters and their victims who have, by and large, been referred by solicitors, court and probation services.

SUFFOLK

Family Planning Association Regional Office
For details, *see* the FPA Regional Office (Eastern England) in Norwich.

Bury St Edmunds

Marital Sexual Therapy Services
West Suffolk Marriage Guidance Council, 67a St Andrews Street North, Bury St Edmunds (Tel: Bury St Edmunds (0284) 67305). *See also* Chapter 15, 'Marriage Guidance'.

Ipswich

Marital Sexual Therapy Services
Ipswich and Suffolk Marriage Guidance Council, 19 Tower Street, Ipswich IP1 3BE (Tel: Ipswich (0473) 54118). *See also* Chapter 15, 'Marriage Guidance'.

Sudbury

Family Planning Clinic
Wavertree Hospital, Sudbury (Tel: Sudbury (0787) 71341).
Services offered: Psychosexual counselling.
Is professional referral required? Yes.
Hours: 6.30 p.m. – 8.30 p.m.
Fees: None.

SURREY (*see also* Greater London)

Family Planning Association Regional Office
For details, *see* the FPA Regional Office (South-east England) in Hove, East Sussex.

Ashstead

Ashstead Clinic
Woodfield Lane, Ashstead (Tel: (037 22) 75259).
Services offered: Psychosexual counselling.
Is professional referral required? Yes.
Hours: Wednesday afternoon and Monday evening.
Fees: None.

Coulsdon

Psychology Department
Netherne Hospital, Coulsdon (Tel: Downland (07375) 56700 ext. 35 and 42).
Services offered: Psychological therapy for a variety of sexual problems in men and women.

Problems dealt with: Non-consummation; impotence; ejaculatory disorders; impaired sexual interest; sexual variations; female orgasmic dysfunction, vaginismus; dyspareunia; victims of sexual abuse,
Is professional referral required? Yes.
Hours: Monday to Friday 9 a.m. – 5 p.m.
Fees: None.

Dr Sarojini Asirdas
58 Brighton Road, Coulsdon CR3 2BB (Tel: 01-668 1968).
Services offered: Psychological therapy for sexual and marital problems.
Problems dealt with: All types of sexual dysfunctions of both female and male, and marital discord.
Is professional referral required? No.
Hours: Evenings: 7 p.m. – 10 p.m; Saturdays 10 a.m. – 5 p.m.
Fees: £40 (1 – 2 hours).

Epsom

Marital Sexual Therapy Services
Epsom and District Marriage Guidance Council, The Cedars, 14 Church Street, Epsom KT17 4QB. (Tel: Epsom (037 27) 22976). *See also* Chapter 15, 'Marriage Guidance'.

Ewell

Bourne Hall Youth Advisory Clinic
Bourne Hall, Ewell. (Tel: 01-394 1301).
Services offered: Youth advisory.
Is professional referral required? Yes.
Hours: By appointment.
Fees: None.

Farnham

Farnham Hospital
(Tel: Camberley (0276) 681636).
Services offered: Help with marital difficulties.
Is professional referral required? No.
Hours: Wednesday evenings.
Fees: None.

Guildford

Marital Sexual Therapy Services
Guildford and District Marriage Guidance Council, 3a Leapale Road, Guildford, Surrey GU1 4JX (Tel: Guildford (0483) 66254).
See also Chapter 15, 'Marriage Guidance'.

Weybridge

Psychosexual Clinic
The Health Centre, Weybridge, Surrey (Tel: Weybridge (0932) 48388).
Services offered: Psychosexual counselling.
Problems dealt with: Any psychosexual problem in the married or unmarried of either sex.
Is professional referral required? No.
Hours: By appointment, Wednesday 4.30 p.m. – 6 p.m.
Fees: None.

Woking

Family Planning Clinic
Beechcroft House, 5 Heathside Road, Woking, Surrey GU22 7ET (Tel: Woking (048 62) 4160).
Services offered: All forms of birth control including IUCD; youth advisory clinic; psychosexual counselling and marital problems; vasectomy unit.
Problems dealt with: Any sexually related matter. Referral to other sources if beyond the Clinic's scope.
Is professional referral required? No.
Hours: By appointment (to be made through office – Monday to Friday 10 a.m. – 12 noon and 2 p.m. – 4 p.m. Sub-clinics held at St Johns' and West Byfleet. Appointments to be made through the office (Tel: Woking (048 62) 4160). Vasectomy enquiries to be made on Fridays only 10 a.m. – 12 noon and 2 p.m. – 4 p.m. (Tel: Woking (048 62) 60734).
Fees: None.

SUSSEX

See East Sussex and West Sussex.

TYNE AND WEAR

Family Planning Association Regional Office
For details, *see* the FPA Regional Office (Yorkshire and North-east England) in Sheffield, South Yorkshire.

Gateshead

Psychosexual Clinic
Dryden Road Hospital, Dryden Road, Gateshead NE9 5BY (Tel: 091 478 3811).
Services offered: Behavioural and analytical psychotherapy for individuals and couples.
Problems dealt with: All forms of psychosexual dysfunction and relationship difficulty.
Is professional referral required? Preferred.

Hours: 9 a.m. – 5 p.m. – later by arrangement.
Fees: None.

Newcastle upon Tyne

Graingerville Family Planning Clinic
Westgate Road, Newcastle upon Tyne NE4 6UJ (Tel: Newcastle upon Tyne 091-273 9560).
Services offered: Family planning and contraception service; psychosexual counselling (insight therapy) on a sessional basis.
Problems dealt with: No restriction initially. Where consultation reveals serious disorders, psychiatric or psychotherapeutic referral is arranged.
Is professional referral required? No, this is an open access clinic.
Hours: By appointment.
Fees: None.

Marital Sexual Therapy Services
Tyneside Marriage Guidance Council, Mea House, Ellison Place, Newcastle upon Tyne (Tel: 091-232 9109).
See also Chapter 15, 'Marriage Guidance'.

South Shields

District Clinical Psychology Service
General Hospital, Harton Lane, South Shields NE34 0PL (Tel: 091-456 1161 exts. 360/434).
Services offered: Behaviour therapy; psychotherapy; counselling.
Problems dealt with: The usual range of psychosexual dysfunctions.
Is professional referral required? Yes.
Hours: Usual hospital/clinic hours.
Fees: None.

Sunderland

Sunderland Clinical Psychology Service
'Denethorpe', Stockton Road, Ryhope, Sunderland SR2 0NB. (Tel: Sunderland (0783) 210541 ext. 3396 or 3416).
Services offered: Treatment of sexual dysfunction; gay counselling; psychosexual counselling; marital counselling, sex education.
Problems dealt with: Homosexuality; transsexual counselling; sexual dysfunctions in men and women (gay or non-gay); sexual problems.
Is professional referral required? Usually (general practitioner must be informed if treatment begun).
Hours: Monday to Friday 9 a.m. – 5 p.m.
Fees: None (but private consultations may be negotiated).

Psychosexual Clinic
Cherry Knowle Hospital, Ryhope, Sunderland (Tel: Sunderland (0783) 656256).
Services offered: Help with all sexual problems.
Is professional referral required? Yes.
Hours: Thursday afternoons.
Fees: None.

WARWICKSHIRE

Family Planning Association Regional Office
For details, *see* the FPA Regional Office (Midlands) in Birmingham, West Midlands.

Leamington Spa

British Pregnancy Advisory Service
Holly Walk Welfare Clinic, Holly Walk, Leamington Spa CV32 4JE (Tel: Coventry (0203) 597344; telephone answering service: Leamington Spa (0926) 25562).
Services offered: Pregnancy testing; pregnancy counselling; abortion assessment; contraception; morning-after birth control. Enquiries about: infertililty problems; artificial insemination.
Is professional referral required? No.
Fees: *See* BPAS, Chapter 3, 'Family Planning'.
For further details of BPAS services *see* Chapter 3.

Marital Sexual Therapy Services
South Warwickshire Marriage Guidance Council, 35 Regent Grove, Leamington Spa CV32 4NN (Tel: Leamington Spa (0926) 24899).
See also Chapter 15, 'Marriage Guidance'.

Nuneaton

Riversley Park Clinic
Coton Road, Nuneaton. (Tel: Nuneaton (0203) 385156.
Services offered: Family planning; psychosexual counselling.
Problems dealt with: Psychosexual
Is professional referral required?: No
Hours: 6.30 p.m. – 10.00 p.m.
Fees: None

Rugby

Marital Sexual Therapy Services
Rugby Marriage Guidance Council, 11 Little Church Street,Rugby CV21 3AW (Tel: Rugby (0788) 65675).
See also Chapter 15, 'Marriage Guidance'.

WEST MIDLANDS

Family Planning Association Regional Office
For details, *see* the FPA Regional Office (Midlands) in Birmingham.

Birmingham

British Pregnancy Advisory Service
Guildhall Buildings, Navigation Street, Birmingham B2 4BT (Tel: 021-643 1461).
Services offered: Pregnancy testing; pregnancy counselling; abortion assessment; contraception; morning-after birth control. Counselling and assessment for: infertility problems; artificial insemination.
Is professional referral required? No.
Hours: Monday to Friday 9 a.m. – 5 p.m; Saturday 9 a.m. – 1 p.m.
Fees: *See* BPAS, Chapter 3, 'Family Planning'.
For further details of BPAS services *see* Chapter 3.

Brook Advisory Centres
Brook Centre, 9 York Road, Edgbaston, Birmingham B16 9HX (Tel: 021-455 0491).
Services provided: As well as the usual contraceptive services this Centre also provides psychosexual counselling and infection testing.
Hours: Monday to Friday 9.30 a.m. – 8.30 p.m; Saturday mornings and afternoons.
City Centre Brook, 12 – 22 Albert Street, Birmingham B4 7UD (Tel: 021-643 5341).
Hours: Monday to Friday 9.30 a.m. – 8.30 p.m; and Saturday mornings.
Handsworth Brook Centre, 102 Hamstead Road, Handsworth, Birmingham B19 1DG (Tel: 021-554 7553)
Hours: Tuesday to Thursday 9.30 a.m. – 8.30 p.m; Monday and Friday 9.30 a.m. – 5.30 p.m; alternate Saturday mornings.
Saltley Brook Centre, 3 Washwood Heath Road, Saltley, Birmingham B8 1SH (Tel: 021-328 4544).
Hours: Tuesday, Wednesday, Friday 10 a.m. – 5.30 p.m; Monday and Thursday 10 a.m. – 8.30 p.m.
Fees: At all Brook Centres the contraceptive service is free, all other services are charged at various fees which are frequently waived or reduced in cases of financial hardship. For further details of Brook Centres, *see* Chapter 3, 'Family Planning'.

BUPA Medical Centre
11 Portland Road, Edgbaston, Birmingham B16 9HN. (Tel: 021-455 6777). For details of BUPA services *see* Greater London (Camden).

Calthorpe Nursing Home
4 Arthur Road, Edgbaston, Birmingham B15 2UL (Tel: 021- 455 7585).
Services offered: Termination of pregnancy; female sterilisation – laparoscopic.
Is professional referral required? No.
Hours. Six days per week – Monday to Saturday.
Fees: Termination – up to 14 weeks, £140; 14 to 20 weeks, £270. Laparoscopic sterilisation, £150.

Carrs Lane Counselling Centre
Birmingham B4 7SX (Tel: 021-643 6363).
Services offered: The Centre has a staff of around 35 professionally supervised volunteer counsellors. The approach is generally client-centred. Although used as an advice-giving and emergency agency for immediate problems, training and supervision are orientated to longer term counselling where emotional reconstruction, with the client doing the work, is indicated. The Centre will if possible, refer to a number of more specialist agencies. Telephone counselling is available during opening hours, but in order to provide more adequate help the Centre would prefer clients to go along to discuss problems.
Problems dealt with: All problems which have to do with self-perception in connection with relationships with other people, above all those that have to do with family, sexuality, ageing, growth and development.
Is professional referral required? No.
Hours: For first interviews, Monday to Friday 11 a.m. – 1.30 p.m. and Tuesday and Wednesday evening 7 p.m. – 9 p.m. Appointments can be made throughout normal office hours, Mondays to Fridays.
Fees: None.

Counselling and Psychotherapy Services
Under the direction of Dr Grahame F. Cooper, 6 Clarence Road, Moseley, Birmingham B13 9SX (Tel: 021-449 2308).
Services offered: A confidential counselling service is available for helping individuals and couples with all types of sexual and relationship problems. Where necessary the service can be provided as a home visit for disabled people. A limited telephone advisory service is available.
Problems dealt with: People with any kind of sexual or relationship problems will be seen. The problems may be of physical or emotional origin and may be long-standing or of short duration. The service is available to people of any sexual orientation, whether disabled or able-bodied.
Is professional referral required? No.
Hours: Monday to Friday 9 a.m. – 4 p.m., with some evening work.

Fees: Normal fee is £15.20 per session of 50 minutes. The fee can be varied for those with financial difficulties. For home visits travelling costs are also charged.

Family Planning Association (Midlands Regional Office)
5 York Road, Birmingham B16 9HX (Tel: 021-454 8236).
See also Chapter 3, 'Family Planning'.
Services offered: Resources – leaflets, posters, fact sheets from the Family Planning Information Service; vasectomy clinic; menopause clinic; specialised book shop on topics relating to sex education; family planning; sexuality and relationships; family health care; telephone information service; talks and courses; film hire.
Problems dealt with: Location of family planning provision services, vasectomy clinics, psychosexual clinics, menopause clinics, other counselling services.
Is professional referral required? No
Hours: Vasectomy – by appointment, Friday 4.30 p.m. – 7.30 p.m. (Coventry). Menopause – by appointment, Wednesday 9 a.m. – 11.30 a.m.; Thursday 3.30 p.m. – 6.30 p.m. All appointments through the Midlands Regional Centre as above.
Fees: Phone for details.

Family Planning Service
Springfield Centre, Raddlebarn Road, Selly Oak, Birmingham 29 (Tel: 021-471 5000).
Services offered: Psychosexual counselling.
Problems dealt with: Female and male sexual difficulties.
Is professional referral required? Helpful but not necessary.
Hours: 9 a.m. – 12 noon alternate Fridays.
Fees: None.

Institute for Sex Education and Research
Under the direction of Dr Martin Cole, PhD, 40 School Road, Moseley, Birmingham B13 9SN (Tel: 021-449 0892).
Services offered: Psychotherapy, behaviour therapy (including surrogate therapy) and marital counselling, in so far as they relate to the treatment of sex disorders.
Problems dealt with: Treatment of specific sex dysfunctions in men, women and married couples.
Is professional referral required? Preferred.
Hours: Monday to Friday – morning, afternoon, evening.
Fees: £15 and upwards per consultation, depending on nature of help; £60 per session for surrogate therapy.
Comment: For a general discussion of surrogate therapy *see* Chapter 1, 'The Helping Therapies', where we draw attention to Dr Cole's pioneering work in this field and describe the broad areas in which surrogate therapy may be helpful. We refer particularly to those people without sexual partners or those whose partners are unco-operative. Treatments are usually provided weekly, the sessions lasting between one and a half and two hours. They may be held at the clinic in Birmingham or in various locations around the country. For educational services, *see* Chapter 13, 'Learning about Sex'.

Marital Sexual Therapy Services
Birmingham Marriage Guidance Council, 74 Broad Street, Birmingham B15 1AQ (Tel: 021-643 1638).
See also Chapter 15, 'Marriage Guidance'.

Psychology Department: Psychotherapy Group for Women
Highcroft Hospital and Marriage Guidance Council using Sutton Coldfield Cottage Hospital as base for this group. (Tel: 021-378 2211 ext. 4307 – Ms A. Fazzani, Dept. of Psychology; or 021-354 1663 – Ms P. Crean, MGC).
Services offered: Long-term psychotherapy for women in mid-twenties to mid-forties.
Problems dealt with: those arising out of incestuous relationships.
Is professional referral required? No.
Hours: Usually between 2 p.m. – 3.30 p.m. Thursdays.
Fees: None.

Out-Patients Department
Dudley Road Hospital, Dudley Road, Birmingham B18 7QH (Tel: 021-554 3801).
Services offered: Psychosexual counselling.
Is professional referral required? Yes.
Hours: Wednesday afternoons.
Fees: None.

Psychosexual Counselling Clinic
Family Planning Clinic, Good Hope Hospital, Birmingham. (Tel: 021-378 2211 on Monday, Wednesday and Friday evenings).
Services offered: Single therapist seeing individuals or couples. Co-therapist occasionally available.
Problems dealt with: Social and marital dysfunction.
Is professional referral required? No.
Hours: Wednesday 7 p.m. – 9 p.m.
Fees: None.

Psychosexual Counselling Clinic
Trethowan Out-Patient Department, Queen Elizabeth Hospital, Edgbaston, Birmingham (Tel: 021-472 1311).
Services offered: Psychosexual counselling and sexual problems of disabled people.
Problems dealt with: Full range of female and male problems.
Is professional referral required? Yes.

Hours: Friday afternoon – assessment; Wednesday evening – treatment.
Fees: None.

Treaford Lane Family Planning Clinic
73 Treaford Lane, Alum Rock, Birmingham 8 (Tel: 021-327 6548).
Services offered: Psychosexual counselling.
Problems dealt with: Wide range of sexual problems.
Is professional referral required? Usual but, not necessary.
Hours: 6.30 p.m. – 8 p.m. alternate Thursdays.
Fees: None.

Coventry

British Pregnancy Advisory Service
Coundon Welfare Clinic, Barker Butts Lane, Coventry CV6 1DU. (Tel: Coventry (0203) 597344).
Services offered: Pregnancy testing; pregnancy counselling; abortion assessment; contraception; morning-after birth control. Enquiries about: infertility problems; artificial insemination.
Is professional referral required? No.
Hours: Monday to Wednesday 6 p.m. – 10 p.m.
Fees: *see* BPAS, Chapter 3, 'Family Planning'. For details of BPAS services, *see* Chapter 3.

Brook Centre
Gynaecological Out-patients, Coventry and Warwickshire Hospital, Stoney Stanton Road, Coventry (Tel: Coventry (0203) 412627 (for appointments); Coventry (0203) 24055 (clinic, evenings only)).
Hours: Thursday 6.30 p.m. – 9 p.m; alternate Mondays 7p.m. – 9 p.m.
Fees: The contraceptive service is free, all other services are charged at various fees which are frequently waived or reduced in cases of financial hardship. For further details, *see* Chapter 3, 'Family Planning'.

Marital Sexual Therapy Services
Coventry and District Marriage Guidance Council, Gorton House, 11 Bayley Lane, Coventry CV1 5RN (Tel: Coventry (0203) 25863).
See also Chapter 15, 'Marriage Guidance'.

Psychological Therapy Service
Psychology Department, Walsgrave Hospital, Coventry (Tel: Coventry (0203) 613232 ext. 7233/7234).
Services offered: Psychosexual therapy for a wide range of problems, including relationship difficulties and sexual dysfunction.
Is professional referral required? Yes.
Hours: 9 a.m. – 5.30 p.m.
Fees: None.

Dudley

Marital Sexual Therapy Services
Dudley Marriage Guidance Council, 16a Stone Street, Dudley (Tel: Dudley (0384) 57392). *See also* Chapter 15, 'Marriage Guidance'.

Psychosexual Clinic
Westhill Clinic, Hagley Road, Stourbridge (Tel: Stourbridge (0384) 396561).
Services offered: Psychosexual counselling.
Is professional referral required? No.
Hours: Monday and Wednesday 2 p.m. – 4.30 p.m.
Fees: None.

Sandwell

Psychosexual Clinic
Control House, Shaftesbury Street, West Bromwich. (Tel: 021-553 1316/3730).
Services offered: Psychosexual counselling.
Is professional referral required? No.
Hours: Monday 1.30 p.m. – 4.30 p.m; Thursday 9.45 a.m. – 12.45 p.m.
Fees: None.

Solihull

Family Planning Centre
51 Grove Road, Solihull B91 3QJ. (Tel: 021-705 0953).
Services offered: Family planning services (including contraception, cytology, vasectomy); psychosexual counselling.
Is professional referral required? No.
Hours: By appointment, Thursday 9.45 a.m. – 12.30 p.m..
Fees: None.

Sutton Coldfield

BUPA Medical Centre
Little Aston Hospital, Little Aston, Sutton Coldfield B74 3UP. (Tel: 021-353 2444). For details of BUPA services *see* Greater London (Camden).

Family Planning Clinic (Psychosexual Counselling Service)
North Birmingham Health District, Good Hope Maternity Hospital, Rectory Road, Sutton Coldfield, West Midlands B75 7RR (Tel: 021-378 2211 Ext 3341).
Services offered: Psychosexual counselling.
Problems dealt with: Any sexual problem which appears to have a psychological element, cause or effect.
Is professional referral required? No.
Hours: Appointments may be made Monday, Wednesday,

Friday 7 p.m. – 9 p.m. Clinic sessions are held Wednesday evening.
Fees: None.

Marital Sexual Therapy Services
Outpost of Sutton Coldfield Marriage Guidance Council, 1 South Cottages, Farthing Lane, Sutton Coldfield (Tel: 021-354 1663). *See also* Chapter 15, 'Marriage Guidance'.

Walsall

Marital Sexual Therapy Services
Walsall and District Marriage Guidance Council, 132 Lichfield Street, Walsall WS1 1SL (Tel: Walsall (0922) 26004). *See also* Chapter 15, 'Marriage Guidance,.

Psychosexual Clinic
Walsall Family Planning Services, 18 – 20 Hatherton Road, Walsall (Tel: Walsall (0922) 20209/32283).
Services offered: Preparing for pregnancy; genetic counselling; psychosexual counselling.
Is professional referral required? No.
Hours: Monday 9.45 a.m. – 12.45 p.m; 1.30 – 4.30 p.m. (for information or to make an appointment – normal working hours daily).
Fees: None.

West Bromwich

Psychosexual Clinic
Control House, Shaftesbury Street, West Bromwich, West Midlands (Tel: 021-553-1316).
Services offered: Psychosexual therapy.
Problems dealt with: Psychosexual.
Is professional referral required? Usual.
Hours: Thursday morning by appointment.
Fees: None.

Wolverhampton

Marital Sexual Therapy Services
Wolverhampton Marriage Guidance Council, 183 Stafford Street, Wolverhampton WV1 1ND. (Tel: (0902) 25082/28447). *See also* Chapter 15, 'Marriage Guidance'.

The Sister Rose Private Clinic
19–21 Queen Street, Wolverhampton (Tel: Wolverhampton (0902) 21479).
Services offered: Examination and assessment for termination of pregnancy; pregnancy tests, both on the premises and also via a postal pack; assessment and examination for female sterilisation which can be performed as a day-care operation; counselling and vasectomy operations; services for routine smear testing; Well-Woman checks; menopausal clinics; contraceptive advice; morning-after pill, etc.
Is professional referral required? No, but general practitioner's referral preferred.
Hours: Monday to Friday 9 a.m. – 5 p.m.
Fees: Counselling, consultation and post-operative check in respect of termination of pregnancy £30; operation fee £107 (up to and including 13 weeks of pregnancy); £239 for prostaglandin termination (up to and including 20 weeks of pregnancy); sterilisation – £25.00 for counselling and £145 for day-care. Comment: Brochures giving brief outlines of treatment available on postal or telephone request.

Red Hill Street Clinic
Red Hill Street, Wolverhampton (Tel: Wolverhampton (0902) 24625 ext. 278).
Services offered: Psychosexual counselling/therapy.
Is professional referral required? Yes.
Hours: Tuesday 9 a.m. – 12.30 p.m.
Fees: None.

WEST SUSSEX

Family Planning Association Regional Office
For details, *see* the FPA Regional Office (South-east England) in Hove, East Sussex.

Chichester

Chapel Street Clinic
Chapel Street, Chichester (Tel: Chichester (0243) 788761).
Services offered: Psychosexual counselling.
Is professional referral required? Yes.
Hours: 1st and 3rd Tuesday 2.15 p.m. – 4 p.m; 2nd Thursday 10 a.m. – 12.30 p.m.
Fees: None.

Marital Sexual Therapy Services
Chichester and Bognor Regis Marriage Guidance Council, Bell House, 6 Theatre Lane, Chichester PO19 1SR. (Tel: Chichester (0243) 788935). *See also* Chapter 15, 'Marriage Guidance'.

Crawley

Family Planning Clinic
Health Clinic, Exchange Road, Crawley, West Sussex (Tel: Crawley (0293) 26212).
Services offered: General family planning advice and supplies; youth advisory counselling; psychosexual counselling.
Problems dealt with: Psychosexual problems and any difficulties relating to family planning, etc.

Is professional referral required? No.
Hours: By appointment.
Fees: None.

Shoreham-by-Sea

Psychosexual Clinic
Southlands Hospital, Shoreham-by-Sea (Tel: Shoreham-by-Sea (0273) 455622).
Services offered: Psychosexual.
Is professional referral required? No.
Hours: Weekly session 9.30 a.m. – 1.30 p.m. or 2 p.m. – 5 p.m.
Fees: None.

Worthing

Marital Sexual Therapy Services
Worthing and District Marriage Guidance Council, 45 South Street, Tarring, Worthing (Tel: Worthing (0903) 202512). *See also* Chapter 15, 'Marriage Guidance'.

WEST YORKSHIRE

Family Planning Association Regional Office
For details, *see* the FPA Regional Office (Yorkshire and North-east England) in Sheffield, South Yorkshire.

Batley

Psychosexual Counselling Clinic
Batley Health Centre, Batley. (Tel: Batley (0924) 479033).
Services offered: Psychosexual counselling.
Is professional referral required? Yes.
Hours: Wednesday mornings.
Fees: None.

Bradford

SAIFLine (Sexual Abuse in the Family Line)
c/o The Link Centre, 7 Southbrook Terrace, Great Horton, Bradford (Tel: Bradford (0274) 309909).
Services offered: Telephone and face-to-face counselling for people who are concerned about child sexual abuse in the family. You may wish to talk about an incident in the past or a present situation. Professionals are welcome to contact the Line for support or advice.
Is professional referral required? No.
Hours: Wednesday 10 a.m. – 1 p.m.
Fees: None.

Halifax

Laura Mitchell Health Centre Family Planning Clinic
Great Albion Street, Halifax HX1 1YR (Tel: Halifax (0422) 63541).
Services offered: Psychosexual counselling.
Is professional referral required? No.
Hours: Tuesday 9.30 a.m. – 11.30 a.m.
Fees: None.

Marital Sexual Therapy Services
Calderdale Marriage Guidance Council, 38 Clare Road, Halifax (Tel: Halifax (0422) 63845). *See also* Chapter 15, 'Marriage Guidance'.

Huddersfield

Family Planning Clinic
Princess Royal Community Health Centre, Greenhead Road, Huddersfield HD1 4EW (Tel: Huddersfield (0484) 45411).
Services offered: Psychosexual counselling.
Problems dealt with: The Clinic is staffed by doctors trained in psychosexual counselling and they deal with all the problems referred to them.
Is professional referral required? No.
Hours: Appointments can be made at any time during working hours through the Family Planning administrative staff. Sessions are twice a month.
Fees: None.

Marital Sexual Therapy Services
Kirklees Marriage Guidance Council, 23 John William Street, Huddersfield (Tel: Huddersfield (0484) 28212). *See also* Chapter 15, 'Marriage Guidance'.

Leeds

British Pregnancy Advisory Service
Second Floor, 8 The Headrow, Leeds LS1 6PT (Tel: Leeds (0532) 443861).
Services offered: Pregnancy testing; pregnancy counselling; abortion assessment; contraception; morning-after birth control. Enquiries about: infertility problems; artificial insemination.
Is professional referral required? No.
Hours: Monday to Thursday 9 a.m. – 5 p.m; Friday 9 a.m. – 3.30 p.m.
Fees: *See* BPAS Chapter 3, 'Family Planning'.
For further details of BPAS services *see* Chapter 3.

BUPA Medical Centre
81 Clarendon Road, Leeds LS2 9PJ (Tel: Leeds (0532) 436735). For details of BUPA services *see* Greater London (Camden).

Marital Sexual Therapy Services
Leeds Marriage and Personal Counselling Service, Rutland House, 38 Cale Lane, Leeds LS1 6DT (Tel: Leeds (0532) 452595). *See also* Chapter 15, 'Marriage Guidance'.

William Merritt Disabled Living Centre
St Mary's Hospital, Green Hill Road, Armley, Leeds LS12 3QE. (Tel: Leeds (0532) 793140; DIAL number Leeds (0532) 795583).
Services offered: Advice and literature available at the Centre. Visitors requiring counselling will be referred to SPOD advisors and marriage counsellors. The DIAL office is staffed by people with disabilities. They are able to advise on general aspects associated with disability.
Is professional referral required? No.
Hours: Disabled Living Centre: Monday to Friday 9.30 a.m. – 4.30 p.m. DIAL: Monday to Friday 10.30 a.m. – 3.30 p.m. (Visits to the DLC are by appointment only).
Fees: None.

The Sister Rose Pregnancy Advisory Centre
4 Albion Street, Leeds 1 (Tel: Leeds (0532) 456914).
Services offered: Examination and assessment for termination of pregnancy; pregnancy tests – both on the premises and also via a postal pack; assessment and examination for female sterilisation which can be performed as a day-care operation; counselling and vasectomy operations; routine smear testing; Well Woman checks; menopausal clinics, contraceptive advice; morning-after pill, etc.
Is professional referral required? No, but general practitioner's referral preferred.
Hours: Monday to Friday 9 a.m. – 5 p.m.
Fees: Counselling, consultation and post-operative check in respect of termination of pregnancy £30; operation fee £107 (up to and including 13 weeks of pregnancy) and £239 for prostaglandin termination (up to and including 20 weeks of pregnancy).
Comment: Brochures giving brief outlines of treatment available on postal or telephone request.

Wakefield

Yorkshire Regional Spinal Injuries Centre
(Registrar in Neuro-Rehabilitation), Pinderfields General Hospital, Aberford Road, Wakefield, West Yorkshire WF1 4DG (Tel: Wakefield (0924) 375217, ask for Spinal Injury Unit).
Services offered: Advice and practical help both with psychological and physical sexual problems associated with spinal injury. Telephone advisory service available.
Problems dealt with: Any problems referred will be dealt with.
Is professional referral required? No.
Hours: Any time by appointment.
Fees: None.

WILTSHIRE

Family Planning Association Regional Office
For details, *see* the FPA Regional Office (South-west England) in Exeter, Devon.

Salisbury

Behavioural Therapy/Family Therapy Department
Nightingale Clinic, Old Manor Hospital, Wilton Road, Salisbury (Tel: Salisbury (0722) 336262 ext. 3136 or 3126).
Services offered: Sexual/family therapy.
Problems dealt with: Sexual dysfunction, sexual deviation.
Is professional referral required? Yes.
Hours: Monday to Friday 9 a.m. – 4.30 p.m.
Fees: None.

Marital Sexual Therapy Services
Salisbury and District Marriage Guidance Council, 2a St Edmunds Church Street, Salisbury SP1 1EF (Tel: Salisbury (0722) 336763). *See also* Chapter 15, 'Marriage Guidance'.

Swindon

British Pregnancy Advisory Service
Priory Road Health Clinic, Priory Road, Swindon SN3 2EZ (Tel: Swindon (0793) 30366).
Services offered: Pregnancy testing; pregnancy counselling; abortion assessment. Enquiries about: infertility problems; artificial insemination.
Is professional referral required? No.
Hours: Monday 5 p.m. – 8.30 p.m.
Fees: *see* BPAS Chapter 3, 'Family Planning'.
For further details of BPAS services *see* Chapter 3.

Marital Sexual Therapy Services
Thamesdown and District Marriage Guidance Council, Friends Meeting House, 79 Eastcott Hill, Swindon (Tel: Swindon (0793) 27664). *See also* Chapter 15, 'Marriage Guidance'.

Seymour Clinic
Kingshill, Swindon (Tel: Swindon (0793) 610510).
Services offered: Psychosexual counselling – contact Consultant Psychotherapist, Dr Amies, direct; Dr Kirkbride also provides counselling at Princess Margaret Hospital at the end of family planning session.
Is professional referral required? No, but preferred.
Fees: None.

WORCESTERSHIRE

See Hereford and Worcester.

YORKSHIRE

See North Yorkshire, South Yorkshire and West Yorkshire.

WALES

Family Planning Association Welsh Office
For details, *see* the FPA (Wales) in Cardiff, South Glamorgan.

CLWYD

Bodelwyddan

Marital Psychosexual Clinic
Glan Clwyd Hospital, Bodelwyddan (Tel: St Asaph (0745) 583910).
Services offered: Counselling; psychotherapy; medication.
Problems dealt with: Interactional/sexual problems.
Is professional referral required? Yes.
Hours: By appointment during working hours of week days.
Fees: None.

Colwyn Bay

Marital/Psychosexual Clinic
Community Hospital, Hesketh Road, Colwyn Bay (Tel: Colwyn Bay (0492) 515218).
Services offered: Counselling; psychotherapy; medication.
Problems dealt with: Interactional/sexual problems.
Is professional referral required? Yes.
Hours: During working hours of week days.
Fees: None.

Marital Sexual Therapy Services
North Wales Marriage Guidance Council, 8 Rivieres Avenue, Colwyn Bay LL29 7DP. (Tel: Colwyn Bay (0492) 33919). *See also* Chapter 15, 'Marriage Guidance'.

Flint

Marital/Psychosexual Clinic
43 Prince of Wales Avenue, Flint (Tel: Flint (035 26) 2183).
Services offered: Counselling; psychotherapy; medication.
Problems dealt with: Interactional/sexual problems.
Is professional referral required? Yes.
Hours: During working hours.
Fees: None.

Rhuddlan

Rhuddlan Family Planning Clinic
Health Clinic, Vicarage Lane, Rhuddlan (Tel: Rhyl (0745) 591039).
Services offered: Psychosexual counselling.
Is professional referral required? No.
Hours: By appointment 1st Thursday in month 7 p.m; 3rd Tuesday in month 10 a.m.
Fees: None.

Rhyl

Marital/Psychosexual Clinic
Day Hospital, Royal Alexandra Hospital, Rhyl (Tel: Rhyl (0745) 55188 ext. 96).
Services offered: Counselling; psychotherapy; medication.
Problems dealt with: Interactional/sexual problems.
Is professional referral required? Yes.
Hours: During working hours of week days.
Fees: None.

GWYNEDD

Bangor

Family Planning Association
Greenhouse, 1 Trevelyan Terrace, Bangor (Tel: Bangor (0248) 352176).
Services offered: Contraceptive; pregnancy tests; womens' health courses and a variety of other educational courses and workshops; vasectomy services.
Is professional referral required? No.
Hours: Phone for details.
Fees: Pregnancy tests £1.50; vasectomy service £60 (counselling £20 and the operation £40).

Menai Day Hospital
Psychology Department, Ysbyty Gwynedd, Bangor (Tel: Bangor (0248) 351177 ext. 4018).
Services offered: Psychosexual counselling.

Is professional referral required? Preferred.
Hours: By appointment.
Fees: £28 per session.

SOUTH GLAMORGAN

Cardiff

British Pregnancy Advisory Service
4 High Street Arcade Chambers, Cardiff CF1 2BE (Tel: Cardiff (0222) 372389).
Services offered: Pregnancy testing; pregnancy counselling; abortion assessment; contraception; morning-after birth control. Counselling and assessment for: infertility problems; artificial insemination.
Is professional referral required? No.
Hours: Monday to Friday 9 a.m. – 5 p.m; Saturday 9 a.m. – 1 p.m.
Fees: *see* BPAS Chapter 3, 'Family Planning'.
For details of BPAS services, *see* Chapter 3.

BUPA Medical Centre
BUPA Hospital, Croescadarn Road, Pentwyn, Cardiff CF2 7XL (Tel: Cardiff (0222) 735515). For details of BUPA services *see* Greater London (Camden).

The Family Institute
105 Cathedral Road, Cardiff CF1 9PH (Tel: Cardiff (0222) 26532).
Services offered: Therapy for emotional, mental health and relationship problems for individuals, couples and families. There are five qualified therapists. Sex therapy usually with couples.
Problems dealt with: Whole range of emotional/psychological difficulties. Most sexual problems.
Is professional referral required? No.
Hours: Monday to Friday 9 a.m. – 5 p.m. Some evening appointments.
Fees: None.

Family Planning Association (Wales)
6 Windsor Place, Cardiff CF1 3BX (Tel: Cardiff (0222) 42766).
See also Chapter 3, 'Family Planning'.
Services offered: Walk-in information/education centre; free leaflets; books to buy; a counselling service for vasectomy operations; telephone advisory service; details of family planning services within Wales; vasectomy clinics in Cardiff and Newport.
Problems dealt with: Everything related to sexual and family planning problems.
Is professional referral required? No.
Hours: Monday to Friday 9 a.m. – 5 p.m. Vasectomy sessions Tuesday evenings at Cardiff and Newport.
Fees: Phone for details.

Marital Sexual Therapy Services
South Wales Marriage Guidance Council, 26 High Street, Cardiff CF1 2BZ. (Tel: Cardiff (0222) 29850). *See also* Chapter 15, 'Marriage Guidance'.

WEST GLAMORGAN

Swansea

Cefn Coed Hospital
Cocket, Swansea (Tel: Swansea (0792) 582054).
Services offered: Psychosexual therapy.
Is professional referral required? Yes.
Hours: By arrangement.
Fees: None.

Family Planning Association
8 St Helens Road, Swansea (Tel: Swansea (0792) 464180).
Services offered: Contraceptive; pregnancy tests; womens' health courses and a variety of other educational courses and workshops; vasectomy service.
Is professional referral required? No.
Hours: Phone for details.
Fees: Pregnancy tests £1.50; vasectomy service £60 (counselling £20 and the operation £40.00).

Marital Sexual Therapy Services
Swansea and West Glamorgan Marriage Guidance Council, 2 De La Beche Street, Swansea SA1 3EY (Tel: Swansea (0792) 55960). *See also* Chapter 15, 'Marriage Guidance'.

SCOTLAND

Family Planning Association Regional Office
For details *see* the FPA Regional Office (Scotland) in Glasgow, Strathclyde.

BORDERS

Jedburgh

Scottish Marriage Guidance Council Marital Sexual Therapy Service
Secretary: Mrs. A. Veitch, Honeyfield, Honeyfield Road, Jedburgh TD8 6JN (Tel: Jedburgh (0835) 62811). *See also* Chapter 15, 'Marriage Guidance'.

CENTRAL

Stirling

Scottish Marriage Guidance Council Marital Sexual Therapy Services
Secretary: Mrs. M. Sutton, 19 Randolph Road, Stirling (Tel: Stirling (0786) 72031). *See also* Chapter 15, 'Marriage Guidance'.

Dumfries

Sex Advisory Service
Johnston House, Crichton Royal, Bankend Road, Dumfries (Tel: Dumfries (0387) 55301 ext. 271).
Services offered: Counselling.
Problems dealt with: Sexual and marital.
Is professional referral required? No.
Hours: Monday to Friday 9 a.m. – 5 p.m.
Fees: None.

FIFE

Dunfermline

Carnegie Clinic
Pilmuir Street, Dunfermline (Tel: Dunfermline (0383) 722911).
Services offered: Psychosexual counselling.
Is professional referral required? Yes.
Hours: Tuesday 5.15 p.m. – 7.15 p.m.
Fees: None.

Kirkcaldy

Loughborough Road Family Planning Clinic
Loughborough Road, Kirkcaldy (Tel: Kirkcaldy (0592) 52133).
Services offered: Psychosexual counselling.
Is professional referral required? Yes.
Hours: Tuesday 5.15 p.m. – 7.15 p.m.
Fees: None.

St Andrews

St Andrews Health Centre
68 Pipeland Road, St Andrews KY16 8JZ (Tel: St Andrews (0334) 77117).
Services offered: Youth advisory service, family planning, Well Woman clinic.
Problems dealt with: Any connected with family planning, including psychosexual and vasectomy counselling and abortion counselling.
Is professional referral required? No.
Hours: Different clinics, on different days, throughout the area of Fife Health Board.
Fees: None.

GRAMPIAN

Aberdeen

Scottish Marriage Guidance Council Marital Sexual Therapy Service
Secretary: Mrs Doris Meston, 10 Belmont Street, Aberdeen (Tel: Aberdeen (0224) 648412). *See also* Chapter 15, 'Marriage Guidance'.

LOTHIAN

Edinburgh

Astley Ainslie Hospital
Rehabilitation Medicine Unit, Astley Ainslie Hospital, 133 Grange Loan, Edinburgh EH9 2HL (Tel: 031-447 6271).
Services offered: Counselling of sexual problems (by clinical psychologist and nursing officer).
Problems dealt with: Sexual problems related to physical disability.
Is professional referral required? Preferred, through a general practitioner.
Hours: Monday to Friday 9 a.m. – 5 p.m.
Fees: None.

Bangour Village Hospital
Broxbourn, West Lothian EH52 6LW (Tel: 031 3300 301).
Services offered: help with sexual dysfunction.
Is professional referral required? Yes.
Hours: Tuesday and Friday afternoon

Brook Advisory Centre
50 Gilmore Place, Edinburgh EH3 9NY (Tel: 031-229 3596).
Services offered: As well as contraceptive services, this Centre offers psychosexual counselling.
Is professional referral required? No.
Hours: Evenings Monday to Friday; mornings Monday to Saturday; lunchtimes Monday to Friday.
Fees: The contraceptive service is free, all other services are charged at various fees which are frequently waived or reduced in cases of financial hardship. For further details, *see* Chapter 3, 'Family Planning'.

BUPA Medical Centre
Murrayfield Hospital, 122 Corstophine Road, Edinburgh EH12 6UD (Tel: 031-334 0363). For further details of BUPA services *see* Greater London (Camden).

Family Planning Services (Psychosexual Services)
Lothian Health Board, Family Planning Centre, 18 Dean Terrace, Edinburgh EH4 1NL (Tel: 031-332 7941 ext. 35).
Services offered: Counselling and treatment for all sexual dysfunctions and problems, both individuals and couples.
Problems dealt with: Male and female sexual dysfunctions and problems.
Is professional referral required? No.
Hours: By appointment, Monday evening, Wednesday afternoon, Thursday afternoon.
Fees: None.
Comment: Women's therapy groups have been established as a useful form of treatment, and are held if there is a need.

Lothian Marriage Counselling Service
9a Dundas Street, Edinburgh EH3 6QG (Tel: 031-556 1527).
Services offered: Counselling in a relationship (whether married or not); group counselling in small groups, meeting on a regular basis; sex therapy.
Problems dealt with: Any relationship problem.
Is professional referral required? No.
Hours: By appointment, Monday to Friday 10 a.m. – 4 p.m.; evenings (except Friday) from 6.30 p.m.; Saturday 9 a.m. – 12 noon.
Fees: Donations are discussed with clients for counselling, group work and sex therapy, but no client is refused help because of inability to pay.

Scottish Marriage Guidance Council Marital Sexual Therapy Service
9a Dundas Street, Edinburgh EH3 6QG (Tel: 031-556 1527).
See also Chapter 15, 'Marriage Guidance'.

Sexual Problems Clinic
Gynaecology Out-patients Department, Royal Infirmary, Lauriston Place, Edinburgh EH3 9YU (Tel: 031-229 2477).
Services offered: Consultations for sexual problems and sexual counselling. Also psychoendocrine clinic for premenstrual syndrome and menopausal problems.
Problems dealt with: Sexual problems of all kinds; premenstrual tension/syndrome; menopausal problems.
Is professional referral required? Preferred.
Hours: Sexual problems, Friday 2 p.m. – 5 p.m. Psychoendocrine clinic, Thursday 9.15 a.m. – 12.30 p.m.
Fees: None.
Comment: Affiliated to the Edinburgh Human Sexuality Group.

Sexual Problems Clinic
Royal Edinburgh Hospital, Morningside Place, Edinburgh EH10 5HF (Tel: 031-447 2011).
Services offered: Counselling and sex therapy for sexual dysfunction, sexual deviation and gender identity problems; training sex counsellors.
Problems dealt with: Male and female sexual dysfunction, sexual deviation, transsexualism.
Is professional referral required? Preferred.
Hours: Thursday afternoon and Friday morning.
Fees: None (but private services are available).
Comment: Affiliated to the Edinburgh Human Sexuality Group.

Western General Hospital
Crewe Road, Edinburgh EH4 2XU (Tel: (031) 332 2525).
Services offered: help with sexual dysfunctions.
Is professional referral required? Yes.
Hours: Tuesday afternoon.
Fees: None.

STRATHCLYDE

Glasgow

British Pregnancy Advisory Service
2nd Floor, 245 North Street, Glasgow G3 7DL (Tel: 041-204 1832).
Services offered: Pregnancy testing; pregnancy counselling; abortion assessment. Counselling and assessment for: infertility problems; artificial insemination.
Is professional referral required? No.
Hours: Monday to Friday 9 a.m. – 5 p.m; Saturday 9 a.m. – 1 p.m.
Fees: *see* BPAS Chapter 3, 'Family Planning'.
For further details of BPAS services *see* Chapter 3.

BUPA Medical Centre
Axton House, 295 Fenwick Road, Giffnock, Glasgow G46 6UH (Tel: (041) 638 4445). For details of services *see* Greater London (Camden).

Department of Child Health
Royal Hospital for Sick Children, Yorkhill, Glasgow G3 8SJ (Tel: 041-339 8888 ext. 368).

Services offered: Medical diagnostic service; advice on psychosexual orientation based on pathological considerations; telephone advisory service in office hours.
Problems dealt with: Chromosomal abnormalities; psychosexual disparity.
Is professional referral required? Not absolutely. Self-referral may be accepted in an emergency.
Hours: Monday to Friday 9 a.m. – 5 p.m.
Fees: None.

The Family Planning Association (Scottish Regional Office)
4 Clifton Street, Glasgow G3 7LA (Tel: 041-333 9696). *See also* Chapter 3, 'Family Planning'.
Services offered: Education, information and resource centre dealing with contraception, sexuality and personal relationships; informal advice and information on family planning services in Scotland; telephone advisory service; provision of bookstalls, displays, free leaflets, speakers.
Problems dealt with: Sex and relationship related topics and questions.
Is professional referral required? No.
Hours: Monday to Friday 9 a.m. – 5 p.m.
Fees: None, except for educational courses and speakers.

Family Planning Centre
2 Claremont Terrace, Glasgow G3 7XR (Tel: 041-332 9144; advisory service: 041-333 9399).
Services offered: Comprehensive family planning contraception service, including vasectomy counselling and operations; pregnancy testing and referral for termination of pregnancy where indicated; Well Woman screening; preliminary advice and investigation of infertility and referral for artificial insemination by donor; counselling on sexual problems; assessment and referral, if required, for hormone replacement therapy and premenstrual tension. A telephone advisory service is available, *see* above.
Problems dealt with: Family planning; infertility; unplanned pregnancies; menstrual and menopausal problems; psychosexual problems. Enquiries from disabled people referred to Family Planning Clinic, Royal Maternity Hospital, Rotten Row, Glasgow G14 ONA (Tuesday evening).
Is professional referral required? No.
Hours: Family planning services by appointment (Monday to Thursday). Pregnancy testing (no appointment) daily. Others by appointment.
Fees: None.

Scottish Marriage Guidance Council Marital Sexual Therapy Service
27 Sandyford Place, Glasgow G3 7NG (Tel: 041 248 5249). *See also* Chapter 15, 'Marriage Guidance'.

Greater Glasgow Health Board
Royal Maternity Hospital Family Planning Clinic, 163 Rotten Row, Glasgow G4 0NA (Tel: 041-552 4511, Tuesday evenings).
Services offered: Contraception and psychosexual counselling for physically handicapped people.
Problems dealt with: Contraceptive and psychosexual problems.
Is professional referral required? No.
Hours: Tuesday 6.30 p.m. – 9 p.m.
Fees: None.

Psychosexual Clinic
Duke Street Hospital, Outpatient Clinic, 5 Oakley Terrace, Glasgow G31 2HX (Tel: 041-554 6267/556 5222).
Services offered: Psychosexual therapy.
Problems dealt with: Any psychosexual problems.
Is professional referral required? Preferable.
Hours: Monday to Friday 9 a.m. – 5 p.m.
Fees: None.

Sexual Problems Clinic
Lansdowne Clinic, 3 Whittingehame Gardens, Glasgow G12 OAA (Tel: 041-334 1734).
Services offered: An NHS clinic offering joint psychology and psychotherapy assessment and treatment of sexual problems. For people within the catchment area of Gartnavel Royal Hospital only. Liaison with family planning, urology, gynaecology, etc.
Problems dealt with: Primarily sexual dysfunctions, but also deviations, and problems arising from sexual abuse.
Is professional referral required? Yes.
Hours: Monday to Friday 9 a.m. – 5 p.m
Fees: None.

The Sister Rose Private Clinic and Pregnancy Advisory Centre
28 St Enoch's Square, Glasgow 1 (Tel: 041-221 9042).
Services offered: Examination and assessment for termination of pregnancy; pregnancy tests, both on the premises and also via a postal pack; assessement and examination for female sterilisation which can be performed as a day-care operation; counselling and vasectomy operations; routine smear testing; Well Woman checks; menopausal clinics; contraceptive advice; morning-after pill, etc.

Is professional referral required? No, but general practitioner's referral preferred.
Hours: Monday to Saturday 9 a.m. – 5 p.m.
Fees: Counselling, consultation and post-operative check in respect of termination of pregnancy £30; operation fee £107 (up to and including 13 weeks of pregnancy); £239 for prostaglandin termination (up to and including 20 weeks of pregnancy); sterilisation £25 for counselling and £145 for day-care.
Comment: Brochures giving brief outlines of treatment available on postal or telephone request.

TAYSIDE

Dundee

Family Planning Clinics (Dundee District)
c/o Ninewells Hospital, Dundee DD1 9SY (Tel: Dundee (0382) 60111 ext. 2137).
Services offered: Family planning methods, youth advisory service, (with separate teenagers clinic), psychosexual counselling.
Problems dealt with: Psychosexual problems and difficulties associated with the sexual relationship.
Is professional referral required? Preferred.
Hours: By appointment.
Fees: None.
Comment: Services are available at a number of clinics and appointments can be made by telephoning the clinic of choice in clinic hours. A list of clinics is advertised in the local press. Such a list is also available from Clinic Area 1.

NORTHERN IRELAND

Family Planning Association Regional Office
For details, *see* the FPA Regional Office (Northern Ireland) in Belfast.

Belfast

Family Planning Association (Northern Ireland Regional Office)
113 University Street, Belfast BT7 1HP (Tel: Belfast (0232) 225488). Derry office: 14 Magazine Street, Derry BT48 6HH (Tel: Derry (0504) 260016).
See also Chapter 3, 'Family Planning'.
Services offered: Bookshop, distribution of information leaflets; telephone informaton service; office open to the public. Courses in relationships and sexuality run by FPA trained tutors.
Problems dealt with: Contraception; pregnancy; women's health; childlessness; sex education.
Is professional referral required? No.
Hours: Monday to Thursday 9 a.m. – 5 p.m.; Friday 9 a.m. – 4.30 p.m.
Fees: Only for courses, not for information service.

Marital Sexual Therapy Service
Northern Ireland Marriage Guidance Council, 76 Dublin Road, Belfast BT2 7HP (Tel: Belfast (0232) 323454). *See also* Chapter 15, 'Marriage Guidance'.

Derry

See Belfast Family Planning Association above.

ISLE OF MAN

Family Planning Association Regional Office
For details, *see* the FPA Regional Office (North-west England) in Liverpool, Merseyside.

The following clinics provide birth control facilities. These are private clinics, but services are provided free for certain patients who are considered 'medical' cases.

Castletown

Family Planning Association
Isle of Man (Castletown) FPA Clinic, Janet's Corner, Castletown, Isle of Man (Tel: Douglas (0624) 833464).

Douglas

Family Planning Association
Isle of Man (Douglas) FPA Clinic, The School Clinic, Murrays Road, Douglas, Isle of Man (Tel: Douglas (0624) 6623).

Family Planning Association
Isle of Man (Douglas), Noble's Isle of Man Hospital, Westmoreland Road, Douglas, Isle of Man (Tel: Douglas (0624) 23526).

Family Planning Association
Woodbourne Road, Douglas, Isle of Man (Tel: Douglas (0624) 76623).

Ramsey

Family Planning Association
Isle of Man (Ramsey) Ramsey Cottage Hospital, Ramsey, Isle of Man (Tel: Douglas (0624) 813952).

CHAPTER 22

Selected Further Reading

Books and publications which are specific to particular chapters are reviewed in those chapters. Those which follow are of more general interest. There are, of course, hundreds of books about sex, of which we have made only a small selection. This is quite deliberate. We believe that long reading lists tend to confuse rather than help. Our choice, naturally, is subjective: we have included the books that we like and have found useful.

Booklists and Bookshops

For those who would like a wider range to consider, the following organisations publish lists of recommended books:

Brook Advisory Centres
– *see* Chapter 3, 'Family Planning'.
Catholic Marriage Advisory Council
– *see* Chapter 15, 'Marriage Guidance'.
Family Planning Association
– *see* Chapter 3, 'Family Planning'
Health Education Authority – *see* Chapter 13, 'Learning About Sex'.
International Planned Parenthood Federation – *see* Chapter 13, 'Learning About Sex'.
National Marriage Guidance Council
– *see* Chapter 15, 'Marriage Guidance'.
SPOD (The Association to Aid the Sexual and Personal Relationships of People with a Disability) – *see* Chapter 12, 'Sexuality and Disability'

In London, there are a number of specialist bookshops which offer a mail order service or where callers can browse at leisure:

Compendium, 234 Camden High Street, London NW1 (for anybody).
Gay's the Word, 66 Marchmont Street, London WC1 (for homosexuals) – *see* Chapter 18, 'Homosexuality'.
SisterWrite, 190 Upper Street, London N1 (for women) – *see* Chapter 8, 'Women Only'.

Publications

Advice to Men by Robert Chartham. Published by Star Books, the Paperback Division of W.H.Allen & Co.Ltd. Price £1.95.
In this book, the author has used letters he has received to demonstrate common sexual problems, and in answering them he provides practical advice. He says

> 'I believe that physical lovemaking should be the visible expression of emotional love. Lovemaking, while a highly skilled and delicate art, only becomes complex if we make it so. . . but once we have developed difficulties, no amount of philosophy on my part or anyone else's helps.'

He goes on to say,

> 'there is scarcely a sexual problem that is not psychologically induced or that does not spring from the man's fear of being rated a failure as a lover.'

The book has chapters on masturbation, penis size, coming off too soon, impotence and partial impotence, circumcision, satisfying a woman, oral intercourse, understanding the sex drive, a discussion on 'normal sex' (which follows letters from individuals worried about certain ways of making love), and the old problem of lack of communication. Some men would be helped and reassured by reading this book, but it may not give them the insight into women's sexuality that is essential to a happy relationship.

The Body Book by Claire Rayner, with illustrations by Tony King. Published by Andre Deutsch, 1978. Price £3.95.
This is a book for young children, but will be a splendid ally for all parents who want to help them, as soon as possible, towards an understanding of human life, or who find their questions difficult to answer. Through

pictures and a simple though ingenious text, it communicates the technicalities of bodily function in a way which young children can readily understand and enjoy. Reproduction comes near the end in a section headed 'Growing and Changing and Making New People. In just five pages, author and artist contrive to present, simply, directly and sensitively, the essential facts of life. It is a notable achievement and admirably appropriate to a much neglected purpose.

The Book of Love by Dr David Delvin. Published by the New English Library, 1975. Price £2.95.
This is one of the books that appears on everyone's lists. It is such a good read that it's not surprising. Dr Delvin's racy style and sensitive insight combine to provide a mass of information in a simple, straightforward way.

He says himself in the introduction:

> 'Despite all the brave talk of a permissive society, the sad fact is that the world is still shrouded in a fog of sexual ignorance. . . So, this book makes an attempt to dispel at least some of the mists of doubt, misinformation and shame. It's intended to give married and unmarried people the basic facts of sex in a clear straightforward way, to tell them how to enjoy intercourse, to teach them techniques of love-play, to explain all the methods of contraception currently available, to tell them how to deal with sexual problems and common infections of the sex organs, and to provide up-to-date helpful information about pregnancy and abortion.'

He does all this and so much more besides, because all he writes is imbued with concern for the readers he sets out to help and encourage. You can tell he wants people to enjoy their sexuality; furthermore, he is writing about loving and not just sex. Some nice line drawings set off the text which is laced with descriptive stories of people having problems which can beset any of us. If we had to recommend only one general book for men and women and young people, this would be it.

Drugs and Sexual Function by M.A.Davies and A.D'Mello. Published by Ridge Publications, 305 Luton Road, Harpenden, Hertfordshire AL5 3LW, 1985. Price £4 plus 50p postage. No one concerned with sexual problems should be without this fascinating little book. While there are many texts on clinical and psychogenic causes of sexual difficulties, this is the only one, so far as we know, that examines the ways that drugs, prescribed or otherwise, can adversely affect sexual function in both men and women. It is written for doctors, pharmacists, pharmocologists, research workers, teachers in medical and paramedical education and students. Sex therapists, surely, will also want to have this book on their shelves.

The authors discuss the nervous and hormonal control of sexual function, and the nature of sexual response, going on to outline possible sexual problems before chapters on the possible effects of various medicinal drugs, alcohol and the drugs of dependence. The book ends with a summary of conclusions and recommendations and a table of drugs, their adverse effects and related literature.

Facts of Life for Children. A Family Doctor booklet published by the British Medical Association, BMA House, Tavistock Square, London WC1H 9JP. Price 95p plus postage.

First Love, First Sex : a Practical Guide to Relationships by Kaye Wellings. Published by Thorsons Publishing Group, 1986. Price £6.99.
Written in conjunction with the Family Planning Association, this copiously illustrated book covers a surprising amount of ground and answers most of the doubts and questions which assail us as young people. It is welcome for the fact that it gets beyond the 'reproductive plumbing' to the area of personal relationships and emotional problems (which can, of course, be acute and exaggerated in youth), and explores the importance of love in sexual union. We found it a very positive book, responsible but never dull, instructive but never condescending, with a happy blend of fact and feeling. The book is also valuable for the way in which it dispels concerns about supposed abnormalities in our bodies, minds and behaviour; 'delicate' subjects are not avoided or glossed over, and Kaye Wellings' handling of such topics as masturbation, fantasies and homosexuality shows refreshing insight and clarity.

How to Last Longer: and Other Sexual Solutions by Michael Castleman. Published by Souvenir Press, 1982. Price £7.95 (hardback). (First published in the USA.)

Don't be put off by the boring cover and a main title which suggests longevity rather than sex. This really is an excellent sex book for men. First to catch the eye are the wholly delightful illustrations by David Passalacqua. How is it that explicit sex is softened and beautified by drawings rather than photographs? The text is non-academic and marvellously down-to-earth.

It is a sensible book, but never stuffy; frank, but never cheap; with a sense of values which embraces a healthy morality within a context of wholehearted enthusiasm for the delights of sex and sensuality – so that pornography, for instance, is not deplored as such, but seen as a leading cause of men's sex problems, perpetuating the myths which the author is trying to dispel.

How to Last Longer, says the cover sleeve with every justification, provides simple, lucid and constructive answers to virtually every sexual situation. It shows how slight shifts in attitude, technique and approach can often eliminate recurrent problems and lead to successful and exciting love-making. Men who are prepared to follow the author's advice on a more leisurely approach to the sensuous areas of the whole body, on more intimate discussion and less concentration on the genitals, will be well on their way to becoming the confident, accomplished and appreciated lovers they have always wanted to be.

It is above all a practical book, which puts sexual love in a true perspective and offers alternative solutions to problems which impede the fulfilment of a satisfying relationship.

How You Began: a Story in Pictures by Lennart Nilsson. Published by Kestrel Books, 1975. Price £5.50.
This remarkable book, first published in Sweden, is obviously intended for children. We think, however, that it will astonish, inform and delight most adults. In only 28 pages, we are shown the wonders of the growth of a foetus inside its mother's womb through a series of superb colour photographs, culminating with a dramatic black and white photograph of the instant of birth. The 'facts of life' are then clearly and straightforwardly explained, and finally, returning to the beginning of things, we see fertilisation in detail: first the father's sperm, then the mother's egg, their meeting (in striking magnification), and the first division into cells.

The Joy of Sex by Alex Comfort. Published by Quartet Books (small black and white format, 1972, price £3.95; full colour illustrated paperback edition, 1982, price £6.50).
During our research this was a book that seemed to be on everyone's list of favourites. Indeed, it is now so well known as scarcely to need recommendation. It gains considerably from its larger format which does better justice to the black and white illustrations of Charles Raymond and Christopher Foss, while the colour plates greatly enhance the sensuality of a book which is itself a hymn to sensuality.

The title is indicative of the contents. This is a book which revels in the pleasure of sexual love. As the author remarks,

> 'love is too seriously joyful a matter to be left to the solemnities of academics, moral authorities and the porno trader'.

Thus the main sections of the Contents are headed 'Starters', 'Main Courses' and 'Sauces and Pickles'. It is indeed a 'gourmet guide to love-making' presented without inhibition and in a style which entertains as much as it instructs. We think that there cannot be anyone who would not find this a life enhancing book and for many it will help to lift the yoke of acquired guilt.

See also details of *More Joy of Sex*, below

Knowing about Sex. A Family Doctor booklet published by the British Medical Association, BMA House, Tavistock Square, London WC1H 9JP, 1986. Price 95p plus postage. Formerly titled *'Sex for Beginners'*.

Make It Happy : What Sex is All About by Jane Cousins. Published by Penguin Books. Price £2.95. (First published 1978.)
An outstanding sex education book, aimed mainly at young people, but instructive for anyone. It presents factual information in a straightforward, unvarnished way and avoids moralising, patronising attitudes. *Make It Happy* won the *Times Educational Supplement* Senior Information Book Award and we can do no better than to quote the judges when they described it as:

> 'Witty upon occasions, wholesome, classless, sometimes moving in its simplicity, gentle and honest in its intentions.'

The author reminds us that our sex lives begin when we are babies, possibly even before we're born, and charts development through puberty to adolescence. She goes on to describe our bodies – genitals and reproductive organs – and discusses the important and often misunderstood question of sexual identity. There is a myth-dispelling chapter on masturbation, an informative one on orgasms and some broad-minded guidance on enjoying sex in various ways. Vital chapters follow on birth control, pregnancy, abortion and having a baby, and the book concludes with a survey of sexually transmitted diseases and other physical disorders, and an explanation of the law relating to sexual offences.

As Jane Cousins writes:

> 'Sex may be a natural instinct – but learning how to express your sexual feelings doesn't always come so very naturally. . . Mostly. . . it's about sharing pleasure. This means treating your partner honestly, fairly and lovingly. That's the only way to make it happy.'

Men and Sex by Bernard Zilbergeld. Published by Fontana. Price £2.50 (paperback).
We began to read this book out of a sense of duty and found we could not put it down. It is wise and funny (in places we were laughing out loud) and so marvellously sensible and practical. It provides a wonderful insight into men's feelings and actions, how they really feel and why they act as they do. We would unhesitatingly recommend it to any man who is experiencing problems and uncertainties in his sexual and emotional life. (We would also strongly recommend it to any woman who would like to understand men better.)

Bernard Zilbergeld unmasks the male stereotype for what it is, a false image, and replaces this with a living, breathing study of men with whom women would be happy to identify. He also sends up hilariously the 'fantasy model of sex'. He talks about erection and ejaculatory problems, promoting and recognising good conditions for sex, understanding women, touching (he's very strong on this, believing it to be all-important to the tough male who spends most of his life 'out of touch'), masturbation, virginity and sexual abstinence, and so on. He doesn't just talk, he gives the reader a whole range of imaginative exercises to do, designed to improve his sensual appreciation and his sexual functioning, but above all to help him be at ease with himself. The author says,

> 'This book is intended for men in all categories – for those who want to learn more about their sexuality, those who want to get more out of sex, those who are looking for ways to integrate sex into their lives in ways consistent with their own values and feelings, and those who want some specific skills for dealing with problems they are experiencing.'

We warmly commend this book.

More Joy of Sex by Alex Comfort. Published by Quartet Books. (First published in 1975, new paperback edition in 1977). Price £3.95.
If *The Joy of Sex* 's encyclopaedic treatment of subjects – particularly of problems – tends to be a bit thin, this is compensated for in the sequel, *More Joy of Sex*, which covers what *The Joy of Sex* left out, namely the elements of development and of relation – sex not merely for fun, but as an instrument of growth and as a shared experience. Alex Comfort believes that

> 'physical sex and the relationships it involves can be the most effective source of self-comprehension if we take the trouble'.

The opening section is concerned with 'body language' – touching, non-verbal communication, massage and so on – discussed not as a separate cult, but 'as part of the education of lovers'. The author then turns to relationships, both conventional and otherwise, ranging over the whole spectrum of heterosexual interaction. 'All good sex', he says, 'is partly relational', and if it is really good 'it generates a relationship'. Even at the level of play, it calls for care and tenderness. Jealousy (where convention encourages us to react like Othello), group sex, sharing sexual experience with another couple, orgies and threesomes are all discussed and the book concludes with a brief consideration of therapies and some of the more common problems (special needs). Throughout, the text is again enlivened with explicit, but gentle, illustrations in all of which affection and tenderness are the keynotes.

Alex Comfort has said that if *The Joy of Sex* was about climbing, then this sequel is about mountaineering. It is fair comment and it is difficult to see how anyone could manage without both.

Sense and Nonsense about Sex. A Family Doctor booklet published by the British Medical Association, BMA House, Tavistock Square, London WC1H 9JP (1986). Price 95p plus postage.

So you Know about Sex. A Family Doctor booklet published by the British Medical Association, BMA House, Tavistock Square, London WC1H 9JP. Price 95p plus postage. For children aged 12 or more.

Teenage Living and Loving. A Family Doctor booklet published by the British Medical Association, BMA House, Tavistock Square, London WC1H 9JP. Price 95p plus postage.

The Visual Dictionary of Sex edited by Dr Eric J. Trimmer with various consultants and contributors. Published by Pan Books, 1978. Price £4.95.
This admirable pictorial guide, with over 400 illustrations, clear layout and ease of reference, is an invaluable companion for anyone who wants technical information on all aspects of sex and wants it fast.

In a series of thematic chapters the Dictionary systematically examines the psychological and physical aspects of our sexual natures, going on to survey, among other subjects, sexual techniques, birth control, fetishes and fantasies, marriage, disability and the interaction of society.

In all, nearly 1,000 concepts, terms and processes are introduced and there is an excellent index.

Index

Note: local services are arranged geographically within Chapter 21 and are not, therefore, further indexed below. Similarly, sex law is arranged alphabetically by subject within Chapter 20 and is not further indexed below.